Shaped by the State

Shaped by the State

*Toward a New Political History
of the Twentieth Century*

EDITED BY BRENT CEBUL,
LILY GEISMER, AND
MASON B. WILLIAMS

THE UNIVERSITY OF CHICAGO PRESS   CHICAGO AND LONDON

The University of Chicago Press, Chicago 60637
The University of Chicago Press, Ltd., London
© 2019 by The University of Chicago
Published 2019

28 27 26 25 24 23 22 21 20 19   1 2 3 4 5

ISBN-13: 978-0-226-59629-7 (cloth)
ISBN-13: 978-0-226-59632-7 (paper)
ISBN-13: 978-0-226-59646-4 (e-book)
DOI: https://doi.org/10.7208/chicago/9780226596464.001.0001

Portions of chapter 1 originally appeared in Sarah E. Igo, *The Known Citizen: A History of
Privacy in Modern America* (Cambridge, MA: Harvard University Press, 2018), copyright ©
2018 by the President and Fellows of Harvard College.

Portions of chapter 5 originally appeared in Julie M. Weise, *Corazón de Dixie: Mexicanos in
the U.S. South since 1910* (Chapel Hill: University of North Carolina Press, 2015).

Library of Congress Cataloging-in-Publication Data

Names: Cebul, Brent, editor. | Geismer, Lily, editor. | Williams, Mason B., editor.
Title: Shaped by the state : toward a new political history of the twentieth century / edited
    by Brent Cebul, Lily Geismer, and Mason B. Williams.
Description: Chicago ; London : The University of Chicago Press, 2019. | Papers based on
    presentations at the conference "Seeing beyond the Partisan Divide," held at the Miller
    Center at the University of Virginia in the fall of 2015. | Includes bibliographical
    references and index.
Identifiers: LCCN 2018032166 | ISBN 9780226596297 (cloth : alk. paper) | ISBN 9780226596327
    (pbk. : alk. paper) | ISBN 9780226596464 (e-book)
Subjects: LCSH: United States—Politics and government—20th century—Congresses.
Classification: LCC E743 .S47 2018 | DDC 973.91—dc23
LC record available at https://lccn.loc.gov/2018032166

Contents

Acknowledgments   VII

INTRODUCTION

Beyond Red and Blue: Crisis and Continuity in Twentieth-Century U.S. Political History   3
Brent Cebul, Lily Geismer, and Mason B. Williams

PART I.   **Building Leviathan**

CHAPTER 1.   Social Insecurities: Private Data and Public Culture in Modern America   27
Sarah E. Igo

CHAPTER 2.   The Strange Career of American Liberalism   62
N. D. B. Connolly

CHAPTER 3.   "Really and Truly a Partnership": The New Deal's Associational State and the Making of Postwar American Politics   96
Brent Cebul and Mason B. Williams

CHAPTER 4.   State Building for a Free Market: The Great Depression and the Rise of Monetary Orthodoxy   123
David M. P. Freund

CHAPTER 5.   *La revolución institucional*: The Rise and Fall of the Mexican New Deal in the U.S. South, 1920–1990   162
Julie M. Weise

PART II.   **Crisis and Continuity**

CHAPTER 6.   The Short End of Both Sticks: Property Assessments and
              Black Taxpayer Disadvantage in Urban America   189
              Andrew W. Kahrl

CHAPTER 7.   Clearing the Air and Counting Costs: *Shimp v. New
              Jersey Bell* and the Tragedy of Workplace Smoking   218
              Sarah E. Milov

CHAPTER 8.   Glocal America: The Politics of Scale in the 1970s   241
              Suleiman Osman

CHAPTER 9.   The Government Alone Cannot Do the Total Job:
              The Possibilities and Perils of Religious Organizations
              in Public-Private Refugee Care   261
              Melissa May Borja

CHAPTER 10.   A Carceral Empire: Placing the Political History of
              U.S. Prisons and Policing in the World   289
              Stuart Schrader

CHAPTER 11.   Fears of a Nanny State: Centering Gender and
              Family in the Political History of Regulation   317
              Rachel Louise Moran

CONCLUSIONS

              The History of Neoliberalism   347
              Kim Phillips-Fein

              Ten Propositions for the New Political History   363
              Matthew D. Lassiter

Contributors   377

Index   381

Acknowledgments

This collection emerged from a conference the editors organized at the Miller Center at the University of Virginia in the fall of 2015. The conference, "Seeing beyond the Partisan Divide," assembled scholars from a range of disciplinary perspectives and at various stages in their careers with the goal of trying to construct alternative frameworks for studying twentieth-century political history. Each of the participants embraced the premise and joined in two days of thought-provoking conversation and enthusiastic debate. In addition to the volume's contributors, we also thank those who took part as panelists, commenters, and audience members, including Brian Balogh, Jamelle Bouie, Merlin Chowkwanyun, Darren Dochuk, Nicole Hemmer, Monica Kim, Andrew McGee, Guian McKee, Quinn Mulroy, Amy Offner, Julia Ott, Daniel Rodgers, Bruce Schulman, James Sparrow, Thomas Sugrue, and Michael Willrich. Their insights influenced this volume in incalculable ways.

We are enormously indebted to the Miller Center and to Will Hitchcock, in particular, for their generosity and support, which made it possible to assemble such a dream group of scholars. The conference also would not have been possible without generous assistance from the University of Virginia's Page-Barbour Interdisciplinary Initiatives Committee. At the Miller Center, Stefanie Georgakis Abbott provided essential logistical support that made us look far more on top of things than we were. We also thank Bruce Schulman and the American Political History Institute at Boston University for providing additional funds, and Bruce for his wide-ranging formal and informal support over the years. We are grateful for the support of our colleagues at the American Academy of Arts and Sciences, University of Richmond, University of North Carolina at Charlotte, Claremont McKenna College, Albright College, and Williams

College (especially the Leadership Studies Program and Political Science Department). Of the countless friends and colleagues who offered advice in less formal settings, we thank especially Leslie Brown, whose comments on the proposal for this volume helped us clear a number of important conceptual hurdles. Her loss has deprived the historical community of a brilliant scholar and a generous spirit.

Our deepest thanks go to Brian Balogh, without whom this project simply would not exist. In addition to introducing all of us to one another when we were graduate students, Brian has provided boundless and energetic mentorship to each of us throughout our careers. Brian has been the greatest champion of and cheerleader for not only this volume but also the resurgence of political history more broadly. We all owe him an immeasurable debt of gratitude.

We also deeply appreciate the efforts and faith of our editor, Tim Mennel, who managed to keep us moving more or less in one direction and more or less on time. And we thank Rachel Kelly; our wonderful and patient copyeditor, Katherine Faydash; and the rest of the staff at the University of Chicago Press for their help making the manuscript come to life. A big thanks to Avery Raimondo, who built our index. We are particularly grateful to the two anonymous readers who provided perceptive, thorough, and generative feedback that helped to strengthen the individual chapters and the collection as a whole. Kevin Kruse organized a panel on the volume's themes at the 2016 Organization of American Historians conference; we are thankful to him; to Matthew Lassiter, who offered incisive comments on that panel; and to the members of the audience for their insightful feedback and challenging ideas. Last but certainly not least, we owe substantial gratitude to the contributors for their patience, for working so hard and efficiently through multiple rounds of revisions, and most of all, for their willingness to contribute their work to this volume.

Lucinda Cebul, Gabriel Geismer, and Emerson Williams all made their debuts in the world during this project's transformation from conference to completed volume. We thank them for making the future far brighter, and we thank our partners, Katherine Treppendahl, Michael Kaufman, and Alexis Schaitkin, for making the present far more wonderful—and also for tolerating "side" projects that sometimes seemed a little more central than initially advertised.

Introduction

Beyond Red and Blue

Crisis and Continuity in Twentieth-Century U.S. Political History

Brent Cebul, Lily Geismer, and Mason B. Williams

D onald Trump's ascent to the White House shocked many Americans—
not least the historical community. Even before the general election,
historians began to converge from a variety of different fields, adopting
a consciously ecumenical approach in the hope that, by placing Trump's
politics in historical context, they might help make sense of a seemingly incomprehensible turn of events.[1] By highlighting the inadequacy of America's political imagination writ large, and hence calling attention to the
need for a more expansive reading of America's political history, Trump's
election has presented both challenges and opportunities with which
scholars of twentieth-century American political history will be grappling
for many years. If they do their work well, historians will not only shed
light on the Trump phenomenon but also add a greater depth to our understanding of modern U.S. history more generally.

The reaction to Trump's rise reminds us of the way historians responded a decade ago, when world capitalism nearly collapsed during the
Great Recession of 2008. In the recession's wake, historians from many
different fields converged around a new history of capitalism; they devised
a common language and set off in search of not only the "prehistory of a
bewildering present" but also a deeper understanding of how power has
worked in American life.[2] As the Great Recession did with capitalism,
the current moment in American politics challenges historians both to
make sense of the present moment and to rethink what it means to study

American political history. Little wonder that the question of what counts as "political history" has recently come to the fore: events have pushed the study of American politics beyond the reach of the existing conceptions of the field.

The "all hands on deck" response to the rise of Trump has built upon (and in turn accelerated) a historiographical phenomenon which was already well under way. Over the past few decades, the call to "bring the state back in" has been so successful that scholars from a wide range of subfields traditionally understood as "social" or "cultural" history regularly make formal structures of state power integral to their analyses.[3] As a result, scholarship on American politics and governance has proliferated as never before. And because it draws on an unprecedented range of perspectives and methodologies, it has never been richer. Yet the fact that much of the best political history is now being written by scholars who would not primarily consider themselves political historians indicates a certain definitional problem in the field of modern American political history—it suggests that the field lacks a set of organizing principles and theories, key questions and debates, and well-established research agendas around which "traditional" political historians and "unofficial" political historians could make common cause.

The scholars who have converged upon the ground of political history, in short, require a language with which they can speak to one another. The key obstacle to developing this language, we believe, lies not in disputes about what counts as political history or which parts of political history deserve the most attention.[4] Rather, it lies in how political historians have thought about politics and historical time.

Explicitly or implicitly, the big narratives of modern American political history as constructed by political historians have been built around the concept of crisis: time and again, our efforts to understand why seemingly stable political orders crack up, and how American politics gets reconstructed in the aftermath of those crack-ups, center on epochal moments when established structures collapse and new ones rise from their ashes. The crisis of the 1850s gave way to the Republican ascendancy, the economic catastrophe of the early 1930s to the New Deal order, the upheavals of the late 1960s and 1970s to the rise of modern conservatism. Most recently, journalists and pundits have drafted a rushed historical framework for the twenty-first century in which the 2016 election of Donald Trump is both the result and the cause of a new crisis—and perhaps a new political era.

In twentieth-century American political history, the concept of crisis rests at the heart of what remains the dominant chronological and historiographical framework: the rise and fall of the New Deal order and its displacement by (depending on how one sees it) the age of Reagan or the era of neoliberalism or both. The New Deal order framework takes its organizing principle from the electoral realignment school of political science, a schema in which periodic "critical elections" (often preceded by social crises) yield relatively durable political systems.[5] Integrating business interests, state institutions, class formation, and political culture fully into the history of American politics, scholars writing in the 1980s and early 1990s charted the development of a liberal "order of ideas, public policies and political alliances" that would shape American politics for four decades, as well as the "missed opportunities, unintended consequences, and dangerous but inescapable compromises" that led to that order's collapse.[6] In the early twenty-first century, historians overlaid the story of the rise of conservatism atop the New Deal order framework, showing how a diverse group of movements blending ostensibly "free-market" economic ideas and practices with staunch anticommunism and a newly assertive Christian social-cultural politics, seized the Republican Party and capitalized on the social and economic crises of the 1970s, riding to national power with Ronald Reagan's election in 1980 and the Gingrich revolution a decade later.[7] Some of the early works on neoliberalism did something similar, positing an abrupt shift in political economy from an "embedded liberalism" crafted in response to the crisis of the 1930s and 1940s to a neoliberalism made possible by the economic restructuring of the 1970s and 1980s.[8]

No one would doubt that American political history contains critical moments, windows during which the established order of things changes abruptly and with permanent consequences. Nor would anyone question the value of the literatures on New Deal liberalism, conservatism, and neoliberalism, which have immeasurably enhanced our understanding of twentieth-century American history. As the essays in this volume make clear, and as ongoing work on topics such as party polarization attest, their influence continues to shape political-historical analysis in profound and productive ways.[9]

But building our historical frameworks around crises comes with significant costs. The very act of invoking "crisis," the anthropologist Janet Roitman notes, begins a subjective process of determining "what counts as history." In the search for proximate causes and clear ruptures, more durable experiences, norms, and institutions can be relegated to the margins. Consequently, the concept of crisis often serves as "an enabling blind-spot for the production of knowledge." By its very nature, crisis implies rift and change, a causal-temporal claim that "makes certain things visible and others invisible."[10] The definitional problems facing political history stem to no small degree from the fact that crisis-centered frameworks have made certain experiences and developments harder to see. Such frameworks have worked relatively well to make sense of those aspects of American politics where rupture really matters: partisan realignments, electoral coalitions, and some (though certainly not all) dimensions of political culture and policy formation, for instance. But they offer less purchase for understanding persistent features of American politics that cut across the usual break points—particularly hierarchies and privileges of race and gender, which are now at the center of scholarship on twentieth-century American history.

As a result, the established paradigms—the New Deal order, postwar liberalism, the rise of conservatism, red versus blue—risk obscuring transformations and continuities that are equally constitutive of American political life and just as central to people's lived experiences under the American regime. Because they tend to obscure deeper forms of consensus around global capitalism, white privilege, patriarchy, and notions of American exceptionalism, these frameworks have never spoken especially cogently to research on radical politics—an obviously important problem in the age of Occupy and the white supremacist "alt-right." They also struggle to illuminate developments that transcend partisan divisions, such as the embrace of "market-based" approaches, the place of the military or the courts in political history, and the vast and decentralized construction of the American carceral state,[11] or to integrate the movement of people, ideas, and institutions that cross the boundaries of the United States.[12] Meanwhile, historians of metropolitan, urban, and rural politics are finding that national partisan and ideological categories sometimes obscure the causes of important developments in local politics and governance, missing the ways in which categories like liberalism and conservatism have often been defined and redefined by a range of other social, cultural, spatial, and economic factors.[13]

The best scholarship on New Deal liberalism, conservatism, and neoliberalism certainly integrated the study of race, gender, property rights, and consumption (among other topics) in histories of American politics and governance.[14] Yet, it remains the case that in much of this scholarship racially unequal and segregated outcomes or gendered policy structures, for instance, have most often been explained as *products* of liberalism or conservatism. More recently, however, a range of other social historians and scholars of American governance have decentered the categories of liberalism and conservatism. They have focused instead on how the American state and its regnant ideologies and parties have been structured by normative values and assumptions, and have in turn embedded or more sharply defined those same deeply rooted values through governance. Often their work intersects with subjects like the New Deal and conservative governance but in ways that do not fit easily into the established red-and-blue frameworks. For instance, Margot Canaday found that the New Deal state played an important role in the production of new categories of sex and gender nonconformity, but not because of any dynamic implied by the concept of New Deal liberalism. Rather, the creation and entrenchment of heteronormative tiers of citizenship was bound up in the state's efforts to govern in areas such as migration, poverty, and crime, embedding in state structures norms that predated the New Deal and continued well after it.[15] Similarly, N. D. B. Connolly recognized the importance of New Deal housing programs in the modernization of Jim Crow's built environment in the city of Miami. But he put the structural politics of property and racial capitalism, rather than New Deal liberalism, at the center of his account.[16] The carceral state literature, which stresses bipartisanship, offers another case in point; so does Mae Ngai's seminal work on immigration and citizenship.[17] These works offer important examples of the possibilities of a political history that cuts across common paradigms, that is sensitive to deeper structures of continuity, and that builds bridges between flourishing subfields that are now home to some of the most exciting new political histories.[18]

Our approach in this book has been to start by identifying the common ground on which these "unofficial" political historians have converged. Although they frame their questions in different ways, much of this scholarship is fundamentally concerned with at least one of three central dynamics of politics in a modern liberal state: the contested relationships between state and economy, state and society, and state and citizen-subject.[19] Rather than seek to uncover the logic and functioning of an "order," we have focused on these dynamics, which are foundational to understanding the problems of democracy within the contexts of the modern state, modern capitalism, and citizenship in an age of globalization. Our contributors have identified important changes and continuities in those relationships, explained how and why they occurred, and examined how those changing relationships in turn reshaped categories, knowledge, group identities, and ideological commitments.

This approach yields no grand narrative of twentieth-century American political history. But by giving us a better sense of the relation of change to continuity, it brings into clearer focus the ways in which phenomena exemplary of a particular historical moment build on and articulate deeper structural forces of American politics. This volume's treatment of neoliberalism, a phenomenon that has moved to the center of twentieth-century U.S. political history in the past decade, offers a case in point.[20] Each of the book's chapters engages with a key theme of neoliberalism: financialization, precarity, public-private partnerships and coadministration, turns toward surveillance and punishment, individual freedoms, and resistance to regulation. But they do not adhere to the standard story of neoliberalization—they posit no abrupt shift toward deregulation, privatization, marketization, and political demobilization in the 1970s. On the contrary, they trace the conditions, assumptions, institutions, and practices associated with neoliberalism across modern American political history, suggesting, as N. D. B. Connolly writes in his chapter, that there is "nothing 'neo' about it."

Indeed, many of the arrangements associated with neoliberalism are not new. State recourse to private or nongovernmental actors, elite preferences for subdued and subjugated labor markets, and broadly shared convictions about the importance of maintaining white supremacy and the government's role in creating markets are, in fact, deeply rooted in American governance. These techniques and assumptions became steadily amplified when the associational state of the nineteenth century became modern "big government" as it responded to the exigencies of depression and war. And as the chapters that follow suggest, the twentieth-century state emerged within these long-standing structures and ideologies of markets and social power defined by race, gender, class, and hierarchies of citizenship.

In stressing continuity, we do not mean to claim that nothing important changed in the 1970s, much less to insist on a neo-consensus framework of political history. But we do wish to highlight some of the problems with making neoliberalism an overarching historical framework rather than a subject of inquiry. And more importantly, we want to suggest some ways to return a sense of historical contingency to a phenomenon which can come to seem totalizing and inescapable. Once we see the ways in which "neoliberal" dynamics are embedded within the deep structures of state-economy, state-society, and state-subject relations, we can understand more fully why these dynamics have become especially prevalent at certain moments in our history—including the current one.[21]

Continuity and Change in Modern American Political History

One of the great strengths of the liberalism-and-conservatism paradigm is that it conceived of American politics as an ongoing contest between multiple traditions. Breaking with the midcentury consensus school's assumptions about the hegemony of liberalism and the inevitable course of modernization, it took conservative and populist ideas seriously, an expansion of vision that allowed it to offer a more nuanced reading of American political history. One of the weaknesses of this paradigm— perhaps its primary weakness—is that it tended to subsume other crises, structures, patterns, and experiences of citizenship and historical development within the framework of these relatively few, unitary political traditions. The development of a Fordist and mass consumption economy, local racial orders, the urban crisis, the rise of law-and-order politics— all of these became subordinated, analytically, to the primary structure of the New Deal order.

Meanwhile, the construction of this paradigm coincided with flourishing studies of the experiences of underrepresented groups. By the 1990s, a variety of emerging subfields took their cues from the "new" social history of the 1970s and 1980s, which had begun focusing on the lived experiences of marginalized groups. More recently mobilized identity groups' rights claims also came to drive the historical inquiry in a range of fields like African American history, Latino history, histories of immigration, and women's and gender studies, to name just a few. Soon, with the arrival of works such as George Chauncey's *Gay New York*, projects proliferated that were profoundly "political" but did not map onto the liberalism-conservatism paradigm.[22] By arguing for the political agency and subjectivity of disfranchised groups, these scholars highlighted patterns of marginalization, identified weapons of the weak, and pinpointed deep continuities of and developments within systems of white supremacy, patriarchy, and economic exploitation both in political history and within the historical profession. Such accounts decentered "big" moments like World War II or the 1980 election. But they also insisted on emphasizing the persistence and adaptability of white supremacy, patriarchy, and economic oppression across the full sweep of American history, even through watershed moments of social or racial political progress.

As they did so, these scholars of what we might call the "newer" social history wrote their way back to structures of state power, which the earlier generation had largely eschewed in pursuit of the linguistic and cultural turn.[23] The newer social historians developed nuanced accounts of particular policies or political processes that were implicated in their historical subjects' experiences of citizenship. Examples include important studies of the creation of public health regimes in San Francisco's Chinatown, radical sharecroppers' role in the Communist Party in the South during the Great Depression, the experiences of civil rights movement figures such as Ella Baker, the role of the border patrol in policing and criminalizing migrants from Mexico, the ideas of citizenship fostered by the migrant labor workers who participated in the bracero program and the families they left behind in Mexico, women's resistance to punitive welfare policies, the transformation of the labor movement into a working-class movement of women, and the role of popular culture in influencing U.S. policy interests in the Middle East.[24] All of these studies and more have provided critical insights into the development and dimensions of policy and political culture, and the role of state power in shaping a wide range of citizenship experiences and state developments. Today, such sustained attention to the experiences of a broad cross section of Americans has cracked open and democratized the very definition of "the political." These histories have expanded the political-historical imagination as never before.

While this cohort illuminated the experiences of groups whose histories had traditionally failed to obtain notice as political history, another group of scholars revitalized scholarship on the processes of governance by placing the state itself at the center of historical political analysis. Beginning in the 1970s, scholars working within the traditions of policy history and the "organizational synthesis" framed their work in ways that cut across epochal crises as well as the frameworks of liberalism and conservatism.[25] A decade later, a multidisciplinary band of scholars of historical institutionalism and American political development drew historians' attention to institutional structures and logics that transcended episodic crises, administrations, realignments, and movements, shaping and constraining political change in ways incomprehensible within, and often directly challenging to, the liberalism-conservatism paradigm. These scholars zeroed in on durable patterns of governance in part because they saw that in the wake of the 1960s, the Vietnam War, and Watergate, social and political movements often failed to penetrate and reform critical features of the American state. Against a tradition that viewed the United States as peculiarly "stateless" and American politics as characterized by a powerful antistatist tradition, these scholars began to illuminate sources of the state's strength and autonomy as well as its significance as a powerful if often subtle social and political actor in its own right, that is, through its agencies, bureaucrats, and extragovernmental partners.[26]

In different ways, then, the newer social historians and historical institutionalists were both writing political histories of *continuity*: continuities of structural racism, continuities of political marginalization and regimes of difference, and continuities of bureaucratic autonomy and state development. Strikingly, too, the approaches represented two sides of a coin undervalued by traditional political historians: a state that continued to grow despite regnant ideologies, a political structure that responded unevenly to minority concerns and social movements, and bureaucracies that constructed their own politics. Yet despite their considerable strengths and their potential for offering powerful insights, especially if paired, historical institutionalism and the various subfields that sprang from social history remained overwhelmingly siloed. While the newer social historians zeroed in on political developments particularly germane to their subjects, the institutionalists too often risked the inverse: writing nuanced analyses of political or economic institutions that did not fully integrate social and cultural history.[27] This siloing also developed in part thanks to different methodological approaches, theoretical frameworks, and disciplinary jargon. "Policy feedbacks" and "subaltern" politics easily passed each other in the night.

Each subfield produced powerful analyses and rich descriptions of particular aspects of political experiences and institutions. Yet at the very moment that explorations of "the political" in U.S. history has flourished as never before, the field of political history has grown decidedly fragmented, lacking unifying concepts, theories, and frames of reference beyond the outmoded red-blue divide.[28] The time is right to integrate these approaches to political history. Such an approach begins from an understanding of the state's development as historically situated within, and in turn acting upon, ideas of race, gender, class, sexuality, and economy; that is, it rejects the notion that institutional structure, political cultures, market forces, and cultural or racial experiences of the state and society can somehow be disaggregated. *Shaped by the State* seeks to offer just such a vertically, socially, and disciplinarily integrated political-historical methodology: sensitive to crises of continuity as well as disjuncture; attentive to political, economic, social, and cultural sites of power and agency; shorn of siloing jargon and connected to the social bases of experience and political authority.[29] A political history attentive to these kinds of continuities and renegotiations can help us make better sense of crucial questions about twentieth-century politics that are irreducible to mere partisanship or ideology.

An Unbounded Political History

The essays that follow proceed chronologically and thematically while also emphasizing themes emerging from our three primary spheres of inquiry: the emergence and experience of a leviathan state as it reoriented politics during the twentieth century (state-society); the persistence, reformation, and influence of the market in American politics as well as in Americans' political imagination (state-economy); and the ways in which these and other forces constrained and constructed differing tiers of rights-bearing citizens and subjects and created forms of governing authority often beyond the reach of popular democracy (state-subjects). The contributions come from scholars working in a variety of different traditions and subfields; some essays are archivally driven while others are more historiographical, blending theory with practice. Together, however, they identify significant lines of political-historical continuities and fruitful comparisons that cut across lines of public and private, of red and blue, and of class, race, and identity.

The chapters in part 1, "Building Leviathan," point to the emergence of the New Deal state and its discontents as they were constructed and reconstructed through the crises of depression and war. The essays suggest that as state builders confronted structural realities and limitations inherited from earlier eras as well as broader contemporary social and structural realities, the state they built entrenched and developed certain governing logics—accommodation with Jim Crow, techniques of surveillance, public-private partnerships, cultivation of highly contingent labor markets, and profound but obscure interventions on behalf of maintaining the fiction of free markets. These chapters emphasize not only the expansive and pervasive dimensions of the New Deal state but also the ways in which Americans understood and grappled with the reality of this powerful and diffuse, yet increasingly distant national government. They also emphasize the overlapping and often constitutive relationships between modern liberalism, modern conservatism, and phenomena associated with neoliberalism.

In the opening chapter, Sarah Igo explores several of the central themes of the volume in her examination of the lived experience of Social Security. As Igo reveals, the New Deal's rollout of Social Security gained cultural legitimacy by its use of the Social Security number, which was quickly embraced by a wide range of citizens as a powerful symbol of inclusion in the national polity. This acceptance of the Social Security Administration's forms of surveillance show the multitude of ways that the New Deal changed the relationship between the public and private. Cultures of state formation and surveillance, Igo suggests, defy easy ideological categorization but can be profoundly consequential in shaping the meaning of politics, the experiences of citizenship, and definitions of liberalism and conservatism as these cultures change over time.

N. D. B. Connolly explores the lived experience of liberalism from a decidedly different vantage point. Yet, like Igo, he demonstrates the analytical fruits of integrating formal state institutions, subjectivity, and the differing forms of mediation between them. Connolly offers important insight into the troubling history of African Americans' relationship to midcentury liberalism. In Connolly's telling, liberalism often cultivated African American partners in its recourse to markets, its endorsement of state violence, its pragmatic embrace of paternalistic alliances, and its reliance on brokered rather than direct democracy. The result was the maintenance of white supremacy that transcended the ostensible high-water marks of the civil rights era. In his exploration of these dynamics, Connolly locates striking lines of continuity between the seemingly distinct political crises of black disfranchisement and modern neoliberalism, which is too often defined as a crisis of the white working class.

In their chapter on the complex legacies of New Deal federalism, Brent Cebul and Mason Williams argue that red-blue binaries, which often took on regional dimensions (e.g., the "conservative" South and the "liberal" North), have led scholars to miss the centrality of the New Deal in creating not only urban liberalism but also Sunbelt conservatism. By mapping the New Deal's reliance on loosely regulated fiscal relationships between national and local governments and public and private actors, Cebul and Williams excavate the importance of local politics in shaping the day-to-day realities of the New Deal and postwar state. In their recounting of New Deal federalism, the legacies of Progressive Era reform, the contingent development of mass democratic publics, Jim Crow, the subtleties of fiscal federalism, the long history of public-private partnerships, and the fierce competition between local elites over the spoils of federal spending emerge as significant factors shaping not only what the New Deal accomplished but also how local actors—urban progressives and Sunbelt boosters alike— remembered and misremembered the importance of the New Deal as they constructed and reconstructed their political ideologies.

As the chapters by Igo, Connolly, and Cebul and Williams all suggest, far from snuffing out the centrality of the market and market actors in Americans' political and cultural imagination, the development of the leviathan state proceeded through market forces and ironically redoubled Americans' recourse to markets as alternatives to increasingly unwieldy or undemocratic governing institutions. As David M. P. Freund argues in his study of New Deal era financial policy, a new economic orthodoxy emerged around public debt and the money supply that justified unprecedented state interventions between 1932, when Herbert Hoover signed the first Glass-Steagall Act, and Franklin D. Roosevelt's passage of the Banking Act of 1935. Yet as Freund reveals, politicians and economists from across the political spectrum masked the implications of the government's new stake in finance, arguing that it mattered not whether public or private assets "stood behind" the currency's value. Instead, Freund argues that the "U.S. state fundamentally remade the financial landscape in the twentieth century by collateralizing it with public resources," and that the state's new powers would be essential to financing unprecedented postwar growth. Freund ultimately contends that policy makers and economists, liberals and conservatives, have been complicit in obscuring this transformation by portraying the value of modern money as purely market driven, further submerging the role of the state and helping maintain fictions of free markets and limited government.

In her chapter, Julie M. Weise highlights how turning to the rural margins can yield new ways of understanding the role of the New Deal state, its transnational dimensions, and its maintenance of contingent labor markets. She explores the experience of Mexican migrant laborers in the Arkansas Delta who came to the United States as part of the bracero program. Begun in 1942 and in effect for twenty-two years, the program was established initially thanks to wartime agricultural labor shortages. But it expanded most rapidly in the decades following the World War II. As Weise suggests, despite New Deal era guarantees of fair wages, humane working conditions, and access to public accommodations, braceros instead faced deplorable working conditions, shelter, and usurious compensation. Denied assistance by U.S. officials, in their efforts to improve their lot, braceros instead turned to the Mexican government, which, as Weise makes clear, more effectively promoted and instituted the New Deal's purported values than did postwar liberals themselves.

In part 2, "Crisis and Continuity," the chapters explore the ways in which earlier techniques of governance and experiences of citizenship became renegotiated and amplified through a subsequent period of crisis, the 1970s. The essays identify not only deep continuities between historical techniques of what we might call neoliberal governance but also continuities and convergences between the experiences of contingent forms of citizenship and citizens' perspectives on the state itself. To be sure, changes in the global political economy and the rights revolutions of the 1960s refashioned the relationships between state and society, state and market, and the lived experience of the leviathan state. But they did not rewrite these relationships on a clean slate. Rather, through a particular emphasis on the 1970s, the chapters suggest ways in which these relationships became recast in the context of earlier state developments and dependencies.

Expanding on themes introduced by Connolly, Andrew Kahrl reveals that racial and ethnic depredations of the U.S. political economy extended and intensified after the Great Society. By focusing on state and local tax-policy administration, Kahrl uncovers a variety of bureaucratic and administrative practices used to punish and exploit the poor and politically disfranchised. Providing a new way to think about the tax politics of the 1970s, Kahrl maps unseen sites of discrimination and chronicles the double injury that myths about black tax delinquency and the undemocratic state have perpetuated: abetting a misguided radical anti-tax, promarket, and antigovernment mood that infects both parties and which simultaneously enforces a locally based, regressively redistributionary tax regime.

In her chapter, Sarah Milov offers a different view of the relationship between the state and citizens seeking new forms of political and workplace rights in the 1970s. Focusing on the battle for smoke-free workplaces, Milov shows how activists often had to go to war with the unions to which they belonged—unions that otherwise bargained for worker health and safety. Milov exposes the complex legal, gendered, and biopolitical forces that could fuse the interests of worker-activists with corporations concerned primarily with efficiency. Ultimately, Milov argues that the workplace battle she uncovers was less a factor in the eclipse of the New Deal order and was instead a legacy of New Deal era "law, administration, and ideas about health and the environment [that] had expanded the realm of the contestable." Crucial continuities, in other words, played an overlooked role in creating labor's decade of crisis.

In his chapter, Suleiman Osman reveals that the "politics of scale" that emerged in the 1970s cut across the ideological and partisan divides and reflected a yearning for both a return to the local and a quest to harness new globalizing capacities. Osman points out the existing limitations in many of the historiographical understandings of that "pivotal decade" and instead calls for an approach that attends to the codevelopment of global and local political outlooks. Through close attention to varieties of political expression and experience on the ground, Osman roots the emergence of neoliberal policy prescriptions not only in the crisis of the national state but also in a multivalent quest to cultivate governing local and global capacities capable of maintaining continuities of rights and opportunity.

Melissa Borja's contribution further demonstrates the complicated ways that global and local scales and state and private organizations interacted in the 1970s. Borja reveals how the federal, state, and municipal governments of the United States joined forces with religious organizations to give relief and resettlement assistance to hundreds of thousands of Indochinese war refugees. Rather than simply discharging responsibility for social services to nongovernmental organizations (as "privatization" narratives would suggest), Borja shows that American governments were able to expand their social welfare capacity by partnering with religious institutions. In the process, voluntary agencies came to serve as an extension of the state, which created new possibilities but also challenges of accountability and coercion. Borja, therefore, offers a more precise understanding of the fault lines in the church-state debate, voluntarism and privatization, and the emergence of the Religious Right in the 1970s and beyond.

Like Weise, Osman, and Borja, Stuart Schrader suggests that looking beyond national boundaries can provide new ways of understanding how the New Deal state evolved over time and ultimately generated what is perhaps the fundamental social and political crisis of our time: the crisis of black, male incarceration. Like Freund, he explores the way political narratives can obscure forms of state power, and, like Igo, he uncovers roots of the neoliberal surveillance state in New Deal and postwar state-building projects—in his case, abroad. Schrader examines the literature surrounding the "carceral state" and spotlights how the turn toward transnationalism or "the U.S. in the world" has been notably absent. By tracking institutions both inside and outside the state, including law-enforcement agencies and professional organizations, Schrader demonstrates the need for close empirical attention to the transnational dimensions of the carceral state, suggesting that key aspects of the construction of a postwar U.S. empire have come home to roost.

The final essay in the volume, by Rachel Moran, also challenges prevailing ideas of culture wars politics of the last decades of the twentieth century. Moran demonstrates shifting cultural perceptions of the state, following as liberals moved from subsidizing a mass consumer economy in the postwar years to regulatory policing of the family-consumer economy in the 1970s. While scholars have illuminated the gender dynamics of specific policy regimes, Moran reveals how gendered metaphors for specific policies, in this case the Federal Trade Commission's efforts to regulate commercials targeting children, shaped the language Americans used to describe the state itself. While these terms have surely taken on partisan valences, Moran reveals how such gendered metaphors were animated by anxieties about big government that also emerged across the Atlantic in other Western democracies in crisis, and in the process reshaped the very meanings of liberalism and conservatism at home.

The volume ends with two synthetic conclusions. In the first, Kim Phillips-Fein offers a more sharply delineated appraisal of the promise and perils of the emerging neoliberalism paradigm, suggesting as well auspicious new sites of historical study and analysis. In the second, Matthew Lassiter explores how the kind of political history suggested by this volume (and the works that inspired it) will provide ways to move beyond the emphasis on critical elections, partisan realignment, polarization, and totalizing narratives of neoliberalism. Lassiter's is also an implicit call to unify the flourishing if fragmented fields of inquiry concerned with the relationship between state power, capitalism, and the experiences of citizenship—of uniting disciplines attuned to both crisis and continuity in political history.

Notes

1. See, e.g., the "Trump Syllabus" crafted by Keisha Blain and N. D. B. Connolly, which drew from more than one hundred scholars in a wide variety of disciplines (http://www.publicbooks.org/trump-syllabus-2-0/; accessed February 19, 2017).

2. Timothy Shenk, "Apostles of Growth," *Nation*, November 5, 2014, https://www.thenation.com/article/apostles-growth/. For a critical audit, see "Interchange: The History of Capitalism," *Journal of American History* 101, no. 2 (September 2014), 503–36. Thank you to Tim Shenk for suggesting this analogy to us.

3. This pattern was evident by the time of Meg Jacobs, William J. Novak, and

Julian E. Zelizer's landmark volume *The Democratic Experiment*, which included essays by a number of scholars who would have been regarded primarily as social or cultural historians. Since then, the flourishing of research involving the state in the fields of the history of gender and sexuality, the history of capitalism, environmental history, the history of immigration and citizenship, and the history of the African diaspora, to name only a few, has tilted the balance much farther. See Jacobs, Novak, and Zelizer, eds., *The Democratic Experiment: New Directions in American Political History* (Princeton, NJ: Princeton University Press, 2003).

4. For all the real issues at stake in the often-contentious conversation launched by Fredrik Logevall and Kenneth Osgood's widely read op-ed on the place of political history within the discipline, historians on all sides broadly agreed on the importance of state power, institutions, and elite actors. See Logevall and Osgood, "Why Did We Stop Teaching Political History?" *New York Times*, August 29, 2016.

5. The classic statement is Steve Fraser and Gary Gerstle, eds., *The Rise and Fall of the New Deal Order, 1930–1980* (Princeton, NJ: Princeton University Press, 1989). For a critique of the theory on which the concept of political order is built, see David R. Mayhew, *Electoral Realignments: A Critique of an American Genre* (New Haven, CT: Yale University Press, 2004).

6. Fraser and Gerstle, *Rise and Fall of the New Deal Order*, ix–x.

7. They did so in the wake of Alan Brinkley's call to take seriously the history of conservatism. Brinkley, "The Problem of American Conservatism," *American Historical Review* 99, no. 2 (April 1994), 409–29. Two excellent reviews of the vast literature that emerged are Kim Phillips-Fein, "Conservatism: A State of the Field," *Journal of American History* 98, no. 3 (December 2011), 723–43; and Julian E. Zelizer, "Rethinking the History of American Conservatism," *Reviews in American History* 38, no. 2 (June 2010): 367–92.

8. Leading works include David Harvey, *A Brief History of Neoliberalism* (New York: Oxford University Press, 2005); Jefferson R. Cowie, *Stayin' Alive: The 1970s and the Last Days of the Working Class* (New York: New Press, 2011); Greta R. Krippner, *Capitalizing on Crisis: The Political Origins of the Rise of Finance* (Cambridge, MA: Harvard University Press, 2012); and Judith Stein, *The Pivotal Decade: How the United States Traded Factories for Finance in the Seventies* (New Haven, CT: Yale University Press, 2010).

9. For an exemplary recent example, see Sam Rosenfeld, *The Polarizers: Postwar Architects of Our Partisan Era* (Chicago: University of Chicago Press, 2017).

10. Janet Roitman, "Crisis," *Political Concepts: A Critical Lexicon* 1 (2011), http://www.politicalconcepts.org/issue1/crisis/.

11. Daniel T. Rodgers, *The Age of Fracture* (Cambridge, MA: Belknap Press of Harvard University Press, 2011). Historians have recently joined geographers, sociologists, and political scientists in emphasizing the bipartisan nature of the punitive turn. Outstanding full-length works in this vein are Elizabeth Hinton, *From the*

War on Poverty to the War on Crime: The Making of Mass Incarceration in America (Cambridge, MA: Harvard University Press, 2016), and Julilly Kohler-Hausmann, *Getting Tough: Welfare and Imprisonment in 1970s America* (Princeton, NJ: Princeton University Press, 2017); see also the earlier statements by Lassiter, "Political History beyond the Red-Blue Divide," 763; Heather Ann Thompson, "Why Mass Incarceration Matters: Rethinking Crisis, Decline, and Transformation in Postwar American History," *Journal of American History* 97, no. 3 (December 2010): 729–31. In the social sciences, see, among others, Marie Gottschalk, *The Prison and the Gallows: The Politics of Mass Incarceration in America* (New York: Cambridge University Press, 2006); Naomi Murakawa, *The First Civil Right: How Liberals Built Prison America* (New York: Oxford University Press, 2014).

12. A number of scholars have examined the transnational origins of domestic developments. See especially Daniel T. Rodgers, *Atlantic Crossings: Social Politics in a Progressive Age* (Cambridge, MA: Belknap Press of Harvard University Press, 1996); Daniel Immerwahr, *Thinking Small: The United States and the Lure of Community Development* (Cambridge, MA: Harvard University Press, 2015); Mae M. Ngai, *Impossible Subjects: Illegal Aliens and the Making of Modern America* (Princeton, NJ: Princeton University Press, 2004); Andrew Preston and Doug Rossinow, eds., *Outside In: The Transnational Circuitry of U.S. History* (New York: Oxford University Press, 2016); Daniel J. Sargent, *A Superpower Transformed: The Remaking of American Foreign Relations in the 1970s* (New York: Oxford University Press, 2015).

13. In his conclusion to this volume Matthew Lassiter explores this issue in more detail. See also Matthew D. Lassiter, *The Silent Majority: Suburban Politics in the Sunbelt South* (Princeton, NJ: Princeton University Press, 2006); Lassiter, "Suburban Strategies: The Volatile Center in Postwar American Politics," in *The Democratic Experiment: New Directions in American Political History*, ed. Jacobs, Novak, and Zelizer (Princeton, NJ: Princeton University Press, 2003), chap. 13; N. D. B. Connolly, *A World More Concrete: Real Estate and the Remaking of Jim Crow South Florida* (Chicago: University of Chicago Press, 2014); Brent Cebul, *Illusions of Progress: Business, Poverty, and Development in the American Century* (Philadelphia: University of Pennsylvania Press, forthcoming); David M. P. Freund, *Colored Property: State Policy and White Racial Politics in Suburban America* (Chicago: University of Chicago Press, 2007); Lily Geismer, *Don't Blame Us: Suburban Liberals and the Transformation of the Democratic Party* (Princeton, NJ: Princeton University Press, 2015); Andrew Needham, *Power Lines: Phoenix and the Making of the American Southwest* (Princeton, NJ: Princeton University Press, 2014); Robert O. Self, *American Babylon: Race and the Struggle for Postwar Oakland* (Princeton, NJ: Princeton University Press, 2003).

14. In addition to the works cited in the previous note, see especially Lizabeth Cohen, *Making a New Deal: Industrial Workers in Chicago, 1919–1939* (New York: Cambridge University Press, 1990); Gary Gerstle, *Working-Class Americanism:*

The Politics of Labor in a Textile City, 1914–1960 (Princeton, NJ: Princeton University Press, 1989), and Gerstle, *American Crucible: Race and Nation in the Twentieth Century* (Princeton, NJ: Princeton University Press, 2001); Thomas J. Sugrue, *The Origins of the Urban Crisis: Race and Inequality in Postwar Detroit* (Princeton, NJ: Princeton University Press, 1996); Alice O'Connor, *Poverty Knowledge: Social Science, Social Policy, and the Poor in Twentieth-Century U.S. History* (Princeton, NJ: Princeton University Press, 2002); Lisa McGirr, *Suburban Warriors: The Origins of the New American Right* (Princeton, NJ: Princeton University Press, 2001); Joseph Crespino, *In Search of Another Country: Mississippi and the Conservative Counterrevolution* (Princeton, NJ: Princeton University Press, 2009); Kevin M. Kruse, *White Flight: Atlanta and the Making of Modern Conservatism* (Princeton, NJ: Princeton University Press, 2007); Kim Phillips-Fein, *Invisible Hands: The Making of the Conservative Movement from the New Deal to Reagan* (New York: W. W. Norton, 2009); Angus Burgin, *The Great Persuasion: Reinventing Free Markets since the Depression* (Cambridge, MA: Harvard University Press, 2012); Jennifer Burns, *Goddess of the Market: Ayn Rand and the American Right* (New York: Oxford University Press, 2009); Bethany Moreton, *To Serve God and Wal-Mart: The Making of Christian Free Enterprise* (Cambridge, MA: Harvard University Press, 2009); Meg Jacobs, *Pocketbook Politics: Economic Citizenship in Twentieth-Century America* (Princeton, NJ: Princeton University Press, 2007); Lizabeth Cohen, *A Consumer's Republic: The Politics of Mass Consumption in Postwar America* (New York: Vintage, 2003); Alice Kessler-Harris, *In Pursuit of Equity: Women, Men, and the Quest for Economic Citizenship in 20th-Century America* (New York: Oxford University Press, 2001); Nancy MacLean, *Freedom Is Not Enough: The Opening of the American Workplace* (New York: Russell Sage Foundation, 2006); Molly C. Michelmore, *Tax and Spend: The Welfare State, Tax Politics, and the Limits of American Liberalism* (Philadelphia: University of Pennsylvania Press, 2010). More recently, scholars of media have emphasized the importance of emergent forms of mass communication in driving the conservative resurgence. See, for example, Nicole Hemmer, *Messengers of the Right: Conservative Media and the Transformation of American Politics* (Philadelphia: University of Pennsylvania Press, 2016). Several edited collections have offered important contributions as well. In addition to Fraser and Gerstle, *Rise and Fall of the New Deal Order*, see especially Bruce J. Schulman and Julian E. Zelizer, eds., *Rightward Bound: Making America Conservative in the 1970s* (Cambridge, MA: Harvard University Press, 2008); Kim Phillips-Fein and Julian E. Zelizer, eds., *What's Good for Business: Business and American Politics since World War II* (New York: Oxford University Press, 2012).

15. Margot Canaday, *The Straight State: Sexuality and Citizenship in Twentieth-Century America* (Princeton, NJ: Princeton University Press, 2009).

16. Connolly, *World More Concrete*.

17. Ngai, *Impossible Subjects*.

18. For recent examples of scholarship on the history of business and politics that challenge the neat alignment of business and conservatism and limited government orthodoxy, see a number of the essays in Richard R. John and Kim Phillips-Fein, eds., *Capital Gains: Business and Politics in Twentieth Century America* (Philadelphia: University of Pennsylvania Press, 2016).

19. In framing political history this way, we distinguish between a politics involving the state and infrapolitics—what the theorist James C. Scott refers to as "a diagonal politics," a politics of everyday stealth and evasion, "a politics that 'dare not speak its name.'" In emphasizing this distinction, we emphatically do *not* wish to diminish the importance of infrapolitics and other forms of exercising and contesting power apart from the state, nor do we mean to suggest that the history of these forms of power merits less scholarly attention than does the history of politics involving the state. To the contrary, we hope that the treatment of political history offered in this book will help scholars to see that the relationship between the two is essential to the production of "the political": the most profound democratic movements often have their genesis in the transformation of infrapolitics into politics. On infrapolitics, see especially James C. Scott, *Weapons of the Weak: Everyday Forms of Peasant Resistance* (New Haven, CT: Yale University Press, 1985); Scott, *Domination and the Arts of Resistance: Hidden Transcripts* (New Haven, CT: Yale University Press, 1990); Robin D. G. Kelley, *Race Rebels: Culture, Politics, and the Black Working Class* (New York: Free Press, 1994).

20. Kim Phillips-Fein's conclusion to this volume discusses the key works; see "The History of Neoliberalism."

21. We can also better understand how progressive aspects of the New Deal and postwar state persist despite such seemingly sweeping ideological or partisan change since the 1970s. For an influential reading of the wholesale decline and historical exceptionalism of New Deal liberalism, see Jefferson Cowie, *The Great Exception: The New Deal and the Limits of American Politics* (Princeton, NJ: Princeton University Press, 2016). For a critique of Cowie's reading of twentieth-century political history and periodization that emphasizes continuities in the form of the persistence of New Deal institutions and social expectations, see Sam Rosenfeld, "There's No Going Back," *Democracy: A Journal of Ideas*, no. 40 (Spring 2016), https://democracyjournal.org/magazine/40/theres-no-going-back/.

22. George Chauncey, *Gay New York: Gender, Urban Culture and the Making of the Gay Male World* (New York: Basic Books, 1994).

23. These trends are reflected in a variety of disciplines well beyond twentieth-century U.S. political history. See, for instance, Nathan Perl-Rosenthal's exploration of a new generation of social historical interest in questions such as "How does it work? How does it happen?" Perl-Rosenthal, "Comment: Generational Turns," *American Historical Review* 117, no. 3 (June 2012): 807.

24. Nayan Shah, *Contagious Divides: Epidemics and Race in San Francisco's Chinatown* (Berkeley: University of California Press, 2001); Robin D. G. Kelley,

Hammer and Hoe: Alabama Communists during the Great Depression (Chapel Hill: University of North Carolina Press, 1990); Barbara Ransby, *Ella Baker and the Black Freedom Movement* (Chapel Hill: University of North Carolina Press, 2003); Kelly Lytle Hernandez, *Migra! A History of the U.S. Border Patrol* (Berkeley: University of California Press, 2010); Ana Elizabeth Rosas, *Abrazando el Espíritu: Bracero Families Confront the US-Mexico Border* (Berkeley: University of California Press, 2014); Rhonda Y. Williams, *The Politics of Public Housing: Black Women's Struggle against Urban Inequality* (New York: Oxford University Press, 2004); Annalise Orleck, *Storming Caesars Palace: How Black Mothers Fought Their Own War on Poverty* (Boston: Beacon Press, 2005); Dorothy Sue Cobble, *The Other Women's Movement: Workplace Justice and Social Rights in Modern America* (Princeton, NJ: Princeton University Press, 2004); Melani McAlister, *Epic Encounters: Culture, Media, and U.S. Interests in the Middle East since 1945* (Berkeley: University of California Press, 2001).

25. For an overview of the field of policy history, see Julian E. Zelizer, "Clio's Lost Tribe: Public Policy History since 1978," *Journal of Policy History* 12, no. 3 (2000): 371–94. For a substantial revision of the organizational synthesis which nonetheless shares its critical approach to the conventional periodizations, see Brian Balogh, *The Associational State: American Governance in the Twentieth Century* (Philadelphia: University of Pennsylvania Press, 2015).

26. Among many others, see Stephen Skowronek, *Building a New American State: The Expansion of National Administrative Capacities, 1877–1920* (New York: Cambridge University Press, 1982); Peter B. Evans, Dietrich Rueschemeyer, and Theda Skocpol, eds., *Bringing the State Back In* (New York: Cambridge University Press, 1985); Theda Skocpol, *Protecting Soldiers and Mothers: The Political Origins of Social Policy in the United States* (Cambridge, MA: Belknap Press of Harvard University Press, 1992); Daniel P. Carpenter, *The Forging of Bureaucratic Autonomy: Reputations, Networks, and Policy Innovation in Executive Agencies, 1862–1928* (Princeton, NJ: Princeton University Press, 2001); William J. Novak, "The Myth of the 'Weak' American State," *American Historical Review* 113, no. 3 (June 2008): 752–72 (esp. 752–63); Brian Balogh, *A Government out of Sight: The Mystery of National Authority in Nineteenth-Century America* (New York: Cambridge University Press, 2009); Balogh, *Associational State*; Karen Orren and Stephen Skowronek, *The Policy State: An American Predicament* (Cambridge, MA: Harvard University Press, 2017); James T. Sparrow, William J. Novak, and Stephen W. Sawyer, *Boundaries of the State in US History* (Chicago: University of Chicago Press, 2015); Suzanne Mettler, *The Submerged State: How Invisible Government Policies Undermine American Democracy* (Chicago: University of Chicago Press, 2011); Christopher Howard, *The Hidden Welfare State: Tax Expenditures and Social Policy in the United States* (Princeton, NJ: Princeton University Press, 1997); Gail Radford, *The Rise of the Public Authority: State Building and Economic Development in Twentieth-Century America* (Chicago: University of

Chicago Press, 2013); Jennifer S. Light, *From Warfare to Welfare: Defense Intellectuals and Urban Problems in Cold War America* (Baltimore: Johns Hopkins University Press, 2004).

27. As Margot Canaday notes in her landmark book, "The best work on the state by historians takes state institutions seriously, but incorporates rather than jettisons the 'society' or 'culture' side of the binary, blending social and cultural with legal and political history." Canaday, *Straight State*, 5. For a powerful example of blending institutional and social historical methodologies that sheds light on cultures of state building, see James T. Sparrow, *Warfare State: World War II Americans and the Age of Big Government* (New York: Oxford University Press, 2011).

28. As the cultural and intellectual historian Daniel Rodgers has argued, the result of such disaggregated attention to agency, institutions, and experience was that "notions of structure and power thinned out." Likewise, Nell Irvin Painter warned social historians about the risks of attending to experience and agency without corresponding attention to institutionalized power and scale ironically risked obscuring historians' subjects' full humanity. Rodgers, *Age of Fracture*, 5; and Nell Irvin Painter, "Soul Murder and Slavery: Toward a Fully Loaded Cost Accounting," in *Southern History across the Color Line*, ed. Nell Irvin Painter (Chapel Hill: University of North Carolina Press, 2002), 15–39.

29. We borrow the notion of vertically integrated history from Peter James Hudson in his participation in the *Journal of American History*'s "Interchange: The History of Capitalism," 504.

PART I

Building Leviathan

CHAPTER ONE

Social Insecurities

Private Data and Public Culture in Modern America

Sarah E. Igo

How are Americans known by their state, and with what ramifications for individual privacy and political culture? Asked urgently today, the question surfaced as early as the first censuses of the population.[1] But it captured broad public attention in the decades defined by the Depression and World War II, provoked by the U.S. government's new—or at least newly open—methods of tracking its people. Honed during the Philippine-American War at the turn of the century and refined through the Bureau of Investigation's domestic surveillance activities during World War I, such techniques were in this era extended to a much broader swath of the citizenry.[2] From birth certificates to passports, administrative tracking was becoming part of the bureaucratic everyday.[3] In the New Deal, it would come wrapped in the guise not of social order but of social benefit—indeed, social *security*.

What scholars have termed the *administrative state* entered citizens' lives in new ways and to novel ends in the 1930s.[4] It ballooned further during World War II, when the scale of government activity came to dwarf the New Deal programs "that had seemed gargantuan only a few years earlier."[5] The state had been a locus for fears about centralized authority since the first days of the American republic, of course. But the state understood as administrator or bureaucrat was a product of the twentieth century.[6] As federal agencies loomed larger in Americans' lives, they also became a focal point for reflecting on individual privacy. How much knowledge about its own citizens ought a government possess? And what would an administered society mean for the people caught in its net?

These questions became less abstract with the passage of the Social Security Act of 1935. A landmark piece of legislation, still considered "the most expansive and important social welfare program in the United States," the act ushered in old-age and unemployment benefits for a large segment of the population.[7] Less noticed, it also marked the U.S. government's first widespread use of personal information to identify and administer specific individuals, in the form of the Social Security number (SSN). The SSN was an essential mechanism of the ambitious new program, which as reformer and social scientist Sophonisba P. Breckinridge put it in 1935, "contemplates the participation in all of our lives of the federal, state, and local governments and puts, for the first time, a degree of validity into the expression 'American standard of life.' "[8]

Standard here referred to a minimum threshold for subsistence, but it implied a kind of standardization common to large-scale administrative projects. Unprecedented though it was in scope, Social Security was in step with a set of identification and documentation practices well advanced by the early decades of the twentieth century.[9] Indeed, its planners drew from other nations' experiments with administering citizens' identities, particularly those of France, Britain, and Brazil.[10] "Seeing like a state," in James C. Scott's influential formulation, hinged on making citizens "legible" and thereby amenable to the designs of officials and planners.[11] The expansion of "paper identities" was thus intertwined with a mode of governance able to register and recognize specific persons.[12]

States were never the only authors of this documentary impulse. Life insurance outfits and credit agencies were two of the powerful private entities driving the creation of what we would now call "personally identifying information."[13] Through the efforts of private as well as public agencies, modern Americans were becoming deeply enmeshed in webs of bureaucratic verification. A columnist for an Atlanta newspaper wryly testified in 1942 that "every law-abiding citizen today" had "his vest pockets . . . crammed with credentials," including "a draft registration card, a social security card, a driver's license, a hospitalization card, an insurance card, a gasoline ration book, a sugar ration book, a finger-print identification card, a shopper's credit card," and so on. "Practically all of these items stress the fact that I am me and nobody else; without them, I would officially cease to exist," he quipped.[14]

For this columnist, Social Security cards were just one piece of a "thoroughly classified, documented, and cross-indexed" modern existence.[15]

Yet these cards warrant special scrutiny for the fashion in which the numbers imprinted on them bound data to entitlements and individuals to the state—enlisting Americans in their own bureaucratic visibility by making manifest the benefits of identification. The federal government's numbering of individuals, and the potential tracking it permitted, did not escape public notice. Quite apart from discussions over Social Security's substantive merits, this feature of its operation engendered sharp questions from a strange set of bedfellows: the Republican opposition as well as African Americans, labor unions, working women, and religious groups. But we must not read backward from our anxious contemporary stance toward identity documents; nor should we assume that state surveillance loomed large for most citizens in the 1930s and 1940s. Concern about Social Security numbers in that era, while evident, competed with another view, in which the nine digits were broadcast, even cherished, as proof of membership in a newly generous polity. This was, we might say, legibility with benefits.

The proud claiming of a Social Security number, a bureaucratic instrument of the expanding welfare state, may today strike us as strange. That dissonance compels us to recognize the ways that the New Deal state has been remembered differently—both in our partisan political culture and in our scholarly accounts—than it was experienced at the time. The lived history of the SSN reveals that earlier Americans' relationship with their identity cards, and with the agencies that tracked their affairs, diverged markedly from our own. It also helps us appreciate the fungibility of the very contents of the public and the private. Understanding how, in those decades of depression and war, "private" data could advance a public claim or identity requires an imagination tempered by time.

The Early Days of Tracking

Franklin D. Roosevelt signed the Social Security Act on August 14, 1935, in the midst of the worst economic crisis in American history.[16] Intended to provide benefits for the elderly, dependent, and unemployed through a payroll tax, it pledged—in a word—security for millions of Americans.[17] A vast scholarly literature now examines the impulses behind, the architects of, and the ideological assumptions built into Social Security and other institutions of the New Deal state. Considerably less attention has been paid to the by-products of the new administrative system, and particularly the assigning of unique identifying numbers to citizens. What did this intersection of numbering and state building mean for the Americans newly in Social Security's embrace?

Given its exclusion of certain classes of workers—agricultural laborers and domestics, and thus African Americans, most prominently (and deliberately)—Social Security was not a national system in the sense that it covered all citizens or residents.[18] Initially, only those in commercial and industrial employment, roughly 60 percent of the nation's paid workforce, were encompassed by the program.[19] Nevertheless, the legislation's reach was unparalleled, establishing something akin to a "national enumeration system."[20] It also differed in kind from most prior state ventures to gather information from Americans. The U.S. Census, although it aggregated reams of personal information, made no decisions pegged to *particular* individuals' data. The Social Security system was designed to do just this: track specific workers' payroll contributions over their entire lifetimes in order to pay out appropriate benefits. Not only, that is, did Social Security need to enlist millions of workers into the program; it also had to keep those individuals in its sights for decades to come.

As a result, SSNs raised in an early form the dilemmas of a society organized around the collection and maintenance of what the agency itself described as "considerable personal and confidential information."[21] It was an issue tailor made for partisan combat, and Social Security's opponents did not squander the opportunity. Republican operatives seized upon the issue of state-issued identification numbers, whipping up fears of regimentation and improper state invasion into Americans' private lives.

This was the point of a colorful political stunt engineered by the publisher William Randolph Hearst and the Republican National Committee (RNC) chairman John D. M. Hamilton on the eve of the 1936 presidential election. Not only would workers hand over to the state a stash of sensitive private information, including—the RNC (falsely) claimed—one's religious and union affiliations, "physical defects," and marital status. They would soon also be required to wear "dog tags" listing their Social Security number. A central exhibit in the Republican campaign against Social Security was a fabricated photograph of the offending item, pictured on a chain around a young man's neck.[22] "If the Roosevelt administration is returned to power, we shall see two groups of citizens in this nation," thundered the RNC chair at a rally in Boston: "those who are numbered and those who are not numbered." The former were the unlucky "27 million men and women who will be forced to report to a politically appointed clerk, every change of their residence, every change in their wages, every change of their employment." For at least some in the crowd of twenty thousand at the Boston Garden who responded with "repeated waves of applause" to Hamilton's invocations of police cards and state surveillance, this was the road to European-style despotism.[23] As Americans watched developments unfold in Hitler's Germany, associating Social Security with other forms of state coercion was a charge with some potency.

The episode fits neatly with conventional wisdom about Americans' reflexive antistatism—their jealous resistance to infringements of their individual liberty—not to mention American historians' received view of the New Deal as cementing the modern liberal-conservative divide.[24] Indeed, even before the Republican attack, the Social Security Board (SSB) was highly sensitive to the public relations of numbering the population, certain it served a people who had "always been fearful of anything that might suggest the loss of some personal freedom through formal records of identities."[25] Thus the board scrupulously avoided the term *registration* to describe the enrollment effort, instead favoring *enumeration*—an attempt to assimilate the new practice with the long-standing one of census taking. It also insisted, somewhat disingenuously, on the "entirely voluntary" nature of applying for an account number.[26] Moreover, that number, it was stressed, was for the holder's convenience and *not* for identification. In response to the RNC "forgery," planners stated emphatically that Social Security did not "intend nor had it ever intended to issue identification disks to American workers."[27] Finally, the SSB described information about marital status and union ties as "matters private in their nature and of no legitimate concern to the Federal Government," adding that "no such questions would be asked now or at any time in the future."[28]

Evidently, the board believed that it was tightly constrained by the public culture in which Social Security was taking root and needed to tread carefully. Each decision it made regarding the rollout of the SSN was carefully weighed not just for its administrative implications but also for its political ones. Internal debates over how best to track Social Security's beneficiaries, vigilant attention to questions of public reception, and strenuous avoidance of fingerprinting or anything that resembled "registration" all point to a bureaucracy focused on exerting the lightest touch possible.[29] But was the Social Security Board—or the RNC, for that matter—correct in its estimation of the American public? Evidence suggests that citizens were not nearly as anxious about "registration" as either Social Security's strongest advocates or bitterest opponents suspected. Indeed, a mere twenty-eight days after the initial distribution of employee forms, Social Security

FIGURE I.I. Social Security records, late 1930s (courtesy of the Social Security Archives)

reported the receipt of more than twenty-two million completed applications out of an expected twenty-six million.[30] Moreover, it seems clear that those who did worry about the gathering and use of their personal data did not direct that worry at the state.

Certainly some concerns were raised about the government's information collection project: the fact that it would, under the auspices of Social Security, possess files on millions of Americans, with more to be added every year. The Social Security Board was aware that "a great many employees were naturally very anxious to know how the information on the employee's application was to be used."[31] Alert to potential criticism, the SSB had determined early on that the "minimum necessary" information was to be requested in order to set up a Social Security account. Only the worker's name, address, date and place of birth, sex, "color," parents' names, and name and address of employer were ultimately deemed "essential for either identification or the actuarial studies required of the Board."[32] This was a considerably less capacious list than the RNC had manufactured in its campaign against Social Security, but even it was too long for some.

African American leaders were particularly incensed about the inclusion of a racial designation on the application form. "The element of color was inserted for one reason and for only one reason," charged an editorial in the *Pittsburgh Courier*: "to more easily discriminate against Negroes."[33] The National Association for the Advancement of Colored People (NAACP) vigorously but unsuccessfully challenged the agency on this point, convinced that such information would "inevitably be used in various ways, both obvious and subtle, to practice discrimination based on race."[34] Being tagged bureaucratically by one's race, these writers understood, was to be made more visible and thus more vulnerable in a society still structured along caste lines. A desire to keep aspects of one's identity private—whether age, marital status, religion, work history, politics, or ethnicity—was apparent in other citizens' reactions to being "registered" as well.

This was not precisely a worry about a Big Brother state, however. It soon became clear that many potential account holders were concerned not about what the government might do but about what *employers* would do with their newly divulged personal information. In order to obtain a Social Security number, workers were to fill out an application blank and return it to the Post Office—which was spearheading the initial enumeration effort—either directly or through their union or workplace. Just as soon as enrollment began, the board began handling questions about employer coercion. Numerous workers complained of having been instructed to return their forms via their employer or else be fired.[35] Employees keenly understood the threat this posed. Details of their work histories and personal backgrounds were items they often kept carefully shielded.

It was a particular worry for women and Jewish workers, Social Security administrators noted, "because they have falsified their age to their employers or because they are married women representing to be single in order to retain their positions or they are jews [*sic*] who have changed their names because the organization for which they work is anti-semitic."[36] Here the board simply acknowledged well-known facts. Religious minorities occupied a precarious place in American society in the 1930s: one 1934 study documented still-high levels of discrimination against Jews in employment and housing and against Catholics in political and civic affairs.[37] Divulging information about one's religion or ethnicity via a telling surname on an official form would have been especially worrisome for these Americans—particularly the chance that it would make its way back to employers. On their part, hundreds of working women called the Social Security Board to ask whether their bosses would be alerted to their age or marital status, information female workers often falsified in order to get or keep a job.[38] An anonymous letter to the *Chicago Daily Tribune*, signed by "The 'Fibbers,'" fretted over this problem, asking whether Social Security applications had to be handed over to employers or could be sent to the agency directly, and whether discrepancies between what was reported to Social Security and to the company would be discovered.[39]

The risk of registration for women and Jews stemmed not from state surveillance or even mismanagement, then, but from the possibility of accurate data maintained by the government being uncovered by employers. The Social Security system in this way imperiled not just workers' job prospects but also their tried-and-true practices for keeping certain kinds of information private. Labor unions harbored a similar concern, namely that an individual's previous position might be divulged to a prospective employer, along with a clue to that person's union affiliation.[40] As the SSB knew from conferences with state administrators of unemployment insurance even before the program was launched, "a good deal of fear was evidenced . . . that the identification token given to the employee would be used for black-listing."[41] When it came to their bosses, African American, Jewish, female, and unionized workers alike had no trouble grasping the dark side of legibility.

The advent of the Social Security system made evident that workers were right to worry. It soon came to light that opportunistic employers were circulating their own official-looking forms demanding additional pieces of data. These could include the worker's nationality, health record, years of residence in the United States, religious background, educational level, home ownership, number of dependents, relatives employed in the same plant, or political and trade union affiliations. An early such example, from December 1935—nearly a year before the actual enumeration began—was the Ferris Tire and Rubber Company, which disseminated a questionnaire inquiring about age and union history "for government purposes only."[42] A New Jersey firm created a spurious "Form C-53-A," titled "Social Security Record System: Employee History Record," intended to glean similar sorts of data. Another company's form was titled "United States Federal Society Security Act—Compulsory Information from All Employees"; still another stated that personal information (of a sort never entertained by the New Deal agency) was required "to make you eligible for social security benefits."[43]

Clearly, some businesses used the prospect of federal information gathering as a foot in the door for their own, more probing inquiries. A Social Security spokeswoman put the number of incidents in which firms fished for detailed data "under the pretext that such information was demanded by the Federal Government" in the hundreds.[44] Concern about whether Social Security data would be available to employers or others outside the agency was common enough to prompt the board to issue in June 1937 its first regulation—Regulation No. 1—formalizing its pledge of confidentiality for information collected and maintained.[45] Strikingly, the agency also offered assistance in bypassing intrusive bosses. The SSB made it known that individuals' "cards need not be returned through the employer," and even suggested that incorrect data supplied via the workplace could be corrected later, so that the employer and Social Security might have different "facts" on file about particular employees.[46]

That so many businesses masqueraded as the state in order to more closely surveil their employees is a reminder of how routine, even normative, it was for companies to pry into employees' personal affairs during this era. The practice inverts our expectations about whom Americans worried about most as invaders of their privacy in the 1930s, at least in the realm of personal data. What now seems remarkable is how readily Americans entrusted sensitive information to the federal government. This was because private employers—not public agencies—were the target of their apprehension.

It should be noted that even as Social Security publicized the protection of personal information in its charge, it was buffeted by requests for its records—not just by employers but by all manner of private citizens. As the board reported it, "immediately following the registration . . . a considerable volume of 'domestic relations' inquiries began to be received. . . . pleas for help in locating missing husbands, wives, relatives, or friends."[47] The board's records show that it refused all such requests.[48] It also, at least in the early days, rebuffed all official ones from the Federal Bureau of Investigation and U.S. Attorney General, carefully safeguarding its storehouse of citizens' data.[49] What surfaces much more clearly in existing sources than the fear or the fact of state tracking is both the reality of corporate surveillance and workers' recognition of such. Contemporary debates—real or fabricated—centering on "state regimentation" masked a far more serious sort of prying into citizens' affairs from the private sector. They continue to distort our vision of New Deal–era attitudes toward identification practices even today.

The Material of Identity

This is not to say that the prospect of improper state surveillance via Social Security numbers was a phantasm of the RNC, conjured solely for political effect. Some Americans did object to being numbered. Beginning
in 1936, there were critiques of the new bureaucratic apparatus and what
it seemed to imply about the contracting realm of freedom in modern
life. Aware of the SSB's carefully chosen language to refer to enumeration, *Time* magazine explained at the outset of the enrollment effort that
"each employe [*sic*] will be issued a numbered identification card. Not
tags (they have no strings) nor discs (they are not round), these cards
will bear a triple hyphenated number." Not so reassuringly, it added, "lest
workers feel they are being numbered like convicts, each number is called
an 'Account Number.' "[50] Similarly, in one columnist's telling, "the only
difference" between a Social Security account holder and "the boys at the
federal prison" was that the former "has to buy his own clothes and meals,
pay rent and doctor bills."[51]

Such complaints were regularly coupled with nostalgic reflections about
a time when "you could get yourself a job, at least, without the necessity
of registering with the government and being assigned a 'Social Security'
number."[52] Referring to the draft in 1940, the *New York Times* mused:
"We are a much more registered and classified people than we were in
1917. Most of us have a social security number."[53] That same year, an editorialist judged the arrival of SSNs a sign that "maybe liberty is shrinking"
in the United States: "When father was a boy, he needed neither union
card nor social security number to get a job. And when he took his girl
riding of a Sunday afternoon, he didn't have to hold a driver's license to
navigate the horse and buggy."[54] Other critics placed the number at the
core of their protest against documentation itself. Sometimes humorously
and sometimes with more bite, they wondered whether the advent of Social Security numbers meant that individuals had relinquished their indi-
viduality altogether. The *Santa Fe New Mexican*, which had supported the
Republicans in the 1936 election, afterward made its political stance clear
by identifying the editor and each of its reporters in their bylines by SSN
rather than name.[55]

Yet public—rather than narrowly partisan—discussion about Social
Security numbers in the 1930s and 1940s was typically less fraught, and to
focus solely on the problems the new digits stirred up would be to miss the

other ways they traveled through American culture. Social Security numbers garnered a fair amount of other kinds of publicity in their early years, owing to both their instrumental value—their link to social benefits—and their novelty. As a Colorado editorial observed in the fall of 1936: "'What's your number?' may easily become the form of greeting among El Paso county residents after the election Tuesday, the same as it may become the greeting among 26,000,000 million [*sic*] Americans." Its author paused to underscore the still-unfamiliar fact: "In short, men and women will be numbered in the United States."[56] Like the editorialist, most who commented on the new identification numbers were more often intrigued than outraged.[57]

The first and most straightforward way that those numbers entered into public life was through the early campaigns to alert Americans to the enumeration process.[58] The Social Security Board kept up a constant drumbeat of announcements about obtaining an SSN. Showcasing the steady uptick in enrollments was a favored public relations strategy. The first person to receive a number and a card—a Republican and "capitalist's son" who had voted not for FDR but for Alfred Landon—was profiled in the press.[59] James Anderson Murray, a forty-three-year-old painter who was issued the 1,000,001st Social Security card from the New York Post Office (and believed that the program was "the greatest thing that ever happened to this country") was the subject of a special ceremony, complete with photographers and reporters.[60] The assigning of the twenty-five-millionth account number (to Roland Jones of Williamsport, Pennsylvania) was touted by the Social Security Board as representing the "remarkable progress" of the enumeration operation in its less than four months of existence.[61] Laggards were also brought to light. It was reported in the summer of 1937, for instance, that Mayor William B. Hartsfield of Atlanta, up to that point negligent in filing his Social Security application, had finally gotten on board. In this fashion, he "became a number just like all other common American citizens." The article that reported this detail also matter-of-factly published his number: 252-12-4939.[62]

The Social Security number was not an incidental aspect of discussions of the new legislation. It was understood, rather, as the entry point to benefits—and even economic rights. The board was eager to get the first old-age benefits checks out to recipients in 1937 precisely because it would "help considerably in efforts to get all the Nation's workers catalogued by number and into the social security files."[63] This message about the number's benefits came through especially strongly in the black press.

Robust criticism had greeted the Social Security Act for its categorical exclusion of many African American workers. Nevertheless, Social Security
was described in some quarters as "the hope of the Negro in America"
and the "major program" of the federal and state governments pertaining
to African Americans, given its focus on the "economic security of the
masses of this country."[64] Readers fortunate enough to be covered by the
program were regularly reminded of their right to request a statement of
wages reported to the government, what to do if they suspected any errors, and, most important, how to proceed if one's number had been lost.[65]

The SSN in this sense was a nine-digit claim on equal personhood, especially for those long excluded from that category. It proved membership in the national polity and helped one lay claims on the state. Given
that not all workers were covered, the SSN could also be seen as a badge
of a particularly coveted form of economic citizenship.[66] The *New York
Amsterdam News* counseled African American workers: "Do not lose
your Social Security number. This number is important. It is important
both to you and your government . . . and evidence of your rights under
this law."[67] News outlets often focused on the number as the tangible sign
of and means to social protection.[68] In this light, an SSN could appear less
like an identifier useful to a state agency and more like an entitlement to
be jealously guarded by the holder. Certainly, many working-class Americans viewed it this way. In the words of a 1937 essay in *American Labor
World*, "Probably second in importance only to 'your daily bread,' in the
lives of working men and women in New York State is the individual possession of a Social Security Account number."[69] Never simply a means of
tracking citizens, the SSN—by remapping the population via exclusions
and benefits—helped produce a specific kind of social citizenship, one
that carried substantive privileges. If, from one angle, "seeing like a state"
could reduce and standardize, then from another it could shore up particular individuals' rights and dignity.

Social Security numbers' arrival in popular culture provides another
window onto the ways the new digits were woven into American life. The
number cropped up as early as 1937 in a Nancy Drew mystery, *The Whispering Statue*, in which the young detective is trying to get a job at a rare-
book shop in order to do some sleuthing ("Nancy was fearful that [the
shop owner] might ask her for a social security number or other type of
identification but he said nothing about it and she bubbled eagerly, 'How
soon may I start?'").[70] Hollywood heroines also paid it tribute: "Well, I
still have my social security number," exclaimed one in 1939 when all else

seemed lost. As a commentator observed, "The audience smiled in com-
prehension."[71] Such accounts suggest how quickly the SSN was becoming
a matter-of-fact part of the social landscape. Adding glamour to the number were reports in 1939 that actress Bette Davis wore a gold link brace-
let bearing hers, and in 1940 that film star Lana Turner's "favorite wed-
ding present from husband Artie Shaw is her social security number—in
diamonds!"[72]

A thicker sense of what the new numbers were coming to mean can be
glimpsed in the curious commercial bonanza that followed the passage of
the Social Security Act. A host of businesses cropped up in the mid- to
late 1930s to offer protection or security for one's SSN for a small fee. This
was not security in the sense we might imagine it today, that is, protecting
the number from the eyes of others. Rather, it was security in the form of
preserving the account number for its holder. Republicans had warned
Americans in 1936 that Social Security would result in "dog tags" bearing
their state identifier. In the years that followed, such tags would become a
reality—but not because the federal government had issued any. Instead,
it became clear that there was a ready private market for them.

"Is the Card bearing your Permanent Social Security Number torn,
smeared, perhaps already Worn Out?—If Not, In Time It Will Be!," advertised one such outfit in 1937 in the AFL-CIO's journal *American Federationist*. The solution was a nickel-silver badge, which "would not rust or
tarnish."[73] The *Chicago Defender* similarly offered to its African American readership a "lifetime" bronze plate, "lasting" but also "beautiful and
serviceable," engraved with the Social Security account holder's number,
in the name of its protection.[74] As another *Defender* ad explained: "You
know the importance of having your Social Security number handy at all
times. You probably are aware that over 50,000 people each month lose
trace of their Social Security card either as a result of wearing it out or
losing it, and therefore, are embarrassed and perhaps hurt financially in
case they need it suddenly when applying for a new position." The newspaper offered a further service should the "etched bronze plate" be lost:
it would maintain an individual's number on "permanent file" with the
engraver.[75]

Commercial outfits sought to capitalize on the fact that the account
cards, devised after much discussion by the early Social Security Board,
were surprisingly flimsy, despite the cards' evident significance. The products for sale, by contrast, were invariably fashioned of more durable stuff
than paper—"lasting bronze metal" complete with a leather carrying

case, in one instance—with the spare nine digits embellished or otherwise dignified.[76] In so doing, these goods restored the proper weight and gravitas to a number that represented an individual's ticket to economic rights, whether unemployment insurance or a guaranteed retirement pension. Something as ephemeral as "security," especially future security, perhaps required this sort of tangible proof.

Social Security–themed tokens could provide shorter-term benefits as well. A cottage industry dangled the allure of extra income from selling such items, playing to the demand for supplemental work during the Depression. The Key Tag Specialty Company of New York City, for example, advertised in 1937 "a complete business for twenty dollars" based on a "new social security number specialty."[77] The J. P. Routier Company of Rochester similarly offered in 1938 a "lightweight and attractive" chrome-plated identification tag that could be affixed to a key ring after being stamped with one's Social Security number, auto and operator license numbers, name, and address. The ad urged, "You should have one"— but also that the company was seeking independent agents to peddle them.[78] Yet another company in 1939 trumpeted a "rare opportunity for clerks, factory, mill or office workers to earn extra money," namely a 50 percent commission selling "social-security life-time plates and cases." Simply order the necessary kits and accessories for making red, white, and blue metal plates with a worker's name and Social Security number stamped on it, and the seller could count on earning "$35 a Week or More at Home . . . In Spare Time!" (with a "big profit on each sale"). Even during the Depression, the pitch suggested, this was an item that "sells on sight to working people everywhere."[79] Ads selling a piece of such businesses—whether the product was a chrome plate or a twenty-five-cent metal pocket token, and whether in Wichita Falls, Texas, Lansing, Michigan, or Baltimore, Maryland—testify to a going market in SSN keepsakes.[80] These outfits banked on the notion that, far from rejecting or resenting identification numbers, workers would pay for the privilege of protecting them.

Browse the advertising pages of any number of newspapers or middlebrow journals from the late 1930s and early 1940s and such items appear. Products appearing in *Popular Mechanics* in August 1938 included one's "Social Security account number engraved and enameled on beautiful brass key ring tag" (the ad continued: "Send 25c coin with security number for sample").[81] The *Atlanta Constitution* ran an ad for one's "Social Security Record made permanent on a solid bronze plate," guaranteeing that "your name and Social Security number" would be "pressed into metal forever" for only nine cents.[82] In 1942, *The Billboard*, the "World's Foremost Amusement Weekly," similarly advertised for $1.98 a high-quality black calfskin billfold, with one's name, "lodge emblem," and army or navy insignia and address, as well as one's "Social Security number Engraved in Gold ABSOLUTELY FREE!" (the ad mentions four pockets, "each protected by celluloid to prevent the soiling of your valuable membership and credit cards"). Sweetening the deal was a free bonus gift: a "beautiful three-color lifetime Identification Plate" that "carries your full name, address and social security or draft number exactly the way you want it." Pitched to consumers during wartime, alongside Hitler pin cushions, "victory heat pads," and service banners, the SSN may here have taken on additional connotations of patriotism and civic inclusion—a badge of membership to be proudly announced alongside one's draft number.[83]

Commodification of the Social Security number can be linked to a new kind of problem Americans were faced with after 1936: how to recall one's digits? Working Americans were urged to hold tight to their number, and account holders seemed to take that responsibility seriously. Scattered reports suggest that mastering the new system included committing the nine-digit number to memory, so that the bearer would be prepared when asked for it by an employer. Emblazoning one's number on a luggage tag or wallet (if not a frosted bronze plate) was arguably simply a mechanism for recalling a bureaucratic identifier without having to depend on an easily lost card or one's own memory. Accounts of Americans recording their Social Security numbers on their dentures attest rather startlingly to this trend. An Omaha man "reporting in for his disabilities pension check" simply removed his "upper plate, where he had had the number engraved."[84] A Minnesotan likewise had his SSN "imprinted on his lower denture" so he would "always have it handy."[85]

But other products and uses of the Social Security number argue for more expansive meanings. What, for example, to make of women's fashion billed as the height of "Social Security Style"? A 1942 piece that ran in the *Los Angeles Times* described a jersey shirtwaist dress, "suitable for the career woman," in exactly this way. It opened: "Are you supporting yourself? Do you have locked in your purse a social security number? Do you spend your daytime hours in an office?" If so, "you're in the market for today's career woman dress . . . designed especially for the business woman."[86] As scholars of gender and the welfare state have extensively documented, much New Deal legislation presumed a masculine labor force, with women as dependent or at best irregular workers.[87] In this light, possessing a Social Security number could stand as an emblem of female economic independence. Already in 1937, women of means could purchase a "tiny gold wafer, to wear on your charm-bracelet," engraved with their Social Security number. This product was advertised as "a new species of identification-disk" that would mark the wearer as an "honest working-girl."[88] If, fearing political fallout, the Social Security Board had shied away from issuing such disks, department stores would not. Merchandisers, employing the familiar rhetoric of self-determination to sell goods, clearly understood the SSN as a signifier with resonance for the modern working woman.

And what of "the latest in Rings," advertised in 1938 for $3.95, made of sterling silver, embedded with the wearer's birthstone, and engraved with his or her Social Security number? "The S. A. Meyer Company offers them first . . . on easy terms with weeks to pay." Perhaps such jewelry was intended to help people remember their numbers. It seems more likely, however, that "a really *personalized* ring for men and women," as the manufacturer billed it, held a different appeal. Here, the SSN identified its wearer uniquely and even proudly.[89] In ways difficult to perceive now, a number could be a mark of individuality. Rings and other items "personalized" by a SSN suggest that some Americans were taking ownership of what in another guise was a bureaucratic tag.

Most striking of all, however, were those who sought a still more intimate bond to their nine-digit number by permanently inking it on their bodies. Scholars of tattoos note that they have "long been a way to mark one's membership in a group" and to "signal belonging."[90] Dorothea Lange's iconic 1939 photograph of an unemployed lumber worker in Oregon, Social Security account number imprinted on his bicep, raises the question. Could a tattoo express a vital stake in the welfare state, a claim on what were still only future "earned benefits"—and perhaps the bureaucratic project itself?[91]

Whether because they affirmed a patriotic link to the nation, or simply the pressing need to remember, Social Security numbers appeared on American bodies in the 1930s and 1940s more often than we might expect. Indeed, SSNs were widely thought to be behind the uptick in business for tattoo parlors in the 1930s.[92] "Sailors, stevedores and sideshow freaks no longer have a corner on the tattoo market," declared the *Washington Post*. "Social security numbers have changed all that." This was because "persons in all walks of life . . . have taken to the social security numerals—indelibly inked on their epidermis—as a handy means of identification."[93] An observer at the *Nation's Business* noted the same: "Tattooing is having quite a boom. It is quite the fashion for the safe carrying of your Social Security number."[94] And a tattooing expert confided on a radio show that he was getting "a lot of calls . . . from customers who want to have their serial numbers stenciled on their chests."[95] Confirming reports came from both coasts. Mildred Hull, a former burlesque dancer turned tattoo artist who set up shop in New York in the 1920s, found that although her business lagged during the Depression, it "picked up again in the late 30s thanks to FDR." The President supplied Hull "10 customers a day . . . wanting their newly issued social security numbers to be made permanent."[96] A San Francisco practitioner averaged "two social security clients a day" in 1937.[97] And two tattoo artists working in Portland, Oregon, in the early 1940s reported that their business had "practically doubled since the issue of Social Security numbers."[98]

Accounts that circulated in the second half of the 1930s and early 1940s speak to the fact that the practice—if by no means common—was not unknown. The *Atlanta Constitution* reported in 1939, for instance, that a receptionist in a public employment office was startled to have a "neatly dressed" job seeker of about thirty years old begin to strip off his shirt when asked for his Social Security number. "Already reddening profusely, the startled Miss Bledsoe tried to head him off," but the man replied: "My social security number is tattooed on my back. I was afraid I'd lose it."[99] A "husky applicant for a job" in La Porte, Indiana, responded similarly to a request for his number at a state employment office, "peeling back his jacket and shirt, baring a number tattooed on his chest."[100] Other evidence comes from instances of individuals easily identified after their death because of an inked SSN: a musician from Lake Worth, Florida, for example, who fell or jumped to his death in the summer of 1943; and a Washington, DC, man, whose heavily tattooed body included both the name "Agnes" on his left arm and the number 579-09-3713 on his left leg.[101]

Treated as humorous or informative rather than offensive, these incidents of identification numbers printed on the body suggest a sensibility not yet shaped by images of concentration camp victims or other totalitarian visions.[102] They signal, instead, a surprising willingness to be numbered and stamped. SSNs in these early years were likely most typically regarded as necessary and unobjectionable, the price of admission for a guaranteed check in retirement.[103] But when emblazoned on a chrome plate, a pocket token, a watch, a ring, or a bicep, the SSN signified something more: not merely an identity document but personal *identification* with the project of making citizens visible to authorities.

Although it is impossible to know how many Americans engraved or displayed their SSNs, it is clear that numbering—and legibility to the state—could have its rewards. As a Census Bureau official noted in 1940, "Each step we take toward the goal of social and economic security for everyone makes more precious each individual's proof of his rights to such benefits."[104] To think of a Social Security number as precious demands that we rejigger our assumptions. In an age of increased social provision, the embrace of one's bureaucratic ID could express a pride in belonging as well as an anxiety now difficult to summon up: the fear of being unidentifiable.

The Afterlife of a Number

Well into the postwar era, Social Security account holders seem to have worried less about the possibility of others using or discovering one's number than about forgetting or losing it themselves, along with the benefits it promised. One finds few references, for example, to keeping that unique identifier safe from others' eyes.[105] Indeed, the digits' status as a quasi-public fact about the holder was almost uncontested. Americans were advised by *Popular Science* in 1947 to engrave their wristwatches with their Social Security number, as this would "identify it in case of loss or theft."[106] Radio stations in the 1950s commonly employed listeners' SSNs to boost their ratings, announcing strings of numbers on the air and offering cash prizes to the matching holders. One enterprising man in Tulsa, Oklahoma, even formed a short-term business to listen for his clients' SSNs on the radio while they went about their day.[107] Other promotions used Social Security numbers to dole out door prizes or invited employers to send in their employees' numbers as entries for drawings. Testifying to the regularity of this gimmick, Social Security officials considered the possibility of "legislation which would prohibit the use of social security account numbers for contests and other promotional purposes" in 1959.[108] Throughout this period, SSNs featured regularly in the missing-person sections of newspapers.[109] And specific individuals' digits were routinely printed in the newspaper without raising any hackles.[110] These examples speak to an understanding of the number as personal but not yet private.

This remained true even as SSNs evolved in the post–New Deal era "from a single-use identifier to the identification number of choice for the public and private sector."[111] Social Security did not at first permit nonagency uses of the identification numbers, but that stricture would loosen over time.[112] FDR furthered this process via a 1943 executive order encouraging the use of SSNs in federal agency record keeping.[113] Consequently, the storing of sensitive data and the sharing of confidential files carried risks for Social Security account holders almost from the beginning. Yet for the first three decades of the program's existence, there would be little public discussion of these risks. Nor was much attention paid to the weaving of SSNs throughout the society's filing systems. It is possible that a lack of concern over the proliferating uses of SSNs was the result of public ignorance of this fact. It seems equally likely, however, to have stemmed from a high level of trust in the federal government's administration of individuals' information. Either way, we are left with the curious case of a bureaucracy more agitated about the potential disclosure of its records than were the subjects of those records themselves.

It would be in the mid-1960s, not the 1930s, that the federal housing of citizens' information became the object of protest. One portent was the hostile public reaction to a proposed federal data center that would pool information held by the Social Security Administration, the Census Bureau, the Internal Revenue Service, the Bureau of Labor Statistics, and the Federal Reserve Board. First recommended in 1965 by the Social Science Research Council, and endorsed by the Bureau of the Budget, the idea of a national warehouse of Americans' data was, for some, concrete proof of the state's aspirations to omniscience. A series of like proposals would each be scuttled.[114] Once again, private data surveillance accelerated the critique. The privatization of public bureaucratic instruments like the SSN to track individuals' financial history (a by-product of the requirement that all federal tax reporting include a Social Security number in 1962) was decried by a number of best-selling exposés in the 1960s.[115] Assured that the SSN was "private" and tied to their personal financial information, citizens suddenly questioned why they were constantly asked to disclose it for purposes ranging from voter registration to credit applications and driver's licenses to death certificates.

And so, in the 1970s, decades after their debut, Social Security numbers themselves erupted as a political issue, prompting the creation of a federal task force and congressional hearings.[116] This timing stemmed in part from the numbers' key role in linking newly computerized record systems and from the corresponding recognition that SSNs had spread far beyond their original purpose in American society. Much like the earlier period, disquiet about the stash of information available through the SSN was voiced by groups on both the left and the right, transcending any clear-cut partisan divide. Senator Sam J. Ervin Jr., of South Carolina, a Democrat and one of the most vocal privacy crusaders in Congress, explained that the "increasing use of this number to identify the individual has made it one of the prime symbols of the computer age."[117] As even Social Security's commissioner acknowledged in 1977, the agency's "records contain one of the world's largest concentrations of personal data, all of it indexed according to SSN, and much of it instantly retrievable from computer records."[118]

As important as technological advances in linking data were, the fresh attention to SSNs cannot be disentangled from broader political shifts. One of the most important was a newfound distrust of the U.S. state on the part of its citizens, a legacy of left social movements, campus rebellions, and the Vietnam War. Mounting suspicion of society's gatekeepers and credentialing systems—ranging from mortgage programs to the credit industry to the Selective Service—was everywhere apparent by the 1970s.[119] Even though public and private agencies alike increasingly depended on Americans' personal data in this period, government practices came under special scrutiny. Ervin's comments were made during well-publicized Senate hearings on computerized records and data banks, which he chaired, in February and March 1971.[120] Much like the systems they investigated, the hearings ranged far and wide. The committee heard expert testimony on the most recent national data center proposal as well as U.S. Army surveillance of domestic political activity, the New York State Identification and Intelligence System, and the national computerized data bank of driver's licenses. It was in this context that Congress took up the problem of the escalating uses of Social Security numbers.

Only in the case of this last topic, perhaps finding a rich vein of sentiment to exploit, did Ervin marshal citizens' own words for his cause, entering into the record numerous letters from the public. One man from Indiana, for example, listed the range of queries for his Social Security number: a car dealer, his dog's veterinarian, the county clerk, the Internal Revenue Service, the bank, the driver's license bureau. He closed: "Since I have lost my personal identity (name) I will sign off with only my number. Punch your computer if you want to know who I am." A college student from California worried about the way universities used the number, through which "a large amount of personal data presumably is widely available to interested parties, without the individual being able to control who sees what." A Rhode Island man similarly revealed that he was "extremely apprehensive of the widespread use of one number to represent all sorts of transactions. . . . How long will it be before one person needing to know only this number will be able to retrieve information which must at least be considered privileged if not none of their business?" The only words of support for the wider use of identification numbers that Ervin quoted perhaps made the senator's case best of all. One Maryland man praised the utility of SSNs for criminal tracking, proposing that "everyone at birth should be given a Social Security number and told that they will be watched for honesty for the remainder of their lives." A woman from Michigan was more specific. She argued for the systematic surveillance of citizens through numbers, fingerprints, and "maybe a dog tag"—an evocative symbol again as the Vietnam War dragged on—to facilitate a lifetime record in which all activities (education, earnings, driving record, affiliations, banking, bankruptcy, welfare, marriage, divorce, misdemeanors, felonies, and convictions) "would be categorically recorded."[121]

These letters, though no doubt carefully culled, still manage to capture the range of concerns citizens voiced about their Social Security numbers. Complaints about the annoyances of bureaucracy and red tape mingled with existential human concerns about freedom and control, standardization and dehumanization. Palpable in this period was the sense that power was shifting in American society in favor of the institutions that controlled citizens' data—and thus also their daily lives and opportunities—and away from individual citizens themselves.[122] No longer was the government assumed to be the wise steward of Americans' information; nor was it deemed capable of protecting citizens from the manifold entities seeking access to their data. Indeed, citizens had come to understand the state to be one of those entities. Certainly, many more Americans were prepared to see the menace rather than the promise in what had become a de facto national identity number: few, if any, contemplated a Social Security tattoo.

Some of these threats were anticipated by labor unions, African Americans, and working women, who early on grasped the link between numbering and surveillance. The infrastructure of tracking, as we have seen, was present from Social Security's inception. But other threats were the product of new times. A report of the federal Social Security Task Force in 1971 framed the issue elegiacally. The problem of the SSN concerned not only "the impact of a single common identification number on legal rights" but also "the psychological impact of such a number on individuals and on the 'quality of life' in America." If some Americans had once claimed a stake in New Deal security through their SSNs, those same numbers now impinged on the citizenry's psychic "life space."[123] By the later twentieth century, even the idea that individuals might once have welcomed identification by the state was impossible to countenance. As a commentator mused in 1990, "Fifty years ago, the idea of identification numbers would have ignited instant horror among citizens proud of their stubborn independence and resistant to regimentation."[124]

*   *   *

The political theorist Itty Abraham notes that "there are few words in our modern political lexicon as parasitic as 'security.'" He adds that the word travels with an inescapable shadow—"insecurity"—since the "process of securing can never be known to be complete."[125] Abraham's recognition that security and insecurity come tethered together well predicts the career of the SSN in U.S. public life in the decades after 1935.

Multiple ripple effects, mostly unanticipated, flowed from the assigning of Social Security numbers. A bureaucratic tag for a specific administrative purpose, the number came to serve as a de facto national identifier. A semipublic article of information in the early decades of the program, it became—paradoxically, precisely because the number became so firmly stitched into the social fabric—fiercely private. A potent symbol of security, it became the cornerstone for a future, yet-to-be-imagined species of insecurity. As the contents but also the context of governance changed, an item that many Americans had once literally burnished and broadcast became something they carefully concealed.

But since we have forgotten, it is worth recalling that a piece of data Americans now treat as one of the most private facts about themselves started out as a visible and tangible part of public culture. There was a time when visibility to the state, and tracking itself, was regarded by many as a positive technology of citizenship. The SSN thus helps us chart Americans' shifting relationship to their state—and to the state of their personal information—across the twentieth century.

Paying close attention to how individuals were knitted into a new system of documentation highlights the unpredictable, unfixed boundary between state and society, public and private. It also reveals the critical importance of popular reception to state formation, the ways citizens collaborate with official agencies in shaping expressions of public authority.

It may even clarify the underpinnings of contemporary dilemmas around data privacy. How Americans assess the security of their "private" information can be pinned to technological developments but also to less easily defined changes in political culture bound up with institutional legitimacy and social trust. The conviction today that society's accountants know too much about us is certainly the result of ramped-up surveillance and the technologies pressed into its service. But it is also a product of altered relations among citizens, state, and society that are not reducible to those developments alone.

Notes

I am grateful to the volume editors, Brent Cebul, Lily Geismer, and Mason Williams, as well as to Michael Willrich and Brian Balogh, for their insightful comments on an earlier draft of this chapter.

1. See Margo J. Anderson, *The American Census: A Social History*, 2nd ed. (New Haven, CT: Yale University Press, 2015).

2. Alfred W. McCoy, *Policing America's Empire: The United States, the Philippines, and the Rise of the Surveillance State* (Madison: University of Wisconsin Press, 2009); Mark Ellis, *Race, War and Surveillance: African Americans and the United States Government during World War I* (Bloomington: Indiana University Press, 2001); David Kennedy, *Over Here: The First World War and American Society* (New York: Oxford University Press, 1980). Christopher Capozzola argues that the "wartime assault on enemy aliens laid the foundations of twentieth-century political surveillance," in *Uncle Sam Wants You: World War I and the Making of the Modern American Citizen* (New York: Oxford University Press, 2008), 201.

3. Birth certificates by the 1920s would be a local- and state-administered program coordinated by the U.S. Children's Bureau. See Susan J. Pearson, "'Age Ought to Be a Fact': The Campaign against Child Labor and the Rise of the Birth Certificate," *Journal of American History* 101, no. 4 (March 2015): 1144–65; and Shane Landrum, "The State's Big Family Bible: Birth Certificates, Personal Identity, and Citizenship in the United States, 1840–1950" (PhD diss., Brandeis University, 2014). On the rise of the passport regime, see Craig Robertson, *The Passport in America: The History of a Document* (New York: Oxford University Press, 2011); and more generally, Jane Caplan and John Torpey, eds., *Documenting Individual Identity: The Development of State Practices in the Modern World* (Princeton, NJ: Princeton University Press, 2001).

4. The increasing scope and reach of governance took place at all levels, and it preceded the New Deal. For the classic work, see Stephen Skowronek, *Building a New American State: The Expansion of National Administrative Capacities, 1877–1920* (New York: Cambridge University Press, 1982). Yet David Graeber writes

that the New Deal was "the moment when bureaucratic structures and techniques first became dramatically visible in many ordinary people's lives." Graeber, *The Utopia of Rules: On Technology, Stupidity, and the Secret Joys of Bureaucracy* (Brooklyn, NY: Melville House, 2015), 13–14.

5. James T. Sparrow, *Warfare State: World War II Americans and the Age of Big Government* (New York: Oxford University Press, 2011), 6. See also Anne Kornhauser, *Debating the American State: Liberal Anxieties and the New Leviathan, 1930–1970* (Philadelphia: University of Pennsylvania Press, 2015) and Gary Gerstle, *Liberty and Coercion: The Paradox of American Government from the Founding to the Present* (Princeton, NJ: Princeton University Press, 2015).

6. The exception is the once-a-decade administration of the U.S. Census.

7. Larry DeWitt, Daniel Béland, and Edward D. Berkowitz, *Social Security: A Documentary History* (Washington, DC: CQ Press, 2008), 1.

8. Sophonisba P. Breckinridge, "Home Economics and the Quest for Economic Security," *Journal of Home Economics* 27, no. 8 (October 1935): 491.

9. Lisa Gitelman, borrowing from Michel de Certeau, writes of an "ever growing, ever more intricate scriptural economy . . . harnessed to the interests of officialdom," in *Paper Knowledge: Toward a Media History of Documents* (Durham, NC: Duke University Press, 2014), ix–x. For accounts of how documentation works (and doesn't), see Annelise Riles, ed., *Documents: Artifacts of Modern Knowledge* (Ann Arbor: University of Michigan Press, 2006); Cornelia Vismann, *Files: Law and Media Technology*, trans. Geoffrey Winthrop-Young (Stanford, CA: Stanford University Press, 2008); Ben Kafka, *The Demon of Writing: Powers and Failures of Paperwork* (New York: Zone Books, 2012); Caplan and Torpey, *Documenting Individual Identity*; Simon Szreter and Keith Breckenridge, eds., *Registration and Recognition: Documenting the Person in World History* (Oxford: Oxford University Press, 2012); and Ilsen About, James Brown, and Gayle Lonergan, eds., *Identification and Registration Practices in Transnational Perspective: People, Papers and Practices* (New York: Palgrave Macmillan, 2013).

10. See, for example, Pierre Tixier and R. C. Davison, "Suggestions on the Administration of the Social Security Act and State Unemployment Compensation Laws," December 14, 1935, p. 8, Stanford Ross Papers, private collection of Stanford G. Ross, Commissioner of Social Security, 1978–1979.

11. Legibility, as Scott defines it, is a central tool of modern statecraft; he uses the term to refer to state attempts to organize both land and population, dramatically simplifying them in order to facilitate the "classic state functions of taxation, conscription, and prevention of rebellion." James C. Scott, *Seeing like a State: How Certain Schemes to Improve the Human Condition Have Failed* (New Haven, CT: Yale University Press, 1998), 2. The same insight is the starting premise of recent studies of biopolitics and governmentality inspired by the work of Michel Foucault.

12. I borrow this language from Simon Szreter and Keith Breckenridge, cited earlier, who regard recognition and registration as the "infrastructure of

personhood" in modern states, and in the process recuperate the often overlooked beneficial functions of registration, contra works like Scott's *Seeing like a State.*

13. See Jonathan Levy, *Freaks of Fortune: The Emerging World of Capitalism and Risk in America* (Cambridge, MA: Harvard University Press, 2012); Dan Bouk, *How Our Days Became Numbered: Risk and the Rise of the Statistical Individual* (Chicago: University of Chicago Press, 2015); and Josh Lauer, *Creditworthy: A History of Consumer Surveillance and Financial Identity in America* (New York: Columbia University Press, 2017).

14. Weare Holbrook, "Unmistaken Identity," *Atlanta Constitution*, November 15, 1942, 11.

15. Holbrook, "Unmistaken Identity," 11.

16. The act established three separate programs, two to be administered by the states (Old Age Assistance and Unemployment Compensation) and one to be administered by the federal government (Old Age Benefits). Histories of the act include Edwin E. Witte, *The Development of the Social Security Act* (Madison: University of Wisconsin Press, 1963); DeWitt, Béland, and Berkowitz, *Social Security*; Charles McKinley and Robert W. Frase, *Launching Social Security: A Capture-and-Record Account, 1935–1937* (Madison: University of Wisconsin Press, 1970); Arthur J. Altmeyer, *The Formative Years of Social Security* (Madison: University of Wisconsin Press, 1966); and Gerald D. Nash, Noel H. Pugach, and Richard F. Tomasson, eds., *Social Security: The First Half-Century* (Albuquerque: University of New Mexico Press, 1988).

17. Jennifer Klein argues that grassroots movements and New Dealers alike "generated an ideology of security" in the mid-1930s, making security "an essential goal in the task of national reconstruction." It was a year into the New Deal (1934) that Roosevelt announced that the federal government would offer a plan for "security against the hazards and vicissitudes of life" and established the Committee on Economic Security, and thus "catapulted the politics of security to the center of American political and economic life." *For All These Rights: Business, Labor and the Shaping of America's Public-Private Welfare State* (Princeton, NJ: Princeton University Press, 2003), 78–79.

18. The most important factor in this exclusion was, in Ira Katznelson's words, "southern power." Southern Democrats' investment in and ability to protect traditional racial hierarchies through congressional votes is thoroughly documented in his *Fear Itself: The New Deal and the Origins of Our Time* (New York: Liveright, 2013); quote on 386.

19. See DeWitt, Béland, and Berkowitz, *Social Security*, 4. Also excluded were seamen, federal and state employees, and employees of religious and charitable organizations. It was not until 1950 that the Social Security Act was amended to extend coverage to self-employed farmers and workers in a number of other professions, including domestic employees, bringing coverage to about three-quarters of the workforce.

20. Robert Ellis Smith, *Ben Franklin's Web Site: Privacy and Curiosity from Plymouth Rock to the Internet* (Providence, RI: Privacy Journal, 2000), 284–85.

21. "Historical Summary of Rules, Regulations and Provisions of the Law Relating to Disclosure of OASI Information," undated, Folder: Confidentiality, Carrier #7, Social Security History Archives, Woodlawn, MD (hereafter, SSHA).

22. "Snooping-Tagging," *New York American*, November 2, 1936.

23. "Hamilton Predicts Tags for Workers," *New York Times*, November 1, 1936; "Hamilton Shows Sample Tag for Workers' Necks," *Chicago Daily Tribune*, November 1, 1936, 5; "Snooping-Tagging," *New York American*, November 2, 1936; "Benefits of Security Act Called Only Dream," *Boston American*, November 2, 1936; " 'Dog Tag' Workers May Have under Social Security Act," *Boston Herald*, November 2, 1936. For the SSB response, see "Social Security Form Condemned as 'Fraud': Board Denies It Seeks Personal Data from Workers, as Republicans Charged," *New York Times*, November 1, 1936. For Arthur Altmeyer's account, see *Formative Years of Social Security*, 69.

24. See, for example, Steve Fraser and Gary Gerstle's edited collection, *The Rise and Fall of the New Deal Order, 1930–1980* (Princeton, NJ: Princeton University Press, 1989).

25. Birchard E. Wyatt and William H. Wandel, *The Social Security Act in Operation: A Practical Guide to the Federal and Federal-State Social Security Programs* (Washington, DC: Graphic Arts Press, 1937), 48. This sense of constraint stemming from the public's fear of "formal records" crops up occasionally in the SSB records but always as conventional wisdom, and as an abstraction. Having examined the public response to SSNs in some detail, I am skeptical.

26. In fact, the Treasury Department issued regulations making the SSN mandatory on November 6, 1936. McKinley and Frase note that while the Social Security Board claimed that registration was voluntary, "it had been negotiating with the Treasury Department to induce that department to require employees and employers to secure account numbers under regulations carrying considerable penalties." *Launching Social Security*, 346, 351–52, 360. In this, Social Security squares with scholars' descriptions of the early twentieth-century U.S. government as an "improvisational hybrid state that reconciled its coercive and voluntarist elements by concealing the conflict between them." Capozzola, *Uncle Sam Wants You*, 210–11.

27. " 'Forgery' Charged to Security Foes," *New York Times*, November 3, 1936, 17. The spokesperson here was Anna Rosenberg, regional director of the Social Security Board. Just months before the board had indeed considered issuing metal registration discs, but that is another story.

28. " 'Forgery' Charged to Security Foes," 17.

29. By contrast, the 1940 Smith Act (Alien Registration Act) required that all aliens be registered and fingerprinted.

30. The Post Office's figure was 22,129,617. Wyatt and Wandel, *Social Security Act in Operation*, 62–63.

31. "Running Record of Board Meeting," Friday, November 20, 1936, 2:45 p.m., Folder: SSN-Enumeration, Carrier #12, SSHA.

32. Memorandum from Executive Committee of the Committee on Assignment of Social Security Account Numbers to the Board, May 5, 1936, Folder: SSN-Enumeration, Carrier #12, SSHA. McKinley and Frase note that race was included for "both identification and actuarial purposes" and that most of the debate over its inclusion was not in fact about whether to include it but about whether to use the word *race* or *color* on the forms; the SSB opted for the latter. *Launching Social Security*, 326.

33. "Insulting Our Intelligence," *Pittsburgh Courier*, December 5, 1936, 12. The writer scoffed at the explanation, given by a Social Security information officer, that the requirement was put in place to distinguish among applicants with the same name.

34. Winston Smith, "Social Security Act, Taking in All Races, Explained by Writer, as Post Office Starts Sending Out Blanks," *New York Amsterdam News*, November 14, 1936, 15.

35. "Running Record of Board Meeting," Friday, November 20, 1936, 2:45 p.m., Folder: SSN-Enumeration, Carrier #12, SSHA.

36. "Running Record of Board Meeting," Friday, November 20, 1936, 2:45 p.m., Folder: SSN-Enumeration, Carrier #12, SSHA. The agency discussed options for reassuring employees, including a strong statement from the board and having the U.S. Treasury state that it would not accept returns from employers "where there was any evidence of coercion."

37. The study was Claris Edwin Silcox and Galen M. Fisher's *Catholics, Jews and Protestants: A Study of Relationships in the United States and Canada* (Westport, CT: Greenwood Press, 1934). As Kevin Schultz writes of the interwar years, "Employment agencies said they found it necessary to secure information concerning an applicant's religion before they sent an applicant to an interview, fearing that a Catholic or Jewish applicant would not have a chance to secure employment at a Protestant-dominated firm." Schultz, *Tri-Faith America: How Catholics and Jews Held Postwar America to Its Protestant Promise* (New York: Oxford University Press, 2011), 23. See also David Sehat, *The Myth of American Religious Freedom* (New York: Oxford University Press, 2011). A handful of others objected over the years to being numbered because of religious warnings regarding the "mark of the beast."

38. Frederick Lane, *American Privacy: The 400-Year History of Our Most Contested Right* (Boston: Beacon Press, 2009), 110. For an argument about disclosure of age as an invasion of privacy, particularly for women (and women workers), see Della T. Lutes, "Why I Don't Tell My Age," *Forum and Century* 97, no. 4 (April 1937): 244.

39. The "Fibbers," "Your Age, Madam," *Chicago Daily Tribune*, November 30, 1936, 8. The SSB's answer was that the account holder's information would not in that case be disclosed.

40. "Historical Summary of Rules, Regulations and Provisions of the Law

Relating to Disclosure of OASI Information," undated, Folder: Confidentiality, Carrier #7, SSHA. See also historical section of Social Security Administration, "Confidentiality of Information Contained in Old-Age, Survivors, Disability and Heath Insurance Records," February 2, 1971, p. 3, Folder: Confidentiality (Privacy-Folder 1), Carrier #7, SSHA. McKinley and Frase point out, however, that the U.S. Employment Service had routinely used "coded union and religious affiliations" in its registration of workers. Regarding the latter, "the Employment Service took the position that it was better to send the employer people he wanted rather than to let an employee begin a job and then be fired because of religious prejudice." As for union affiliation, "there had been no protest from the labor unions." *Launching Social Security*, 326.

41. McKinley and Frase, *Launching Social Security*, 326.

42. McKinley and Frase, *Launching Social Security*, 451–52.

43. "Time Is Extended on Security Form," *New York Times*, December 6, 1936, 3.

44. Anna M. Rosenberg, regional director of the Social Security Board, is quoted in "Time Is Extended on Security Form," at page 3. The *Times* reported that investigation "substantiated these complaints in the cases of more than fifty concerns."

45. Much amended over the years, Regulation No. 1: Disclosure of Official Records and Information, permitted disclosure from Social Security records only to claimants or their representatives; the Treasury Department, responsible for taxation under the act; state unemployment agencies for use in the administration of their programs; and for the publication of statistical data "not relating to any particular person." When Congress amended the Social Security Act in 1939, it implemented section 1106, which provided that "information could not be divulged except as the Board by regulation prescribed."

46. "Government Will Take First Steps Today to Enroll Workers," *Washington Post*, November 16, 1936, X1; and "Running Record of Board Meeting," Friday, November 20, 1936, 2:45 p.m., Folder: SSN-Enumeration, Carrier #12, SSHA.

47. Social Security Board, "Survey Relative to Requests for Information from the Confidential Board Files," January 1938, Folder: Confidentiality, Carrier #7, SSHA.

48. See the running record of SSB meeting minutes in Folder: Confidentiality, Carrier #7, SSHA.

49. I write elsewhere about the pressures on Social Security to allow other state agencies into its files; I have not included a discussion here in the interest of brevity.

50. "National Affairs: Labor: Social Security," *Time*, November 16, 1936, 25.

51. Ralph T. Jones, "Numerous Possibilities," *Atlanta Constitution*, December 16, 1936, 6.

52. Ralph T. Jones, "Silhouettes: Life under a Monarchy," *Atlanta Constitution*, November 5, 1939, 18A.

53. "Topics of the Times: Many American Figures," *New York Times*, September 25, 1940, 25.

54. "Is It Too Late?" *Atlanta Constitution*, June 16, 1940, 10B.

55. "The Santa Fe New Mexican . . . came out with full recognition of the Social Security Act today. From E. Dana Johnson down to reporters, social security account numbers were used for bylines. Over the editor's 'Jobs in the Solar Plexus' was: 'By 525-10-9454.' In the personal columns were such items as: 'No. 525-10-9363 is recovering from an attack of the flu'"; Associated Press, "Social Security Figures Are Newspaper By-Lines," *New York Times*, December 11, 1936, 29. See also Jones, "Numerous Possibilities."

56. "Every Employed Person to Be Given 'Number' by Costly, Cumbersome Security Plan," *El Paso County–Colorado Springs Gazette*, undated clipping from November 1936; Folder: SSN-Enumeration, Carrier #12, SSHA.

57. See, for example, stories about newly married women immediately rushing to the Social Security office from the altar to sign up for a number; a couple discovering that their Social Security numbers, issued by different employers two years before, were only one digit apart; and the discoveries SSNs made possible regarding the most frequent as well as longest and shortest family names on record. "Bride of an Hour Applies Social Security Education," *New York Times*, March 13, 1938, 2; "Social Security Numbers Matched," *Washington Post*, October 27, 1939, 4; "Joneses Trailing 5 Other Names in Age Pension Lists," *Washington Post*, June 26, 1938, M11.

58. See, for example, "Directions to Employes," *New York Times*, November 6, 1936, 21; "Social Security Deadline: Every Employe [*sic*] Must Have Account Number by June 30," *New York Times*, June 20, 1937, 14.

59. "Republican Gets No. 1 Security Card: Capitalist's Son, His Name Chosen by Lot, Becomes Dean of New Labor Class," *New York Times*, December 2, 1936; "Social Service: Pensioners," *Time*, December 14, 1936.

60. "Painter Gets 1,000,001st Security Card and Is Rushed to Ceremony in Overalls," *New York Times*, December 9, 1936, 1.

61. "25,000,000th Card in Security Files," *New York Times*, March 17, 1937, 26. See also "27,704,396 Now Listed," *New York Times*, June 21, 1937, 5; "Social Security Spread," *New York Times*, June 28, 1937, 19 (noting that twenty-nine million have cards); "Security Numbers Given to 29,954,821," *New York Times*, July 26, 1937, 5; "Ask Security Numbers," *New York Times*, September 26, 1937, 24 (noting that thirty-four million have been issued); "Social Security Filings," *Wall Street Journal*, March 15, 1938, 11 (reporting national total as 37,781,710); "39,000,000 in Social Security," *Wall Street Journal*, June 20, 1938, 3; "5,700,000 New Yorkers on Social Security Roll," *New York Times*, January 1, 1939, 23 (total number at forty-two million); "Security Board Reports Advance," *Atlanta Constitution*, July 17, 1939, 3 (44,727,520). In 1940 the *New York Times* reported that fifty million people held Social Security account cards; "Twenty News Questions," *New York Times*, August 18, 1940, 58. And by early 1944 that number had climbed to sixty-three million; "Peace Will Test Social Security," *Los Angeles Times*, March 19, 1944, 12.

62. "Mayor Hartsfield No. 252-12-4939," *Atlanta Constitution*, July 15, 1937, 9.

63. "The news that John Smith got $10 by having a social security number will not be slow in getting around, and it will bring in applicants from all unnumbered workers in that area," claimed a board member. "20,000 Old-Age Benefit Checks Going Begging," *Washington Post*, August 3, 1937, 8.

64. A. M. Wendell Malliet, "'Social Security Is Hope of Negro in America,' Says Cohron," *New York Amsterdam News*, December 24, 1938, 4. See also "Negro Democrats Hail Roosevelt as Modern Savior," *New York Amsterdam News*, June 27, 1936, 1.

65. For a later example, see "Tips on Checking Social Security," *New York Amsterdam News*, September 11, 1948, 5.

66. On this point, see Suzanne Mettler, *Dividing Citizens: Gender and Federalism in New Deal Public Policy* (Ithaca, NY: Cornell University Press, 1998).

67. "Social Security," *New York Amsterdam News*, April 15, 1939, 10. See also "Social Security: What It Means—How It Works," *Baltimore Afro-American*, August 16, 1941, 9.

68. "The New Social Security Act," *Crisis* 47, no. 2 (February 1940): 42–43, 59.

69. "Get Your Social Security Number before You Are Unemployed," *American Labor World* (1937), 216.

70. Carolyn Keene, *The Whispering Statue* (New York: Grosset & Dunlap, 1937), 56.

71. As reported in Ernest R. Bryan, "America Advances with Social Security," *Health Officer* 4 (May 1939): 104.

72. "Costume Jewelry Requires Art in Wearing," *Washington Post*, August 5, 1939, 8; Sheilah Graham, "Colleen Moore Lends Home to Former Film Millionaires," *Atlanta Constitution*, March 27, 1940, 16.

73. AFL-CIO, *American Federationist* 44, no. 1 (1937): 570.

74. Advertisement: "Free! Protection for Your Social Security Number," *Chicago Defender*, October 22, 1938, 5.

75. Advertisement: "Hurry! Join the Hundreds Who Have Taken Advantage of This Free Gift," *Chicago Defender*, November 12, 1938, 5.

76. Advertisement: "A Lifetime Gift for You," *Chicago Defender*, October 15, 1938, 5.

77. Advertising section, *Popular Mechanics* 67, no. 5 (May 1937): 48A, Key Tag Specialty Company, 91 Wall Street, New York City.

78. Advertising section, *Popular Mechanics* 70, no. 4 (August 1938): 43A, J. P. Routier Co. 221 Frost Ave, Rochester, NY. A similar product gets a mention as "a gadget which appeared last year" and "turns up again, much improved," in "New Things in City Shops," *New York Times*, March 31, 1940, 53.

79. Advertising section, *Popular Mechanics* 71, no. 4 (April 1939): 168A. Company is Roovers Bros, Inc., Dept. M41, 258 Broadway, New York, and 3611-14th Ave., Brooklyn, NY. Interestingly, the ad asked potential sellers to "send 10c

with your social security number." This was William Hament, 665 W. Lexington Street, Baltimore, MD.

80. See Advertising section, *Popular Mechanics* 69, no. 3 (March 1938): 58A. The contact information was listed as Napeus, 1303 Austin St., Wichita Falls, Texas. Another seller, "Stanley-Engraving" of Lansing, Michigan, was listed for similar products in 1944: Advertising section, *Popular Mechanics* 82, no. 6 (December 1944): 59A.

81. Advertising section, *Popular Mechanics* (August 1938): 43A. Company listed was H. I. Laboratories, 1451 Broadway, New York, NY.

82. Advertisement: "Social Security Record Made Permanent on a Solid Bronze Plate," *Atlanta Constitution*, July 23, 1939, 4A.

83. *The Billboard*, November 28, 1942, 65. Company was Illinois Merchandising Mart, Dept. 117, 54 W. Illinois Street, Chicago, IL. The same advertisement (this one a full page) appears in *American Legion Magazine* 32–33 (1942); *Popular Mechanics Magazine* 78, no. 6 (December 1942): 40A; *Popular Science* 141, no. 5 (November 1942): 21, and various others.

84. "Good-by, Old Pal," *Chicago Daily Tribune*, January 1, 1950, 8.

85. Reported by Doe Richards in Arch Ward, "In Wake of the News," *Chicago Daily Tribune*, October 18, 1950, C1.

86. Sylvia Weaver, "Shirtwaist Dress Fits Needs of Career Woman," *Los Angeles Times*, January 8, 1942, A6. This was not the only link made between fashion and Social Security numbers. An article in the *Atlanta Constitution* on "smart outfits" of Hollywood stars, for example, profiled June Travis (Ronald Reagan's leading lady in his first film, that year), who favored "simple dresses with novel belts," one of which had a pocket for a "silver locket engraved with her social security number." Sheilah Graham, "Sheilah Graham Describes Smart Outfits of the Stars: Hollywood Today," *Atlanta Constitution*, July 20, 1937, 14.

87. On the encoding of gender dependence in the Social Security Act and other New Deal legislation, see Ruth Feldstein, *Motherhood in Black and White: Sex and Race in American Liberalism, 1930–1965* (Ithaca, NY: Cornell University Press, 2000); Mettler, *Dividing Citizens*; and Alice Kessler-Harris, "In the Nation's Image: The Gendered Limits of Social Citizenship in the Depression Era," *Journal of American History* 86, no. 3 (1999): 1251–79.

88. "Shop-Hound around the Town," *Vogue* 89, no. 10 (May 15, 1937): 118. The disk sold at the Lord and Taylor department store for six dollars.

89. These rings were produced by the S. A. Meyer Company of Washington, Pennsylvania, as advertised in the *Washington Observer*, March 3, 1938.

90. Christine Rosen, "The Flesh Made Word: Tattoos, Transgression, and the Modified Body," *Hedgehog Review* 17, no. 2 (Summer 2015).

91. Dan Bouk offers the most extended analysis of this image in the conclusion to his *How Our Days Became Numbered*, suggesting that we "consider the ways that some Americans grasped those numbers as their own" (210–11). Also see

David Peeler, *Hope among Us Yet: Social Criticism and Social Solace in Depression America* (Athens: University of Georgia Press, 1987), 103–4. The photograph can be found in Ann Whiston Spirn, *Daring to Look: Dorothea Lange's Photographs and Reports from the Field* (Chicago: University of Chicago Press, 2008), 154.

92. The anthropologist Margo DeMello notes: "After the first Social Security card was issued in 1936, men and women flocked to tattoo shops to have their number tattooed on them." *Bodies of Inscription: A Cultural History of the Modern Tattoo Community* (Durham, NC: Duke University Press, 2000), 65.

93. "Social Security Act Increases Tattooing," *Washington Post*, April 15, 1937, 20. See a poem that nods to the "fad" of tattooing one's social security number; H. I. Phillips, "The Once Over: Oh, Say, Can You See?" *Washington Post*, May 3, 1937, 9. And also the casual mention of "holders of social-security numbers" as customers for tattoos in "Decorative Art," *New York Times*, June 20, 1937, 54.

94. "Through the Editor's Specs," *Nation's Business* (December 1937): 7.

95. "Radio Comedians Turn to Mocking Daytime Shows," *Chicago Daily Tribune*, February 11, 1938, 28.

96. Margot Mifflin, *Bodies of Subversion: A Secret History of Women and Tattoo*, 3rd ed. (New York: powerHouse Books, 2013), 35. Hull's leading tattoo image request from women in 1939, however, was reportedly Mickey Mouse.

97. "Through the Editor's Specs," 7.

98. "Red Gibbons, then tattooing in Portland, Oregon, stated in a 1937 news article, that he and Sailor Walter were working overtime in their Burnside Street shop just tattooing Social Security numbers on the arms and legs of folks who didn't want to be caught without their numbers." C. W. Eldredge, "Identification," *Tattoo Archive* (2000), http://www.tattooarchive.com/tattoo_history/identification.html.

99. "Job Applicant Has Social Security Number on Back," *Atlanta Constitution*, August 31, 1939, 8.

100. "Tattooed Man Bares His Social Security Number," *Chicago Daily Tribune*, February 16, 1938, 8. See also "Miscellany: Red Tape," *Time*, May 16, 1938.

101. "Identified by Tattooing: Musician Had Social Security Number on His Forearm," *New York Times*, August 22, 1943, 33; "Tattoo Marks on Arm Identify Florida Man," *Atlanta Constitution*, August 22, 1943, 10A; "Body in Lot Starts Slaying Probe Here," *Washington Post*, December 17, 1939, 3.

102. Needless to say, these were the years before serial numbers printed on arms came to be associated with Holocaust survivors. It is unclear when precisely those numbers made it into Americans' consciousness. As Peter Novick has observed, the Holocaust loomed much larger in American life in the 1970s and beyond than it did in the 1940s or 1950s; Novick, *The Holocaust in American Life* (Boston: Houghton Mifflin, 1999), 20. The comparisons I have found between Social Security numbers and "Nazi tattoos" or "totalitarianism" come from the 1990s and after; see discussions of the dangers of identity cards in "America, Doubled,"

New York Times, April 1, 1990, E18; and Robert Ellis Smith, "The True Terror Is in the Card," *New York Times*, September 8, 1996, SM58. Recent critiques of biometrics and identity registration have been articulated most forcefully by Giorgio Agamben in *State of Exception*, trans. Kevin Attell (Chicago: University of Chicago Press, 2005). I have found no reports of new SSN tattoos in the 1950s, but this may be because tattooing's popularity dropped off in that decade in both the military and the general population. DeMello, *Bodies of Inscription*, 65.

103. Note the considerable doubts in the 1930s that this was in fact a guarantee, however. Brian Balogh cites one insider, Edwin Witte, as claiming that for "nearly two years after the Social Security Act became law, serious doubts continued to exist about its ever coming into full operation." See "Securing Support: The Emergence of the Social Security Board as a Political Actor, 1935–1939," in *Federal Social Policy: The Historical Dimension*, ed. Donald T. Critchlow and Ellis W. Hawley (University Park: Pennsylvania State University Press, 1988), 65.

104. Robert F. Lenhart, quoted in Pearson, " 'Age Ought to Be a Fact,' " 1165.

105. For one potential such instance from 1950, see the recommendation for putting "personal affairs in shape for an emergency," which included placing "old income-tax returns, canceled checks, savings bank books, birth certificate, social security card, and similar papers in a locked file drawer or similar safe place," in Kathleen A. Johnston, "Family Economics—Home Management," *Journal of Home Economics* 42, no. 6 (June 1950): 462. A similar list appears in "Tips to Wives on Business Management," *Atlanta Constitution*, June 8, 1943, 12. But both notices, it seems clear, concerned being able to get to the number and other important documents when needed—rather than worries about theft or public knowledge of the SSN.

106. "Just as soldiers' 'dog tags' gave vital information in emergencies, your wrist watch can carry your name, social security number, and other data"; "Keeping the Home Shipshape," *Popular Science* 151, no. 1 (July 1947): 207. Notice here the favorable comparison to dog tags.

107. Sonia Stein, "What Became of Banned Giveaways?" *Washington Post*, April 23, 1950, L4; "Tower Ticker," *Chicago Daily Tribune*, May 10, 1950, 28; Roy Touchet to J. S. Futterman, "Account Number Issuance Procedure—Status Report," November 30, 1959, 3, Folder: SSN-Process, Carrier #12, SSHA.

108. "Mercury Sets LP Bonus Plan," *Billboard*, November 18, 1950, 14.

109. "Lost: One Wife; Clue: Her Social Security Figure," *Atlanta Constitution*, January 7, 1940, 11A; "Looking for Someone?" *Baltimore Afro-American*, February 3, 1940, 10; "Courier Missing Persons Bureau" (entry for Taylor, Nathaniel Edward), *Pittsburgh Courier*, January 28, 1950, 26.

110. See "History Repeats," *New York Times*, February 9, 1947, SM44, in which it was reported that "the shoe number of a pair of red slippers which Annie Ruth Hight, Cedartown, Ga., bought was familiar to her. It was the same as her Social Security number—258-24-2173." See also the listing of athletes' SSNs by *New*

York Times columnist Arthur Daley: "Sports of the Times," *New York Times*, June 10, 1945, S2, and April 24, 1950, 34.

111. Philippa Strum, *Privacy: The Debate in the United States since 1945* (New York: Harcourt Brace, 1998), 46–47.

112. See, for example, Memorandum from Oscar M. Powell and John J. Corson to the Board re: "Revision of Regulation No. 1 to Permit Closer Cooperation with Other Government Agencies," July 9, 1940, Folder: Confidentiality, Carrier #7, SSHA.

113. This was Executive Order No. 9397, "Numbering System for Federal Accounts Relating to Individual Persons," 8 Fed. Reg. 16095–97, 3 C.F.R. (1943–1948 Comp.) 283–84 (1943). The specific agencies mentioned in the discussions leading up to the executive order were the Bureau of Internal Revenue of the Treasury Department, the Railroad Retirement Board, and the Civil Service Commission. It would not be until the 1960s that federal agencies began to employ the SSN as a general identifier in other contexts. See Kathleen S. Swendiman, "The Social Security Number: Legal Developments Affecting Its Collection, Disclosure and Confidentiality," *CRS Report for Congress*, updated January 21, 2005, 2.

114. See, for example, Nan Robertson, "Data-Center Aims Scored in Inquiry," *New York Times*, July 28, 1966, 24. Helen Nissenbaum, *Privacy in Context: Technology, Policy, and the Integrity of Social Life* (Stanford, CA: Stanford Law Books, 2010), 39.

115. Carolyn Puckett, "The Story of the Social Security Number," *Social Security Bulletin* 69, no. 2 (2009), http://www.ssa.gov/policy/docs/ssb/v69n2/v69n2p55 .html. Myron Brenton, *The Privacy Invaders* (New York: Coward-McCann, 1964); and Vance Packard, *The Naked Society* (New York: David McKay, 1964).

116. Social Security Task Force, "Report to the Commissioner, Social Security Administration," May 1971, Folder: SSN-Early History, Carrier #12, SSHA.

117. "Federal Data Banks, Computers and the Bill of Rights," *U.S. Senate Hearings* (1971), pt. 1, 776. See also Flavio Komuves, "We've Got Your Number: An Overview of Legislation and Decisions to Control the Use of SSNs as Personal Identifiers," *John Marshall Journal of Computer & Information Law* 16, no. 3 (1998): 529–77.

118. Memo from Commissioner of Social Security to Secretary of Health, Education, and Welfare, "Social Security Number Misuse—Possible Congressional Interest," February 15, 1977, Folder: SSN-Process, Carrier #12, SSHA. This included "identifying information on 256 million peoples . . . earning histories for 90 percent of the work force; family, financial, and in some cases, medical details on the 38 million people who are entitled to a benefit under one of the programs administered by SSA."

119. For key contributions to this dialogue, see Alan F. Westin, *Privacy and Freedom* (New York: Atheneum, 1967); Arthur R. Miller, *The Assault on Privacy: Computers, Data Banks, and Dossiers* (Ann Arbor: University of Michigan Press,

1971); and James Rule, *Private Lives and Public Surveillance* (London: Allen Lane, 1973).

120. See, for example, "Senator Tells Plans to Probe U.S. Snooping," *Los Angeles Times*, February 8, 1971, 28; and James J. Kilpatrick, "Ervin Gives Privacy a Boost," *Los Angeles Times*, February 23, 1971, C7.

121. Excerpts from letters concerning universal identifiers and misuses of Social Security numbers are from "Federal Data Banks, Computers and the Bill of Rights," *U.S. Senate Hearings* (1971), pt. 1, 777–81.

122. Here there may be some resonance with Cornelia Vismann's argument that files are "the medium instrumentally involved in the differentiation processes that pit state against society and administration against citizenry. The state compiles records, society demands their disclosure." Vismann, *Files*, 147.

123. Social Security Task Force, "Report to the Commissioner, Social Security Administration," May 1971, p. 16, Folder: SSN-Early History, Carrier #12, SSHA. The report here quoted Milton R. Knovitz, "Privacy and the Law: A Philosophical Prelude," *Law and Contemporary Problems* 31 (Spring 1966): 272–80, and Westin, *Privacy and Freedom*, 31–32.

124. "America, Doubled," *New York Times*, April 1, 1990, E18. The writer, reporting on transformations revealed by the U.S. Census, suggested that one of the most notable was Americans' more resigned "attitude toward being treated as numbers," evidenced in part by the fact that they willingly submitted their Social Security number every time they took a new job—something that had been required since 1937.

125. Itty Abraham, "*Segurança*/Security in Brazil and the United States," in *Words in Motion: Toward a Global Lexicon*, ed. Carol Gluck and Anna Lowenhaupt Tsing (Durham, NC: Duke University Press, 2009), 21, 22–23.

CHAPTER TWO

The Strange Career of American Liberalism

N. D. B. Connolly

In addition, I feel that a rule which discriminates between students on the basis of race is not consistent with the liberal tradition of the Johns Hopkins campus."[1] With these words, a young history professor at Hopkins, C. Vann Woodward, closed a 1947 letter, an argument, really, for the Johns Hopkins Club to admit its first black member.[2] Founded nearly a half century earlier, the Johns Hopkins Club served as a private haunt for faculty, graduate students, and, tellingly, "faculty wives."[3] It had nearly 1,500 members, and not a single African American among them.[4] In his letter, Woodward, a member of the club, noted how "quietly and effectively" the college had added its first black undergraduate only two years before. Hoping to make way for "a Negro graduate student," Woodward looked to initiate a similarly smooth defense, both of a single black hopeful and of the university's "liberal tradition."

But that was precisely the problem with liberalism. Its transformations, transitions, and even its continuities were hardly smooth, its workings never really tethered to tradition. Liberalism, rather, was contingent, held in place through power and, often, clumsy practice. Nearly a decade after his letter to the Hopkins Club, Woodward himself would point out America's crooked-line history of racial segregation in perhaps his most famous work, a collection of three 1954 lectures that eventually became *The Strange Career of Jim Crow* (published in 1955).[5] There, the professor painstakingly documented just how conditional and uneven white supremacy and American liberalism had been. He reminded Americans of the fact of black voting power in the late nineteenth century and detailed how white backlash, not black incompetence, stood responsible for unmaking the promise of Reconstruction. Woodward also dropped *Strange Career* in response to a possible *second* Reconstruction, hearkened by the May 1954 racial desegregation ruling in *Brown v. Board of Education.* Aware that any challenge to *Brown* would likely characterize racial apartheid as a timeless "Southern" value, Woodward maintained that, if Jim Crow had been so recently made, it could just as assuredly be unmade. Indeed, he said further, it *would* be, through careful uses of Congress and the courts, eloquent suasion, and rigorous argumentation in defense of "the Negro's" individual rights. With no small sense of inevitability, "A unanimous decision [in *Brown*]," he remarked, "has all the moral and legal authority of the Supreme Court behind it, and it is unthinkable that it can be indefinitely evaded."[6]

Alas. Both the impact of Woodward's 1947 letter and his 1955 book would be dampened by the very liberalism he'd hoped, twice over, to marshal. His call to desegregate a private university club elicited only "a committee to study the matter and report back at a later date."[7] "The Board [of Governors] does not disapprove of admitting Negroes as members and guests as a matter of principle," Woodward was assured, "but [it] feels that it must consider the wishes of the club members at large."[8] The club's membership guidelines did not explicitly reference race at all, in part because they never had to.[9] The preferences of the members were enough. A few informal inquiries were made; no report was written. Segregation held.[10]

Similarly, the U.S. Supreme Court, in *Brown*, expressed disdain for segregation, again as a matter of principle. But, in observance of the stated wishes of white opposition, the Court drew on vague language to outline how desegregation might be implemented, deploying the now-infamous phrase "with all deliberate speed." Even before attorneys made their closing arguments before the Court, Southern strategists planned the establishment of private schools, or "segregation academies." According to the plan, the state defense of privacy and free association, combined with the "market" of tuition, would keep black people out of white schools. (The key to those private schools remaining a possibility, of course, lay in their ability to draw state funding until the Supreme Court told them otherwise.)[11]

These two responses—one interpersonal, once societal—have more in common than their admittedly asymmetrical connection to C. Vann Woodward. They represent articulations of what one might call the strange career of American liberalism. It is a career with which we continue to grapple, both analytically and politically. Dependence on white benefactors, opaque procedures, indefinite timetables: these serve as but a few of the elements that made up the Jim Crow world. And it's a world that, oftentimes wrongly, we think we understand and have left behind. In our rush to canonize the upheavals of the 1960s and to lament the apparently more pressing problems of the 1970s and beyond, we emphasize privatization, conservative political ascendancy, mass incarceration, or so-called neoliberalism, as if these represent sharp breaks from liberalism's better days. To better understand what even Woodward once missed, one would do well to revisit and revaluate Jim Crow's political culture, with an eye not toward democracy's apparent inevitability, as Woodward did, but toward the stubborn durability of racist, capitalist political culture.

Much has changed since the age of Jim Crow, to be sure, not the least of which being the broad rejection of explicit racial segregation in American discourse and politics. However, much about racism and capitalism under Jim Crow continues to confine our unfolding political future. One can never forget that, when segregationists finally surrendered the Democratic Party in the late 1960s, they did so without having to give up many of the institutional protections they and their predecessors had built around white supremacy over the preceding several decades.[12] Just looking at the half century between the Progressive Era and the Great Society, one finds civil rights liberalism, growth liberalism, and older, laissez-faire forms of nineteenth-century liberalism being fought over, worked out, and, I maintain, reconciled through the everyday practices of systemic, institutional, and interpersonal white power. The need for white political favor and friendship remains an indispensable ingredient in American institution building, and capital (more benignly referred to as "the business community") continues to have outsized influence in determining what counts for political "common sense."[13] Indeed, for all our contemporary teeth gnashing about neoliberalism—about the apparent novelty of privatization, excessive policing, and market logics in our otherwise democratic institutions in and following the 1970s—we would do well to consider fundamental elements in liberalism, writ long and writ large: the primacy of private clubs, property ownership, extralegal violence, and state-sponsored segregation.[14] What happens, in fact, if we elect not to take at face value the presumed divides between classical liberalism, growth liberalism, civil rights liberalism, and neoliberalism, and choose instead to unpack the economic reasoning and political culture undergirding liberalism's sundry, contingent variations? How do we account, even now, for American society's stubborn adherence

to contract relationships, "market solutions," and degrees of white supremacy without locating at least some of this within segregationist statecraft?

Even at its most lofty, the "liberal tradition" Woodward invoked and
fought for in the 1940s and 1950s might best be understood as a set of political and cultural habits steeped in the state protection of private property rights and contract rights. Its history includes an emphasis on localism and the elevation of individual rights over group rights. Liberalism, in
practice, involves, too, preserving the broad state power of white people
over their black counterparts specifically, and over professedly democratic
politics in general.[15] By turns, folkways and state ways served as the glue
holding liberalism together. Where white power and property rights could
be, as at the Hopkins Club, held together by mere adherence to "the private," no laws were needed. But where people's everyday goings and com-
ings in the public marketplace might challenge white predominance (as at
a lunch counter or in a train station, for instance), Jim Crow laws needed
to be written, ratified, and posted publicly. The peaceful consummation
of capitalism's various contracts demanded such regulation.

The mid-twentieth century represented something of a turning point in
liberalism's biography, but only a modest one. Beginning in the 1930s, activists and their allies had begun successfully turning the government defenses
of contract and individual liberty toward brokering more on behalf of groups
on society's margins. And yet, even here, as America's segregationists slowly
lost on the question of overt racial apartheid, they preserved, over several
decades, the white racial power that slavery and classical liberalism had first
affixed to capitalism.

Jim Crow *was* liberalism. It supported and depended on the economic
rescue agenda of New Deal liberalism, the spending of growth liberalism,
and it even drove certain cultural elements of civil rights liberalism, particularly the strategic use of white shame through nonviolent direct action.[16]
In our more conventional narratives about modern liberalism, we describe
the history of the New Deal Era as if it were Southern or business conservatives versus Northern liberals, or as if nineteenth-century liberalism—
with its emphasis on property rights and local control—just disappeared
through the sheer passage of time or the weight of Roosevelt's, Truman's,
and later Lyndon Johnson's expanding federal government. During the age
of Jim Crow, however, Southern segregationists fought mightily against
black activists and organized labor for control over the Democratic Party
(a fight they initially lost) and the soul of American liberalism (which arguably they won). Indeed, if our so-called neoliberal moment offers any

indication—with its anemic defenses of civil rights and capitalists reigning over American politics—it's that Jim Crow's defenders successfully preserved a distinct, if troubling, continuity in the country's political and economic values.

*   *   *

The inhabitants of Jim Crow America lived between the cracks in the U.S. Constitution. And into those cracks white politicians crammed every manner of state, county, and municipal regulation restricting the movements, love lives, political fortunes, and economic prospects of so-called colored people. The state of Alabama had over forty such segregation statutes; Georgia, not to be outdone, had nearly sixty, to say nothing of the hundreds passed by county and municipal governments in both states.[17] A 1911 Arkansas statute made interracial sex a felony and defined a "mulatto child" born to any woman as *prima facie* evidence of guilt without further proof . . . justify[ing] conviction" of that woman.[18]

The lack of enforcement did the rest. Laws *forbidding* segregation, like an 1872 prohibition against the segregation of public accommodations in Washington, DC, were openly ignored for nearly a century.[19] In one state after another, the slavery prohibitions of the Thirteenth Amendment meant nothing to black convict laborers and debt peons, even during the labor reforms of the New Deal. Racist courts cleaved African Americans' human rights into social and political halves, effectively blunting the Fourteenth Amendment for a hundred years.[20] And the Fifteenth Amendment, with all its faith in the franchise, failed to guarantee colored people the positive right to vote. Coming into the twentieth century, then, white political rule remained a central feature of American governance.[21]

Subsequent articulations of white power in Congress, the presidency, and the courts ensured those nineteenth-century cracks would, in some respects, widen in the twentieth century, creating the possibility (and now historical fact) of mass incarceration, voter disempowerment, and ongoing racial segregation in housing, employment, and education. When one considers the centrality of government policy to these developments, they seem to occur not in spite of liberalism but because of it.

By means of its ability to regulate black people since the time of slavery, liberalism shored up capitalism's extractive qualities, preserving and quite often mystifying white people's economic dependence on racism. Jeffersonian liberalism, for example, relied on, among other things, associations of planters taking out mortgages on enslaved black people and then grouping and floating those mortgages to Britain, *as securities*, within an international investment chain: British capital to the United States and Southern cotton to British textile mills.[22] Progressive Era liberalism relied on imperialism in the Caribbean and Jim Crow at home. White policy makers held together the plantation economy through incarceration and debt peonage. They enabled the development of the first "whites only" garden suburbs, ensuring that those, too, could flourish from foreign investment and local racial restriction.[23] White people also protected their power on the factory floor through strengthening segregated, whites-only labor unions.[24] Through agricultural restructuring programs and federal mortgage guarantees for single-family homes, 1930s New Deal liberalism had officially used the housing sector to supplant the plantation as the heart of American capitalism. In all these contexts the controlled placement of black people underwrote national economic growth and international flows of capital.

As it concerned liberalism internationally, white officials constantly modified colonial management to preserve the idea that white nations should oversee the affairs of "colored" ones. In that way, as one founder of *Foreign Affairs* admitted, "international relations meant race relations."[25] What had begun the twentieth century as "the White Man's Burden," would evolve during the 1930s and 1940s into what Franklin Roosevelt's and Harry Truman's administrations referred to as the Good Neighbor Policy, or what South Africa's prime minister Jan Smuts called "trusteeship."[26] Take, for example, the Atlantic Charter: a joint U.S.-U.K. policy statement from 1941 defining the post–World War II goals of the Allied forces, which included professed commitments to the "restoration of sovereignty, self-government, and national life." Winston Churchill made sure to clarify that such sovereignty, as in the United States and South Africa, was not "applicable," in Churchill's words, "to Coloured Races in colonial empire."[27] Instead, the colonies and developing world got promises of broad economic growth, lubricated by tax structures favorable for white investment. A general absence of public spending, too, made colonial civil society structurally dependent on white beneficence and philanthropy.[28] Even in the emergent postfascist world, apparently, paternalism would have its place.

In some key respects, preserving liberal notions of racial paternalism became harder with the arrival of the Cold War. America's standing as a global defender of democracy seemed compromised by the persistence of racial terrorism following World War II. It also remained true, though, that Cold War politics muted many who might espouse more strident class critiques and antiracism. The Red Scare did much, in other words, to suppress and hem in the left, democracy's racial contradictions be damned. As Woodward explained in a 1991 interview, "If the Cold War hadn't come when it did and with such force[,] . . . there were forces in the South that would have become more vocal and more courageous than otherwise."[29] Stuart Hall made a similar claim from the vantage point of being a leftist in Britain: "We didn't foresee at all how the global imperatives of the Cold War would overwhelm the liberatory promise of decolonization."[30]

Cold War struggles over black freedom and capital's relationship to labor precipitated battles within the Democratic Party over how to define liberalism itself. As Florida senator George Smathers explained to a crowd of Oklahoma voters in 1952, "In recent years . . . there have been those who have come into our Democratic Party who have adopted our Democratic slogans and regalia, but they espouse and advance a philosophy which is foreign to that of true Democrats." Smathers argued "these false Democrats"—speaking of the National Association for the Advancement of Colored People (NAACP) and labor leftists—"have appropriated unto themselves the name of 'Liberal.'"[31] "A true Democrat," Smathers continued, "could not subscribe to the Federal Employment Practices Commission [sic], for in its essence it smacks of the autocratic, the dictator, and the tyrant."[32] It moved us closer to the socialism and communism of our dreaded Cold War enemy, the Soviet Union. For Smathers and other New South Democrats at midcentury, true liberalism was not that envisioned by Franklin Roosevelt or Harry Truman but rather that of Thomas Jefferson: propertied white men setting the country's political agenda through local government structures, sound adherence to enterprise, and political and racial mastery over those in need of a white patriarch's strong, guiding hand. And in the course of conducting the country's business, whenever Smathers and other Southern power brokers saw an opportunity to assert their particular liberal vision—classical, racial liberalism—they seized it.

Going back, again, to yet another fundamental element of Jim Crow's political culture, extralegal violence, specifically lynching, cut with particular sharpness through apparent partisan divides. Under a Jim Crow system, the supreme authority of white people, as a group, rested in their ability to determine, often on a whim, which black people would live or die.[33] This was "white popular sovereignty," an especially strong notion in American politics that placed white citizens above the state.[34] Such

visions of mob rule—not restricted to the United States, to be sure—
relied on the perception that all government power and authority flowed
first from white citizens, not from classes (in the Marxian sense) or leaders, but rather from elective, often-extemporaneous associations committed, as needed, to bloodletting. In the later twentieth and twenty-first
centuries, assertions about the will of "the people" usually got whipped
up by authoritarian populists hoping to exhibit the will of "the market,"
thereby undermining the "defensive organizations of the working class."[35]
In the thick of Jim Crow America, that populism—the market, such as it
was—made lynching a principled, albeit extreme, expression of politics.

To be sure, African Americans developed their own principled responses. The black radical tradition includes African Americans in armed
self-defense, fighting through the courts, and laying their own reputations,
bodies, and lives on the line to secure freedom (however defined). It also
includes, we know, everyday forms of deception, subterfuge, and clandes-
tine sabotage.[36] Such were the instruments of black survival under white
supremacy.

We must consider, too, other tools of survival, such as interracial sham-
ing, moral suasion, demonstrations of ownership, fealty, favors, and, naturally, each of these approaches' many drawbacks and limitations. These
constituted liberalism as well.

The constant threat of popular white violence meant that racial governance hung not on objective government oversight but on interracial
relationships, at times even on friendships. Whites in power often knew
the most successful black business people quite well and consulted them
regularly. It was, indeed, middle-class Negroes' job to broker deals and social pacts with wealthy white people to get (or keep) resources coming into
black communities. Information, too, circulated between white and black
politicos, and a lynching could serve as evidence of the networks working
very well (in the case of a planned interracial lynching) or of those networks
breaking down, as occurred in, say, the pogroms of Tulsa, Oklahoma, in
1921 or Rosewood, Florida, in 1923.[37]

In 1895, the educator and entrepreneur Booker T. Washington famously
articulated a vision of Southern economic progress that did not threaten
social contact or equality between blacks and whites: "In all things that
are purely social we can be as separate as the fingers." Negroes and whites
could then be "one as the hand" in matters of mutual regional progress.[38]

The lived experience of this political formulation—the hand of the collective South—remained attached to the arm of large property holders.

White owners of large farms and timberlands, city real estate, mills, and railroads ran Southern towns.[39] Black owners of rental properties, professional services, and insurance companies helped them do it. John Merrick, Aaron Moore, and Charles Spaulding, three generations of presidents for America's most successful black business, North Carolina Mutual Life Insurance Company, built their respective fortunes by helping poor black people insulate themselves from economic ruin and by continuing to make powerful white friends.[40] And in pushing for improvements to black schools and building scores of homes for black people, these men counted among their friends and supporters Durham's largest white banking, newspaper, and tobacco interests.[41] Many Negro capitalists, in short, built personal fortunes and Southern liberalism simultaneously.

In the eyes of African American civic leaders, good white leaders ran interference when lynching loomed. Bad ones, like South Carolina's Cole Blease, allowed practices of lynching to carry the day. Blease, who was governor of South Carolina during some of that state's bloodiest years of lynching, made a habit of pardoning black men from prison by the hundreds because he believed that white citizens, not the state, should be the ultimate arbiter of death for colored people.[42] Blease, whose own campaign posters described him as "A Governor Who Lauds Lynching," reflected and protected widely held notions that white Americans served as the source of all political authority in the United States.[43]

In theory, the job of political liberalism was to facilitate capitalism. Yet in the shadow of white popular sovereignty, the black encounter with American capitalism undercut several features assumed about the free market. Capitalism, as an ideal type, is supposedly made up of individuals who are free to pursue self-interest in a market-oriented economy. Capitalism persists, too, only through state protections of private property and transactions ensured through legally enforceable contract. Under capitalism, unequal distribution of wealth is not just allowed but encouraged.[44] Black people in the United States were not allowed to simply pursue self-interest, however; they had to do so in observance of white power. They also did so in an economy built on the disposability of black persons in the first place, and the exploitation of black labor in the second. At the hands of white persons, black people suffered the forcible redistribution of wealth under cover of darkness, sometimes by torchlight, and just as often through unscrupulous business transactions done in broad daylight.[45] As political scientist Michael Dawson describes it, African Americans historically entered a marketplace in which "their lives were in danger if they attempted to participate successfully, let alone equally."[46]

At times, such conditions of terrorism deepened black affirmations of white state authority. In June 1918, Robert R. Moton, Booker T.'s successor at Tuskegee, wrote President Woodrow Wilson asking him to condemn lynching. A series of murders, including the hanging of a pregnant black woman in rural Georgia, prompted Moton to plead, "I think a strong word definitely from you on this lynching proposition will have more effect just now than any other one thing." In keeping with the conventions of the day, Moton then professed to Wilson his "loyalty absolutely to you" and begged forgiveness "for writing frankly, or for adding another ounce to your already too heavy burden."[47] A moral plea wrapped in palpable racial deference: such often served as the script between black elites and their more powerful white counterparts.

Southern liberalism included affluent whites coming to the defense of African Americans so as not to allow poor whites, in their "barbarity," to create social unrest or, in even more high-minded terms, to besmirch the reputation of Anglo-Saxon civilization. Wilson eventually made that public denunciation of lynching. In it he noted, "There have been many lynchings, and every one of them has been a blow at the heart of ordered law and humane justice." The president continued, "Every American who takes part in the action of a mob or gives it any sort of countenance is no true son of this great Democracy, but its betrayer." Wilson then queried, in the context of his internationalist vision, "How shall we commend democracy to the acceptance of other peoples, if we disgrace our own by proving that it is, after all, no protection to the weak?" He then accused Germans, who had been encroaching on U.S. interests, of having "outlawed herself among the nations and . . . made lynchers of her armies." American lynchers, the president then intoned, "emulate [Germany's] disgraceful example."[48]

Broad, bold terms to be sure. But in casting African Americans as "weak," Wilson affirmed a strain of Southern paternalism that became common to the evolution of American liberalism. State actors needed to temper mob rule or regulate the white power exercised through lynching. To be a liberal meant protecting an apparently feeble Negro—once known widely as "the Lady of the Races"—from an overreach of Anglo-Saxon strength. At least in theory. Neither Woodrow Wilson nor any other president would push for an *actual* antilynching bill, especially not one that extended punishments to Southern states for mob violence. Through the 1920s, the NAACP conducted a broad antilynching campaign that included trying to shame the White House, Department of Justice, and Congress into action. Southern senators killed a 1922 effort at an antilynching bill by way of filibuster.[49]

FIGURE 2.1. Louis Dalyrmple, "The Lynching Problem," *Puck*, vol. 45, no. 1162, June 14, 1899

Black and white Southern women used their ties to elected officials to curtail the lynching problem. Even without a hard law, it was becoming increasingly evident as the 1930s wore on that, in the court of public opinion, many Southern politicians no longer felt comfortable openly celebrating lynching. In 1930, Jessie Daniel Ames, a white Georgia woman, founded the

Association of Southern Women for the Prevention of Lynching (ASWPL), a group that eventually ballooned to more than forty thousand members. The ASWPL used projections of middle-class womanhood and Christian morality to affirm the more general liberal commitment to localism and paternalism. On the other end of liberalism's political spectrum, Mary McLeod Bethune, closely collaborating with Eleanor Roosevelt, continued the work of Ida B. Wells and others by demanding new antilynching legislation as part of the New Deal. Franklin Roosevelt remained reluctant to advance such a measure. As he explained to NAACP activists: "I've got to get legislation passed by Congress to save America. The Southerners by reason of the seniority rule in Congress are chairmen or occupy strategic places on most of the Senate and House committees. If I come out for the anti-lynching bill now, they will block every bill I ask Congress to pass to keep America from collapsing. I just can't take that risk."[50]

On the question of racial violence, liberals North and South maintained for decades that they could end the lynching problem without federal intervention. In city politics, even up North, during the late 1910s and 1920s, this sometimes looked like Ku Klux Klan chapters infiltrating local police departments and at times even running for higher municipal office.[51] In Congress this looked like yet another Senate filibuster against an antilynching bill, this one in 1938. Among benevolent associations like Jessie Ames's Association of Southern Women for the Prevention of Lynching, it looked and sounded much like speeches coming from Southern senators that were full of robust defenses of localism and states' rights.[52] Much of the more genteel opposition also maintained, in fact, that any antilynching bill unfairly punished Southern states for what were ultimately the actions of individuals.[53]

In the universities and state legislatures, "experts" in criminology and the social sciences took to changing the very nature of lynching statistics. Since the 1920s, any white person who suffered a mob attack simply stopped counting in public records, so, too, did anyone who survived an attempted lynching. Black people killed under unverifiable circumstances were not really victims of lynching either, at least not in the official sense. "Lynching is not dying out," Thurgood Marshall explained in immediate response to the ASWPL's 1940 report. Taking a clear jab at the tactics of Southern congressmen, "lynchers," Marshall maintained, "have simply adopted a subcommittee technique." Instead of a large, noisy mob, "a small group of five or six persons now kidnap the victim and maim or kill him. If it's a killing party, the body is sunk in water with heavy weights."[54]

(In 1955, the killing of fourteen-year-old Emmett Till in Money, Mississippi, followed this lynching model to the letter. In place of spectacle lynching, disposing of black victims' bodies had become the template for disappearing rebellious colored people. And true to the agreed-on stance relative to "New South" statistics, Mississippi's governor, in Till's case, insisted to the media that the boy was "murdered, not lynched."[55])

Jim Crow liberalism often worked in this way—preserving the broader legitimacy of the racial state through the parsimonious release of certain goods for black people or the creative use of statistics or terminology. In this way, the lynching problem highlighted a principal racial contradiction at the heart of twentieth-century liberalism—where, exactly, did African Americans fit into the broader political calculus?

The Roosevelt years serve, by most accounts, as the fountainhead of contemporary liberalism and the big bang for African Americans' joining of the Democratic Party en masse. Yet, given the Democrats' record on race, such realignments came slowly and unevenly. In 1932, black voters withheld electoral support from Franklin Roosevelt, providing him with only 25 percent of the black vote. Black voters cited FDR's 1913 signing of segregation directives in the Department of Navy, which came as part of President Woodrow Wilson's Jim Crowing of the federal bureaucracy. They also noted Roosevelt's unilateral rewriting of the Haitian constitution a few years later, also done on Wilson's orders.[56]

In response to the Great Depression of the 1930s, the U.S. Congress and President Franklin Roosevelt ratified countless pieces of legislation and established more than three-dozen new federal agencies to pull the country out of a deep economic depression. In every city and state where new government agencies popped up, African Americans had to navigate an exclusively or majority-white bureaucracy that distributed benefits at best unevenly. Still, Southern members of Congress ensured that the labor and old-age protections being granted to white Americans under Washington's avalanche of new legislation would not reach black people. They excluded agricultural workers and domestics—the very folks working the fields and kitchens of Southern senators—from the right to unionize, as outlined under the Wagner Act.

In the area of housing, white staffers at the Home Owners Loan Corporation (HOLC), the Federal Housing Administration (FHA), and the Public Housing Administration similarly built color lines into their programs, making sure to preserve the separation of the races. As the political scientist Robert Lieberman described, "Any possibilities for broader racial inclusion in [New Deal] policy evaporated before the ink from the president's pen was dry on 14 August 1935, the moment Franklin Roosevelt affixed his signature to the Social Security Act."[57] Within a year of Roosevelt's initial bundle of programs, many black Americans across the country took to referring to the National Recovery Act as the "Negro Riddance Act," the "Negro Removal Act," and "Negroes Rarely Allowed."[58] The *Chicago Defender* noted that the " 'New Deal' [was] rapidly becoming [a] 'Raw Deal' for dark Americans."[59]

Roosevelt's proposed recovery was not being managed by color-blind technocrats who were free from self-interest; it served as an extension of existing white power over African Americans. This seemed especially true in the nation's Southern states. "So far as the Negroes in the South are concerned," the *Defender* reported, "the [Agricultural Adjustment Act], the [Federal Emergency Relief Administration], the HOLC, the [Civil Works Administration] etc., just might as well be administered by the Ku Klux Klan."[60] In government-funded flood-control zones in Mississippi, black workers suffered seven-day workweeks, lack of proper sanitation, irregular wages, forced labor conscription, and whippings.[61] In 1933, the family of James Eastland, the eventual U.S. senator and heir to a massive cotton plantation in Sunflower County, Mississippi, received $26,000 in government subsidies for not producing cotton. Relief efforts for all of Sunflower County's poor amounted to only $6,000.[62] For Southern sharecroppers, only three of every thousand relief checks, according to one University of North Carolina study, made it into croppers' hands. By one report's telling, "the other 997 were secured by fraud, deceit and common thievery by large plantation owners."[63] In many instances county agents delivered sharecroppers' checks directly to landlords on the notion that "it isn't customary for niggers to get checks."[64] This meant that for planters like the Eastlands, who had some eight hundred black field hands, the New Deal, as executed, proved instrumental in advancing black dependency. Southern Democrats, as one historian explained, "made fealty a condition of WPA employment."[65] White relief agents threatened to cut aid to African Americans who chose to vote Republican. Powerful white bosses could also lean on African Americans and force them to enter unofficial "slavery compacts," with complicit relief agents buying black labor, off the books, with government money. In other words, the very same U.S. senators who kept labor, as a whole, weak did so as part of a three-step process of exploitation: taking subsidies, repelling federal civil rights protections, and demanding political loyalty. The bureaucratization of Southern life did not necessarily root out white racists. In some cases, it merely armed them with new instruments.

It could also reshuffle the deck about which white relationships black people should cultivate. With the arrival of New Deal housing programs in North Carolina, the president of the North Carolina Mutual Life Insurance Company, Charles Spaulding, "increasingly . . . found himself thoroughly frustrated by unwieldy layers of racist bureaucracy and a southern intractability that would not bend to his style of personal politics."[66] Robert Clifton Weaver, a longtime housing bureaucrat based in Washington, began his career working for Spaulding's company, calculating risk as an actuary. Weaver, through his own white connections, gave Spaulding fresh access to the new housing agencies and helped advance Spaulding's efforts to delay farm foreclosures of black landowners in and around Durham.[67] Given the interpersonal elements within the political sphere, it often fell, yet again, to elite interracial groups to alleviate some of the New Deal's worst abuses.

The Federal Council on Negro Affairs, or the so-called Black Cabinet of President Franklin D. Roosevelt, offered a handful of accomplished African Americans their first taste of federal power. Arguably the first official representatives of what present-day observers might call Black America, Roosevelt's Black Cabinet provided the president and First Lady Eleanor Roosevelt with a moderate black voice on matters of race relations and Negro poverty. As members of civic and civil rights groups, such as the National Urban League and black Greek organizations, members of the Black Cabinet stood among the most well-connected black people in their respective hometowns. They also appeared often in the black press. As part of an emergent generation of nationally visible black liberals, they were tasked with selling the New Deal's benefits to colored people in cities and rural areas across America.[68] In the election of 1936—the fateful campaign in which FDR targeted the black vote and helped claim it for the Democratic Party into the foreseeable future—the Black Cabinet generated black votes in the North, South, and West. The Roosevelts even sent their maid, Lizzie McDuffie, onto the campaign trail. "But I don't know anything about politics, Mr. President," McDuffie allegedly protested. "All you have to do is talk Roosevelt," the president assured.[69] What that largely meant was talking access and ownership.

As liberals, Black New Dealers, such as Mary McLeod Bethune, and Truman Democrats, like the NAACP's Walter White, advanced the importance of property through the 1930s and 1940s. In a 1941 report, the NAACP cited property ownership as "*the* substantial basis of freedom" and claimed that any economic program African Americans hoped to advance would have to address black people's status as a "landless proletariat in the country[side] and a propertyless wage-earner in the city."[70] The federal government, many hoped, would expand the path of ownership and political power. Federal redlining would thwart many of these efforts. Still, even in the face of federally underwritten housing discrimination, New Deal public housing projects created the first government posts granted African American entrepreneurs at the local and federal level following Reconstruction.

Black liberalism was on the march. Chicago's Robert Taylor or Miami's James C. Scott were just a few among dozens of black Americans appointed as administrators within new municipal housing authorities.[71] At the federal level, housing offices also proved uniquely receptive to black staffers, and, as in cities, men and women joining the government housing sector tended be pulled from the ranks of business.[72] Robert Weaver's early work as an actuary and real estate consultant represented a common beginning for those who would rise to high-level government positions, in Weaver's case the first African American to secure an *actual* cabinet position for a U.S. president, in 1966.

The occasional black federal appointee aside, it presented a genuine political problem—to say nothing of the procedural impossibilities—to have local governments across the United States suddenly recognize the citizenship claims of black people en masse. One way this occurred more incrementally was through the politics of "taxpayer rights," usually considered a conservative or "neoliberal" question—that is, one of opting out of taxes.

That history of opting out represents only part of the story, though. Suffice it to say that black property owners had long made arguments for taxpayer rights, likely since their earliest negotiations with white elites in the late nineteenth century. Accumulating property and paying property taxes brought certain advantages. It made one eligible to vote in freeholder elections. It also got one's name in the real estate sections of city and county newspapers, an important requirement for building local political influence. Absent wider voting protections, however, taxpayer arguments for equality in parkland, street quality, or schools had only moderate effect. As one Florida councilman responded to a black mortician flaunting his rights as an American taxpayer: "We are responsible to the *voters* in the city. *You* people didn't put us in here and you people can't put us out."[73]

Once black voter power expanded with the end of the all-white political primary in 1944, taxpayer-rights arguments gained additional political

heft. And once black people began to gain improved economic wherewithal to expand their property ownership in a growing postwar economy,
taxpayer-rights arguments became more frequent. Indeed, during those
complicated years immediately after World War II, African American
property owners used tax receipts and taxpayer-rights arguments in city
after city to show the literal price they paid for citizenship. In Chicago,
some 1,600 black homeowners formed what they called the Property Owners Improvement Association. The group, touting their status as "taxpaying citizens," fought to reduce crime and substandard housing in their
neighborhoods. They also actively ferreted out corrupt politicians and
organized to reduce mafia influence over black votes.[74] In the post–World
War II South, black suburban communities often petitioned as "residents,
homeowners, [and] taxpayers" to improve roads and control the placement of neighborhood businesses and churches.[75] Paper tax receipts actually became critical weapons in waging direct action campaigns against
racial exclusion from public amenities and recreation. Activists looking
to desegregate beaches or public parks usually brought an attorney, a
churchman, cash for bail, and a pocket full of tax receipts to potentially
keep protesters out of jail. As one Southern black newspaper editor explained, "We brought along our [property] tax receipts [so everyone]
could see that we were freeholders [property owners] and we had paid
our taxes."[76]

Even the most racist white Americans had little rebuttal for taxpayer
arguments. For one, they drew on the hallowed language of capitalism
and contract. But just as important, they allowed whites to alleviate certain political pressures without conceding black equality in moral or social
terms. Miami's H. Leslie Quigg was a city commissioner who had a record
as an open Klan member and a murderer and torturer of black people
during his years as Miami's police chief in the 1920s and 1930s. Yet when
approached by black businessmen in 1953 for city funds to attract Negro
tourists to the city, Quigg quickly conceded, "The Negroes [are] taxed just
like anybody else for these publicity funds and they should be entitled to
some benefit from them."[77] Southern white police chiefs could celebrate
the appointment of black cops or judges as an entitlement of taxpaying
citizens and, in the very same breath, deem such appointments necessary
for those who "are more closely related to their savage forefathers of the
jungle."[78] Certain racial conditions, in other words, remained intact.

Loyalty to white business leaders and white run institutions still served
as liberalism's political glue. For instance, in matters of labor, white bosses

expected their black employees to trade rights for whites' protection and, through fealty, to court white paternalism instead of troublesome union membership. As one railroad company representative remarked in 1927: "We were the first company in this vicinity to employ Negroes as molders, cranemen or locomotive engineers. The better class of Negroes recognize this and have shown a peculiar loyalty to our company." Their black workers, he continued, "have always felt that they could get a fair deal and justice in every way."[79] Compromises, as one might expect, were uneven. In 1940, black carpenters sued a Southern housing authority and, after two years of "extensive negotiations," under nascent federal fair employment guidelines. Yet even there, the white carpenter's local agreed to extend "temporary work permits" to only a few Negro craftsmen.[80] Most often, employers considered a kind of antiunion "loyalty" from their black workers to be the surest formula for tranquil race relations.[81]

Once New Deal programs got under way, informal patronage networks found themselves flush with federal dollars. As an upside of this development, new monies made available under federal housing programs allowed black and white entrepreneurs and civic leaders to fold Jim Crow liberalism into the modernization of American residential life. Across the country, public housing projects strictly observed Jim Crow principles, of course. But even in the context of that commitment, preexisting commercial relationships between black and white entrepreneurs allowed Negroes (even in the South) to have especially strong voice in the New Deal's evolving federal-local partnerships. Two of America's first public housing projects, the "colored only" Techwood Homes in Atlanta and Liberty Square in Miami, empowered local African Americans to assume the first government leadership positions offered in the South since Reconstruction. Federal Housing Authority leadership also saw fit to extend mortgage insurance to "a group of Atlanta builders and financier, all Negro," for "the development of housing for Negroes in Atlanta."[82]

The housing situation for African Americans remained so dire that practically any relief was welcome. "Liberal" actions, as reformist actions, could be either public or privately executed. They could come from an earnest reformer or a blockbuster concerned only with his bottom line. Relative to the segregationist approach to housing reform, orchestrating "progress" on a white or colored basis made the government a benign fomenter of antiblack sentiment. It affirmed a certain status regarding African Americans, by default, as undesirable neighbors. So strong became the conventions of residential segregation that, as Kevin Boyle describes, to break them "took

more courage—or more avarice—than many real estate agents and landlords had." "Discriminatory practices," he explains further, "passed from
office to office, property to property, and racial hatred gradually turned
into common business practice, the way things were done."[83]

Across the twentieth century, the pursuit of real estate most often
prompted upwardly mobile African Americans to affirm a vision of liberalism rooted in the right to be treated as individuals rather than as a "race."
"Instead of just thinking of Negroes as Negroes," argued one black Miami
activist in 1962, "homeowners and real estate people [should] treat them
as individuals."[84] Seaside black communities with gates, private streets,
and opposition to relocation housing for the displaced—these exclusion-
ary practices and more served as expressions of black liberalism under
Jim Crow. They also tended to fall in line with perceived white sentiment,
following what one Urban League staffer called in 1948 "gradual, har-
monious population movement." Harmony, "good community relations,"
and "intelligent understanding" seemed possible, the argument went, if
realtors based their discrimination on "individual family standards rather
than race."[85] Merely tweak the housing market, in other words, to regulate
the aspiring black buyer "differently," more "fairly."

Market-based governance was, of course, a talking point, not a statement about an especially novel or efficient approach to the problems of the
color line. In perhaps the most glaring example, schools in many Southern
counties had run in accordance with "the market" since at least the 1890s.
Boards of education across the Deep South closed black schools months
early so African American children could pick cotton and edible cash
crops for local agribusiness.[86] Until the mid-1940s, white kids in Broward
County, Florida, attended school nine months a year, with summers off.
Black kids went for only seven months, and through the summer, so as to
maximize farmers' use of their labor during the growing season.[87]

Market adherence in education was not invented, but rather deepened,
in response to *Brown* and subsequent school desegregation decisions. In
the 1950s and 1960s, when racist, all-white school boards did close public
schools completely, the number of private schools throughout Dixie ex-
ploded. One 1969 desegregation ruling in Mississippi prompted, within
weeks, thirty-nine new private schools across the state.[88] One county,
Holmes, saw student enrollments drop by 97 percent. Public money proved
essential to that and similar developments across the South. In the 1950s
and 1960s, such money was "liberal" in that white private schools drew
state funds for any nonreligious content in their curriculum.[89] By the late

1960s and 1970s, those subsidies to private schools were "conservative," in that they came in the form of tax exemptions. Whether talking about the late nineteenth or late twentieth century, however, the fact remained: segregation—white power—came at the general public's expense.

In many, if not most, instances, white politicians and power brokers ensured that increased government spending and federal involvement in Southern life would shore up the power of white owners. At the very same time, African Americans found ways to take advantage of paternalism's implied social contract, variously building, bending, and breaking Jim Crow's rules.[90] Understanding liberalism's evolution thus requires examining the overlaps around liberty, property, and violence that white and colored people governed on, agreed on.

Or at least seemed to agree on. As political practice, paternalism's legitimacy depended on white people asserting that, through segregation, they had also garnered black consent. Such claims may strike us as odd today, but when faced with challenges about the precarious condition of black schools or businesses, white Southerners pointed to black people's "freedom" to create their own institutions. When called out about the paucity of "colored only" infrastructure, whites highlighted their efforts, often conducted in concert with Negroes, to make separate equal. And when filibustering antilynching legislation or campaigning on the stump about the traditions of racial separateness, Southern politicians bragged of having black buy-in for Jim Crow's incremental progress. They also claimed a certain cultural sameness with black elites, as both endeavored to uplift what one Southern senator described as a "race that had known only savagery and slavery."[91] These alleged points of concert were, undoubtedly, white paternalists' most specious claims. They were also easily refuted by activists' willingness to protest, suffer public humiliations and beatings, engage in armed struggle, and, in all this, risk death to end Jim Crow. Black people gave no consent, really; they survived.

Among the most remarkable "achievements of American liberalism" (to borrow from the historian William Chafe) stood the modernization of antiblack violence across these years. Again, slowly and unevenly, black Americans within and outside of the federal government worked with white allies to appropriate pieces of state's monopoly on administrative violence. Not since Reconstruction had African Americans been allowed to mete out punishments as representatives of the state. But these efforts, to be successful, had to be coordinated in concert with Southern Democrats and had to abide by Jim Crow's clear racial guidelines.

In the 1940s, this looked, in part, like a "Negro Officers for Negroes" movement, which saw cities across the Jim Crow South hiring African American patrolmen and judges during the late 1940s and early 1950s.[92] While campaigning for the Senate, George Smathers noted proudly in 1949, "We set up a complete and almost autonomous negro police force which operates exclusively in the colored sections of Miami."[93] Miami would get its first black judge a year later. Black officers could not arrest white offenders, of course, nor could black judges try whites in court. For lynching to disappear, other means of disciplining Americans, largely in observance of white power, had to take its place.

When direct action campaigns did emerge, the most successful ones tended to secure gains by using the embarrassing fact of white violence and terrorism against more civilized white obstructionists. To cite just one theater of contest, Bayard Rustin, Martin Luther King Jr., and the advocates of nonviolent direct action used publicized white intolerance and violence during the 1960s to cast a light on the lie of Jim Crow's peacekeeping power. In laying their bodies on the line against racial terror and excessive policing (and in doing so in full view of the American media and international community), Rustin, King, and other activists did not just shame politicians into action. They tapped into what had been a set of political beliefs about civil white rule going back to the 1890s. They showcased the moral insufficiency of white liberalism, drawing a direct line between the worlds of Woodrow Wilson, Franklin Roosevelt, and John F. Kennedy. If individual rights had been one of the defining points of contrast with Soviet totalitarianism, the brutality of Jim Crow made a lie of American exceptionalism. Civil rights activists, in effect, used a holdover of New South political culture—paternalism—to weaponize the "white man's burden" and secure allies North, South, and worldwide.

As African Americans made white political violence increasingly unacceptable in the 1950s and 1960s, Southerners stepped further away from the violent defense of Jim Crow, elevating, in its place, the morality of "the market." Hoping to fend off "federal coercion [to] put the Negro in the South . . . on a plane of equality with the white people," the intellectual defenders of Southern segregationists argued, as early as the mid-1950s, for the fairness of social "competition" between the races.[94] They cast segregation as a product of cultural merit earned by whites. And they retreated ever deeper into the property rights and individual liberty arguments that Jim Crow liberalism had long preserved. Letting the "market" decide became the meeting place of segregationist, liberal, and libertarian defenses of white power.

The idea that one should let "the market" rule preceded even the 1950s. It came from erroneous, popular recollections—the as-told history of that great calamity of black governance: Reconstruction. "Legislation cannot make mores" went the old adage. And in the 1940s and 1950s, this Dixie "common sense" represented perhaps the most charitable (and durable) interpretation of Reconstruction's apparent failure.[95] It also became the default legislative argument once the Truman White House began taking concrete steps, as articulated in the 1947 report *To Secure These Rights*, to make civil rights a formal part of federal regulation. Whereas the South maintained its commitment to equalization—making separate actually equal—Truman's Committee on Civil Rights, in *Secure*, vowed the "elimination of segregation, based on race, color creed, or national origin, from American life."[96] Many Northern states also broke from their Southern counterparts and began repealing segregation statutes, often enacting in their place legislation and local ordinances forbidding racial discrimination in education, public accommodations, and employment.[97]

Any efforts to bring about greater equality seemed to raise the specter of unnatural competition between "the races" and threatened, as perceived of Reconstruction, the institutionalization of black inferiority. Federal efforts to initiate fair employment, for example, seemed to tamper with an otherwise fair, peaceful, and just labor market. As the state legislators of Alabama decreed in 1945, "the experience if [*sic*] this state in reconstruction times and since has shown that no good can come from changing the course of evolution and development of race by arbitrary legal means."[98] Or as Florida senator George Smathers explained, "forced employment" could never work because "the Negro as a group does not have the industrial qualification of the white workers—that is a fact."[99] This negative "fact" of blackness rang out from Jim Crow's more well-heeled defenders in the North as well. William F. Buckley, in a 1957 issue of the *National Review*, maintained that, given black inferiority, paternalism, not equality, should remain the centerpiece of effective American governance. "The South confronts one grave moral challenge," Buckley explained. "It must not exploit the fact of Negro backwardness to preserve the Negro as a servile class."[100] Anything, he avowed, that unjustly tried to put black people on the same plane as whites represented an adulteration of what the founding fathers intended.

During the Great Society of the Johnson era, individual programs developed different measures of efficacy, depending on their institutional homes, the presence and prominence of black and antiracist staffers, and the ability and willingness of those drawing benefits from such programs to demand bureaucratic accountability administrative responsiveness.[101] The broader political culture of government spending, however, consistently moved away from considering welfare and the regulation of capital acceptable and necessary features of economic growth, racial equity, and national security. By the 1960s, "the public" had become blacks. This fanned an ideological dimension in which Republicans and Southern Democrats blocked housing, welfare, and employment programs and then blamed those same programs for their own limits. The racialization of the War on Poverty as a "black" program similarly contributed mightily to white opposition to government social spending in the abstract, particularly in light of increasingly vocal black radicalism, urban and suburban riots, and other apparent expressions of black ungratefulness.[102]

In the abstract, the War on Poverty threatened to sever the racial paternalism that shaped liberalism and welfare benefits over previous generations.[103] In particular, the initiative's Community Action Programs (CAPs) were supposed to empower poor people toward greater self-sufficiency via federal grants and partnerships between businesses and community groups. And in some critical instances they did. In Mississippi, African American women took advantage of Head Start programs in a dual effort to expand basic childcare to poor black families and, just as critically, to provide black women with alternatives to the coercive domestic and agricultural labor being offered by white employers. Offices of Economic Opportunity also represented a new level of oversight on employment discrimination, renter exploitation, and other potentially coercive aspects of black life under white supremacy.

Yet even within the War on Poverty, the kinds of power white capital had amassed over the preceding decades made it easy for exploitative business interests and discriminatory bosses to control local implementation of Johnson-era liberalism. Where black people had solidified a measure of control, whites worked to undermine it. After four steady years of pressure from white Mississippians, Office of Economic Opportunity (OEO) officials in Washington withdrew their support for Head Start in the Magnolia State. They opted, instead, for a more "market based" (i.e., white controlled) alternative.[104] In a move that had analogues across the country, the barons of Florida's segregated rental markets made sure to appoint a man named Charles Lockhart as the state's chief OEO "consultant." Lockhart, the black longtime rent collector for Greater Miami's most powerful white property manager, actively undermined the formation of tenant unions throughout the state and kept government responsiveness to black poverty moving at a glacial pace.[105]

Looking back, one would be hard pressed to consider the enemies of Head Start programs or tenant unions "liberals." But, critically, that is largely because by the late 1960s the discourse around liberalism itself had been changed. Some thirty years of political conflict with small-business libertarians, big-business corporate lobbyists, red-baiting politicians and their backers, grassroots religious organizations, and dug-in segregationists created a Cold War crucible that effectively transformed the very meaning of the term *liberal*. Thus, well before the end of the Johnson presidency in 1968, Southern Democrats had given up their fight over the meaning of *liberal*; the term *conservative* would work just fine.[106]

There was, under Jim Crow, a certain set of ideas and political projections that the South helped preserve for the nation as a whole. Nancy MacLean notes how the modern Republican Party drew its strength from notions of a mythical South in which "classes never clashed, whites took care of blacks, planters shared the interests of city dwellers, [and] men presided over orderly households." "The architects of the conservative movement," she maintains, "enlisted a mythical Southern past" to create a world of "untrammeled property rights"; small, punitive states; and Judeo-Christian hierarchies built into every aspect of public life.[107] That the modern GOP built its present-day political blocs from the splintering of Jim Crow's Northern and Southern Democrats is a fact that few could plausibly deny (although many GOP sympathizers try).

The obstructionism orchestrated against fair employment in the 1940s and 1950s by dyed-in-the-wool Southern politicians like George Smathers, James Eastland, and John Stennis easily became, by the mid- to late 1960s, the purview of business lobbyists, conservative Republicans, and their white suburban constituents. "When [Congress] finally did act" on fair employment, Tony Chen notes, "it was too little too late." "The consequence," Chen continues, "was affirmative action."[108]

Passed through compromise and eroded through the courts, affirmative action, today, stands as an elective not federally required measure. It is meant to mediate competition between institutions seeking a competitive edge by way of "diversity." It is not intended to end structural racism or redress historical wrongs, and it includes no clear antidiscrimination benchmarks. Rather, individual employers set their own incremental "goals and timetables" and, depending on in-house institutional climate, pursue them with waxing levels of urgency. None of this, of course, has kept affirmative action from serving as a lightning rod for any number of new "massive resistance" efforts to roll back gains made by people of color in American institutions.[109] The policy is, in other words, "all deliberate speed" by another name—smeared as "liberal," politically polarizing, but utterly unenforceable—a perfect post–Jim Crow program.

We now talk about a thing called neoliberalism. Present-day observers have become committed to describing the post-1970s as a period marked by distinct engagements with the market, one might even say the marketization of politics. But neoliberalism as a notion—really, a story—is not wholly unlike public-private governance of the "white man's burden." It serves mostly as a wistful scrap of nostalgia, accompanying lamentations about the apparent arrival of privatization, deregulation, fiscal austerity, and market logics in the distribution of social goods. Such stories accompany other tales about the good old days of the Keynesian mixed economy, replete with its welfare state, labor protections, and ostensibly robust social safety net.

For the vast majority of African Americans living under the life and afterlife of Jim Crow, however, such halcyon days never came. How does one explain the ostensible newness of neoliberal market logics to a Jim Crow–era sharecropper or the costs of fiscal austerity to a "colored only" schoolteacher? Afro-America did not need the stagflation of the 1970s, Reagan-era austerity, or Clinton-era "triangulation" to experience a world of meager welfare benefits, privatized law enforcement, disproportionate imprisonment, the outsized political influence of capital, the apparent common sense of adhering to "market principles," or tax obligations that no way proved commensurate to the entitlements they supposedly guaranteed. Simply being black in the age of Jim Crow did that well enough on its own. Indeed, to live as a "Negro" under Jim Crow was to live in a so-called neoliberal age before the term had become fashionable. What we are experiencing today may simply be the *black* side of liberalism writ large, the blackening of the American polity as a whole. Whatever it is, there is nothing "neo" about it.

Rather than discuss federal redlining or, say, the exclusion of African Americans from most of the economic protections offered by the Social Security Act, as an exception to a broadly progressive expansion of liberal state power, we should understand these historical developments as expressions of a particular and durable form of American liberalism, one that preferred to keep the regulation of black life in the hands of powerful whites, both in the halls of power and at the grass roots. When you examine the actual consequence of liberalism in action, and not simply the democratic ideals that one may *believe* should abide, the integral place of racial paternalism and white power in the liberal political calculus becomes undeniable. In matters of housing, employment, welfare, and even redressing racial violence, twentieth-century liberalism, as a feature of Jim Crow, served to tighten certain paternal bonds—or perhaps, better, standardized them—in ways that left black people, structurally anyway, ever in search of white favor.

It was that constant searching that led one black graduate student at Johns Hopkins University in 1947 to seek out the support of one C. Vann Woodward. During the 1930s, 1940s, and 1950s, Woodward belonged to a group of faculty at Hopkins—and indeed, around the country—whose efforts, at various turns, helped institutionalize a measure of racial progressivism. These included sociologist Broadus Mitchell, who lost his job at Hopkins in the 1940s advocating for desegregation at the university, and the political scientist V. O. Key, who, in the late 1940s, helped conceptualize how to use federal grants (and their withdrawal) as an instrument to reduce discrimination.[110] Their particular form of liberalism would, at least for a time, come to define liberalism as a whole. So would the political convictions of arguably their most sterling member.

By the 1990s, not surprisingly, perhaps, C. Vann Woodward seemed nowhere near describing himself as a liberal. "No sooner have we placed ourselves as left-of-center," the historian explained to a former student in 1998, "than center turns out to be where right was the day before yesterday."[111] Noting the shifting political terrain of the late twentieth century, he claimed that, "except for the fleeting moment of the civil rights movement," he had "never been a liberal."[112] *Brown* seemed necessary; race-based redressive policies, not so much. Once the 1964 Civil Rights Act mandated that African Americans and other minorities finally be treated as self-maximizing individuals, there seemed no need for any further legislative, institutional, or political solutions. To this effect, Woodward in his later years professed himself an enemy of "political correctness." And where he once offered his considerable scholarly reputation to blacks aiming to integrate a private club, by the 1990s, he had taken to backing on-campus movements defending right-wing "free speech" and opposing affirmative action.[113] Woodward went so far as to imply that John Hope Franklin, whose work he had cited by name in *Strange Career of Jim Crow*, had been hired by Duke University merely on account of Franklin's race.[114] A strange career, indeed.

Notes

The author wishes to thank the editors of this volume, attendees at the "State Categories/Social Identities" conference at Austria's Leiden University (2014); the "Seeing beyond the Partisan Divide" conference at the University of Virginia (2015), the "New Materialisms" conference at the University of Michigan (2016), and the "Race and Capitalism: Global Territories, Transnational Histories" conference at UCLA (2017), especially Robert Chao Romero, Ananya Roy, Michael C. Dawson, Tianna Paschel, Megan Ming Francis, Jemima Pierre, and Aisha Finch.

1. C. Vann Woodward to Board of Governors of the Johns Hopkins Club, December 18, 1947, in *The Letters of C. Vann Woodward*, ed. Michael O' Brien (New Haven, CT: Yale University Press, 2013), 114–15.

2. John Egerton interview with C. Vann Woodward, January 12, 1991, Southern Oral History Program Collection (interview A-0341), http://docsouth.unc.edu /sohp/html_use/A-0341.html.

3. Meeting of the Board of Governors, November 12, 1952, *The Johns Hopkins Club Board of Governors Collection*, "1952," July 1952–December 1952, Johns Hopkins University, Baltimore, MD.

4. Membership Committee Report: Annual Meeting, December 6, 1947, *The Johns Hopkins Club Board of Governors Collection*, January 1946–December 1946 (the December 1947 document here is likely misfiled), Johns Hopkins University, Baltimore, MD.

5. C. Vann Woodward, *The Strange Career of Jim Crow* (Oxford: Oxford University Press, 1955).

6. Woodward, *Strange Career*, 149.

7. Meeting of the Board of Governors, January 13, 1948, *The Johns Hopkins Club Board of Governors Collection*, January 1948–December 1948, Johns Hopkins University, Baltimore, MD.

8. Meeting of the Board of Governors, January 13, 1948, *The Johns Hopkins Club Board of Governors Collection*, January 1948–December 1948, Johns Hopkins University, Baltimore, MD.

9. "Application for Membership," *The Johns Hopkins Club Board of Governors Collection*, January 1953–December 1953, Johns Hopkins University, Baltimore, MD.

10. Meeting of the Board of Governors, May 11, 1948, *The Johns Hopkins Club Board of Governors Collection*, January 1948–December 1948, Johns Hopkins University Baltimore, MD.

11. Charles Wallace Collins, "Confidential: Outline of a Plan . . ." February 1, 1954, p. 11, "General Information Concerning FEPC 1950, 52–53" folder, box 302, George A. Smathers Papers, University of Florida, Gainesville.

12. Nancy MacLean, "Neo-Confederacy versus the New Deal: The Regional Utopia of the Modern American Right," in *The Myth of Southern Exceptionalism*, ed. Matthew D. Lassiter and Joseph Crespino (Oxford: Oxford University Press, 2010), 308–29; Matthew D. Lassiter D., *The Silent Majority: Suburban Politics in the Sunbelt South* (Princeton, NJ: Princeton University Press, 2006); and Kevin M. Kruse, *White Flight: Atlanta and the Making of Modern Conservatism* (Princeton, NJ: Princeton University Press, 2005).

13. Noliwe Rooks, *White Money/Black Power: African American Studies and the Crises of Race in Higher Education* (Boston: Beacon Press, 2007); Karen Ferguson, *Top Down: The Ford Foundation, Black Power, and the Reinvention of Racial Liberalism* (Princeton, NJ: Princeton University Press, 2013); and Kim Phillips-Fein and Julian E. Zelizer, *What's Good for Business: Business and Politics since World War II* (Oxford: Oxford University Press, 2012).

14. Neoliberalism, we are led to believe, has converted the "distinctly political character" of our society and made "democracy's constituent elements into economic ones." The history of Jim Crow—indeed, of racial capitalism—contradicts such a clean notion of historical rupture. Wendy Brown, *Undoing the Demos: Neoliberalism's Stealth Revolution* (Cambridge, MA: MIT Press, 2015), 17.

15. Thomas C. Holt, *The Problem of Freedom: Race, Labor, and Politics in Jamaica and Britain, 1832–1938* (Baltimore: Johns Hopkins University Press, 1992).

16. On the successful claiming of the political center by Southern segregationists, see Joseph Crespino, *In Search of Another Country: Mississippi and the Conservative Counterrevolution* (Princeton, NJ: Princeton University Press, 2009); and Joseph Crespino, *Strom Thurmond's America* (New York: Hill and Wang, 2012). See also Brent Cebul and Mason Williams's chapter in this volume, "'Really and Truly a Partnership': The New Deal's Associational State and the Making of Postwar American Politics."

17. Pauli Murray, *States' Laws on Race and Color: and Appendices Containing International Documents, Federal Laws and Regulations, Local Ordinances and Charts* (Cincinnati, OH: Women's Division of Christian Service, Methodist Church, 1952), 21–34, 89–117.

18. Highlighting the sexism that often accompanied racism, this same law continues, "no person shall be convicted of the crime [of concubinage] upon the testimony of the female, unless the same is corroborated by other evidence." Murray, *States' Laws*, 39.

19. *District of Columbia v. John R. Thompson Co.*, 346 U.S. 100 (1953).

20. Slaughterhouse Cases, 83 U.S. (16 Wall.) 36 (1873), *United States v. Cruikshank*, 92 U.S. 542 (1876).

21. *United States v. Reese*, 92 U.S. 214 (1876).

22. Edward E. Baptist, "Toxic Debt, Liar Loans, and Securitized Human Beings," *Common Place* 10, no. 3 (April 2010), http://www.common-place-archives.org/vol-10/no-03/baptist/.

23. Paige Glotzer, "Who Bankrolled Jim Crow? Global Capital and American Segregation," *Public Seminar*, http://www.publicseminar.org/2015/09/who-bankrolled-jim-crow/#.WhrelrQ-d-U.

24. Peter James Hudson, *Bankers and Empire: How Wall Street Colonized the Caribbean* (Chicago: University of Chicago Press, 2017).

25. William Langer, *In and out of the Ivory Tower: The Autobiography of William L. Langer* (New York: Neale Watsun Academic Publications, 1977), 81, cited

in Robert Vitalis, *White World Order, Black Power Politics: The Birth of American International Relations* (Ithaca, NY: Cornell University Press, 2015), 19.

26. N. D. B. Connolly, *A World More Concrete: Real Estate and the Remaking of Jim Crow South Florida* (Chicago: University of Chicago Press, 2014), 103; Vitalis, *White World Order, Black Power Politics*, 111.

27. Penny Von Eschen, *Race against Empire: Black Americans and Anticolonialism, 1937–1957* (Ithaca, NY: Cornell University Press, 1997), 26.

28. Vanessa Ogle, "Archipelago Capitalism: Tax Havens, Offshore Money, and the State, 1950s–1970s," *American Historical Review* 122, no. 5 (December 2017): 1431–58.

29. John Egerton interview with C. Vann Woodward, January 12, 1991, Southern Oral History Program Collection (interview A-0341), http://docsouth.unc.edu/sohp/html_use/A-0341.html.

30. Hall, *Familiar Stranger*, 232.

31. Sen. George Smathers to State Convention in Oklahoma, October 1952, p. 7, "Speeches, Talks, and Addresses, various subjects, 1951–1952" folder, box 302, George A. Smathers Papers, University of Florida.

32. Smathers to State Convention in Oklahoma, 13.

33. Achille Mbembe, "Necropolitics," *Public Culture* 15, no. 1 (2003): 11–40.

34. Ashraf H. A. Rushdy, *American Lynching* (Oxford: Oxford University Press, 2012).

35. Stuart Hall, "Great Right Moving Show," in *Selected Political Writings: The Great Moving Right Show and Other Essays*, ed. Sally Davison, David Featherstone, Michael Rustin, and Bill Schwarz (Durham, NC: Duke University Press, 2017), 179.

36. Robin Kelley, "'We Are Not What We Seem': Rethinking Black Working-Class Opposition in the Jim Crow South," *Journal of American History* 80, no. 1 (June 1993): 75–112; Tera W. Hunter, *To Joy My Freedom: Southern Black Women's Lives and Labors after the Civil War* (Cambridge, MA: Harvard University Press, 1997); and Glenda Elizabeth Gilmore, *Defying Dixie: The Radical Roots of Civil Rights, 1919–1950* (New York: W. W. Norton, 2008).

37. Karlos K. Hill, *Beyond the Rope: The Impact of Lynching on Black Culture and Memory* (Cambridge: Cambridge University Press, 2016).

38. Booker T. Washington, "Atlanta Exposition Address [1895]," in Henry Louis Gates Jr. and Jennifer Burton, eds., *Call and Response: Key Debates in African American Studies* (New York: W. W. Norton, 2011), 207.

39. Timothy B. Tyson, *Blood Done Signed My Name* (New York: Three Rivers Press, 2004), 227.

40. Leslie Brown, *Upbuilding Black Durham: Gender, Class, and Black Community in the Jim Crow South* (Chapel Hill: University of North Carolina Press, 2008).

41. Weare, *Black Business in the New South*, 20n54.

42. Bryant Simon, *A Fabric of Defeat: The Politics of South Carolina Millhands, 1910–1948* (Chapel Hill: University of North Carolina Press, 1998); and Rushdy, *American Lynching*, 7.

43. Rushdy, *American Lynching*, 116.

44. Stanley Buder, *Capitalizing on Change: A Social History of American Business* (Chapel Hill: University of North Carolina Press, 2009), 10.

45. Between 1890 and 1900, whites bearing legal authority and, at times, hoods, or "white caps," seized more than two thousand acres from black farmers in Quitman County, Georgia. It was more than half of all the black-owned land in the county; W. E. B. Du Bois, "The Negro Land-holder of Georgia," *Bulletin of the United States Department of Labor* 35 (July 1901): 755.

46. Michael C. Dawson, *Black Visions: The Roots of Contemporary African-American Political Ideologies* (Chicago: University of Chicago Press, 2001), 286.

47. R. R. Moton to Woodrow Wilson, June 15, 1918. "President Wilson Correspondence, Statement, and Press Releases regarding Lynching, 1918," Federal Surveillance of Afro-Americans (1917–1925): The First World War, the Red Scare, and the Garvey Movement, History Vault.

48. Woodrow Wilson, "Mob Action," July 26, 1918. "President Wilson Correspondence, Statement, and Press Releases regarding Lynching, 1918," Federal Surveillance of Afro-Americans (1917–1925): The First World War, the Red Scare, and the Garvey Movement, History Vault.

49. Megan Ming Francis, *Civil Rights and the Making of the Modern American State* (Cambridge: Cambridge University Press, 2014).

50. Walter White, *A Man Called White: The Autobiography of Walter White* (London: Viking, 1949), 169–70.

51. Kevin Boyle, *Arc of Justice: A Saga of Race, Civil Rights, and Murder in the Jazz Age* (New York: Henry Holt, 2004).

52. Walter White to Arthur Raper, April 22, 1940, NAACP Correspondence Regarding Jessie Daniel Ames, of the Association of Southern Women for the Prevention of Lynching, Papers of the NAACP, pt. 7, Antilynching Campaign, 1912–1955, Series B: Anti-lynching Legislative and Publicity Files, 1916–1955, ProQuest History Vault.

53. Correspondence from E. M. Martin, Secretary of Atlanta Life Insurance Company, to Mary McLeod Bethune, June 10, 1943, ProQuest History Vault.

54. "NAACP Cites Three Lynchings in 1940 in the Answer to Women's Claim of 'Lynchless Year,'" May 10, 1940, NAACP Correspondence Regarding Jessie Daniel Ames of the Association of Southern Women for the Prevention of Lynching, Papers of the NAACP, pt. 7, Anti-lynching Campaign, 1912–1955, Series B: Anti-lynching Legislative and Publicity Files, 1916–1955, Proquest History Vault; and "Lynching Goes Underground: A Report on a New Technique," January 1940, Papers of the NAACP, pt. 7, The Anti-lynching Campaign, 1912–1955, Series A: Anti-Lynching Investigative Files, 1912–1953, ProQuest History Vault.

55. Rushdy, *American Lynching*, 7.

56. N. D. B. Connolly, "Franklin Roosevelt: A Candidate of Questionable Constitution," *Talking Points Memo*, October 14, 2015, http://talkingpointsmemo.com/primary-source/haiti-constitution-fdr.

57. Robert C. Lieberman, *Shifting the Color Line: Race and the American Welfare State* (Cambridge, MA: Harvard University Press, 1998), 216.

58. Lewis Caldwell, "What the NRA Is Doing to the Race!" *Chicago Defender*, May 26, 1934, 10.

59. Caldwell, "What the DRA Is Doing to the Race!" 10.

60. Caldwell, "What the DRA Is Doing to the Race!" 10.

61. "Conditions among the Negro Laborers in Mississippi Flood Control Camps," *New Republic*, September 21, 1932, 72, 137; and "The Government's Job," *Survey*, October 1932, 68, 498—both cited in John G. Van Deusen, *The Black Man in White America* (Washington, DC: Associated Publishers, 1938), 115.

62. Christopher Myers Asch, *The Senator and the Sharecropper: The Freedom Struggles of James O. Eastland and Fannie Lou Hamer* (New York: New Press, 2008), 81.

63. The remarks of John P. Davis, July 1, 1935, 26th Annual NAACP conference, St. Louis, MO, Papers of the NAACP, Part 01: Meetings of the Board of Directors, Records of Annual Conferences, Major Speeches, and Special Reports, History Vault.

64. Van Deusen, *The Black Man in White America*, 120.

65. Nancy J. Weiss, *Farewell to the Party of Lincoln: Black Politics in the Age of FDR* (Princeton, NJ: Princeton University Press, 1983), 199.

66. Walter B. Weare, *Black Business in the New South: A Social History of the North Carolina Mutual Life Insurance Company* (Urbana: University of Illinois Press, 1973), 220.

67. Weare, *Black Business in the New South*, 219.

68. Edgar G. Brown, *What the Civilian Conservation Corps (CCC) Is Doing for Colored Youth* (Washington, DC: Government Printing Office, 1941).

69. Weiss, *Farewell to the Party of Lincoln*, 201.

70. "Future Plan and Program of the NAACP," n.d., ca. December 1941, box 439, file "NAACP Programs: General, 1941–42," Papers of the NAACP, cited in Carol Anderson, *Eyes off the Prize: The United Nations and the African American Struggle for Human Rights, 1944–1955* (Cambridge: Cambridge University Press, 2003), 18 (my emphasis).

71. N. D. B. Connolly, *A World More Concrete: Real Estate and the Remaking of Jim Crow South Florida* (Chicago: University of Chicago Press, 2014), 90–91; Robert Taylor's granddaughter is Valerie Jarrett, an adviser to former president Barack Obama.

72. See Charles Abrams, "The Segregation Threat in Housing," *Commentary* 7, no. 2 (February 1949): 123–31; Wendell Pritchett, *Robert Clifton Weaver and the*

American City: The Life and Times of an Urban Reformer (Chicago: University of Chicago Press, 2008), 121–29.

73. Ted Poston, "And Now, Negroes of Miami Not Only Register and Vote, but Are Showing the Way," *Pittsburgh Courier*, June 22, 1940, 22 (my emphasis).

74. Robert M. Lombardo, "The Black Mafia: African-American Organized Crime in Chicago, 1890–1960," *Crime, Law and Social Change* 38, no. 1 (July 2002): 33–65, 45.

75. "Petition," Neighborhoods and Communities #2, Richmond Heights folder, The Black Archives History and Research Foundation of South Florida, Miami.

76. Garth Reeves, quoted in Connolly, *World More Concrete*, 208.

77. "Request for Publicity—Negro Tourist Facilities," Office of the City Clerk, 4 November 1953, Office of the Miami City Clerk, *Resolutions and Minutes of the City Commission, 1921–1986*, box 43, State Archives of Florida, Tallahassee.

78. Arthur E. Chapman, "The History of the Black Police Force and Court in the City of Miami" (PhD diss., University of Miami, 1986), 132.

79. Correspondence of February 23, 1927, quoted in Sterling D. Spero and Abram L. Harris, *The Black Worker: The Negro and the Labor Movement* (1931; rpt., New York: Atheneum, 1968), 129.

80. "Employment of Negro Construction Labor on Public Housing Projects," p. 14, record group 196, box 1, Folder: Correspondence Re: History, National Archives and Records Administration (NARA), College Park, MD.

81. Perhaps not surprisingly, black small businesses often made the same claim, preferring a well-paid customer base generating revenue than having to deal with an organized workforce driving up labor costs.

82. Philip Sadler, "History of Public Housing for Negroes," January 6, 1954, record group 196, box 1, Folder: Correspondence Re: History, NARA.

83. Boyle, *Arc of Justice*, 108.

84. "Dade NAACP Puts Shoe on Other Foot," *Miami News*, March 4, 1962, cited in Connolly, *World More Concrete*, 239.

85. Reginald Johnson, "The Restrictive Covenant," May 17, 1948, "Restrictive Covenant, May 1948–May 1953, January 1960" folder, National Urban League Papers, Room, pt. 3, box 76, Library of Congress. Johnson was the director of field services and housing co-coordinator for the National Urban League of New York City.

86. Jim Anderson, *Education of Blacks in the South*, 1860–1935 (Chapel Hill: University of North Carolina Press, 1988), 96.

87. Deborah Work, *My Soul Is a Witness: A History of Black Fort Lauderdale* (Virginia Beach, VA: Donning Co., 2001), 33–36; *Clarence C. Walker Civic League et al. v. Board of Public Instruction for Broward County, Fla.*, 154 F.2d 726 (1946).

88. Crespino, *In Search of Another Country*, 227–28.

89. Collins, "Confidential: Outline of a Plan . . . ," 11. "General Information Concerning FEPC 1950, 52–53" folder, box 302, George A. Smathers Papers, University of Florida, Gainesville.

90. The record of black subterfuge and sabotage in racist workplaces is as old as the history capitalism in the New World. During the U.S. occupation of Haiti, for example, one white bank vice president for the National City Bank of New York describes how one of his black servants, in her "naiveté and restricted mentality" mismanaged a trip to buy beef in a local market. Given money for buying three pounds of beef filet, she brought back far less, professing "there are big cows and small cows . . . this piece is from a small cow." Allen laments, unaware he's been deceived, "she was satisfied and we had to be." John H. Allen, "American Co-operation Assures a Better Era for Haiti," *Americas* 6, no. 8 (May 1920), 8–9.

91. Russell, cited in Keith M. Finley, *Delaying the Dream: Southern Senators and the Fight against Civil Rights, 1938–1965* (Baton Rouge: Louisiana State University Press, 2009).

92. Earl Lewis, *In Their Own Interests: Race, Class, and Power in Twentieth-Century Norfolk, Virginia* (Berkeley: University of California Press, 1991), 197; N. D. B. Connolly, "Games of Chance: Jim Crow's Entrepreneurs Bet on 'Negro' Law-and-Order," in *What's Good for Business: Business and Politics since World War II*, ed. Phillips-Fein and Zelizer, 140–56.

93. George A. Smathers, "Memorandum," December 6, 1949, "Political—1950 Campaign—misc." folder, box 319, George A. Smathers Papers, Special Collections, George A. Smathers Libraries, Gainesville, FL.

94. This particular charge of "coercion" comes from Charles Wallace Collins, a eugenicist and political strategist who helped orchestrate massive resistance measures for Southern politicians. "Confidential: Outline of a Plan . . . ," February 1, 1954, p. 12, "General Information Concerning FEPC 1950, 52–53" folder, box 302, George A. Smathers Papers, University of Florida.

95. Woodward points to this adage from William Graham Sumner as central to what became the orthodox, liberal read on Reconstruction's implications, in *Strange Career* (90).

96. Woodward, *Strange Career*, 117.

97. Davidson M. Douglas, foreword to Murray, *States' Laws*, xxi.

98. "Fair Employment Practices—Joint Resolution against Enactment of F.E.P.C. Legislation," *General Acts of the State of Alabama* (1945), 725, cited in Murray, *States' Laws*, 29.

99. George Smathers, "FEPC in the South," "FECP [*sic*], General Information folder 1 of 2 1953" folder, box 302, George Smathers Papers, University of Florida.

100. William F. Buckley, "Why the South Must Prevail," *National Review*, August 24, 1957, 149.

101. Crystal R. Sanders, *A Chance for a Change: Head Start and Mississippi's Black Freedom Struggle* (Chapel Hill: University of North Carolina Press, 2016); Lieberman, *Shifting the Color Line*; Premilla Nadasen, *Welfare Warriors: The Welfare Rights Movement in the United States* (New York: Routledge, 2004); and

Rhonda Y. Williams, *The Politics of Public Housing: Black Women's Struggles against Urban Inequality* (Oxford: Oxford University Press, 2005).

102. Judith Russell, *Economics, Bureaucracy, and Race: How Keynesians Misguided the War on Poverty* (New York: Columbia University Press, 2004), 7.

103. Lieberman, *Shifting the Color Line*, 221.

104. Sanders, *Chance for a Change*, 7–8.

105. Connolly, *World More Concrete*, 225–26.

106. Barry Goldwater, *The Conscience of a Conservative* (Wheaton, IL: Victor Publishing, 1960). The term *conservative* has proved to be quite capacious in American politics, with its latest standard-bearer, President Donald J. Trump, having made donations to the Hillary Clinton campaign for U.S. Senate as recently as 2007. Nick Gass, "Trump Has Spent Years Courting Hillary and Other Dems," *Politico*, June 16, 2015, https://www.politico.com/story/2015/06/donald-trump-donations-democrats-hillary-clinton-119071.

107. MacLean, "Neo-Confederacy versus the New Deal," 311, 312.

108. Anthony S. Chen, *The Fifth Freedom: Jobs, Politics, and Civil Rights in the United States, 1941–1972* (Princeton, NJ: Princeton University Press, 2009), 232.

109. George Derek Musgrove, "Good at the Game of Tricknology: Proposition 209 and the Struggle for the Historical Memory of the Civil Rights Movement," *Souls* (Summer 1999): 7–24.

110. Broadus Mitchell, "Excluded Because of Color," *Frontiers of Democracy*, March 15, 1940, in Discrimination against Black Applicants at Johns Hopkins University, Papers of the NAACP, Part 3: The Campaign for Educational Equality, Proquest History Vault; V. O. Key to Jack Dunham, May 7, 1947, *Federal Grants-in-Aid Program for Civil Rights*, President Truman's Committee on Civil Rights, April 25, 1947–May 7, 1947, History Vault.

111. C. Vann Woodward to Cushing Strout, January 19, 1998, in *The Letters of C. Vann Woodward*, ed. Michael O'Brien (New Haven, CT: Yale University Press, 2013), 405.

112. Michael O'Brien, introduction to *The Letters of C. Vann Woodward* (New Haven, CT: Yale University Press, 2013), xl.

113. In a string of apologies for what he admits is a very flawed book, Woodward writes the following about D'Souza's *Illiberal Education*: "Its moderation in tone and style may put readers off guard for its occasional stretching of evidence and logic to score a point. That does occur, but on the whole, for a subject so heatedly debated up to the last moment, the investigation seems reasonably thorough, the rhetoric comparatively temperate, and the documentation fairly detailed, if sometimes very selective." C. Vann Woodward, "Freedom & the Universities," *New York Review of Books*, July 18, 1991, http://www.nybooks.com/articles/1991/07/18/freedom-the-universities/; O'Brien, introduction to *Letters of C. Vann Woodward*, xl.

114. John Hope Franklin, *Mirror to America: The Autobiography of John Hope Franklin* (New York: Farrar, Straus & Giroux, 2005), 325–28.

CHAPTER THREE

"Really and Truly a Partnership"

The New Deal's Associational State and the Making of Postwar American Politics

Brent Cebul and Mason B. Williams

A s the first calendar year of his presidency wound to a close, Franklin Roosevelt convened a meeting of America's mayors and relief officials to explain the Civilian Works Administration (CWA)—the temporary work-relief program he had designed to see the nation's unemployed workers through the winter of 1933–1934. "This work is really and truly a partnership," Roosevelt said. "Most of the responsibility for the practical application of the plan will fall on you rather than on us in Washington."[1] Looking back on the experience, CWA director Harry Hopkins (who later headed the longer-lived Works Progress Administration, or WPA) echoed Roosevelt: "We would have been awful damned fools . . . if we thought for a minute that we have either the power or the ability to go out and set up 100,000 work projects as we are going to have to do, probably 200,000 before the year is over, without the complete cooperation of local and state officials. We couldn't do it if we wanted to."[2]

Sometimes of choice and sometimes of political and institutional necessity, the New Dealers made state and local governments, private contractors, and members of civil society their local partners in administering many of their initiatives. This was particularly so in the New Deal's social welfare and developmental programs like the WPA and Public Works Administration (PWA), which, between 1933 and 1939, constituted the bulk of federal emergency expenditures. The PWA operated through some fifty-five thousand contracts with twenty thousand private companies and in all but three of the nation's 3,071 counties. The WPA, meanwhile, constructed nearly five hundred airports and seventy-eight thousand new bridges, employing some 8.5 million Americans on projects directed by leaders of the local public and private sectors.[3] Roosevelt's cheery invocation of partnership was born out by local elites. The Augusta, Georgia, Chamber of Commerce liked to joke that WPA actually stood for "We Protect Augusta." The manager of the Liberty, Texas, Chamber of Commerce was fired for criticizing a WPA project, lest he jeopardize future federal funding. In larger cities like Dallas, too, business elites happily sought partnerships with the New Deal state.[4]

Reading the history of the New Deal and its political legacies, however, one might easily miss these robust partnerships between local elites and the national government—and not simply because we lack fine-grained social histories of the local administration and implementation of New Deal works programs. More significant, perhaps, has been historians' tendency to read the New Deal through historiographical categories that risk obscuring as much as they reveal. The "New Deal order" literature tended to couple centralization with progressive policy goals and construed localism or decentralism primarily as sources of conservative drag on reform. The rise of conservatism literature, meanwhile, described a rather narrow story in which all state developments were perceived as anathema by business constituencies such as chambers of commerce. And each of these literatures developed regional biases—the Northeast and Midwest were hubs of liberalism (and sites of case studies of its crack-up), while the Sunbelt was home to burgeoning antistatist conservatives. Yet the above examples—all drawn from the emerging Sunbelt—suggest a far more complicated story than those generally written within the traditional frameworks of political history, characterized as they are by overly neat distinctions between red and blue, North and South, public and private.

While localism and devolution are often associated with late twentieth-century new federalism or neoliberalism, the pragmatic and political utility of local administrative autonomy and public-private partnerships were an essential part of the New Deal. The American federal structure simultaneously presented the New Dealers with both a tool and a barrier. It made possible the New Deal's most ambitious (and politically powerful) programs; it helped bind a wide variety of local elites to the New Deal project; and it enabled some of the most progressive parts of the New Deal to persist at the state and local levels once the winds of national

politics had changed. But beneath the cheery language of partnership
often lay a bitter truth: as two generations of scholars have amply documented, the prerogatives of localism and partnership built into the New
Deal, thanks to a blend of preference and pragmatism, embedded new
forms of racial and gender inequalities in the American state and social
structure.[5]

The New Deal's politics of partnership also introduced a number of
important dynamics into local politics: It changed local interest-group
politics, elevating the power of some actors and diminishing that of others; it introduced resources that allowed elites to govern in new ways; and
it encouraged actors of all different sorts—from civic boosters to industrial workers—to demand more of their governments. Over time, these
dynamics would reshape local, state, and regional politics, shaping key
contours within which postwar American politics would unfold.

How precisely these dynamics reshaped local politics depended on
institutional factors—that is, the New Deal produced a range of local,
state, and regional outcomes that often depended on the legacies of local pre–New Deal social and political developments. Region and history
mattered greatly. Many cities in the North had been home to strong Progressive Era reform movements, possessed capable, well-resourced social
welfare institutions and boasted empowered labor and consumer movements. These relatively democratic local polities were more likely to in-
corporate redistributive and regulatory features of the New Deal state
along with developmental ones—public housing and fair employment laws
along with public works. The result was a momentary flourishing of urban
liberalism characterized by commitments to labor and decommodified social goods—progressive commitments that coexisted uneasily with rampant (and federally supported) racial segregation, racialized disinvest-
ment, and powerful local efforts to maintain the color line (struggles over
which New Deal projects themselves became key sites, as in cases where
public housing projects accelerated racial segregation in the North). In
less democratic polities, like much of the Jim Crow South, characterized
by large numbers of disenfranchised and marginalized citizens led by
closed ranks of elites, the New Deal was shorn of its more redistributive
elements. In these communities, many of which became the citadels of
the Sunbelt, the New Deal's unprecedented investments in infrastructure
fueled a frenzy of booster politics, and growth-oriented state-business
coalitions developed relatively unencumbered by challenges from labor
or minority groups.[6] Hardly antigovernment, these elites enjoyed much

smoother administration of many New Deal initiatives precisely because Jim Crow and low rates of labor organizing constrained and quieted broader enfranchisement.

These are idealized types, of course; the local politics of most postwar American cities, states, and regions would best be placed at some point on a spectrum that stretched between them. But thinking in terms of types helps illuminate the key point: because of the particular ways in which the New Dealers rebuilt the American state, the New Deal organized a range of new styles of governance into the American system.[7] Political modes typically thought of as quite antithetical—urban liberalism and Sunbelt conservatism—each took root through partnerships with the New Deal state. Recognizing those shared origins helps to unlock some of the mysteries of postwar politics: why, for instance, did Sunbelt politicians whose districts reaped a disproportionate share of federal spending come to preach a gospel of small government? It also helps historians transcend the regional essentialism implied by categories like "Sunbelt conservatism" and "urban liberalism." And not least, it helps us see beyond "red versus blue" narratives of American political history to identify more precisely the relation between political ideologies and the American state. Because the post–New Deal state was contested terrain, a disparate scope of subnational regimes depending on it, local and national politicians devised powerful languages—a language of urban liberalism and a language of small-government conservatism—to stake their claims on fiscal federalism and legitimize their own vision of how the New Deal's legacy ought to unfold. Governance did not follow from ideology, but rather the reverse.

Yet the New Deal did not develop a robust political and ideological commitment to the national state among a wide range of local elites. Rather, the New Deal's politics of partnership enabled local authorities to enjoy the benefits of federal spending while obscuring the national government's authority: because federal resources flowed through local intermediaries, local politicians and boosters were encouraged to understand their relation to the national state as a competition for resources and to narrate federally subsidized development as evidence of the wisdom of localism.

The New Deal's reliance on partnerships thus placed a crucial constraint on the post–New Deal national state's political and conceptual legitimacy. Through the postwar era, fiscal federalism and partisan affiliation held the New Deal coalition together. Amid the economic turmoil of the 1970s, however, conflict broke out between the New Deal's

Northern and Southern wings as politicians scrambled for resources—a conflict from which a new generation of Sunbelt politicians, who combined quiet support for New Deal–style developmentalist spending with a strident antistatist rhetoric ultimately emerged victorious. This paradoxical politics of dependence, regionalism, and outrage at federal spending has proved one of the New Deal's most enduring legacies.

*   *   *

When the New Dealers came to power in March 1933, they inherited a remarkably weak set of instruments with which to craft and implement a policy response to the unfolding economic catastrophe. "American leaders," Anthony Badger notes, "had only the feeblest of governmental weapons available to them."[8] Half of all federal employees worked in the Post Office. Government spending "amounted to only 3.5 percent of gross national product"[9]—less than what the New Deal would soon be spending on work-relief and public works projects alone. It may well be, as Margaret Weir and Theda Skocpol have suggested, that the relative underdevelopment of the American national bureaucracy expanded the range of policy options available to the New Dealers.[10] But in any case, the fact that the New Dealers' political reach exceeded their administrative grasp naturally led them to search for auxiliary sources of governing capacity.

The New Dealers found the capacity they required in many places: in agricultural institutions, trade associations, and not least in the military.[11] Ultimately, though, the most important sources of capacity proved to be America's state and especially local governments—municipalities, counties, and public authorities. In the North and West, Jon Teaford has noted, municipal development had been an "unheralded triumph" of American governance in the latter half of the nineteenth century, as city governments had borne the infrastructural burden required by industrialization and urbanization.[12] By the end of the 1920s, this infrastructural capacity was far more advanced still; the bureaucratization of governments, the expanded role of experts wrought by the efficiency movements of the Progressive Era, and the creation of new public authorities had greatly expanded the capacity of local governments to access capital markets and undertake technically demanding megaprojects.[13] At the same time, cities had been the key sites of social welfare politics dating back to the Progressive Era;[14] by the time the New Dealers came to power, many of the social policies introduced in American cities by the Atlantic crossings of the 1890s and 1900s—ranging from small parks to infant health clinics to low-cost housing—had begun to be implemented, often in ways that had garnered support from social reformers and civic elites alike.[15] The New Dealers turned to local governments as administrative partners in the first instance because they recognized that local governments possessed the operational, planning, and legal capacities the New Dealers needed to realize their national policy objectives. Charles E. Merriam typified a number of New Dealers, who had decades of practical experience working with or in local governments and viewed these partnerships not merely with pragmatism but with optimism.[16] Cooperative federalism, as it later came to be called, paired federal spending power and local planning and operational capacity to make possible exercises of governance that neither level would have been capable of on its own, underpinning a policy response to the Great Depression that, as Edwin Amenta notes, had no equal in the capitalist world.[17]

If the New Dealers' eagerness to build partnerships with local governments represented a pragmatic response to the underdevelopment of the American national state, it also reflected a sound political strategy. This was true in at least three ways. First, and most obvious, local administration facilitated the extraordinarily wide range of local outcomes necessary to accommodate a political coalition that included everyone from urban social democrats to the political trustees of Jim Crow. National lawmakers wrote local flexibility into the New Deal works agencies in the form of regional wage differentials; but more than that, the executive branch created an administrative structure in which localities could exercise relatively broad discretion as to the number and type of projects and the ways in which the works programs interacted with local labor markets.[18]

Intergovernmental partnerships facilitated New Deal state building by creating an administrative structure within which the New Deal political coalition could hold together, but they also worked to bind local elites to specific New Deal initiatives—if not the entirety of the New Deal's social project. Mayors became the strongest defenders of the New Deal works programs; the U.S. Conference of Mayors (USCM) developed in its early years in large measure to do precisely that, and by the time the mayors' conference helped line up the votes for Roosevelt's 1938 spending program (which consisted largely of higher work-relief and public works spending, justified in new Keynesian terms), many observers considered the USCM the strongest lobby in Washington.[19]

The works programs also found strong support among local chambers of commerce. In 1929, the U.S. Chamber of Commerce counted more than 1,500 dues-paying local chambers, and many more business-oriented associations—Lions, Kiwanis, Rotary, and non-dues-paying chambers—concerned themselves with their communities' economic growth.[20] In many localities, these organizations became actively involved in designing, administering, and lobbying for federal programs. Like the USCM, local chambers of commerce helped the New Dealers project community-level support for the works agencies into the legislative arena, where it served as an important counterweight to opposition from national business organizations and advocates of an abstract commitment to the idea of economy in government.[21] In capital-poor and rural regions of the United States, economy in government was most often a fact of life, not a choice. For such communities trapped in austerity, federal funds were manna, and elites hungrily pursued infrastructure improvements they prayed would bring their communities economic escape velocity. A retailer in Gadsden, Alabama (population twenty-four thousand in 1930), for instance, considered federal investments in regional water infrastructure "one of the grandest achievements taking place in the history of the city." "Once we are in the swing of this," he prophesied, "I can visualize a great city in one of the greatest industrial areas in our country."[22]

Finally, intergovernmental partnerships allowed the national New Dealers to tell a resonant story about the nature and ends of national state expansion. This story was analogous to the idea that work relief helped insulate the New Dealers' commitment to income maintenance from the stigmatizing association with "the dole." The idea of community-level improvement and local administration (with its overtones of Tocquevillian local democracy and civic associationalism) allowed the New Dealers to claim that theirs was not the path to continental authoritarian centralization but rather represented "the American way" of meeting the Depression and the broader necessities of modernization. FDR, Harry Hopkins, and other New Dealers sold this narrative unrelentingly in press conferences, fireside chats, and whistle stops across the country. By foregrounding the idea of "partnerships" between the federal government and local communities, and by calling attention to the fact that most projects were not megaprojects but neighborhood-level efforts to enrich local communities—many of which local boosters, community-based organizations, and civic elites had long dreamed of—the New Deal could depict itself as a modern realization of an idealized vision of democratic localism, operating on the basis of cooperation and partnership with local communities.[23]

By the late 1930s, this pragmatic solution to the problem of national state capacity was fast becoming liberals' preferred model for state development. And in the early 1940s, the New Dealers planned to formalize the ad hoc system of local-national, public-private partnerships that had underwritten the rapid expansion of state capacity. The National Resources Planning Board, helmed by Charles Merriam, released a report explaining the importance of "state and local participation in the administration of . . . public aid." Such localism also enabled the flexible adaptation of federal programs "to the peculiar needs of different sections of the country. These objectives," another New Dealer explained, "are necessarily more difficult" in "highly centralized administration." Ultimately, then, New Dealers considered localism a critically important means of maintaining "the democratic tradition."[24] While localism and public-private partnerships are often thought of today as products of a neoliberal age, such tools of governance are better understood as just that: governing tools and arrangements open to appropriation by many differing agendas.[25]

Yet justifying a slate of national initiatives in terms of localism was not without risks. Any generous spending program would engender competition. And without forcefully articulating the broader importance of collective endeavor and collective purse strings, the rhetoric of interregional competition and frustration at federal spending decisions became the dominant discourse surrounding these widely valued programs. Harry Hopkins described this Janus-faced politics of competitive localism in 1938. "There is a curious thing about these operations," he wrote, "which have been dotting the landscape of the United States for the past three years. Although they are attacked constantly in newspapers, people who visit them report that workers, public officials and citizens alike exhibit strong pride in them." "Derision," he concluded, "is reserved for projects elsewhere that they have never seen."[26] Despite their role in fostering such interjurisdictional jealousies, as they looked to the future, many liberals considered these associational and decentralizing aspects of the New Deal ideal models for future state developments.

*   *   *

Thanks to the persistence of localism, there were key differences between the New Deal's durable effects in different regions and different localities. But these should not be understood in terms of big and small government, or even liberalism and conservatism. Rather, they were the product of the different ways in which localities incorporated the redistributive,

regulatory, and developmental or infrastructural elements of the New
Deal into state and local governance. The New Deal produced lasting institutional and political changes in a variety of localities through a common set of mechanisms.[27] By improving local capacity, they led to a resil-
ient shift in the activities of local governments, as functions that had been
developed during the heyday of the New Deal works agencies became
incorporated into local, regional, and state governance, and in some cases
transferred to "warfare state-building," following the works agencies'
liquidation. The experience of New Deal investment also produced new
"common senses" among local elites, who now envisioned a new relation
to Washington and an expanded role for the state in infrastructural investment and economic planning.

In localities that lacked resources and in which local politics were
relatively undemocratic—that is to say, where economic and social authority and political power were tightly intertwined—local business and
civic elites often seized command of the local New Deal administrative
machinery and sought to steer it away from redistributive commitments.
They put New Deal works agencies to the service of local boosterism—to
the development of local economic assets. This was not simply a phenomenon in the South or the Southwest. Elite-led business and civic associations became actively involved in designing, lobbying for, and even administering federal programs; in turn, New Deal spending inspired the
formation of new local associations specifically designed to invite and mediate an expanded federal presence.[28] A Seattle real estate developer and
leader of the chamber of commerce, for instance, directed his regional
WPA. There, as the *Seattle Daily Times* reported, one hundred interested civic leaders joined him "at the Seattle Chamber of Commerce"
to take "steps toward starting the new federal public works program."[29]
Similarly, business boosters in northwestern Alabama and northeastern
Georgia formed a regional lobbying association to secure a $60 million
appropriation for river improvements.[30] In Cleveland, Ohio, meanwhile,
a former railroad executive and chamber leader administered the local
WPA during its peak years. Under his leadership, the WPA drew on the
examples of the chambers of commerce in Columbus and Philadelphia
and established planning committees staffed by "400 to 500 'white collar'
unemployed" to determine economically worthwhile projects.[31]

In the North, however, labor and civil rights groups contested New Deal
projects: witness WPA strikes and work stoppages that flared in cities
like Chicago, Milwaukee, and New York, or NAACP investigations into

and lawsuits targeting discriminatory clearance and housing programs in Cleveland.[32] In the South, meanwhile, the greatest friction in New Deal projects often emerged between factions of local elites. In Atlanta, commercial interests warred with residential real estate concerns over the specifics of New Deal–sponsored slum clearance projects. As Clarence Stone put it, during those years in cities in the Jim Crow South, "private social contacts were as effective as formal associations as ways of planning. Private clubs . . . provided gathering places where informal plans of action could be worked out."[33] Elites in larger Southern cities were hardly alone in jockeying for the benefits of otherwise relatively unfettered administration of the New Deal infrastructural state. Similar patterns played out across the South as state and local elites learned to navigate the unprecedented development opportunities offered through New Deal and wartime fiscal federalism. In doing so, they built Sunbelt booster states: they doggedly pursued New Deal infrastructural support and enjoyed easier administration of the spoils thanks to their maintenance of Jim and Juan Crow within the broader community.[34]

Other cities learned that further limiting local democracy offered advantages when it came to administering federal spending programs. In postwar Phoenix, leaders of the chamber of commerce spurred changes to the city government charter, enhancing the powers of the city manager. They also succeeded in ending the city's less efficient but more democratic system of ward-based council elections in favor of a majoritarian, at-large system that heavily favored downtown business interests. These reforms speeded elites' ability to mediate the liberal state's role in local affairs, limiting its regulatory strictures but magnifying its developmental impact by increasing elites' control over federal infrastructure spending and defense contracting.[35] Other Sunbelt elites learned to deploy this tactic throughout the postwar decades and, especially, following the civil rights movement. In effect, the opportunity to control federal aid incentivized elites' updates of the electoral malapportionment schemes that characterized Southern states' Jim Crow–era legislatures.[36]

This kind of booster politics was very much present in more democratic local polities—places where local states and bureaucracies were more responsive to mass electoral coalitions and citizens' groups, where organized labor and exerted a stronger influence and where women were more fully incorporated into political life. Rural road-building projects had their urban counterparts in projects like New York's Triborough Bridge, the Loop section of the Chicago metro, and the development of

Los Angeles's automotive network. More broadly, as Gail Radford has recently shown, the New Deal encouraged the development of local public authorities, which by design were meant to serve the purposes of economic development, shielded from the pressures of democratic politics.[37]

What was most distinctive about highly democratized localities, though, is the degree to which the New Deal built on and catalyzed the development of local welfare and regulatory states. In turn, its programs reshaped local politics in ways that allowed these local New Deal states to survive the end of the New Deal itself.[38] For the heirs to municipal progressivism and socialism, the New Deal works agencies represented (as one WPA official put it) "a challenge and an opportunity . . . to have done those things which make our cit[ies] more beautiful and useful, and which [we] on [our] own behalf would hardly ever be financially able to do."[39] The New Deal allowed city governments to build new schoolhouses and college campuses, to build new parks and restore old ones, to expand public broadcasting, to create new public health initiatives, to launch local public housing authorities, and much more—as well as, of course, to render employment itself a (quasi) right of citizenship rather than the outcome of market relationships. Later, national wartime policies created local- and state-level rent control and fair employment practices regulation.[40]

The New Deal supplied the legal, administrative, and above all fiscal resources that made such local social efforts possible. It also created political incentives to sustain New Deal experiments at the state and local levels even once the national programs were discontinued. Three political dynamics introduced by the New Deal were paramount. First, the New Deal reorganized local politics across the North and the West by reenergizing the American labor movement, which grew rapidly in the wake of prolabor policies such as the National Recovery Act's section 7(a) and the National Labor Relations Act—particularly as the industrial union movement began to grow in the mid-1930s. As the labor movement mobilized politically to defend the New Deal at the national level, it did likewise in industrial cities and states across the nation, providing political support to prolabor local and state politicians who used the New Deal works agencies to expand local social provision.[41]

Second, New Deal fiscal federalism enabled local bureaucracies to develop strong capacities, professional reputations, and ties to civil society free from the limitations of local budgets and tax resources. The case of Commissioner Robert Moses's New York City Parks Department, though a rather extreme one, illustrates this dynamic well. For several years in the mid-1930s, the WPA bestowed upon Moses's department work-relief labor that amounted in value to more than 800 percent of what the city typically appropriated for the entire Parks Department—while also leaving Moses broad autonomy to use that labor as he wished. Unsurprisingly, Moses's Parks Department quickly exceeded any imaginable standard of agency capacity, and Moses himself had built a reputation as a charismatic bureaucrat capable of doing the impossible. By the time the WPA was curtailed in the 1940s and the Parks Department had to garner from local extraction what it had previously gotten from Washington, Moses was in a far-stronger position to press his case in the public sphere—not least because he could mobilize citizens who had been enjoying the restored city parks.

Third, the very fact that the New Deal had changed what local governments were capable of doing helped build a more democratic local citizenry.[42] In large measure because a wider swath of citizens could imagine circumstances under which governments could be useful to them, they became more involved in their cities. This process of political incorporation fundamentally reshaped state and local as well as national electorates—New York City's mayoral electorate grew by 80 percent between the last pre-Depression election and the first postwar one; Chicago's grew by 57 percent, and Philadelphia's by 71 percent.[43] Because most of these newly mobilized citizens were working-class first- or second-generation Americans or previously disenfranchised African American migrants from the South, and in at least some cases disproportionately women,[44] this process of political incorporation should be thought of as a process of democratization—that is to say, it broadened the range of people who could exercise some measure of influence over political outcomes, bounded and constrained though their influence was.

In relatively highly democratized localities, contenders for power following World War II were forced to grapple with the expanded power of organized labor and consumer groups to appeal to a far larger and more fully mobilized citizenry (whose expectations had been framed by the New Deal era), and to negotiate with larger, more professional, more politically adept, and more ambitious municipal agencies. In this context, local projects begun through cooperation with New Deal works agencies as well as national regulatory regimes established during World War II were sustained by state and local governments in the years to come.

*   *   *

These local and state political developments suggest that the concept of a New Deal order must reckon with federalism and localism. Both forces created for national New Dealers opportunities and constraints, and both reorganized local and state politics in profound ways—with enduring consequences. We conclude with three brief examples of how recapturing New Deal federalism offers valuable vantage points for postwar American political history: national policy, urban liberalism, and Sunbelt conservatism. All three of these histories cut across the standard "liberalism versus conservatism" narrative of postwar American political history: in each, structural forces unleashed by the New Deal were critically important in shaping political developments typically ascribed to ideology.

First, the New Deal's politics of partnership provided a template for postwar national policy making. Thanks to their experience guiding New Deal programs, local interests pressed national policy makers to include local discretion in postwar programs designed to benefit a broad array of local constituencies—from job training or housing programs to infrastructure development initiatives. An example: the Housing Act of 1949 established urban renewal—a program boosters might have applauded— but included housing regulations that undermined local elites' interest in the program. In 1954, following persistent lobbying by local real estate, government, and business interests, Congress amended the 1949 act, loosening the housing stipulations in an effort to motivate more localities to apply for the federal program. Still wary, the Portland, Oregon, Chamber of Commerce hired a lawyer to assess the amended act. He was quite satisfied: "There need be no fear that federal co-operation on these problems entails surrender of self-decision or local and private initiative."[45]

Built on expectations forged in the New Deal, then, local elites succeeded in reorienting the nation's most significant push for affordable and equitable housing away from those goals and toward their own: wholesale redevelopment of their cities. As they had during the New Deal, elites guided urban renewal, simultaneously emphasizing their private-sector, localist bona fides. In Cleveland, urban renewal was the nation's "private-sector solution" for slum removal, housing, and redevelopment.[46] Federal officials joined in. One such official praised the New Orleans Chamber of Commerce; their leadership of urban renewal offered "a national example of what can be done by private enterprise in urban redevelopment."[47] Through local policy feedbacks generated by the New Deal's decentralized associationalism, urban renewal became a key plank in liberals' construction of a postwar "businessman's utopia" of public-private, local-national partnerships.[48]

At the state and local level, the New Deal's impact is perhaps easiest to see in the large industrial cities of the Northeast and Midwest, places that regarded themselves (only partly correctly) as the laboratories in which the New Deal itself was conceived. In many of these cities, New Deal–style regulation and social provision had acquired a powerful political foothold: above all in the labor movement,[49] but also through local political parties and civil society. These groups used their power in both municipal and state politics to sustain New Deal–era labor, social welfare, and regulatory policies. At the same time, the local growth coalitions that the New Deal had inspired extended their efforts, building airports, highway systems, and more; they also extended the New Deal's "slum clearance" programs into a broader effort to redevelop the city itself through urban renewal.[50] Throughout, cities honed a political style that became known in the 1950s as urban liberalism.

If the New Deal established the political conditions for the emergence of post–World War II urban liberalism, it also framed two of its defining features. One was a perennial conflict between political reach and fiscal grasp. In the 1930s, the New Deal works agencies had encouraged the development of local social welfare programs while largely shielding them from the task of having to extract resources locally. When those agencies demobilized during World War II, local governments were faced with the task of raising locally (and at the state level) resources that had once been supplied by Washington—a task to which cities were not equally suited, and which proved a daunting political challenge even for the wealthiest among them. Declining industrial cities were already turning toward a politics of social austerity and "economic competitiveness" by the 1960s—sometimes as a way of generating the tax revenue needed to sustain social services. In some cities, as Guian McKee found in Philadelphia, mobilized groups of citizens pushed local government to make good on New Deal–era promises of full employment and adequate social services even in the face of the crises of deindustrialization.[51] Wealthier cities were able to sustain their "local social democratic polities" into the 1970s, when even a city with as vast a base of taxable capital as New York ran aground on the shoals of fiscal crisis.[52] In the wake of these urban crises, a new generation of liberals would rebuild the public services that had collapsed in the 1960s and 1970s, justifying prodevelopment policies by pointing to the need for local revenue sources to sustain local social welfare functions and drawing on the resources made available by the explosion of wealth in the finance, insurance, real estate, and tourism sectors to form new public-private partnerships. The link among economic competiveness, fiscal capacity, and public services thus in place, the "neoliberal" local state emerged from the institutional legacy of the New Deal.

The second defining feature, of course, was the politics of race. As many scholars have noted, postwar American metropolitan politics was a struggle over the New Deal's contested legacy.[53] The New Deal's embrace of an expanded vision of social citizenship "regardless of station, race, or creed" had suggested a future in which America's egalitarian promises might be more fully realized by people of color. But racial exclusion was built into the New Deal itself: in national programs crafted by Southern congressmen, but also by Northern officials who at best were committed to a narrowly procedural view of racial equality and at worst actually deployed New Deal resources to reinforce the color line. As scholars such as Thomas Sugrue, Rhonda Williams, and Jeff Wiltse have demonstrated, one consequence of this divided legacy was that New Deal projects and programs themselves became key sites where the color line was both constructed and contested: in fights over the location of public housing and the integration of public housing itself, and in neighborhood turf wars over New Deal projects like swimming pools and parks.[54]

The New Deal stimulated a somewhat different state of affairs in what would come to be called the Sunbelt. From Georgia to California, minority constituencies were not simply marginalized like their Northern counterparts; in many regions Jim Crow and eventually Juan Crow policed the boundaries of local democracies. Repression of labor organizing meant that working-class constituencies lacked material and democratic advantages enjoyed by many Northern workers. These patterns of disfranchisement ensured local elites' control over the spoils of New Deal, defense, and postwar spending dollars that disproportionately poured into the South and West. Military Keynesianism and postwar infrastructure programs concretized New Deal–era linkages between Sunbelt boosters and national liberals, a relationship forged less in shared ideology than in a pragmatic convergence around such nonpartisan commitments as national security and the importance of economic growth.

Not surprisingly, then, this relationship between national liberals and local boosters underwrote dual agendas: for federal policy makers, it helped build support for national defense and other national policy objectives like research and development; for local elites, it subsidized a wide range of economic growth initiatives, regional market specialization, and industrial, service-sector, and academic asset development.[55] In Silicon Valley, Southern California, and Atlanta, defense-related research and development was essential to local elites' construction of academic-industrial and defense-contracting economies.[56] Defense contracting provided subsidies for modernizing rural regions, as they did along the Savannah River in South Carolina, where local business leaders secured federal funding for a massive DuPont-operated Atomic Energy Commission facility. Said the secretary of the Augusta, Georgia, Chamber of Commerce, just across the river, the facility would "mean empire-building to us. Augusta is going to grow and grow and be prosperous."[57] By 1973, as the historian Bruce Schulman found, "more southerners worked in defense-related industries than in textiles, synthetics, and apparel combined. Defense dollars permeated nearly every town in the region."[58] And if anything, defense-related stimulus was even more critical for the industrial strategies shaping the postwar West.[59] By harnessing the power of fiscal federalism and extending the local-national, public-private partnerships forged in the New Deal, local elites became the decentralized engines that national liberals depended on to deliver economic growth and ensure national security.

The emphasis on business boosters also risks missing other critical legacies of the New Deal in the Sunbelt, particularly the role of federal dollars and program guidelines in stimulating the modernization of Southern governing institutions. In contrast to expectations created by political rhetoric or ideological categories, perhaps no region of the United States plunged so enthusiastically into regional economic and political planning as did the South. Boosters' appetites for economic plans were whetted by the New Deal, but it was in the 1950s and 1960s that Southern elites fully embraced strategic economic planning by enhancing local governments' ability to positively shape the full range of assets required to recruit industry—investments in higher education, parks, health facilities, and infrastructure.

In the Housing Act of 1954, the national government offered an often-overlooked inducement in this direction. In addition to creating urban renewal as we remember it today, the 1954 legislation was also designed to assist small city, rural, and suburban governments in the process of modernization. The legislation created two-thirds matching grants to fund strategic planning commissions in communities with populations of up to twenty-five thousand residents. In 1957, Congress raised the population

threshold to fifty thousand, and by 1964, the section 701 Planning Grant
Program, as it was called, had distributed $79 million to 4,462 local gov-
ernments.[60] By 1968, the program assisted planning agencies in 65 percent
of the nation's 7,609 local governments.[61] Armed with federal funds,
these commissions and planning agencies developed infrastructure plans,
drafted strategic regional economic reports, and recommended social service improvements that might entice new business and industry. Some of
the most successful examples of postwar planning for economic development and urbanization occurred through the 701 program in states such as
Georgia, North Carolina, and South Carolina.[62] Local economic planning
soon expanded to include regional compacts between counties and even
Southern states; regionalism, public-private partnerships, and cooperative
economic planning were at the heart of the Appalachian Regional Commission, post–New Deal liberalism's longest-lasting effort to ameliorate
rural poverty.[63] Scholars have tended to emphasize Southern regionalism
as a force exerted primarily upon Congress and most often as a check on
national progressivism. Yet in the wake of the New Deal, Southern regionalism kept ablaze the flame of New Deal development and booster politics.
By the late 1960s, the Southern Growth Policies Board (SGPB) emerged as
an interstate, public-private council of governors and industry leaders devoted to developing locally tailored industrial policy. Very much the intellectual heir of the New Deal's National Resources Planning Board, the SGPB
guided state and regional economic planning, investments, and federal lobbying throughout the 1970s and 1980s.[64]

Such widespread enthusiasm for New Deal–style spending and planning
raises some critical questions. Why have historians missed this national, albeit decentralized, story? Why didn't the ubiquity of local-national, public-
private partnerships create national political coalitions capable of sustaining
New Deal–scale programs? And why didn't some of the New Deal's greatest
beneficiaries—local boosters and civic elites—fight to maintain favored
aspects of New Deal liberalism?

The answers lie in the often perverse politics federalism and localism make. As Andrew Needham suggested in his study of Phoenix, the
localism and boosterism that legitimized local elites' quest for federal
largesse often had more to do with interregional and municipal competition over scarce businesses and resources than it did with a coherent Sunbelt or Rustbelt approach to development or a clear-eyed appreciation for
the federal government.[65] Boosters competed against one another for the
spoils of the New Deal state just as they would for the spoils of defense

contracting, urban renewal, and other forms of national spending that might spur local growth. They saved their antigovernment rhetoric for other regions, competitors, or for the bureaucrats who oversaw programs and too often denied their applications. By the 1960s and 1970s, examples of these competitive public-private, local-national partnerships included the state of Georgia's Area Planning and Development Commissions, the Greater Baltimore Committee, Boston's Coordinating Committee, Dallas Citizens' Council, Detroit Renaissance, Minnesota Business Partnership, Greater Philadelphia First, Greater Phoenix Leadership, Pittsburgh's Allegheny Conference on Community Development, and San Francisco's Bay Area Council.[66] These organizations competed with and learned from one another, hungrily pursuing federal subsidies and jealously decrying federal largess wasted on their competitors. Their frequent spasms of antigovernment rhetoric were far from statements of ideological clarity. They instead functioned as a political trope that obscured their true and desired relationship with Washington, DC.

*   *   *

In 1978, forty-five years after Franklin Roosevelt sold America's mayors on the politics of partnership, a very different gathering took place, only a short distance from where FDR had made his pitch. The White House Conference on Balanced Economic Growth was billed as a "national town meeting," intended to generate policy ideas for the age of stagflation. The conferees, one journal wrote, were in search of a "breakthrough idea as dramatic as the New Deal in the 1930s."[67]

But whereas Roosevelt's intergovernmental programs had helped tie together the politically and regionally disparate New Deal coalition, the White House Conference on Balanced Economic Growth dissolved into a highly public family feud. Senator Daniel Patrick Moynihan, of New York, whose hometown was exporting millions more tax dollars than it was receiving in aid and services even during the depths of its "Ford to City: Drop Dead" scrape with bankruptcy, chided Southerners for running out on the New Deal's spirit of regional reciprocity. Moynihan asked pointedly, "What if it turns out that the New Deal was a one-way street, that the policies of the New Deal brought about the downfall of the region which nurtured them and gave them to the nation?" "I will tell you what will happen," he continued. "There will be a response of bitterness and reaction which will approach in duration if not in intensity the response of the South to defeat in what we now call the War Between the States."[68] Georgia governor George Busbee, in turn, accused Moynihan of spouting "bunk, pure bunk."[69]

Arguments about the fate of the post–New Deal state like the one that broke out at the Conference on Balanced Economic Growth were often conducted in regional terms. But they did not spring from indigenous regional ideologies or from deep differences in political culture between Sunbelt and Rust Belt. Rather, they derived from the range of ways in which the New Deal's impact had been institutionalized—dynamics that were less regional than historical. And *pace* Moynihan, the Sunbelt had not run out on the New Deal's spirit of regional reciprocity, for the New Deal had never demanded one in the first place. To the contrary, by cloaking federal policy in localist garb, the New Dealers had impeded the development of a strong sense of the national state and helped naturalize the claims of state and local politicians and boosters who preached the merits of local control.

For three decades, local business elites built their cities and regions on fiscal federalism while preaching the value of localism, business leadership, and small government—rhetoric that became more strident in the 1960s, when the War on Poverty tried to empower marginalized communities of color in a way the New Deal never had. An increasingly embattled set of liberals, mostly in Northern states and cities, had carried the burden of making a positive case for the liberal state even as the balance of federal spending tilted increasingly against them and efforts to extract locally became more and more arduous.

Lacking a shared commitment to the authority of the national state, and even a sense of shared political purpose, this increasingly tenuous political arrangement could not withstand the shocks of the 1970s and the coming of Reaganism. In the 1980s, a new generation of suburban conservatives came of age, heirs not to the New Deal legacy but to the 1970s politics of antigovernment populism; they dealt the deathblow to post–New Deal urban liberalism even as they continued to profit from New Deal–style fiscal federalism. Newt Gingrich, for instance, cited Georgia as a model of limited-government, free-market politics even as his own district continued to garner unparalleled federal aid: in 1992, Cobb County, the bulk of Gingrich's district, received more federal subsidies than any nonurban county in the country—nearly $3.4 billion. As Gingrich blasted New York City's "culture of waste," Cobb County received nearly twice as much federal spending per capita as did New York City.[70] Meantime, New

York City's mayor David Dinkins—whose town, economically battered though it was, was underwriting fiscal federalism to the tune of billions a year—was left pleading in vain for a new era of cooperation between Washington and America's cities.

Gingrich's mastery of the ideological rhetoric of limited-government conservatism and the intergovernmental politics of New Deal federalism reveals a critical contradiction in New Dealers' pragmatic and politically expedient embrace of federalism and localism. The New Dealers succeeded in enhancing the state's reach through decentralized, associative means, but these momentary and expedient compromises created a state that was at once robust and highly contingent; nimble and strikingly porous—whose material basis was dependent on national revenues whose relation to local concerns could be portrayed as simultaneously antithetical and essential. The results were twofold: a localist brand of politics, which disparaged the state not as an expression of ideological preference but as a means of expressing boosters' sense of greater entitlement to state support; and its flip side, an urban politics of disenchantment and "neoliberalization" in places where local democratic aspirations had outlived the national political alignments that had once underwritten them. Public-private partnerships gained renewed purchase as a kind of accommodation, a way of sustaining public goods and services in the context of declining intergovernmental transfers, diminished local revenue raising capacity, and a robust elite countermobilization against midcentury local social states.[71]

To understand these politics—to have a more complete picture of the vast array of developments subsumed within but that ultimately transcend the New Deal order—we must consider not just the structure of the New Deal state, but the intended and unintended uses to which communities, interest groups, and citizens have directed the generous tools of New Deal federalism.

Notes

We would like to thank Lily Geismer and Gary Gerstle for their comments on earlier drafts of this chapter, as well as the many colleagues who have discussed the ideas presented here with us.

1. Franklin D. Roosevelt, "Speech to C.W.A. Conference in Washington, November 15, 1933," http://www.presidency.ucsb.edu/ws/?pid=14555.

2. Quoted in Jason Scott Smith, *Building New Deal Liberalism: The Political Economy of Public Works, 1933–1956* (New York: Cambridge University Press, 2006), 105.

116   BRENT CEBUL AND MASON B. WILLIAMS

3. Smith, *Building New Deal Liberalism*, 1–2.

4. "A New Meaning for W.P.A.," *Augusta Chronicle*, April 6, 1936; "Chamber of Commerce Ousts Critic of WPA" and "Counties Are Told Not to Expect Any State Aid on Roads," *Dallas Morning News*, March 17, 1936.

5. Building on James T. Patterson's classic work, *The New Deal and the States*, Anthony Badger surveyed the vast literature on state- and local-level "little New Deals" and found relatively little in the way of durable change in state activity of the sort implied by the national New Deal project but much in the way of persistent conservatism. See Anthony J. Badger, "The New Deal and the Localities," in *The Growth of Federal Power in American History*, ed. Rhodri Jeffreys-Jones and Bruce Collins (DeKalb: Northern Illinois University Press, 1983), 102–15. Several classic works in political science and history called attention to the way national, state, and local policy makers used local administration to prevent New Deal programs from threatening white supremacy and patriarchy. See especially Thomas J. Sugrue, "All Politics Is Local: The Persistence of Localism in Twentieth-Century America," in *The Democratic Experiment: New Directions in American Political History*, ed. Meg Jacobs, William J. Novak, and Julian E. Zelizer (Princeton, NJ: Princeton University Press, 2003), esp. 305–7; Ira Katznelson, *When Affirmative Action Was White: An Untold History of Racial Inequality in Twentieth-Century America* (New York: Norton, 2005); and Suzanne Mettler, *Dividing Citizens: Gender and Federalism in New Deal Public Policy* (Ithaca, NY: Cornell University Press, 1998). And as "state-centered" modes of analyses filtered into political history by way of the social science subfields of historical institutionalism and American political development, historians came to see local and state authority not just as sites of conservative opposition to New Deal social and economic policy, but also as barriers to the construction of a strong national state. See especially Margaret Weir, "States, Race, and the Decline of New Deal Liberalism," *Studies in American Political Development* 19 (Fall 2005): 157–72; Gary Gerstle, "A State Both Strong and Weak," *American Historical Review* 115, no. 3 (June 2010): 779–85, esp. 781–83. Similarly, political scientist Theodore J. Lowi ascribed to federalism the most salient differences between twentieth-century liberalism and conservatism. As he put it, "A fairly clear distinction has therefore been maintained between state-level conservatism and national-level liberalism that gives concrete reality to the distinction between conservatism and liberalism." See Lowi, "The Reagan Presidency and the Governing of America," in *The Reagan Presidency and the Governing of America*, ed. Lester M. Salamon and Michael S. Lund (Washington, DC: Urban Institute, 1984), 35–36.

6. Jim Crow and the legacies of white supremacy ensured Southern state-business coalitions enjoyed easier access to federal largesse. The economist Mancur Olson argued for the importance of the South's lack of interest-group competition in speeding Southern industrialization: see Olson, "The Causes and Quality of Southern Growth," in *The Economics of Southern Growth*, ed. E. Blaine Liner

and Lawrence K. Lynch (Durham, NC: Southern Growth Policies Board, 1977). On interest groups and the tension between democracy and development in a global context, see Mancur Olson, *The Rise and Decline of Nations: Economic Growth, Stagflation, and Social Rigidities* (New Haven, CT: Yale University Press, 1982).

7. This formulation owes a debt to Richard Valelly's analysis of the fate of state-level radicalism in the New Deal era. See Valelly, *Radicalism in the States: The Minnesota Farmer-Labor Party and the American Political Economy* (Chicago: University of Chicago Press, 1989), xv.

8. Anthony J. Badger, *FDR: The First Hundred Days* (New York: Hill and Wang, 2008), 7.

9. Badger, *FDR*, 7.

10. Margaret Weir and Theda Skocpol, "State Structures and the Possibilities of a 'Keynesian' Response to the Great Depression in Sweden, Britain, and the United States," in *Bringing the State Back In*, ed. Peter Evans, Dietrich Rueschemeyer, and Theda Skocpol (New York: Cambridge University Press, 1985).

11. For an overview of the New Deal's associationalism, see Brian Balogh, *The Associational State: American Governance in the Twentieth Century* (Philadelphia: University of Pennsylvania Press, 2015), introduction and chapter 5.

12. Jon C. Teaford, *The Unheralded Triumph: City Government in America, 1870–1900* (Baltimore: Johns Hopkins University Press, 1984).

13. Keith D. Revell, *Building Gotham: Civic Culture and Public Policy in New York City, 1898–1938* (Baltimore: Johns Hopkins University Press, 2003); Gail Radford, *The Rise of the Public Authority: Statebuilding and Economic Development in Twentieth-Century America* (Chicago: University of Chicago Press, 2013), esp. chap. 3. On the role of experts in Progressive Era municipal state building, see Kenneth Finegold, *Experts and Politicians: Reform Challenges to Machine Politics in New York, Cleveland, and Chicago* (Princeton, NJ: Princeton University Press, 1995).

14. Daniel T. Rodgers, *Atlantic Crossings: Social Politics in a Progressive Age* (Cambridge, MA: Belknap Press of Harvard University Press, 1998).

15. Daniel Amsterdam, *Roaring Metropolis: Businessmen's Campaign for a Civic Welfare State* (Philadelphia: University of Pennsylvania Press, 2016). See also Brian Balogh, "Reorganizing the Organizational Synthesis: Federal-Professional Relations in Modern America," *Studies in American Political Development* 5, no. 1 (Spring 1991): 119–72.

16. On Merriam's pre–New Deal career in Chicago, see Barry D. Kahrl, *Charles E. Merriam and the Study of Politics* (Chicago: University of Chicago Press, 1975).

17. Edwin Amenta, *Bold Relief: Institutional Politics and the Origins of Modern American Social Policy* (Princeton, NJ: Princeton University Press, 1998). Interestingly, administrative frictions in the New Deal works programs tended to occur when relatively strong founts of auxiliary state capacity encountered each other, for instance, in the remarkably heated contest over whether New York City parks projects would be overseen by the band of army officers with which General Hugh

Johnson had staffed the New York City WPA, or by the municipal parks department, which commissioner Robert Moses had quickly made into a highly professional organization. Robert Moses to Victor Ridder, December 17, 1935, Robert
Moses Papers, box 97, New York Public Library.

18. Many historians know that the WPA went to great lengths to avoid competing with the Southern agricultural labor market. Perhaps fewer are aware that
WPA wages in the North often paid more than comparably accessible unskilled
and semiskilled work, especially for communities that suffered acute discrimination
in private employment markets. Cheryl Greenberg, *"Or Does It Explode?": Black
Harlem in the Great Depression* (New York: Oxford University Press, 1997), 152.

19. Mark Gelfand, *A Nation of Cities: The Federal Government and Urban
America, 1933–1965* (New York: Oxford University Press, 1975); and Richard M.
Flanagan, "Roosevelt, Mayors and the New Deal Regime: The Origins of Intergov-
ernmental Lobbying and Administration," *Polity* 31, no. 3 (Spring 1999), 415–50.

20. Robert M. Collins, *The Business Response to Keynes, 1929–1964* (New York:
Columbia University Press, 1981), 23. On the pre–New Deal emergence of local
chambers' sense of civic stewardship, see Alison Isenberg, *Downtown America: A
History of the Place and the People Who Made It* (Chicago: University of Chicago
Press, 2004), 35–37. See also Amsterdam, *Roaring Metropolis*.

21. By the late New Deal, among the leading antagonists of public works was
the U.S. Chamber of Commerce, whose local members' interests were leading
them in the polar opposite direction. In the spring of 1939, as the White House,
the WPA, and the USCM were making a sustained push to protect the WPA from
congressional conservatives, FDR told the White House press corps about a meeting with an ostensibly antigovernment businessperson: "In every case I find what I
suspected. His local Chamber of Commerce, his local newspapers are 'yelling their
heads off' to have those projects built with Federal assistance. And I say to him:
'Consistency, thy name is geography. You believe with the United States Chamber
of Commerce that Federal spending on public works should cease—except in your
own home town.'" Franklin D. Roosevelt, "Address before the American Retail
Federation, Washington, D.C.," May 22, 1939, available online at Gerhard Peters
and John T. Woolley's American Presidency Project, http://www.presidency.ucsb
.edu/ws/?pid=15763.

22. "Coosa Waterway Action Gladdens Local Citizens," *Gadsden Times*, November 9, 1941, box 1, Rome, Georgia Chamber of Commerce Papers, Rome-Floyd
County Library, Rome, GA.

23. The preceding several paragraphs draw on Brent Cebul, *Illusions of Progress: Business, Poverty, and Development in the American Century* (Philadelphia:
University of Pennsylvania Press, forthcoming), introduction and chaps. 1 and 2;
and Mason B. Williams, *City of Ambition: FDR, La Guardia, and the Making of
Modern New York* (New York: Norton, 2013), chaps. 4–5.

24. Seymour E. Harris, *Saving American Capitalism: A Liberal Economic Program* (New York: Knopf, 1949), 497.

25. In a variety of domains—social provision and economic development, for instance—public-private partnerships are even older. And localism is as old as the Union itself. See, for instance, Brian Balogh, *A Government Out of Sight: The Mystery of National Authority in 19th Century America* (New York: Cambridge University Press, 2009).

26. Harry L. Hopkins, *Spending to Save: The Complete Story of Relief* (New York: W. W. Norton, 1936), 169.

27. Although the best synthetic histories of the New Deal acknowledge that New Deal programs and policies led to a growth of government at the state and local levels, the literature offers little in the way of a detailed, conceptually rich understanding of the New Deal's consequences for postwar local and state-level politics and governance. See, e.g., David M. Kennedy, *Freedom from Fear: The American People in Depression and War, 1929–1945* (New York: Oxford University Press, 1999). We are left with the "little New Deal" literature, which tells a story of continuity rather than change, and in which sustained institutional and political changes, where they did occur, are typically treated as the consequences of distinctive local conditions rather than as the products of broader aspects of New Deal state building.

28. Cebul, "They Were the Moving Spirits," in *Capital Gains: Business and Politics in Twentieth-Century America*, ed. Richard John and Kim Phillips-Fein (Philadelphia: University of Pennsylvania Press, 2017), 144–48.

29. "Guenther Named Works Director," *Seattle Daily Times*, July 14, 1935.

30. "Coosa Waterway Action Gladdens Local Citizens," *Gadsden Times*, November 9, 1941, box 1, Rome, Georgia Chamber of Commerce Papers, Sarah Hightower Special Collections, Rome-Floyd County Library, Rome, GA.

31. "Foresight in Traffic," *Cleveland Plain Dealer*, May 18, 1936.

32. Cebul, *Illusions of Progress*, chap. 2.

33. Clarence Stone, *Regime Politics: Governing Atlanta, 1946–1988* (Lawrence: University Press of Kansas, 1989), 15–17.

34. In his history of Southern industrialization, James C. Cobb notes that state-level development organizations that flourished in the postwar South owed an intellectual debt to the National Resources Planning Board. The point is worth underscoring given the frequency with which more recent scholars of conservatism have often uncritically accepted businesspeople's limited government rhetoric. On these development organizations, see Cobb, *The Selling of the South: The Southern Crusade for Industrial Development* (Urbana: University of Illinois Press, 1993), 64–95. On Southern boosters, the New Deal, and the emergence of the Sunbelt, see Bruce J. Schulman, *From Cotton Belt to Sunbelt: Federal Policy, Economic Development, and the Transformation of the South, 1938–1980* (Durham, NC: Duke University Press, 1994).

35. Andrew Needham, *Power Lines: Phoenix and the Making of the Modern Southwest* (Princeton, NJ: Princeton University Press, 2014), 96–106.

36. On the emergence of urban at-large voting, see, for instance, Julian Maxwell Hayter, "From Intent to Effect: Richmond, Virginia, and the Protracted Struggle

for Voting Rights, 1965–1977," *Journal of Policy History* 26, no. 4 (October 2014): 534–67; and Matthew D. Lassiter, *The Silent Majority: Suburban Politics in the Sunbelt South* (Princeton, NJ: Princeton University Press, 2006), esp. 177–84.

37. Radford, *Rise of the Public Authority*, chap. 4.

38. The following discussion is drawn primarily from Williams, *City of Ambition*, esp. chaps. 4–7.

39. "Civil Works Offer to City Is Praised," *New York Times*, December 21, 1933, 4.

40. See especially Anthony S. Chen, *The Fifth Freedom: Jobs, Politics, and Civil Rights in the United States* (Princeton, NJ: Princeton University Press, 2009).

41. For an extraordinarily rich description, see Steven Fraser, *Labor Will Rule: Sidney Hillman and the Rise of American Labor* (New York: Free Press, 1991), esp. chaps. 10–14. See also J. David Greenstone, *Labor in American Politics* (New York: Knopf, 1969). Valelly, *Radicalism in the States*, notes that the rise of industrial unionism had the potential to unsettle (and in many cases, did unsettle) existing labor-based political coalitions.

42. The best account of this process remains Lizabeth Cohen, *Making a New Deal: Industrial Workers in Chicago, 1919–1939* (New York: Cambridge University Press, 1990), esp. chap. 6.

43. James Trager, *The New York Chronology* (New York: HarperResource, 2003), 440, 568; Ralph Caliendo, Janice L. Reiff, Ann Durkin Keating, and James R. Grossman, *Encyclopedia of Chicago*, http://www.encyclopedia.chicagohistory.org /pages/1443.html; City of Philadelphia, Department of Records, http://www.phila .gov/phils/mayorlst.htm.

44. Whereas men had made up a disproportionate share of the newly mobilized in the years leading up to the New Deal, the jump in registration in advance of New York City's 1937 mayoral election was 72 percent female. See Williams, *City of Ambition*, 231–33.

45. "Hurdles to Center in Blighted Area Seen," *Oregonian*, April 1, 1955.

46. Daniel Kerr, *Derelict Paradise: Homelessness and Urban Development in Cleveland, Ohio* (Amherst: University of Massachusetts Press, 2011), 131.

47. "Downtown Area Livening Urged," *New Orleans Times-Picayune*, February 21, 1956.

48. Nicholas Dagen Bloom, *Merchant of Illusion: James Rouse, America's Salesman of the Businessman's Utopia* (Columbus: Ohio State University Press, 2000).

49. See especially Joshua B. Freeman, *Working-Class New York: Life and Labor since World War II* (New York: New Press, 2000), which charts a labor politics that existed in many cities—although New York's economic and residential structures, its open three-party politics, its distinctive ideological heritage, and above all its sheer wealth make it an extreme case, different in degree but only partly in kind.

50. The classic account is John Mollenkopf, *The Contested City* (Princeton, NJ: Princeton University Press, 1983). Important recent historical accounts are Eric

Fure Slocum, *Contesting the Postwar City: Working-Class and Growth Politics in 1940s Milwaukee* (New York: Cambridge University Press, 2015); Cebul, *Illusions of Progress*; and Andrew Diamond, *Chicago on the Make: Power and Inequality in a Modern City* (Berkeley: University of California Press, 2017).

51. Guian A. McKee, *The Problem of Jobs: Liberalism, Race, and Deindustrialization in Philadelphia* (Chicago: University of Chicago Press, 2008). See also Michael Woodsworth, *Battle for Bed-Stuy: The Long War on Poverty in New York City* (Cambridge, MA: Harvard University Press, 2016).

52. Cebul, *Illusions of Progress*; and Kim Phillips-Fein, *Fear City: New York's Fiscal Crisis and the Rise of Austerity Politics* (New York: Metropolitan Books, 2017). Local political structures, themselves very much shaped by the New Deal, made some cities more prone to fiscal crises than others. See Ester Fuchs, *Mayors and Money: Fiscal Policy in New York and Chicago* (Chicago: University of Chicago Press, 1992).

53. Among many others, see Thomas J. Sugrue, *The Origins of the Urban Crisis: Race and Inequality in Postwar Detroit* (Princeton, NJ: Princeton University Press, 1996); Becky Nicolaides, *My Blue Heaven: Life and Labor in the Working-Class Suburbs of Los Angeles, 1920–1965* (Chicago: University of Chicago Press, 2002); and Martha Biondi, *To Stand and Fight: The Struggle for Civil Rights in Postwar New York* (Cambridge, MA: Harvard University Press, 2003).

54. Sugrue, *Origins of the Urban Crisis*, esp. chap. 3; Rhonda Y. Williams, *The Politics of Public Housing: Women's Struggles against Urban Inequality* (New York: Oxford University Press, 2004); Jeff Wiltse, *Contested Waters: A Social History of Swimming Pools in America* (Chapel Hill: University of North Carolina Press, 2007).

55. On military Keynesianism, see especially Michael J. Hogan, *A Cross of Iron: Harry S. Truman and the Origins of the National Security State, 1945–1954* (New York: Cambridge University Press, 1998).

56. Margaret Pugh O'Mara, *Cities of Knowledge: Cold War Science and the Search for the Next Silicon Valley* (Princeton, NJ: Princeton University Press, 2005); Lisa McGirr, *Suburban Warriors: The Origins of the New American Right* (Princeton, NJ: Princeton University Press, 2001).

57. Kari Frederickson, *Cold War Dixie: Militarization and Modernization in the American South* (Athens: University of Georgia Press, 2013), 49.

58. Schulman, *From Cotton Belt to Sunbelt*, 141. For another short case study of a particular region's transformation as a result of its transition to the defense economy, see James T. Sparrow, "A Nation in Motion: Norfolk, the Pentagon, and the Nationalization of the Metropolitan South, 1941–1953," in *The Myth of Southern Exceptionalism*, ed. Matthew D. Lassiter and Joseph Crespino (New York: Oxford University Press, 2010), 167–89.

59. See, e.g., Roger W. Lotchin, *Fortress California, 1910–1961: From Warfare to Welfare* (New York: Oxford University Press, 1992); McGirr, *Suburban Warriors*;

Elizabeth Tandy Shermer, *Sunbelt Capitalism: Phoenix and the Transformation of American Politics* (Philadelphia: University of Pennsylvania Press, 2013).

60. Carl Feiss, "The Foundations of Federal Planning Assistance: A Personal Account of the 701 Program," *Journal of the American Planning Association* 51, no. 12 (1985), 175–84.

61. Cited in Peter Dreier, John Mollenkopf, and Todd Swanstrom, *Place Matters: Metropolitics for the Twenty-First Century* (Lawrence: University Press of Kansas, 2004), 113.

62. Cebul, *Illusions of Progress*, chaps. 3 and 6.

63. Wilson, *Communities Left Behind*; and Cebul, "They Were the Moving Spirits."

64. Cebul, *Illusions of Progress*, chap. 8. See also Schulman, *From Cotton Belt to Sun Belt*, 201.

65. Needham, *Power Lines*, 14.

66. A comprehensive appraisal of these coalitions and their secondary literature is beyond the scope of this chapter. For a brief overview, see James Austin and Arthur McCaffrey, "Business Leadership Coalitions and Public-Private Partnerships in American Cities: A Business Perspective on Regime Theory," *Journal of Urban Affairs* 24, no. 1 (Spring 2002): 35–54.

67. "A 'Hell of an Experiment' in Resolving Economic Growth," *National Journal*, January 21, 1978.

68. "Moynihan Warns on Aid for New York City," *New York Times*, February 1, 1978.

69. "Yankee, Southerner Try to Mend Fences," *Boston Globe*, February 1, 1978; and "Moynihan vs. Busbee: Hoped-for Excitement At Meetings on Growth," *Washington Post*, February 1, 1978.

70. "Traditions and Ideas of Old South Make a Political Comeback," *Chicago Tribune*, February 26, 1997.

71. This kind of local neoliberal state building is the subject of an exciting, rapidly growing literature. For an overview by one of this essay's authors, see Mason B. Williams, "Trickle Down Urbanism," *Dissent* (Spring 2018): 161–68.

CHAPTER FOUR

State Building for a Free Market

*The Great Depression and the Rise of
Monetary Orthodoxy*

David M. P. Freund

The U.S. government transformed American finance between 1913 and 1935 by assuming extraordinary new powers over the banking sector and the money supply. Each wave of reform during these years was controversial, and by the early 1930s the fiercest critics were warning that federal overreach in financial markets threatened to undermine the free-enterprise system. But the critics were silenced, in the end, by an argument about money that helped reconcile contemporaries to the government's new powers and responsibilities. And that view of money has since been foundational to scholarship on financial history and policy. For this reason, the early twentieth-century debate over reform has fundamentally shaped our understanding of state building in the United States. It helped produce a broad consensus about banking and public policy that has prevented scholars from reckoning with some of the federal government's most powerful tools for driving economic growth and allocating its benefits.

The story about reform begins in 1913, when Congress passed the Federal Reserve Act and set in motion a wholesale restructuring of the nation's money supply. The legislation created a new standardized paper currency that was printed by the U.S. Treasury and introduced into the financial system by a central bank called the Federal Reserve (or "Fed").[1] The act also ended the practice of issuing federally sanctioned paper money to banks only when they purchased U.S. government securities and then deposited them (at the Treasury) as reserves. Instead, banks would access notes by handing over specie and commercial assets to the Fed, so that the new currency's supply would be responsive to the market's—not the government's—needs. Finally, the new Federal Reserve System welcomed thousands of banks as chartered "members" and then, in return for controlling their interest rates and reserve requirements, stood at the ready to supplement their reserve accounts with emergency loans. This was radical legislation designed to insulate the banking system against crises but only by a means that limited the government's discretionary powers. And "delinking" the currency from the Treasury's debt was essential in this regard, for it would prevent public officials from manipulating (or simply mismanaging) the financial marketplace. New currency would be issued to meet private-sector demand, and the currency's value would be rooted solely in commercial activity and precious metals. Both money's value and its supply, reformers argued, would be dictated by the free-enterprise system.

But the new central bank would soon defy its founders' vision and forge an unexpected path by again backing monetary issue against government bonds. Financing the U.S. effort in World War I set this change in motion, when the Fed and Treasury helped generate the largest debt in the nation's history and introduced billions of dollars' worth of government securities into the banking system. After the war the Fed came to rely on the purchase and sale of these debts (via "open-market operations") to fulfill its mandate. Then beginning in 1932, the administrations of Herbert Hoover and Franklin Delano Roosevelt shepherded through Congress a series of crisis-driven financial reforms that cemented Treasury bonds' role in American banking while expanding the Federal Reserve's powers and consolidating its decision making in Washington, DC.[2] By 1935, as a result, the nation's bank reserves were collateralized heavily by government securities, monetary authorities had extraordinary new powers to encourage or discourage private lending, and Roosevelt—to the horror of "sound money" advocates—had nullified the domestic gold standard, which meant that the dollar was no longer secured by specie.

In just over two decades the nation's financial markets had been transformed. Federal Reserve notes monopolized the circulating currency. And meanwhile Depression-era reform subverted a guiding principle of the Fed's design: the belief that the private sector, alone, should determine the currency's supply and stand behind the dollar's value.[3] Instead the U.S. government was the ultimate guarantor of the dollar's domestic worth, and a central bank more responsive to federal influence took actively to managing the amount of currency in circulation. The state had assumed unprecedented authority over both the value and supply of American money.

This assault on cherished precedents set off a contentious public debate over federal authority and produced searing condemnations of the state's actions. By 1934, the editors of *Fortune* magazine declared that "the Revolution" had come "to the credit system" and a contributor for *Literary Journal* insisted that "financial news no longer originates in Wall Street." In 1935, the economist Henry Parker Willis—professor at Columbia University and a coauthor of the original Federal Reserve Act—described Roosevelt's latest financial bill, designed to further enhance Washington's influence over Fed policy, as "the most dangerous, the most unwarranted, the most insidious measure" of the New Deal and warned Congress that its passage would be "practically suicide" for the banking industry.[4] But these critics lost the era's battles over both public policy and economic ideas. And they lost to officials and academics who found common cause in a theory that helped them justify the state's expansive new role. Specifically, reform's defenders argued that the type of collateral backing monetary issue was largely incidental—that it need not be tied to commercial activity, per se— because the central bank's primary responsibility was managing the currency's supply. Federal interventions had not "revolutionized" American finance, they explained, but instead tasked authorities with a modest oversight role that posed no threat to capitalist markets.[5]

And today most scholars agree. Historians and economists view Willis and other critics as ill informed, and they describe Depression-era financial policies as prudent and "conservative" measures, especially when compared to the New Deal's famous experiments in economic management. In this standard narrative, financial reform stabilized the banking sector and insulated Americans against some of capitalism's unpredictability without disrupting the market's natural generative powers.[6] Meanwhile, scholars explain how economic knowledge gradually "caught up" with the facts on the ground, as monetary authorities, politicians, and economists gained new insights into money and markets. Experts came to embrace modest state-building efforts and the Fed's new "discretionary" role, the story goes, all in the name of financial stability.[7]

I argue here that reform did revolutionize American finance—indeed, far more than Willis and like-minded critics imagined—by giving the U.S. government new powers to direct and subsidize economic growth. And

I argue that scholars ignore this history because the era's money debate helped to close off inquiry into the subject.

This chapter is not about fiscal policy, a topic that tends to loom large in histories of American politics, in no small part because public spending is readily quantified and involves conflicts that hew to a familiar partisan debate over the merits of "big government."[8] Instead, this chapter examines financial policy and, of equal importance, a debate about banking practices and the nature of money that is largely ignored by historians. An earlier version of that debate was prominent in the first decades of the twentieth century and its terms familiar to the actors discussed here. Critics of Depression-era reform embraced a "commercial" or "real bills" theory of banking, which held that any expansion of the money supply— the result of bank lending and investment—should be collateralized by identifiable commercial activity. Banks could safely lend and invest, according to this view, only when confident that revenues from commercial sales would enable the borrower to repay the debt. And for this reason advocates of real bills saw tremendous danger in any actions by monetary authorities that defied these principles. Defenders of the era's reforms, by contrast, subscribed to the "currency" or "quantity" theory of banking, which holds that the most important monetary variable is the amount in circulation, regardless of its origins or the collateral that backs it. Thus, in their view, it was the Fed's primary task to monitor and, when necessary, help adjust the money supply by encouraging banks to lend and invest, regardless of short-term commercial considerations.

Quantity theory emerged triumphant from the era's policy debates and soon helped forge a bipartisan consensus about finance that continues to dominate scholarly and political treatments. Indeed, since then, liberals and conservatives—including self-described Keynesians and monetarists— have seldom disagreed about what David Laidler calls "fundamental questions of monetary theory."[9] Most important, scholars generally agree that the creation of money by the banking system does not actively drive the growth process but rather enables people to fulfill their desires to produce and exchange—and that these choices about production and exchange, in the final analysis, spur wealth creation. In this conventional— often called orthodox—vision, a well-managed money supply unleashes the market's inherent dynamism; money is useful as a facilitator but it is not essential to economic growth.[10] And this orthodox model has distorted profoundly our understanding of the modern American state by assigning to financial policy the narrow goal of adjusting that supply—the quantity of money in circulation—so that the private sector can go about its business.

This consensus is a product of developments in American politics, policy, and intellectual life that converged during the 1930s to address an economic emergency. The orthodox vision of money began to assume its modern, textbook form during the Great Depression in part because it helped validate—by disguising—a radical expansion of state authority. Monetary orthodoxy helped usher in federal powers that it also helped to explain away, and this is consequential for our understanding of the modern state and party politics. For it has led scholars of the post–New Deal United States to erase the ways that monetary and credit policies actively rebuilt the productive economy and drove the growth process. Orthodoxy's ascendance has blinded economists and historians alike to money's complicated history—specifically its origins in debtor relationships and its continued function as a credit instrument—and thus to an arena of state power that makes markets and thereby creates new wealth.[11] Indeed, for most scholars who accept orthodox assumptions about money, the claim that Depression-era financial reform "revolutionized" the American economy is unintelligible.[12]

The orthodox consensus and the "real bills" challenge to it—both of which I detail here—are incorrect.[13] But scrutinizing this debate over money and the era's seemingly arcane financial reforms forces us to reconsider a familiar story about American state building. Depression-era monetary and banking policies transformed the American economy by tethering the growth process, in unprecedented fashion, to speculative investment practices and federal authority. And scholars' indifference to this subject is a product of a debate over money that has largely been forgotten.

The Asset and Policy Revolutions

The money debate was sparked by controversial changes to banking practice and federal policy. In the first decades of the twentieth century, many banks were experimenting with new investment strategies while monetary authorities and the federal state were modifying their relationships to the financial system. The end result was that a trade in Treasury debt became integral to American finance, and the U.S. government became the guarantor of the currency's domestic value. In response to bankers' new priorities and pressing public needs, the state gained unprecedented authority over the market for money.

This story hinges on a seemingly mundane facet of the banking business: the collateral deemed acceptable for extending a loan. Banks make profits by purchasing revenue-generating assets, and historically, their primary earning assets were loans to private customers. Commercial bankers purchased a promise of repayment (let's say, $1,100) by advancing a lesser amount (say, $1,000) to a customer and then earned a profit when the debt was repaid (this was the interest charge). Banks demanded collateral for each purchase (for each loan), something to replace its value should the borrower fail to meet their commitment. And before World War I, the lion's share of lending was secured by commercial collateral, often taking the form of a document known as "commercial paper." This paper was the borrower's contractual pledge to repay the debt with anticipated revenues from the production and/or sale of specific goods. A borrower might pledge an existing inventory, for example, or the expected earnings from a planned venture. Seen another way, bank loans traditionally represented an investment in a commercial promise, with the understanding that the lender could recoup potential losses (were the borrower to default) by taking ownership of the specified goods. Lending on these terms was supported by the "commercial"—or "real bills"—theory of banking,[14] which was rarely codified (it was more of a traditional consensus view) but nonetheless "expresse[d] very well the professional ideology of bankers," particularly those who saw themselves as "helpmate[s] of the commodity trade."[15]

And it was these assumptions that generally discouraged bankers from investing in stocks, bonds, and landed property, which were viewed as risky—or "speculative"—purchases because the revenue-producing potential was uncertain. The future sales price of a security or real estate was far less predictable than that of, say, durable goods or an agricultural commodity. Moreover, few securities were less attractive to investors (including bankers) than U.S. Treasury bonds, given that they were another step removed from the world of private exchange; their value was rooted not in specific commercial transactions or a company's performance per se, but in the federal state's promise to collect taxes.[16] Invoking this conventional wisdom in a 1912 manual for securities traders—an industry standard titled *The Work of the Bondhouse*—Lawrence Chamberlain reminded his readers that "nothing but unfamiliarity with investment principles is an excuse for private buying of United States bonds."[17]

But conventions changed after a series of World War I–era bond drives introduced billions of dollars in Treasury debt into the American financial system. Banks were among the most important buyers, with the result that government securities came to represent, on average, about 8 percent of the banking system's total investment portfolio between 1923 and 1929 (and 21 percent in the latter year, when the stock market collapsed). Then federal reform heightened their strategic importance. By 1934 the nation's banks invested 58 percent of their funds in government obligations and over the following three years those investments accounted for an average of 31 percent. By 1936 the Fed's chartered institutions alone had more money invested in Treasury debt than in their loan portfolios. Just three years into Roosevelt's first term, the Fed's member banks were devoting more funds to the purchase of federal debt instruments than they were lending to commercial customers.[18]

To understand the significance of this development requires some familiarity with contemporaneous trends in American banking and—more broadly—with the relationship between banking and the money supply. It turns out that loyalty to real bills had already been eroding in some sectors of the financial community by 1914, when the Federal Reserve began operations. Many banks were extending fewer commercial loans in favor of investing directly in both real estate and securities. The strategy became far more popular in the 1920s until, by decade's end, investments represented 29 percent of the banking system's assets. Then crisis conditions swiftly accelerated the practice, until they accounted for 56 percent in 1934. "The importance of commercial banks as lending institutions," the American Bankers Association (ABA) would soon report, "ha[d] . . . become markedly secondary to their importance as investing institutions."[19]

And this trend, coupled with the growing importance of Treasury securities, helped fuel a subtle but decisive change in the composition of banking assets, because it meant that institutions were both lending against and investing in comparatively "illiquid" types of debt. These were the "speculative" debts that might be difficult to sell quickly, if necessary, for cash or checkable deposits. For example, just after the war most loans were still issued on real bills principles: that is, against self-liquidating (called "good") commercial paper. The bank accepted this collateral—it purchased or "discounted" the paper by putting funds (the loan) in the borrower's account—because the contract referenced a presumably saleable form of wealth. But profits from commercial lending had been drying up, which sent bankers in search of alternative revenue sources. By 1929, when the stock market collapsed, only 47 percent of banks' loans (45 percent by one estimate) were extended against commercial paper, and the remaining 53 percent (or 55 percent) were issued for so-called capital purchases, in which the loans' collateral consisted of the stocks, bonds, or real estate being purchased with the borrowed money.

This was a comparatively risky arrangement, of course, because collateral is only as "good" as its market price. Skeptics feared that these speculative purchases threatened to undermine the economy's robust postwar performance, and they were vindicated in 1929, when security and real estate prices began their free fall and a sizable share of the banking system's earning assets simply disappeared.[20] The crisis did not end the practice, however, because banks were in the business of making profits and continued to seek the highest return. By 1934 they were lending 79 percent of their funds for capital purchases and only 21 percent against commercial collateral. Put simply, the nation's banking system was no longer focused on extending traditional "commercial" loans. Such loans had made up more than half of the assets of the Fed's member institutions in 1923 but represented only one-fifth of the total in 1937.[21]

Banks lend and invest—that is, they purchase earning assets—by creating checkable deposits ("check book money") in a customer's account, and it is through this process that they create new money. New currency enters circulation not in the form of paper notes but as a bookkeeping entry. And this means that by the mid-1930s, both the mechanics of monetary issue (creation) and the federal state's role in the process had been remade. To earn profits, banks were steadily leaving the market for commercial lending in favor of lending against or making direct investments in securities and real estate. The collateral for bank operations, for day-to-day lending and investment activity, was represented less by commercial assets, more by securities and real property, and more by public securities in particular—in other words, by debt instruments long deemed "illiquid" or "speculative" in the world of finance.[22] To hear financiers explain it, market pressures—what the American Bankers Association called the "force of circumstance"—had narrowed their options and led to the "development of non-liquidity" during the 1920s. "Because of the drying up of the springs of traditional commercial credit," the ABA reported, lenders had "found it necessary to enter into [the] field of credit related to capital assets."[23] Meanwhile a wave of federal reform in the early 1930s accelerated these trends and ensured their lasting significance.

The changes outlined above matter because the supply of the domestic currency increases only when banks lend and invest. The Fed does not inject new money directly into the economy but supplements the banking system's reserves, which represent a small percentage of the institution's total assets.[24] A bank with $1,000 in reserves (Federal Reserve notes or an accounting equivalent) can lend $10,000 to a borrower by purchasing a debt (the promise to repay) and creating a bookkeeping entry in the customer's account. With a ledger entry—or, nowadays, an electronic keystroke—the bank invents $9,000 and the nation's overall money supply increases by that amount. And by 1935 banks not only were pursuing new profit-making strategies but also the character of their reserve accounts had been transformed. Before passage of the Federal Reserve Act, most reserves were either precious metals (with a recognized value) or banknotes and debt instruments collateralized by a combination of commercial and public assets. Meanwhile federal debt represented a small and shrinking component of that asset base. Yet just two years into the New Deal, and largely as a result of government action, reserves increasingly took the form of bank notes collateralized by federal debt obligations. A large proportion of the banking system's reserves were investments in Treasury securities, the value of which is rooted in nothing more than the U.S. government's promise to raise revenues through taxation. And these reserve accounts sustained the creation of new money in the U.S. economy.

In simplest terms, the era's asset and policy revolutions—fundamental changes both in banking practice and state power—can be described this way. Before the 1910s, domestic currency was introduced into circulation, for the most part, when individual banks had faith in their borrowers' commercial assets as well as sufficient reserves (of mixed origin) to justify the loan. Most monetary creation was "commercial" in origin and the federal government's debt played a limited as well as increasingly untenable role in maintaining the money supply. Yet by the mid-1930s, the nation's currency was increasingly created against comparatively "illiquid" collateral (e.g., securities, real estate) and against reserves collateralized by the government's promise to collect taxes.[25] In the older system, banks generally created money to accommodate the production or exchange of identifiable commercial wealth, either existing or anticipated. In the new system, banks increasingly created money to accommodate the production or exchange of comparatively "risky" assets and U.S. government obligations backed a far larger proportion of the banking system's reserves.

This change in banking practices was inseparable from the swift expansion of state capacity. In 1913, the Federal Reserve Act assigned the U.S. government unprecedented authority to stabilize the banking sector but tasked it neither with determining how much money circulated in the economy nor with "backing" that supply, that is, securing its worth. The central bank's architects were adamant that these were not public responsibilities.[26] Jump ahead to the 1930s and the federal state had assumed the power to adjust actively the money supply and to ensure its value.

Financial Reform and Its Critics

Here was the "revolution" that, in the view of many contemporaries, posed an existential threat to the free-enterprise system. Now these critics were not questioning the Federal Reserve's legitimacy or a sovereign government's responsibility to protect its currency. They were not challenging the principle of central banking. But they balked when the Fed actively incentivized private lending, and they resisted the liberal use of government debt to collateralize the banking system's reserves. They viewed monetary creation—the act of introducing more currency into circulation—as a job for bankers and investors responding to market imperatives, free from interference by legislators or regulators. And so they objected whenever that model appeared to be under threat and then, during the 1930s, led the "bitter editorial and Congressional opposition" to financial reforms viewed as "contrary to principles in central banking widely taught and firmly held."[27] A careful examination of these changes to finance and the struggle over their meaning highlights public policy's transformative impact on the banking sector as well as the considerable intellectual work required to reconcile Americans to the state's new powers.

*   *   *

It was not supposed to be controversial. Indeed, in 1913 the Fed's architects were confident that they had addressed the banking system's most pressing structural problem: much of the circulating currency—including federally sanctioned paper notes—was tied to a market for government debt. Congress had created the problem during the Civil War when it decided to raise revenues by selling Treasury bonds to the banking system. Desperate for funds to battle the Confederacy, legislators passed the

National Banking Acts of 1863 and 1864, which manufactured a market for the government's debt by introducing a standardized currency (the National Bank Note) and conditioning banks' access to it. Banks that opted to issue and lend this paper—and thereby earn profits—were required to purchase U.S. government securities and deposit them, immediately, at the Treasury. The new paper's supply increased only when the government sold its bonds. But this made the supply "inelastic," meaning that it often failed to adjust to the economy's needs and thus keep pace with the nation's commercial, industrial, and territorial expansion. Reformers viewed this inelasticity as a source of instability and a trigger of the era's recurring financial crises. Finally, a particularly severe panic in 1907 helped legislators overcome long-standing divisions on the "money" question and reach the consensus that created a new central bank.

The Federal Reserve Act of 1913 created another standardized and government-sanctioned paper money, this one printed by the U.S. Treasury (and still used today). It invited individual banks to "join" the new Federal Reserve System by applying for a charter and then required these "member" institutions to maintain a minimum reserve of the new currency in their vaults, equal to a percentage of their total assets. The Fed issued this paper to members in exchange for specie or commercial debts; it "delinked" the currency's issue from the sale of Treasury bonds. Meanwhile, Congress set strict terms for the Fed's lending operations, which were a centerpiece of the experiment and would be a focus of considerable controversy during the Great Depression. If a member bank's reserves dropped below the required minimum, it could cover the deficit by arranging a short-term loan from its regional Fed branch (there were twelve branches, in all). For member banks, the Federal Reserve System served as the "lender of last resort" and the terms by which it did so were crucially important. The branches advanced funds by purchasing a bank's commercial paper (its earning assets) in an operation known as rediscounting. Here the commercial paper was accepted a second time, in this case by the Fed to collateralize its loan to the bank. The presumption was that a private loan backed by "good" commercial paper would likely be repaid by the bank's customer, thus allowing the bank in turn to repay its debt to the Fed.[28]

And so, in theory, reserve accounts and in turn bank lending would expand only in response to private-sector demand. Or as the act's coauthor H. Parker Willis explained, note issue by the Fed to its members would be "based upon commercial assets" and thus "in accordance with the volume

of business."[29] Meanwhile the Fed was given a hybrid, public-private structure—its branches answered to government oversight but were privately
owned and operated—to ensure that bankers and not politicians made
decisions about the money supply. Reformers envisioned a central bank
that would achieve its public charge (maintaining financial stability) while
respecting the laws of a private market for money. It would manage a uni-
form currency and insulate the financial system from crises, while tasking
the private sector with adjusting the money supply and securing its value.
The Federal Reserve's Conference of Governors shared this vision, and the
board's early actions demonstrate their commitment as well.[30]

Staying true to this imperative proved difficult in practice, however, because Progressive Era governance was unusually expensive. And again a
war spurred monetary innovation, when financing the nation's contribution to World War I required abandoning commercial banking principles.
Between 1917 and 1919, Congress raised about two-thirds of its war-related
costs through a series of "Liberty" and "Victory" bond campaigns, drawing in $21.3 billion from individuals and corporations. The securities were
marketed at the time—and still are portrayed in most histories—as government "borrowing" from American citizens. But most accounts down-
play or ignore the fact that much of the money spent on those purchases
was created by monetary authorities specifically to finance these sales. On
September 7, 1916, the Fed's Board of Governors suspended the Federal
Reserve Act's real bills requirement for rediscounting and authorized advances to member banks against U.S. bonds or notes. This allowed banks
to expand their reserve accounts—and thus potentially expand their
lending—even if they lacked sufficient commercial collateral. Next the
Fed, under pressure from the Treasury, encouraged its members to lend
for the singular purpose of buying war bonds. As the Fed board explained
in its 1918 annual report, "discount policy . . . has necessarily been coordinated . . . with Treasury requirements and policies, which in turn have
been governed by demands made upon the Treasury for war purposes."[31]

This coordination resulted in a sustained campaign of government debt
sales on margin. Traditionally, investors bought bonds by drawing upon
their personal savings. Here, by contrast, they completed the purchases
with borrowed money; banks accepted the bond as collateral for the loan
that was used, simultaneously, to buy it. Or as James Grant aptly notes,
the banking system was "more than accommodating to the would-be saver
who happened to be without money."[32] And it was this financial sleight of
hand that expanded the federal debt burden exponentially while introducing into banks' portfolios a financial instrument that would in time

prove to be of great consequence. Between 1916 and 1919, ownership of U.S. securities within the national bank system increased from $729 million—most of it representing the 2 percent bonds issued since 1863 to secure National Bank Notes—to $2.4 billion worth of Liberty bonds, Victory notes, and short-term certificates. Outside of the national system, bank holdings of government debt rose from $7.4 million to $986 million during that same period. By 1919 the nation's commercial banks held approximately $5 billion in Treasury obligations, representing 20 percent of the total in circulation, as well as $3 billion in loans made to finance purchases of war bonds.[33] These bond sales were a prime driver of monetary expansion. Among the Fed's member institutions, total credit outstanding (the money that entered circulation when banks lent or invested) increased from about $280 million when the United States entered the war to $2.5 billion by war's end. Overall, the nation's demand deposits and circulating currency expanded by $7 billion (44 percent) between June 1916 and June 1919.[34]

In simplest terms the Federal Reserve helped banks create much of the money—secured by nothing more than the government's promise to redeem its obligations—that was in turn used to purchase the government's debt. That debt ballooned from $1.3 billion in 1917 to $26.6 billion in 1919. And 70 percent of the war's costs, as John Kenneth Galbraith writes, were "covered by methods not appreciably different from [the greenback sales that financed] the Civil War."[35]

Contemporaries seldom used this kind of language to explain wartime finance operations, however, because this was a real bills generation. Instead, they justified the margin sales as an expedient necessary to promote government "borrowing." In April 1917 the Fed reasoned that citizens would assume the burden of covering current government expenditures by committing their future earnings (savings) to the cause. A patriotic public would pay later for spending that was required now, and meanwhile the board "felt it to be its duty to adjust its discount rates," in order "to assist the distribution of the . . . Treasury issues." Then in 1919 the secretary of the Treasury announced the ultimate goal of "wiping out . . . the war debt" and insisted that "any thought" of delaying the process by marketing additional securities would be a "breach of faith with every [bond holder]" as well as "unwise in the extreme from the standpoint of the Government's finances." "Whatever may be necessary in the future financing of the government," he concluded, "nothing must be permitted to interfere with . . . retirement of the war debt."[36]

But the U.S. government proved unable to "wipe out" that debt and so revenue requirements again trumped a commitment to real bills principles. The central bank continued to accommodate the Treasury after the war by artificially lowering discount rates, that is, the interest (fee) that Fed branches charged member banks for short-term advances. This made commercial borrowing less expensive for customers—and less profitable for bankers—which in turn ensured that war bonds (which had low rates of return) would remain competitive with other investment opportunities. Seen another way, the Fed manipulated the discount rate to prop up the value and thus marketability of federal bonds, so that bankers would finance their purchase instead of seeking profits from commercial lending. Its actions were not a secret and prompted concern among the Fed's leadership that this path might be encouraging speculation. "Ordinarily this could be corrected by an advance in discount rates," one board member noted at a June 1919 meeting, only to concede that it was "not practicable to apply this check at this time because of Government financing."[37]

Equally troubling to advocates of real bills was a postwar development in monetary management that transformed a wartime exigency—expanding banks' reserve accounts against the sale of government debt—into standard practice. The practice is called "open market" operations and refers to Fed-initiated purchases of Treasury securities from its member banks. The mechanics of open-market sales were identical to rediscounting: the Fed received debt instruments (government obligations in one case, commercial paper in the other) and transferred Federal Reserve notes to the issuing bank,[38] thus replenishing its reserve account. The original legislation sanctioned this practice—despite its open defiance of real bills principles—so that the twelve Fed branches could supplement their revenues. These were for-profit institutions that needed a reliable source of income. And while our contemporary discussions of Fed policy rarely address this, open-market purchases were never intended to figure prominently in the system's operations, nor could such a role have been envisioned in 1913, given that the federal debt was small and Treasury bonds were hardly coveted investments. But war financing created an investment demand for the Treasury's debt and opened the door for branches to increase their purchases as an investment strategy. Meanwhile, postwar recessions provided the impetus by discouraging commercial borrowing and setting off a chain reaction. When private firms borrowed less, the nation's banks held less commercial paper and lacked incentive to rediscount it with the Fed. The drop-off in rediscounting then took a bite out of the branches' revenues, so they compensated by increasing their open-market purchases of Treasury securities.[39]

This practical, profit-driven response would have unintended consequences, ultimately altering the Federal Reserve's approach to monetary management and, years later, the collateral structure supporting investment nationwide. For the system's founders had installed a mechanism that was now steadily supplementing banks' reserves against the sale of government debt. Already by the early 1920s, increases in open-market purchases were reliably reducing member borrowing—that is, the rediscounting of commercial paper—because the banks' reserve requirements were covered. Fed leadership saw an opportunity to strategically harness the trend and in 1923 created the Federal Open Market Investment Committee to coordinate the branch banks' purchases. Between December 1923 and November 1924 alone, open-market operations increased the system's holdings of Treasury securities from $84 million to $582 million. Then throughout the rest of the decade these purchases contributed immeasurably—and far more than traditional commercial lending—to the growth of the domestic money supply. That expansion was necessary to sustain the era's spectacular growth, of course, but it also fueled speculative investment and thus inflated real estate and security prices.

The cycle was unstoppable. Banks steadily curtailed their commercial lending in favor of financing purchases of stocks and real property. Banks created the money that was helping inflate prices across the board, yet they did so without the backing of "good" commercial paper. Meanwhile, the Fed was financing the banks—at a rate after 1924 that alarmed contemporaries—by supplementing their reserve accounts through open-market purchases and by reducing discount rates.[40]

For defenders of real bills these were ominous developments. Among the critics was John U. Calkins, the Ohio-born banker and governor of the Fed's San Francisco branch who in 1922 reaffirmed the system's "commercial" principles and described monetary creation backed solely by federal debt as a "fiat currency"—that is, a money form with no real wealth behind it. A year later, the *Chase Economic Bulletin* accused the Fed of substituting bank credit for "real" (i.e., commercial) capital, thus disguising the economy's shortage of the latter and further fueling speculative investment. And tellingly the Fed's leadership again conceded that its "easy money" policies might encourage risky behaviors, specifically in the stock market, but defended them as necessary to sustain the flow of credit to commercial borrowers for "productive" purposes.[41] Reflexively invoking real bills to justify their actions, Fed officials nonetheless acknowledged the theory's failure to explain how investors behaved—and thus how the money supply expanded—in the real world.[42]

It was in this context that the Great Depression began and a wave of emergency measures set off a contentious debate over money and state power. Hoover signed the Glass-Steagall Act in 1932 and then change came swiftly under Roosevelt, who declared a "bank holiday" on his second day in office and shepherded through the Emergency Banking Act of 1933, the Glass-Steagall Act of 1933, the Gold Reserve Act of 1934, and the Banking Act of 1935. All told these executive and legislative actions rejected formally the Fed's real bills requirements by broadening the categories of assets eligible for accessing reserves (commercial paper and Treasury securities became virtually indistinguishable for this purpose) while also reconstituting the Federal Reserve Board (it became the Board of Governors) and consolidating its powers over discount rates and open-market policy. The Fed gained unprecedented authority to encourage or discourage private lending, and a trade in Treasury securities became integral to financial stability. Of equal importance, a government guarantee replaced specie as the ultimate collateral for the U.S. dollar in its domestic uses. Three years of frenetic state building accelerated—in part by materially supporting—a long-standing trend: the nation's banks were increasing their investments in noncommercial assets, especially real property and securities, and the debt of the federal government now represented a sizable share. Meanwhile the U.S. government was responsible for securing the value of the domestic currency.[43]

Critics sounded the alarm about a credit "revolution." Congressional opponents of the first Glass-Steagall bill claimed that it assaulted traditional collateral safeguards and "struck at the very foundation of the Federal Reserve System," in the words of a *Post* reporter. The chief economist of Chase Manhattan Bank, Benjamin Anderson, decried reform in the pages of the *Chase Economic Review* and in testimony before the U.S. Senate. Even Roosevelt's budget director, Lewis Douglas, was reportedly so outraged by the president's position on the gold standard that he predicted "the end of Western Civilization" (and would soon resign from the administration).[44] But perhaps the most telling critique came from Senator Carter Glass of Virginia, who with Willis had coauthored the original Federal Reserve Act and now, two decades later, helped secure passage of key New Deal–era financial reforms. For, throughout these years, Glass remained a staunch defender of real bills and a prominent spokesperson among the officials, businessmen, and pundits who believed that disregard for commercial banking principles was prolonging the economic crisis.[45]

The senator's sponsorship of two landmark banking acts—the Glass-Steagall Acts of 1932 and 1933—tends to obscure his role as a vocal New

Deal critic and reluctant reformer who supported those measures only under considerable political pressure.[46] But real bills' champions were well aware of his dissent, and they flooded his office with letters encouraging defiance. Bankers, business owners, and other professionals warned that efforts to liberalize the Fed's lending operations would "destroy business confidence," as an accountant from New York City explained. They condemned pending bills that called for "any permanent broadening of the [banking system's] rediscount base," and they considered acceptance of "worthless stocks and bonds" (in the words of a "cashier in a small country bank") as especially dangerous. "Liberalizing the rediscounting privilege," wrote a financial reporter from Springfield, Massachusetts, in 1932, "could only result in an expansion of credit for stock gambling purposes." An investment banker from Cleveland agreed that it was "time to force the banks out of the security business."[47]

This conventional wisdom was captured succinctly in a letter that Glass received in 1931 from the president of the Florsheim Shoe Company, who insisted that Congress's first priority must be to keep the central bank "untainted and sound." The Fed's policies and practices, wrote Milton Florsheim, must remain "in keeping with . . . public opinion and . . . the thinking business men of the country." That same year one of these "thinking" men, financier and presidential adviser Bernard Baruch, implored Glass not to "let . . . the Federal Reserve system be destroyed by issuing credit against things which are not liquid." The senator agreed. "The trouble with this country," Glass noted in one exchange, "is not too little credit but too much."[48] As Congress and two presidents assigned the state vast new authority over banking and the money supply, a generation of critics insisted that these new federal powers threatened to devalue the currency and open the floodgates of "speculative" investment. New money should enter circulation, they insisted, only when commercial actors demanded it.

Monetary Orthodoxy Makes Reform "Safe" for the Market

Carter Glass, H. Parker Willis, and other real bills advocates lost these battles to people who insisted that monetary issue has no integral relationship to wealth creation. And that view remains conventional wisdom, to this day, among academic economists. College textbooks explain that growth is fueled by choices about production and consumption made in the "real" economy. Then they explain how the "financial" sector (the arena of money and credit) aids the growth process by facilitating real-sector exchanges, say, of investment capital for materials, or labor for wages, or wages for other goods. Most economists depict money as "exogenous"— external and not determinant—to wealth creation, arguing that the supposedly barter-like market activities that drive growth would continue (theoretically, at least) if money forms did not exist.[49] According to this calculus, money is useful but not essential to growth. And it follows logically that the type of collateral backing monetary issue is unimportant, as long as the amount of acceptable money in circulation satisfies a market's requirements for intermediation.

Why, then, should historians concern themselves with the early twentieth-century money debate? Glass and his supporters were mistaken about many things and commercial banking theory, as Mark Blaug writes, was one of the "longest lived economic fallacies of all time."[50] But their dissent is nonetheless revealing because these critics insisted on a claim that is correct: monetary issue by the banking system is inextricably linked to the productive process. Contrary to the orthodox model, the creation of financial instruments is essential to economic growth, and this point has been documented in a multidisciplinary heterodox scholarship that explores money's properties as a credit form. (The most prominent branches—chartalism and post-Keynesian monetary theory—were not fully articulated until the decades following World War II.[51]) Proponents of this heterodox view share little in common, in the final analysis, with advocates of real bills; they define money differently (the real bills view is quite narrow) and disagree about the importance of sovereign authority (real bills advocates cautioned against government overreach, whereas credit-money theories see state power as integral to both the value and the function of sovereign currencies).[52] But in the 1930s, real bills theory inspired resistance to reforms that assigned to the federal government unprecedented powers over money creation and this dissent was shot down by a theory (the "quantity" model) that helped justify the expansion of state capacity.

And so while we should by no means lament the demise of commercial banking theory, the era's policy debate demonstrates that scholars' embrace of monetary orthodoxy is deeply indebted to the politics of crisis management during the Great Depression. Moreover, the outcome of that debate has prevented historians from exploring money's complicated role in American economic development. The history of economic thought looms large here. Indeed, early twentieth-century financial reform is inseparable from a history of ideas and of economists' desire for professional legitimacy. Our modern financial system and the rise of an orthodox consensus about money share an origins story.

*   *   *

The backdrop for the Depression-era controversy was a methodological dispute among professional economists that had long been transforming assumptions about research and evidence. Until the late nineteenth century, most practitioners of "political economy" (as the field was known at the time) were engaged in a capacious intellectual project that differs both in aim and substance from the modern discipline. To explain how modern economic systems create and distribute wealth, political economists considered a wide range of evidence, much of it qualitative, about the institutions, decision making, and social processes that produced and allocated goods deemed valuable in the marketplace. But by the early twentieth century the object of inquiry had narrowed considerably and many scholars focused instead on measuring the efficiency with which markets created and distributed wealth. Meanwhile, scholars were now privileging quantifiable evidence and quantitative methods, part of a wide-ranging effort to bolster the profession's "scientific" credentials. Together these developments marked what is known as the marginal revolution in economics, describing a new focus on calculating the satisfaction or benefit derived from the purchase of goods and services. That benefit is recorded as a product's "marginal utility." A new generation of scholars argued that by isolating and calculating this measure, they could assess a market's ability to satisfy consumers' preferences.[53]

Foundational contributions to marginal theory by writers including Marie-Esprit-Léon Walras and Alfred Marshall were published in the latter half of the nineteenth century and would give rise to an analytical model—called neoclassical—that has long dominated economic inquiry in the United States.[54] The neoclassical model views markets as sites of exchange among individuals who are seeking to fulfill their preferences about work and consumption. Markets are seen as the aggregation of countless, self-interested economic choices. And the model holds that this aggregated self-interest, all other things being equal, produces an efficient and fair distribution of wealth. The neoclassical market self-calibrates, constantly moving toward what economists call a state of general equilibrium.

This turn had profound consequences for the study of finance and specifically for an old theory about money, commonly known as the currency or quantity school. Quantity theory's intellectual lineage dates back at least to Aristotle, but the pioneers of marginalism—among them Marshall and an American economist, Irving Fisher—reconciled it with the equilibrium model and the new emphasis on quantification.[55] To do so, they worked from common assumptions about the marketplace, viewing money's original (and still primary) function as facilitating the exchanges that satisfied people's needs and wants. ("Money is only a mechanism," Marshall would later write, "by which [a] gigantic system of barter is carried out."[56]) And they viewed prices as an accurate measure of goods' market value, that is, the willingness of a consumer to (work and) pay for things produced by the economic system.[57] It followed logically that general price stability indicated a market's efficiency, for this meant that the money supply was expanding or contracting at a rate appropriate to the economy's natural growth or contraction, and that instability (inflation or deflation) was a sign of market imbalances. Building on these premises, scholars looked to prices—and their movements—as a valuable metric for social-scientific analysis. By measuring changes in price levels for particular goods, they claimed to gauge—to literally calculate—an economy's ability to satisfy efficiently peoples' preferences.[58]

Fisher's iconic status stems from his work on what soon became one of the profession's most powerful tools of measurement. After earning a PhD from Yale in 1891—notably, in mathematics—with a thesis on Walras's theory of general equilibrium, Fisher joined the faculty in 1898 as a professor of political and social science and later as professor of political economy. Then in *The Purchasing Power of Money* (1911) he outlined a formula for gauging the relationship between the money supply (described as banknotes and checking deposits), the "velocity" of that supply's circulation (basically how often these money forms changed hands), and price levels. And he documented how, at least theoretically, if one were to hold the amount of goods constant, monetary expansion would trigger a proportional increase in prices (because there would be more money to spend on a finite selection of goods). Finally, Fisher designed a new calculus for determining general price levels, or what economists call the price index, and insisted that monetary authorities could use it to fashion policies that would all but eliminate price inflation. Application of sound economic analysis, he argued, would create optimal market conditions and prevent financial crises.[59]

Turning to advocacy in the 1920s, Fisher founded the Stable Money League and sponsored bills designed to give federal legislators direct influence over the Fed's discount rates and open-market purchases. The central bank, he insisted at a congressional hearing in 1926, could achieve a "man-made stabilization" and serve as "the greatest public service institution in the world."[60] To his chagrin he found few receptive audiences. Central bankers and political leaders rarely consulted with economists (meanwhile the Fed's leadership had long been skeptical of Fisher's scholarship), and pundits agreed that prices should be set by market forces. "When has the regulation of prices [either by central bankers or politicians] been successful?" asked the editors of the *New York Times* in 1923. "What confidence could be felt in price movements if it were announced that they were under control by anything but the free movement of trade?"[61] The crisis unleashed in 1929 did little to test these views. President Hoover rejected Fisher's ideas, arguing instead that inflation and "easy credit conditions" were anomalies created by a flood of gold imports, and he stood by that assessment in February 1932, when a looming gold crisis helped him persuade Congress to pass the first Glass-Steagall Act.[62] Meanwhile, there was hardly an academic consensus about the Depression's origins and the best path forward. Writing to Carter Glass in 1931, the Harvard economist F. W. Taussig admitted that scholars, bankers, and politicians alike were "feeling their way tentatively" about the next steps, because their "ide[a]s of what a central bank organization might or could accomplish have been revolutionized since the war."[63]

This generation came to embrace reform not because of Fisher's insights but rather because crisis conditions required a new kind of federal commitment. In the early 1930s a radical expansion of state capacity was simply necessary to rescue and then sustain American financial markets. But in the meantime, the new iteration of quantity theory had gained a well-positioned advocate in a young economist named Lauchlin Currie, whose work helped assure contemporaries that reform was compatible with the free-enterprise system.

Currie's early career offers a road map to monetary orthodoxy's political and intellectual ascendancy. And the institutional context proved decisive because of changes in the professional setting since the days of Fisher's apprenticeship. By 1925, when Currie entered Harvard's graduate program in economics, the field's leading scholars were proudly asserting their scientific and policy credentials, and Currie, throughout his career, was notable among his peers for linking scholarship to the public purpose.[64] Meanwhile, his doctoral dissertation made waves by rigorously applying quantity theory to the study of the ongoing crisis. In a thesis examining American and British bank assets, Currie tracked Federal Reserve policy from 1928 and through the early years of the Depression and concluded that the Fed's "tight money" policies (restricting the supply's growth) were largely to blame for domestic conditions.[65] He updated and published this research in 1934 as *The Supply and Control of Money in the United States*, which combined a rebuttal of real bills theory with a defense of the government's expansive new powers. The book articulated core premises of the orthodoxy that would come to dominate academic and political discussions of finance.

Central to that orthodoxy and to the argument in *Supply and Control* is a narrow definition of money. And Currie's exegesis of the subject, seen in light of the controversy over New Deal financial reform, helps explain the work's analytical coherence and political appeal. Specifically, the book draws a sharp distinction between two categories of financial instruments: the true "money" forms that permit people to buy things, on the one hand, and instruments that represent a promise of future payments, on the other hand. Put simply, Currie provides a social-scientific vocabulary for distinguishing money from credit. There is "an important distinction," he writes, "between means of payment and what may be regarded . . . as *equivalent* to means of payment." The first category—"money"—is limited to bank paper (cash) and demand (or checking) deposits: instruments widely accepted for the completion of a purchase. And they are different, Currie explains, from money "equivalents"—savings accounts ("time deposits") and a range of credit forms, including promissory notes, stocks, and bonds—which performed some of money's vital functions (namely measuring and holding value) but did not directly facilitate exchange. "Time deposits . . . do not differ essentially from holdings of government securities, call loans, or indeed, any property possessing good marketability which by sale can be converted into means of payment," he writes. For "it is no more correct that one can 'spend' a time deposit than a government security. . . . [B]oth must first be exchanged for cash or [checkable] deposits." True money, Currie argued, enabled people to make purchases—to buy things "now"—while money "equivalents" enabled them to plan for future monetary exchanges.[66]

This broad distinction was not new to economists,[67] but Currie's deep dive into the mechanics of contemporary financial markets coupled with his stature and disciplinary rigor validated an appealing political narrative about reform. For his categories described alternatively a sector of American finance over which the state had come to exercise considerable

authority since World War I and another to which it remained essentially
a bystander. In those two decades monetary authorities had gained significant new powers to influence the creation of paper currency and checking
deposits: the tools identified by Currie as means of payment. By contrast,
public authorities still had minimal direct influence on people's decisions
to save or on the creation of private credit forms, such as promissory notes
or private securities: instruments that, according to Currie, could be used
to make strategic decisions about spending.[68] Again, money facilitated
exchange, while credit (and savings) provided flexibility for making decisions about when to complete exchanges—that is, when to use money.
And by this logic, the evolution of Federal Reserve practices and the wave
of Depression-era financial reform left their mark solely on the mechanics of market exchange, that is, on people's short-term ability to buy and
sell things. Reform enabled authorities to adjust the amount of money
"tokens" in circulation so that people were free to act on their needs and
preferences. But reform did not shape the creation of the money "equivalents" and with it peoples' economic choices.[69] The market's dynamism,
Currie assured his readers, remained secure in the private sector and free
from government interference.

Highlighting the policy implications of this argument is *Supply and
Control*'s categorical rejection of real bills. There was "no theoretical justification for the attempt to tie notes to commercial loans," Currie explained,
"as was done in the Federal Reserve Act." There was no justification because money's creation bore no intrinsic link to wealth creation. He even
relegates commercial lending "to a past era" and scolds writers who fail
"to realize that the loaning activity of banks are becoming more and more
concerned with security loans and bonds."[70] In Currie's vision, money creation helped people pursue their preferences and those choices fueled
economic growth, thus it was imperative that monetary authorities properly manage and calibrate the money supply to make market exchanges
optimally efficient. In a consequential contribution to the theory of market
equilibrium, Currie refuted "scientifically" the real bills view that monetary expansion need be grounded in an expectation of any specific wealth-
creating activity. Most important for the history of economic thought and
public policy, he helped codify the belief—at a notably precarious moment
in American political development—that money creation by the banking
system had no direct relationship to the productive process.[71]

This move goes a long way in explaining the appeal of quantity theory
to political leaders and economists during the Great Depression. Between

1932 and 1935, public policy ensconced Treasury securities as collateral for the nation's banking reserves, expanded federal power to encourage or discourage private lending, and tasked the government with guaranteeing the currency's (domestic) value. And such powers would have been deemed quite radical—indeed, they would still be seen as radical today—if the banking system's creation of cash and checking deposits was deemed essential to economic growth. Instead, Currie parceled out the supposedly essential (i.e., decision making) facets of financial exchange and situated them in the realm of private "credit," preserving the narrative that money—narrowly defined—was a token that simply made exchange more efficient. The result was that Depression-era financial reforms could be cast as unobtrusive "stabilizing" measures designed to unleash private market forces. Transformative policy interventions were viewed—and have been viewed by most observers since the 1930s—as minimally interventionist and, in the final analysis, market-friendly.

Currie also served as a New Deal adviser and in this capacity wrote quantity theory—literally—into the American financial system. Recruited away from Harvard and into the Treasury in 1934, Currie prepared the memorandum that Utah banker Marriner Eccles handed to Roosevelt when they discussed Eccles's interest in directing the Federal Reserve System. That memo recommended a permanent expansion of the types of paper eligible for rediscount. Eccles was appointed days later, and Currie followed him to the Fed, where he drafted "the main lines" of what would become the Banking Act of 1935.[72] When its provisions met with a now-familiar resistance, Fed officials—including the general counsel Walter Wyatt—consulted with Currie and others to legitimate the changes and assure Eccles that the bill was sound. (One Fed official privately accused critics of attributing a "mysterious and nefarious purpose" to the bill's redefinition of "sound assets" and recommended avoiding the conflict by simply removing those words from the text.[73]) Eccles drew on this expert consensus in his defense of the measure before a Senate subcommittee in May 1935. The proposals were "definite and limited in scope and arise out of the experience of the past twenty years," Eccles explained. "They are not revolutionary . . . and they do not, as has been asserted by critics, make the Federal Reserve System a football of party politics . . . or an engine of inflation."[74]

Here was the legislative culmination of a policy and asset revolution that assigned to the state unprecedented authority over money and that made the U.S. government's debt an integral component of the financial system. It also provides a revealing snapshot of the intellectual work required to rationalize this dramatic expansion of state power.

*   *   *

The real bills generation would soon be sidelined and their theory of banking rejected almost universally by professional economists.[75] Meanwhile the standard narrative concerning the Fed's mandate was revised in light of the new consensus thinking. A telling document appeared as early as 1936, when W. Randolph Burgess updated his influential study, *The Reserve Banks and the Money Market*, to reflect ongoing shifts in policy and intellectual fashion. The original edition, published in 1927 as the stock market reached new heights, offered a full-throttled endorsement of real bills thinking. "All paper presented to [Fed banks] for rediscount or as collateral for an advance" was carefully scrutinized, Burgess wrote at the time, to ensure that "the concerns whose paper is presented are in liquid condition." In other words only "good" commercial paper was "liquid" and thus acceptable for the purposes of Fed rediscounting. But that model soon fell to pieces, of course, and so Burgess revised this section for the 1936 edition, adding that the Fed could also "put reserve money to work by purchasing government securities . . . and certain other types of securities." And he noted that Treasury securities could "be sold promptly," thus putting banks "in a safer and more liquid position" than they would be by accepting the "best quality" commercial paper.[76]

Here was a clear marker of the sea change in views about the investment quality of Treasury debt and a far cry from Lawrence Chamberlain's observation, a quarter century earlier, that U.S. government bonds were unsuitable for the purpose of private investment. Recognizing that his readers would demand an explanation, Burgess conceded that "it has indeed been necessary to change some ideas formerly held, especially as to the nature of the collateral for note issues." Why? Because central bankers learned that the key to ensuring the money supply's elasticity was not "the specific [type of] collateral held." This had "proved less important," they discovered, "than the mechanism by which notes are issued."[77]

These assumptions about money and central banking have since dominated academic and policy discussions in the United States. Scholars portray true "money" narrowly, as an instrument that captures existing private-sector wealth and that facilitates exchange. Meanwhile, they depict credit forms as contracts that afford people and institutions temporal flexibility in

their spending choices. And with the exchange and contractual components
of finance separated for purposes of economic analysis, scholars describe
the most important monetary variable in narrow terms: as the quantity of
Federal Reserve notes and checkbook money in circulation. Moreover,
the source of those instruments' creation—the conditions under which
they are produced and who or what collateralizes them—has become
largely insignificant.[78] Thus, Milton Friedman and Anna Schwarz, in their
Monetary History of the United States, dismiss Glass and like-minded
peers for approaching Fed policy from a "qualitative, 'real bills' point of
view." They made "invalid distinctions," the authors argue, between "dis-
counts, bills, and government securities," because they failed to recognize that the nature of the credit supporting money creation was largely
irrelevant.[79]

*   *   *

This seemingly arcane disagreement about finance would be a footnote
to the story of American political and economic development if not for
the fact that orthodoxy—the "victor" of the era's money debate—invokes
a history of money that cannot be documented. The evidentiary record
does not support orthodoxy's claim that money and debt are distinct instruments that have historically performed different functions. What the
record shows, instead, is that modern money forms evolved from credit
instruments (essentially IOUs) and that our state-sanctioned currencies
continue, in many contexts, to do the work of contracts. All monetary
instruments—including the Federal Reserve's notes—are best described
as "credit money" forms. Of course, modern sovereign currencies serve as
mediums of exchange. But they are also economically productive, because
their creation and circulation are essential to the contractual relations—
the negotiations between creditors and debtors—that fuel the growth
process. This history of money "in the real world," as Paul Davidson calls
it, is explored in a heterodox scholarship written by economists, historians, sociologists, and anthropologists.[80] And it challenges scholars to
rethink the history of American financial policy. The creation of credit-
money instruments (including the nation's legal tender) is essential to
the creation of wealth. Thus when the federal government gained new
means of collateralizing money creation and simultaneously guaranteed
the currency's domestic value, the state gained unprecedented power to
finance economic growth. It did so, as the history of credit-money forms

demonstrates, because financial assets deemed "liquid" in our economy owe their value to an implicit promise: that a person or an institution— either public or private—will eventually exchange them for another thing of value, even if that valuable thing does not yet exist.[81]

This represents a radical departure from the orthodox view, in which a liquid asset has value on far narrower grounds: because it is readily converted into cash or checking deposits, which are tokens that measure and "stand in" for existing private-sector wealth. Orthodoxy sees money not as a contract that promises future access to things of real value but rather as an exchangeable commodity—it could be a precious metal, or a paper currency, or even a good such as grain—that symbolizes things of real value. And so orthodoxy depicts newly created money by banks as a representation of surplus wealth that will be "saved" later—to repay a debt—once the growth process generates it. In the standard narrative about banking, financial assets are the "stuff" against which banks create new money tokens (by lending), confident that any increase in the money supply will be matched, in the future, by real-sector growth.[82] And it follows that American banks stopped lending during the Great Depression because they were caught off guard, without sufficient "liquid" assets to support adequate (and necessary) monetary expansion. The state then stepped in, this story continues, and created those assets by fiat when it declared that, for the purpose of stabilizing the financial system, public debt had the same liquidity as commercial paper. Orthodoxy claims that this strategic intervention insulated and thereby sustained a system that is designed, in the final analysis, to circulate private wealth.

The politics of the Great Depression helped validate and refine a theory about finance that has since dominated our histories of American economic life. As a result, financial policy has received minimal attention in the study of American state building. Most economists—and the historians who follow their lead—treat finance as important but nonessential to the wealth-creation process and so they view Depression-era reforms as "conservative" responses to the market's stubborn instability. The real-world history of money—its history as a credit instrument—demonstrates, instead, that the U.S. state fundamentally remade the financial landscape in the twentieth century by collateralizing it with public resources: with the promise that the federal government, when push comes to shove, would both adjust the (narrow) money supply and stand behind the currency's value. And this reading alters fundamentally our view of the state's impact on economic development in the twentieth and twenty-first centuries.[83]

During the 1930s, economists joined politicians in attributing the Depression's endurance to a liquidity crisis that was sparked, in large measure, by a collapse of confidence. They reaffirmed orthodox assumptions about liquidity (that it describes nothing more than an asset's convertibility into cash) and about money (that its primary role is to facilitate exchange). And they revised the working definition of "sound assets" for monetary expansion, claiming that the change was prompted by advancements in their understanding of money. Necessity and the insights provided by a new economic science, they explained, helped them recognize the Fed's responsibilities for monetary management and so they adjusted public policy accordingly.

Most accounts of early twentieth-century financial history repeat this story. They argue that American monetary authorities were slow to recognize their responsibility for stabilizing the money supply because of their misconceptions about money. And scholars portray the ascendance of monetary orthodoxy as a triumph of economic science, not a product of politics and reform itself.[84] But orthodoxy's triumph was in no small part a function of policy debates over the state's response to an economic emergency. The conventional wisdom about money changed in this era because orthodoxy told a story that many people wanted to hear. A reformulation of the classical "quantity" theory appealed to contemporaries and later to postwar Americans who were anxious to reconcile the government's heavy hand in finance with a desire to protect the sanctity of the "free market."

Notes

Thanks to the many audiences and readers who have contributed to this chapter. I owe a special debt to Karen Caplan, Brent Cebul, Nathan Connolly, Lily Geismer, Greta Krippner, Stephen Mihm, Eric Tymoigne, David Weiman, Mason Williams, and L. Randall Wray. This chapter is dedicated to the memory of Arnold Hirsch.

1. Prior to this—and since the American Revolution—the nation's currency circulated in multiple forms, some more secure and reliable than others. Paper currency took the form of notes issued by state-chartered banks, notes issued by federally chartered banks, and occasionally Treasury notes issued to cover budgetary shortfalls. Meanwhile other circulating instruments (e.g., checks, promissory notes) were denominated in dollars. After 1913 a number of these older note forms remained in use—including National Bank notes and both gold and silver certificates—but the new Fed paper rapidly dominated circulation. See Board of

Governors of the Federal Reserve System, *Banking and Monetary Statistics* (Washington, DC, 1943), table 110, 408–9.

2. I discuss the Glass-Steagall Acts of 1932 and 1933, the Emergency Banking Act of 1933, the Gold Reserve Act of 1934, and the Banking Act of 1935 later in this chapter.

3. Federal debt had been used before to provide banks' initial capitalization (famously, for the First and Second National Banks). But only the National Banking Acts of 1863 and 1864 had given federal authorities discretionary authority to adjust the supply of bank paper and this experiment—as discussed in this chapter—proved unsustainable.

4. Speaking about the same bill that so concerned Willis, former secretary of the Treasury Ogden Mills predicted that its passage "would throw us back five hundred years." It would soon become the Banking Act of 1935. "Federal Reserve," *Fortune*, May 1934; Ferdinand Lundberg, "Wall Street Dances to Washington's Tune," *Literary Digest*, May 12, 1934, 46; Arthur Schlesinger, *The Politics of Upheaval, 1935–1936*, vol. 3, *The Age of Roosevelt* (New York: Marriner Books, 2003), 297; and James Grant, *Money of the Mind: Borrowing and Lending in American from the Civil War to Michael Milken* (New York: Farrar, Straus & Giroux, 1992), 242.

5. Roosevelt set the tone in his first "fireside chat" in March 1933, when he assured a national radio audience that "there is nothing complex, nothing radical" about the government's financial interventions. The secretary of the Treasury described the wave of emergency financial measures as a means to "insur[e] that the banks will be put in apple-pie order." Russell D. Buhite and David W. Levy, eds., *FDR's Fireside Chats* (Norman: University of Oklahoma Press, 1992), 16; *Brooklyn Daily Eagle*, March 14, 1933, 2.

6. New Deal reformers, according to Anthony Badger, sought "a return to conservative banking practices which would foster investor confidence." Susan Estabrook-Kennedy agrees that financial policy "restored banking . . . without radical change." Badger, *The New Deal: The Depression Years* (Chicago: Ivan R. Dee, 2002), 66–73, 98–100; Estabrook-Kennedy, *The Banking Crisis of 1933* (Lexington: University Press of Kentucky, 1973), 189. See also Price V. Fishback, "The New Deal," in *Government and the American Economy: A New History*, ed. Price Fishback, Robert Higgs, Gary D. Libecap, John Joseph Wallis, Stanley L. Engerman, Jeffrey Rogers Hummel, Sumner J. La Croix, Robert A. Margo, Robert A. McGuire, Richard Sylla, et al. (Chicago: University of Chicago Press, 2007), 384–430; Jonathan Hughes and Louis P. Cain, *American Economic History*, 7th ed. (Boston: Pearson Education, 2007), 507–8; Milton Friedman and Anna Jacobson Schwartz, *A Monetary History of the United States, 1867–1960* (Princeton, NJ: Princeton University Press, 1971), 433–34; and Eugene N. White, "Banking and Finance in the Twentieth Century," in *The Cambridge Economic History of the United States*, ed. S. Engerman and R. Gallman (Cambridge: Cambridge University Press, 2000), 3:743–802. An important exception is Eric Rauchway, *The Money*

Makers: How Roosevelt and Keynes Ended the Depression, Defeated Fascism, and Secured a Prosperous Peace (New York: Basic Books, 2015), which nonetheless shares the "orthodox" view of money discussed in this chapter. See also William J. Barber, *Designs within Disorder: Franklin D. Roosevelt, the Economists, and the Shaping of American Economic Policy, 1933–1945* (Cambridge: Cambridge University Press, 1996), 24–26, 93–95; and Elliot A. Rosen, *Roosevelt, The Great Depression, and the Economics of Recovery* (Charlottesville: University of Virginia Press, 2005), chaps. 3–4.

7. By contrast, "early monetary policymakers," writes Robert L. Hetzel, "had no sense of their responsibility for the price level." "The Real Bills Views of the Founders of the Fed," *Federal Reserve Bank of Richmond Economic Quarterly* 100, no. 2 (2014): 159–81, at 177. See Friedman and Schwartz, *Monetary History*, chap. 7; and Allan H. Meltzer, *A History of the Federal Reserve*, vol. 1, *1913–1951* (Chicago: University of Chicago Press, 2003), 727–42.

8. That familiar story pits "liberals" (usually Democrats), who support state activism to stimulate growth and redistribute its benefits, against "conservatives" (usually Republicans), who argue that federal restraint, by unleashing market forces, will generate prosperity and equitable outcomes. See Herbert Stein, *The Fiscal Revolution in America: Policy in Pursuit of Realty* (Washington, DC: AEI Press, 1990); and Robert Collins, *More: The Political Economy of Growth in Postwar America* (New York: Oxford University Press, 2002).

9. See, e.g., David Laidler, ed., *The Foundations of Monetary Economics* (Cheltenham, UK: Edward Elgar, 2000), 1:xvi.

10. Paul A. Samuelson and William D. Nordhaus, *Economics*, 18th ed. (New York: McGraw-Hill Irwin, 2005), 510–15; Don Patinkin, "Neutrality of Money," in *The New Palgrave Dictionary of Economics*, ed. Steven N. Durlauf and Lawrence E. Blume, 2nd ed. (Basingstoke, UK: Palgrave Macmillan, 2008); and David Laidler, *Taking Money Seriously and Other Essays* (New York: Cambridge University Press, 1990), 1–23.

11. On "credit money" theories of finance, see discussion later in this chapter and David M. P. Freund, "Money Matters: Financial Policy and Economic Growth in American History" (article manuscript, January 2018). On Depression-era credit and monetary reforms, see Ira Kaminow and James M. O'Brien, eds., *Studies in Selective Credit Policies* (Philadelphia: Federal Reserve Bank of Philadelphia, 1975); David M. P. Freund, *Colored Property: State Policy and White Racial Politics in Suburban America* (Chicago: University of Chicago Press, 2007), chaps. 3–5; and Robert Guttman, *How Credit-Money Shapes the Economy: The United States in a Global System* (Armonk, NY: M. E. Sharpe, 1994), 78–86.

12. Instead, most observers attribute the era's financial innovations to new private-sector activity—most notably the expansion of consumer credit and call loans—by "nonbank" financial intermediaries. See Martha L. Olney, *Buy Now, Pay Later: Advertising, Credit, and Consumer Durables in the 1920s* (Chapel Hill:

University of North Carolina Press, 1991); Hughes and Cain, *American Economic History*, 472–73; Friedman and Schwarz, *Monetary History*, 240–45; and Robert A. Degen, *The American Monetary System: A Concise Survey of Its Evolution since 1896* (New York: Lexington Books, 1987), 53–54.

13. This chapter is not a defense of real bills. Rather, it demonstrates how a debate over the theory's merits helped validate ideas about money that distort our understanding of financial policy.

14. Thomas M. Humphrey, "The Real Bills Doctrine," *Federal Reserve Bank of Richmond Economic Review*, September–October 1982, 3–13; Lloyd W. Mints, *A History of Banking Theory* (Chicago: University of Chicago Press, 1945); Anna J. Schwartz, "Banking School, Currency School, Free Banking School," in *The New Palgrave Dictionary of Economics*, 2nd ed., ed. Steven N. Durlauf and Lawrence E. Blume (Basingstoke, UK: Palgrave Macmillan, 2008); Robert Craig West, *Banking Reform and the Federal Reserve, 1863–1923* (Ithaca, NY: Cornell University Press, 1977), chap. 7; and Mark Blaug, *Economic Theory in Retrospect*, 5th ed. (New York: Cambridge University Press, 1997), 53, 128–29, 194–96.

15. Joseph Schumpeter, *History of Economic Analysis* (1954; rpt., New York: Oxford University Press, 1996), 729–31; West, *Banking Reform*, 140–48.

16. See *supra* note 3.

17. Lawrence Chamberlain, *The Work of the Bondhouse* (1912; rpt., New York: Arno Press, 1975), 148; Grant, *Money of the Mind*, chap. 6.

18. James S. Olson, *Saving Capitalism: The Reconstruction Finance Corporation and the New Deal, 1933–1940* (Princeton, NJ: Princeton University Press, 1988), 82; American Bankers Association (ABA), *The Earning Power of Banks: A Study of Changes in Political, Social and Economic Conditions Affecting Banking, Resulting Modifications in the Structure and Necessary Adjustments in Practical Bank Operations* (New York: American Bankers Association, 1939), 10; Paul Studenski and Herman Edward Krooss, *Financial History of the United States*, 5th ed. (1952; rpt., Washington, DC: Beard Books, 2003), 400–401; Freidman and Schwartz, *Monetary History*, chap. 6.

19. Meanwhile banks had long relied on "speculative" credit instruments to sustain their daily operations. ABA, *Earning Power*, 12–14, 43–46; ABA, *Changes in Bank Earning Assets* (New York: American Bankers Association, 1936), chap. 2; West, *Banking Reform*, 156–58, 162. See also Perry Mehrling's discussion of "shiftability" in *The New Lombard Street: How the Fed Became the Dealer of Last Resort* (Princeton, NJ: Princeton University Press, 2011), esp. 30–37. Compare Roy Green, "Real Bills Doctrine," in *The New Palgrave Dictionary of Economics*, 2nd ed., ed. Steven N. Durlauf and Lawrence E. Blume (Basingstoke, UK: Palgrave Macmillan, 2008).

20. White, "Banking and Finance in the Twentieth Century," 748–49; ABA, *Changes*, 14; and Olson, *Saving Capitalism*, 5. Compare Friedman and Schwartz, *Monetary History*, 245.

21. ABA, *Earning Power*, 14–15; Studenski and Krooss, *Financial History*, table 52; Benjamin M. Anderson, *Economics and the Public Welfare: A Financial and Economic History of the United States, 1914–1946* (Indianapolis: Liberty Press, 1979), 135, 140–41; John Kenneth Galbraith, *Money: Whence It Came, Where It Went* (Boston: Houghton Mifflin, 1975), 177–78; John Kenneth Galbraith, *The Great Crash: 1929* (Boston: Houghton Mifflin, 1972), 25–27; White, "Banking and Finance," 747–52; Committee on Recent Economic Changes of the President's Conference on Unemployment, *Recent Economic Changes in the United States* (Washington, DC: National Bureau of Economic Research, 1929), vols. 1–2, sec. I, ix and 661–712.

22. Investment in U.S. Treasury securities also transformed the portfolios of nonbank intermediaries (including trusts, savings and loans, and finance companies). See Raymond W. Goldsmith, *Financial Intermediaries in the American Economy since 1900* (Princeton, NJ: Princeton University Press 1958), 134–37.

23. ABA, *Changes*, 11, and see chap. 2 generally. By 1932, the ABA was appealing directly to Congress to "broaden the rediscount base and provide the acceptance of Government securities." ABA to Glass, February 15, 1932, box 305, "Glass-Steagall correspondence," Glass Papers, University of Virginia, Charlottesville.

24. When individual banks need to supplement their supply of circulating cash (to meet their customers' demand), they draw it from those reserve accounts.

25. By then "strictly eligible commercial paper" accounted for only 7 percent of member banks' portfolios. W. Randolph Burgess, *The Reserve Banks and the Money Market*, 2nd ed. (New York: Harper & Brothers, 1936), 67.

26. The Federal Reserve Act's coauthor considered the U.S. government's "guarantee" of Federal Reserve notes to be meaningless, since the currency was ultimately backed by commercial activity. See Carter Glass, *An Adventure in Constructive Finance* (Garden City, NY: Doubleday, Page, 1927), 124–25.

27. Burgess, *Reserve Banks*, 52.

28. Meltzer, *Federal Reserve*, chaps. 2–3; Degen, *American Monetary System*, chap. 2; and Jane W. D'Arista, *The Evolution of U.S. Finance*, vol. 1, *Federal Reserve Monetary Policy: 1915–1935* (Armonk, NY: M. E. Sharpe, 1994).

29. Henry Parker Willis, *The Federal Reserve System: Legislation, Organization and Operation* (New York: Ronald Press, 1923), 11–12; Glass, *Adventure*, 62. Real bills advocates dominated the planning efforts that eventually produced the Federal Reserve Act. See Meltzer, *Federal Reserve*, 74–77; Schumpeter, *History of Economic Analysis*, 729–31; Richard Timberlake, "Gold Standards and the Real Bills Doctrine in U.S. Monetary Policy," *Independent Review* 11, no. 3 (Winter 2007): 325–54; Glass, *Adventure*, 69–70; and Elmus Wicker, *The Great Debate on Banking Reform: Nelson Aldrich and the Origins of the Fed* (Columbus: Ohio State University Press, 2005).

30. D'Arista, *Evolution*, 16, 86–87; Meltzer, *Federal Reserve*, 74–77; West, *Banking Reform*, 184–86.

31. Alexander Dana Noyes, *The War Period of American Finance, 1908–1925* (New York: G. P. Putnam's Sons, 1926), 183–87, 193–96; *Fifth Annual Report of the Federal Reserve Board: Covering Operations for the Year 1918* (Washington, DC: Government Printing Office, 1919), 4–5; D'Arista, *Evolution*, 31–32; Meltzer, *Federal Reserve*, 84–90; Degen, *American Monetary System*, 32–33; Walter S. Logan, "Amendments to the Federal Reserve Act," *Annals of the American Academy of Political and Social Science* 99 (January 1922): 114–21.

32. Grant, *Money of the Mind*, 151–53. By contrast, most accounts characterize the bond drives strictly as a means of government "borrowing" from the public. See Tilford C. Gaines, *Techniques of Treasury Debt Management* (New York: Columbia University and the Free Press of Glencoe, 1964), 23–24; Robert Higgs, "The World Wars," in *Government and the American Economy*, ed. Price Fishback, Robert Higgs, Gary D. Libecap, John Joseph Wallis, Stanley L. Engerman, Jeffrey Rogers Hummel, Sumner J. La Croix, Robert A. Margo, Robert A. McGuire, Richard Sylla, et al. (Chicago: University of Chicago Press, 2007), 431–55; and Ajay K. Mehrotra, "Lawyers, Guns and Public Moneys: The U.S. Treasury, World War I and the Administration of the Modern Fiscal State," *Law and History Review* 28 (2010): 173–225.

33. Other incentives included a "borrow and buy" policy that allowed investors to delay payments. Noyes, *War Period*, 183–91, 202–14; D'Arista, *Evolution*, 31–37; Degen, *American Monetary System*, 34–35; Meltzer, *Federal Reserve*, 85–87; Logan, "Amendments," 114–21; Ray Bert Westerfield, *Money, Credit and Banking*, rev. ed. (New York: Ronald Press, 1947), 633; and Lester Vernon Chandler, *Benjamin Strong: Central Banker* (Washington, DC: Brookings Institution, 1956), 116.

34. Gaines, *Techniques*, 24.

35. D'Arista, *Evolution*, 31–32; Galbraith, *Money*, 141–42. Compare Grant, *Money of the Mind*, 153; Friedman and Schwarz, *Monetary History*, 216–17; Meltzer, *Federal Reserve*, 86; and Hugh Rockoff, "Until It's Over, Over There: The US Economy in World War I," in *The Economics of World War I*, ed. Stephen Broadberry and Mark Harrison (New York: Cambridge University Press, 2005), 310–39.

36. D'Arista, *Evolution*, 15–17, 34 (on the origins and influence of the Governors' Conference and their 1917 meeting); *Fifth Annual Report of the Federal Reserve Board*, 4–5; Secretary Andrew Mellon's comments reprinted in *Bankers Magazine* 99, no. 1 (July 1919): 471; Anderson, *Economics and the Public Welfare*, chap. 4; Gaines, *Techniques*, 27–35; Burgess, *Reserve Banks*, 118–19.

37. Studenski and Krooss, *Financial History*, 328–29.

38. Or registered credits in the branch bank's ledger, which were a promise of those notes.

39. Not until March 1919 did the board propose using open market operations "as a tool of policy," and the initial proposal was real bills compatible (it recommended use of bankers' acceptances rather than government obligations). D'Arista, *Evolution*, 80–81; Meltzer, *Federal Reserve*, 140–43.

40. Anderson, *Economics and the Public Welfare*, 95–96, 135; D'Arista, *Evolution*, 80, 92–101, 130; Grant, *Money of the Mind*, 184–86; Degen, *American Monetary System*, 42–50, 47–51; Guttman, *Credit Money*, 80–81; and Studenski and Krooss, *Financial History*, 328.

41. In 1923 the board reaffirmed that member banks were in "little danger" of creating an "excessive volume" of credit if it was "restricted to productive uses." *Tenth Annual Report of the Federal Reserve Board (1923)*, excerpted in D'Arista, *Evolution*, 223–33, and 228. Meltzer, *Federal Reserve*, 68–73, 143–45 (citing Calkins on 70); Anderson, *Economics and the Public Welfare*, 97–99; Degen, *American Monetary System*, 54–55; and Studenski and Krooss, *Financial History*, 332.

42. Here I invoke Paul Davidson's *Money in the Real World*, 2nd ed. (New York: Palgrave Macmillan, 1978), a key text in the heterodox scholarship introduced in this chapter.

43. William J. Barber, *From New Era to New Deal: Herbert Hoover, the Economists, and American Economic Policy, 1921–1933* (New York: Cambridge University Press, 1985), 112–13; Grant, *Money of the Mind*, 217–24; Guttman, *Credit Money*, 78–86; Peter Conti-Brown, *The Power and Independence of the Federal Reserve* (Princeton, NJ: Princeton University Press, 2016), chap. 1. See also Mehrling, *New Lombard Street*, 43–47.

44. Grant, *Money of the Mind*, 242; J. B. M'Donnell, "Reserve System Credit Expansion Passed by House: Glass-Steagall Bill Wins by Vote of 350 to 15," *Washington Post*, February 16, 1932; Douglas's response is discussed in Raymond Moley, *After Seven Years* (New York: Da Capo Press, 1972), 160. See also A. U. Romascu, *Politics of Recovery* (New York: Oxford University Press, 1983), 45–51; and Schlesinger, *Politics of Upheaval*, 295–301.

45. Glass, *Adventure*, 60–90, 130–31, 172; Friedman and Schwarz, *Monetary History*, 388–89; West, *Banking Reform*, 146–47; Estabrook-Kennedy, *Banking Crisis*, 46–47.

46. "Liberalizing the Credit Facilities of the Federal Reserve System," 72nd Congress, H.R. 9203, February 12, 1931, 1; Herbert Hoover, *The Memoirs of Herbert Hoover* (New York: Macmillan, 1952), 3:117; "Operation of the National and Federal Reserve Banking Systems," 72nd Congress, S. 4115, pt. 1, March 23–25, 1932; Conti-Brown, *Power and Independence*, 28–32.

47. All the following citations are found in the Carter Glass Papers at University of Virginia: Martin W. Walbert to Glass, May 10, 1932, box 297; Henry A. Horne to Glass, May 20, 1935, box 304; Thomas C. Boushall (Morris Plan Bank of Virginia) to Glass, December 20, 1932; J. H. Ellis (Malden State Bank, Malden, MO) to Glass, October 12, 1931; Arthur Hoyt Bogue (*Springfield [MA] Daily News*) to Glass, October 8, 1931; Julian Tyler to Glass, April 5, 1932—all in box 278, "Corr. Re. Eligible Paper Requirements."

48. Milton Florsheim to Glass, October 9, 1931, in Glass Papers, box 284, "Corr. Re. Glass Banking Bill." Bernard M. Baruch to Glass, October 10, 1931, and Glass

to Alfred L. Aiken, November 14, 1931, in Glass Papers, box 278, "Corr. Re. Eligible Paper Requirements."

49. A standard college text explains: "As economies develop, people no longer barter one good for another. Instead, they sell goods for money and then use money to buy other goods they wish to have." Samuelson and Nordhaus, *Economics*, 511–12. For an introduction and critical assessment of the barter-origins story, see L. Randall Wray, "Money and Inflation," in *A New Guide to Post Keynesian Economics*, ed. Richard P. F Holt and Steven Pressman (London: Routledge, 2001), 79–91.

50. Blaug, *Economic Theory in Retrospect*, 53.

51. These heterodox—or "credit money" theories—demonstrate that money forms have their origins in credit instruments and then show how a range of financial instruments (including sovereign currencies) continue to perform credit functions. Excellent introductions include Davidson, *Money and the Real World*; L. Randall Wray, *Money and Credit in Capitalist Economies: The Endogenous Money Approach* (Aldershot, UK: Edward Elgar, 1991), and Geoffrey Ingham, *The Nature of Money* (Cambridge, UK: Polity, 2004).

52. Real bills advocates did not draw a sharp distinction between money and credit—thus their hostility to reform—but they did argue that bankers "had no influence on credit or prices," preferring to see themselves as "neutral intermediaries" who "merely served the needs of business and trade." West, *Banking Reform*, chaps. 7–8, citing 141.

53. R. D. Black, A. W. Coats, and Craufurd D. W. Goodwin, eds., *The Marginal Revolution in Economics: Interpretation and Evaluation* (Durham, NC: Duke University Press, 1973); Phyllis Deane, *The Evolution of Economic Ideas* (Cambridge: Cambridge University Press, 1978), 71–124. On economists' challenge to the marginal turn, see Michael A. Bernstein, *A Perilous Progress: Economists and the Public Purpose in the Twentieth Century* (Princeton, NJ: Princeton University Press 2004), chap. 2; and Dorothy Ross, *The Origins of American Social Science* (Cambridge: Cambridge University Press, 1992), 408–27.

54. Deane, *Evolution of Economic Ideas*, 71–124; Dimitris Milonakis and Ben Fine, *From Political Economy to Economics: Method, the Social and the Historical in the Evolution of Economic Theory* (London: Routledge, 2009), chaps. 6, 7, and 14; and Geoffrey M. Hodgson, *How Economics Forgot History: The Problem of Historical Specificity in Social Science* (London: Routledge, 2001).

55. "Much of standard neoclassical theory today," writes James Tobin, "is Fisherian in origin, style, spirit, and substance." Tobin, "Irving Fisher (1867–1947)," in *Celebrating Irving Fisher: The Legacy of a Great Economist*, ed. Robert W. Dimand and John Geanakoplos (Malden, MA: Blackwell Publishing, 2005), 19–20, 31; David Laidler, *The Golden Age of the Quantity Theory* (Princeton, NJ: Princeton University Press, 2016), chaps. 2–4; Blaug, *Economic Theory in Retrospect*, 194–96, 613–16, 633–37, 645; Patinkin, "Neutrality of Money"; and William J. Barber,

"Irving Fisher of Yale," in *Celebrating Irving Fisher*, ed. Dimand and Geanakoplos, 44–47.

56. A. Marshall, *Official Papers of Alfred Marshall*, ed. J. M. Keynes (London: Macmillan, 1926), 115; and Laidler, *Golden Age*, 83.

57. Prices were seen to reflect the preferences and capacities of economic actors, acting in the context of available resources, capacity, and knowledge.

58. These neoclassical premises still guide the discipline. Economics, according to a standard college text, is "the study of how societies use scarce resources to produce valuable commodities and distribute them among different people." Both scarcity and efficiency are determinant. An economy "is producing efficiently when it cannot make anyone economically better off without making someone else worse off." Samuelson and Nordhaus, *Economics*, 4.

59. Tobin, "Irving Fisher," 33; Barber, *New Era*, 25; Samuelson, "Irving Fisher and the Theory of Capital," in *Ten Economic Studies in the Tradition of Irving Fisher*, ed. William Fellner, Challis A. Hall Jr., Tjalling C. Koopmans, John Perry Miller, Marc Nerlove, Richard Ruggles, Paul A. Samuelson, Herbert Scarf, James Tobin, and Henry Wallach (New York: John Wiley and Sons, 1967); Barber, "Irving Fisher of Yale," 54; and Blaug, *Economic Theory in Retrospect*, 614–16.

60. Barber, *New Era*, 23–28; Stein, *Fiscal Revolution*, 142; William R. Allen, "Irving Fisher, F.D.R., and the Great Depression," *History of Political Economy* 9, no. 4 (1977): 560–87; and David Laidler, "The Neoclassical Theory of the Price Level: The Cambridge School and Fisher," in *The Golden Age of the Quantity Theory* (Princeton, NJ: Princeton University Press, 2016), 49–88.

61. Bernstein, *Perilous Progress*, 34–39, chap. 2, 211n2; Barber, *New Era*, 71–77, 59–61, 112; "Bank Credits and Prices," *New York Times*, August 24, 1923, 10. See also Rauchway, *Money Makers*, 20–21.

62. *Recent Economic Changes*, 664–69, quoting 669; Estabrook-Kennedy, *Banking Crisis*, 46; Hoover, *Memoirs*, 3:115–17; "Action to Aid Bank Credits and Free Billions in Gold Agreed on at White House," *New York Times*, February 11, 1932, 1–2; "President Signs Bank Credit Bill; Lauds Both Parties," *New York Times*, March 28, 1; Barber, *New Era*, 96–97, 140–41.

63. Taussig to Glass, March 21, 1931, box 278, "Corr. Re. Eligibility Requirements," Glass Papers, University of Virginia.

64. Bernstein, *Perilous Progress*, chap. 2; and Roger Sandilands, *The Life and Political Economy of Lauchlin Curie: New Dealer, Presidential Advisor, and Development Economist* (Durham, NC: Duke University Press, 1990), chaps. 1–3.

65. This portion of the research appeared as "The Failure of Monetary Policy to Prevent the Depression of 1929–1932," *Journal of Political Economy* (April 1934): 145–77. See Sandilands, *Lauchlin Currie*, 18–19, 23, 28, and 39–45 (on Currie's departure from Fisher's work on velocity).

66. Money was any instrument "possessed by the public by delivery of which debt contracts and price contracts are discharged." Lauchlin Currie, *The Supply*

and Control of Money in the United States: A Proposed Revision of the Monetary System of the United States (1934; rpt., New York: Russell & Russell, 1968), 10–24. Note that prior to 1914 "there was no legal distinction between [checking deposits and time deposits]" and "no mention of time or savings deposits in the national banking laws." Burgess, *Reserve Banks*, 34.

67. On the intellectual precedents see Laidler, *Golden Age*, esp. chap. 5.

68. Other New Deal initiatives would soon change that. See Kaminow and O'Brien, *Studies in Selective Credit Policies*, and Freund, *Colored Property*.

69. For Currie, private credit was a tool for planning and contracting to engage in commercial activities, whereas the government used its existing debt strategically to protect the payment system. Private credit was "market making," whereas public credit was a convenient tool for stabilizing that private market.

70. Currie, *Supply and Control*, 36, 152.

71. Karl Brunner, "On Lauchlin Currie's Contribution to Monetary Theory," in Currie, *Supply and Control*, ix–xxvi. See also Thomas M. Humphrey, "Monetary Policy Frameworks and Indicators for the Federal Reserve in the 1920s," Federal Reserve Bank of Richmond Working Paper No. 00-7 (August 2000).

72. Sandilands, *Currie*, 56–60, 62–64.

73. "To eliminate this criticism . . . we could strike out the words 'secured by any sound assets of such member banks' and substitute . . . 'secured to the satisfaction of such Federal Reserve bank.'" "Section 206. Eligibility of Paper for Discount or Advances by Federal Reserve Banks. What it does and why it is needed" (memo), in Banking Act of 1935 (folder 4/4); Typescript of Wyatt's revisions to the banking act ("1934 Dec"), in Banking Act, 1935 (1/4); Wyatt to Eccles, March 16, 1935, in Banking Act, 1935 (2/4); Wyatt to Eccles, April 2, 1935 (4/4); "Alternative for Open-Market Committee Provisions of Banking Act of 1935," in Banking Act, 1935 (3/4), in Walter Wyatt Papers, University of Virginia. See also Economists' National Committee on Monetary Policy, "Memorandum in Opposition to Title II, Banking Bill of 1935," box 108, folder 1-3 (43/70-114 Money), Raymond Moley Papers, Hoover Institution, Stanford University, Stanford, CA.

74. "Statement on Title II of the Banking Bill of 1935 (S.1715) by Marriner Eccles, Before Committee on Banking and Currency of the United States Senate, May 10, 1935."

75. Anderson, *Economics and the Public Welfare*, 362n1; and Frederic S. Mishkin, *The Economics of Money, Banking, and Financial Markets*, 3rd. ed. (New York: Pearson, 2013), 481–82.

76. W. Randolph Burgess, *The Reserve Banks and the Money Market* (New York: Harper & Brothers, 1927), 44; Burgess, *Reserve Banks* (1936), 28, 53, 55–56, 73.

77. Burgess, *Reserve Banks* (1936), 75–76. By contrast, Gilbert Harold's *Bond Ratings as an Investment Guide: An Appraisal of Their Effectiveness* (New York: Ronald Press, 1938) did not discuss government bonds because, in the author's view, major ratings agencies still distinguished them from commercial debt

(82–83). Jump ahead twelve years and Herbert V. Prochnow and Roy A. Foulke, in *Practical Bank Credit*, 2nd ed. (New York: Prentice-Hall, 1950), describe Treasury debt as "liquid reserves": "Government securities are to the business enterprise what paper eligible for rediscount is to a member commercial bank or trust company" (183).

78. For an introduction to quantity theory's intellectual history, see Patinkin, "Neutrality of Money."

79. Friedman and Schwartz, *Monetary History*, 267. Most historical treatments of American finance depict government interventions as efforts to "shore up" or "protect" a system of private-sector intermediation. The creation of money is cast as a market-fueled function of a banking system that is attending, above all else, to the "real" sector's needs. The creation of private credit instruments is parceled off analytically while federal debt is treated as distinct: as a useful instrument for pursuing monetary policies designed to protect a private market. See Freund, "Money Matters."

80. Good introductions to this vast literature include Davidson, *Money and the Real World*; Wray, *Money and Credit*; and Ingham, *Nature of Money*.

81. "Money is essential not just to exchange or to accumulate," writes L. Randall Wray, "but to make production possible because production takes time." *Money and Credit*, 9–10.

82. Standard economic theory imagines all calculable monetary exchanges occurring simultaneously; strictly speaking, its models do not account for the passage of time. Of course it describes fractional reserve bank loans as creating money that represents future earnings. Critically, however, it depicts lending not as the creation of a "promise" but instead as a contemporaneous exchange of debt for money. The loan-financed purchase is treated as a separate exchange—again, made in the present—using "someone else's money." In this story, lenders risk their (existing) wealth to make these transactions possible, because they will have to absorb the cost of loans that go unpaid. Thus, the real-world promise "across time"—which is a premise of a credit-theory of money—is reduced to a financier's calculated risk in the present. Put another way, orthodoxy insists that monetary instruments themselves do not make promises. Again, "money" is not "credit." Instead, it holds that investors take chances with their own money.

Moreover by delinking wealth creation from the banks' creation of a sovereign currency, orthodoxy erases the federal state's integral role in sustaining productive activity. But sovereign states have always helped finance production by managing state-money forms. Indeed, the so-called financialization of the capitalist economy in the late twentieth century is one episode in a much longer history of money-financed (and often state-financed) growth. For an essential introduction to this topic and careful reconstruction of money's capitalist history in early modern England, see Christine Desan, *Making Money: Coin, Currency, and the Coming of Capitalism* (Oxford: Oxford University Press, 2015). I explore why historians of the American experience need to revisit money's long history in "Money Matters."

83. For example, deficit spending does not represent the strategic use of "future savings," but rather the government's contractual commitment to financing growth. Also, economists do not describe federal credit programs (which facilitate private lending) as wealth creating but as a way to "improve the efficiency of markets by correcting market imperfections and encouraging innovations." According to this model, the federal contribution simply demonstrates how existing markets can be "operated profitably." See Barry P. Bosworth, Andrew S. Carron, and Elisabeth H. Rhyne, *The Economics of Federal Credit Programs* (Washington, DC: Brookings Institution Press, 1987), 6–8. I examine the impacts of federal mortgage insurance programs in *Colored Property*.

84. See *supra* notes 6 and 7. Economists have long debated the Fed's culpability for the Great Depression and the obstacles to learning a "proper approach to monetary policy." For introductions to this vast literature, see Michael D. Bordo and David C. Wheelock, "The Promise and Performance of the Federal Reserve as Lender of Last Resort 1914–1933," and "Charles W. Calomiris, "Volatile Times and Persistent Conceptual Errors: U.S. Monetary Policy 1914–1951," both in *The Origins, History, and Future of the Federal Reserve: A Return to Jekyll Island*, ed. Michael D. Bordo and William Roberds (Cambridge: Cambridge University Press, 2013), 59–98 and 166–218 (quoting 167); and Julia Ott, "What *Was* the Great Bull Market? Value, Valuation, and Financial History," in *American Capitalism: New Histories*, ed. Sven Beckert and Christine Desan (New York: Columbia University Press, 2018), 63–95.

CHAPTER FIVE

La revolución institucional

The Rise and Fall of the Mexican New Deal in the U.S. South, 1920–1990

Julie M. Weise

In the midst of the 1952 cotton-picking season in the Arkansas Delta, seventeen cotton pickers awoke at 3 a.m. to the sound of frantic yelling. Their cabin was on fire. The men quickly fled, although three sustained painful burns. All escaped with their lives, but their hard-earned cash went up in smoke, along with their clothes, hats, and one man's radio.[1]

The fire, they reasoned, was their boss's fault. The men had repeatedly requested more and warmer blankets, but planter Coy E. Scott gave them a tin woodstove instead. The stove, in turn, had ignited the blaze. The workers wanted Scott to absorb the fire's consequences by reimbursing them for their losses.[2]

Forty years earlier, a deadly fire in New York's Triangle Shirtwaist Factory had helped union activists and Progressive reformers push through a host of new protections for industrial workers: workplace safety regulations, a child labor law, and a fifty-four-hour workweek for women. These measures, together with other state-level initiatives (like workers' compensation and unemployment insurance) provided a kind of template for the federal labor regulations and government insurance programs of the New Deal, which shifted many of the risks once borne by ordinary workers to their employers and the federal government. In 1938, the Fair Labor Standards Act guaranteed a minimum wage and maximum hours to all the country's industrial workers.

As historians have long noted, rural workers received no such New Deal. Whether white, black, or brown, their negligible electoral power left them out of the era's Democratic coalition, rendering their interests easily ignored even by senators and representatives otherwise sympathetic to labor.[3] So in a compromise with the Democratic Party's Southern wing, domestic and agricultural laborers were excluded from the New Deal's signature labor laws.[4] No federal standards governed the work or housing conditions of agricultural laborers anywhere in the United States in 1952, and none would do so for another fifteen years. And while the Southern Tenant Farmers Union (STFU) reorganized and reemerged during and after World War II, its impact on cotton working conditions remained extremely limited.[5] Thus, no regulations governed the working and living conditions of the men who escaped the fire on Scott's farm. Furthermore, because these men were not white, their concerns also would receive no hearing in the offices of local politicians. In theory, neither the three workers hospitalized with burn wounds nor the fourteen who lost property in the blaze stood much chance of forcing Scott to pay.

The men saw things differently. Incensed by Scott's disregard for their life and property, they went on strike and refused to pick cotton. They filed a complaint with the U.S. Employment Service (USES), which paid them little heed. And then, worker spokesmen Dagoberto Caballero Calderón and Heriberto Salas Ochoa appealed to a representative of their own government: the consul of Mexico at the time, Ángel Cano del Castillo, stationed in Memphis with the express purpose of overseeing his conationals' working conditions.

Mexican nationals like Caballero Calderón and Salas Ochoa have performed agricultural labor throughout the United States, and even in the Deep South, from the early twentieth century through the present. Millions worked in the country during the mid-twentieth century, the supposed heyday of "big government" in which liberal reformers were extending the power of the state into countless areas of the American economy, often in the name of protecting workers from the vicissitudes of modern capitalism. Yet the U.S. federal state played almost no role in their lives. The characterization of the mid-twentieth century as a time of strengthened bonds between citizens and the state falls woefully short in any discussion of agricultural laborers' lives; after all, not until the Great Society—in hindsight, the waning days of the political order the New Deal had forged—did U.S. agricultural workers acquire any meaningful relationship to the state at all.

Yet unlike their white and black counterparts, Mexican agricultural workers in the midcentury Deep South did reap the benefits of a robust relationship to a state. Their power, however, hinged not on Democratic coalition politics but on the interpretation of a liberal ethos across the border and a set of historical contingencies that gave this ethos real clout in the Arkansas Delta. Theirs was a meaningful citizenship at midcentury, but it was not the U.S. government that recognized their claims—it was the Mexican state.

Recovering the histories of the Deep South's Mexican workers across the twentieth century challenges our understanding of the histories of the rural South and Latino migration, in turn reorganizing our historical geographies of liberalism and neoliberalism. In particular, it disrupts the narratives of U.S. historians who have failed to consider the evolution of twentieth-century liberal politics across borders. As U.S. Southern historians have shown, Jim Crow was not just a social and cultural system. Just as important, Jim Crow was the labor system that underwrote the rural South's business model.[6] Observers of Latino migration have noted that over the course of the 1980s, low-skilled labor became increasingly foreign and Latino not just in the West but throughout the country, including the South.[7] The overarching narrative of this progression, which scholars have located at the intersection of "Juan Crow" and "neoliberal globalization," posits that the gains of the civil rights movement and the Great Society created a rural low-wage labor market crisis whose resolution came when noncitizen Latinos replaced second-class citizen blacks as an exploited class of less-than-free workers at the bottom rungs of the economy.[8]

Yet a longer view of agricultural labor and international migration in the Deep South, including Chinese and particularly Mexican migration, shows that noncitizen and second-class citizen labor have coexisted empirically, rhetorically, and with the sanction of the federal government since Emancipation. Critically, however, because domestic agricultural workers were excluded from New Deal labor protections until 1966, foreign agricultural laborers potentially had more rights than their U.S. citizen counterparts. Mexicans, for example, were citizens of a state whose midcentury liberal project, *la revolución institucional*, embraced a much wider swath of society than its U.S. American cousin, the New Deal. In the United States, the Mexican state's power was felt most strongly in places like the Arkansas Delta. Unlike their counterparts closer to the Mexico-U.S. border in the Southwest, the Deep South's farmers did not enjoy unfettered access to a pool of Mexican American or undocumented Mexican workers, thus heightening the capacity of the Mexican government to play a mediating role there. Indeed, in the era before the minimum wage

in agriculture, Mexican contract workers were the first Southern rural laborers to have any economic rights at all thanks to the intercession of the
Mexican, not the U.S., government.

It was therefore the transition of Mexican political culture from liberal to neoliberal, rather than its U.S. counterpart, that ushered in the era
of extreme Latino labor exploitation that has persisted to this day. And
rather than in the 1980s, this transition began two decades earlier. Indeed,
these most vulnerable transborder citizens witnessed the effects of the
Mexican state's retreat long before most other members of the working
and middle classes. By the 1960s, Mexican citizens in the United States
asked for and received much less from their state than the victims of the
Scott plantation fire had in 1952.

Deeper Histories of the Deep South

From the moment of blacks' emancipation and particularly in times of
their out-migration, rural Southern plantation owners and managers fan-
tasized about importing immigrants to their fields. As they grudgingly removed the shackles from their slaves' limbs, Southern planters sought out
Chinese workers rather than confront the newfound need to actually negotiate the terms of employment with blacks. "To bring coolie labor in
competition with negro labor—to let the negroes see that laborers can be
had without them—is the main feature of the plan," explained a reporter
in 1865.[9] But Chinese were unwilling to work on planters' terms and
quickly left the plantations; those who remained in the area opened small
grocery stores rather than pick cotton.[10] In the 1880s and 1890s, Southern
planters, still unable to exert total control over the lives of African American laborers, tried to attract Italian immigrants. The Italians did arrive,
but once again, the "experiment" with immigrant labor yielded conflict
and controversy.[11] Planters' hopes of attracting a permanent and pliant
immigrant workforce remained mere fantasies, leaving them dependent
on poor African American and white cotton pickers.[12]

Yet as Southern planters plainly saw, the rapidly growing, better-
capitalized cotton industry in the U.S. Southwest relied increasingly on
immigrant labor from Mexico.[13] Following the lead of their competitors,
Mississippi planters first recruited small numbers of Mexican workers in
1904–1905. They, too, proved unwilling to tolerate the region's abusive
conditions, and most left the area.[14] The small handful who remained in

Mississippi or came there in the 1910s, the early years of the Mexican Revolution, attracted little attention and encouraged few in Mexican America
to follow their routes.[15]

Although white Southern planters had complained of "labor shortages" since Emancipation, World War I gave their anxieties renewed urgency. Cotton production in the Delta had increased dramatically in the
years preceding the war, just as African Americans headed north.[16] To
resist the flight of their black labor force to military posts and northern
industrial jobs, planters pressured draft officials, attacked northbound African Americans at train stations, and in one case, closed down pool halls
in an attempt to force black workers back into the fields.[17] The federal government intermittently supported their efforts, approving of "work-or-
fight" orders that all men not enlisted in the army pick cotton or go to jail,
and creating the U.S. Employment Service to ensure that adequate labor
was available in rural areas.[18]

Soon, planters appealed to the U.S. federal government to help them
secure a new labor source: Mexican immigrants. Cotton planters in Louisiana, Mississippi, and Arkansas asked the federal government to foot
the bill for the importation of Mexican laborers during World War I. With
hopes that up to five thousand Mexican workers could "solve [the] question of common labor in the South," a federal labor official invited three
hundred Arkansas farmers to attend a New Orleans meeting about the
promise of Mexican labor for the region's rural areas in 1918.[19]

The U.S. government's Mexican labor recruitment policy during World
War I was largely informal: approaching Mexican government officials
to ask for their cooperation in recruiting workers. But these efforts were
fragmented and amounted to little more than allowing private labor recruiters to operate along the border. U.S. laws that prohibited the entry
of previously contracted workers made U.S. government participation
dicey, while local and state governments in Mexico attempted to manage
migration according to their own labor and remittance needs, not Mexico
City's agenda.[20] Neither the U.S. nor Mexican federal states exerted much
influence over migration routes or conditions before World War II, and
Southern planters' hopes for a massive federal effort on their behalf were
dashed.

Unable to secure federal subsidy for their labor recruitment plans,
Delta planters invested their own resources in the effort. In the 1910s
and 1920s, they followed the lead of agricultural bosses elsewhere in the
United States: they hired *enganchadores*, labor recruitment agencies that
operated in Texas and along the Mexican border. These agents promised

Mexican and Mexican American workers set wages and transported them to the agricultural fields of California, Arizona, the Midwest, and now the South. Whatever the destination, wages and conditions of work often bore little resemblance to those promised.[21]

During the 1920s, the loosely coordinated efforts of *enganchadores*, Mexican consuls, and the U.S. Employment Service brought thousands of Mexican workers to the Deep South—primarily to the Mississippi Delta, but also to rural Arkansas and Louisiana. At first these workers traveled there seasonally from Texas, with the largest number making the journey for the fall picking season. Their numbers peaked in 1925, when observers noted their presence on every plantation in the Mississippi Delta.[22]

Like their counterparts in 1950s Arkansas, interwar Mexican immigrants in 1920s Mississippi found the Mexican consulate to be their most useful source of political power. Yet the regime that the consulate represented was still young. The Mexican Revolution of 1910–1917 had ousted a development-focused dictatorship seen as "mother to foreigners and stepmother to Mexicans" and heralded a new era of working-class Mexican nationalism. The postrevolutionary government's paternalistic concept of *protección*, or protection of emigrants, grew out of its ideological commitment to being the authentic representative of Mexican workers from all social, economic, racial, and geographical backgrounds as well as its political need to gain legitimacy in the eyes of these diverse citizens.

The consulate in New Orleans did respond to the appeals of rural Mexican workers, but the help offered in the interwar years was usually more symbolic and rhetorical than it was concrete. If the force of a request from a foreign government to a state or local official was enough to sway the outcome, as in the case of the consul's successful efforts to win Mexicans' admission to white schools in Mississippi, then the consul was useful to its citizens in the Deep South. Yet in this period, consuls had little to offer their compatriots in the way of resources, and they almost never journeyed to visit them in their rural communities.[23] The Mexican federal state was still preoccupied with the basic work of consolidating its power domestically and helping the country's economy recover from the destruction of the revolution.

Liberal States and Migration Management

Once World War II began, labor recruitment cooperation between the Mexican and U.S. governments reached a new level of formalization. The two states created a transborder labor recruitment system governed by a bilateral contract and administered directly by federal bureaucrats on both sides of the border. Under the auspices of the bracero program, as it came to be known, the Mexican government would approve and select workers at recruitment centers in the Mexican interior, then transport the men to the Mexico-U.S. border. The U.S. government would then admit the men to the United States, medically inspect and "disinfect" them with pesticides, process them, and distribute them to private labor recruiters, who would, in turn, bring the men to labor sites as near as Texas and far as Washington State. For both the U.S. and Mexican governments, the program was an opportunity to exert control and enhance state authority over a migrant stream that had been, in practice, mostly unregulated.[24] For Mexican men, becoming a bracero meant embarking on an independent adventure or acquiring the capital that would allow him to provide for his family.[25] The program initially promised to alleviate wartime labor shortages and the attendant upward pressure on agricultural wages. But the program continued for two decades beyond World War II, bringing more than four million Mexican men to perform agricultural labor in the United States before it ended in 1964.[26]

While Georgia and Mississippi farmers did recruit small numbers of braceros, Arkansas was by far the most prominent contracting site in the Deep South. Around three hundred thousand braceros worked the Arkansas cotton fields between 1948 and 1964, in some years making up more than a third of all laborers there.[27] For Arkansas planters, the promise of the bracero program was continued access to cheap and available labor even as the postwar boom drew workers to cities and their control over African Americans deteriorated.

Yet the braceros who arrived to Arkansas frustrated white farmers' seemingly strategic use of the U.S. federal government by successfully enlisting the Mexican federal government to help them win greater rights. Thousands of Mexicans struck and protested on farms, and successfully appealed to the Mexican consulate for political support. Historians have either painted 1948–1953 as the period in which the Mexican government steadily lost control and bargaining power in the bracero program, or they have discounted the effectiveness of Mexican consuls entirely. This is because planters in the Southwest quickly learned that if the Mexican government made demands they did not want to meet, they could force its hand by replacing government-sanctioned workers with undocumented workers.[28]

However, more recent research shows that this tactic was only effective in the U.S. Southwest. Farther from the border, in the Pacific Northwest and the Deep South, farmers did not have consistent access to undocumented labor. This economic fact emboldened both direct bracero protest and Mexican consuls' demands for compliance with the bracero contract.[29] During the late 1940s and early 1950s in the Arkansas Delta, the targeted local efforts of activist Mexican bureaucrats effectively curtailed white farmers' unfettered access to low-cost Mexican labor. In so doing, Mexican migrants and bureaucrats placed a transnational weight on the Delta's political scale, promoting the Mexican version of New Deal liberalism to the dismay of farmers who had seen Mexican labor as a way to circumvent it.

Unlike Arkansas' poor white and African American cotton workers, who gained few or no rights in practice from their U.S. citizenship, Mexican braceros had citizenship rights in Mexico.[30] The practical meaning of this citizenship hinged on the ideologies and resources that emerged from a transborder conversation about the meanings of liberalism, nationalism, and rural development. The New Deal and *la revolución institucional* did not each develop in isolation, but rather in relationship with the other. Border-crossing intellectuals and reformers in the New Deal years included U.S. Bureau of Indian Affairs leaders and Mexican thinkers on *indigenismo*, disciples of John Dewey and Franz Boas and Mexican educational policy makers, officials from Franklin D. Roosevelt's U.S. Department of Agriculture and architects of the sweeping land reforms of Lázaro Cárdenas, and countless others.[31] As the U.S. federal government more directly entered the lives of ordinary citizens through infrastructure projects and made citizenship considerably more meaningful to urban workers through social insurance, labor regulation, and political engagement, the Mexican government pursued a parallel process of far greater scope: the integration of indigenous, European, and mestizo Mexicans into a single national identity served and represented by a strong central state. With the years of revolutionary upheaval past and the state well established by midcentury, the ruling Partido Revolucionario Mexicano, the Mexican Revolutionary Party, changed its name in 1946 to Partido Revolucionario Institucional (PRI), the Institutional Revolutionary Party. The change aptly captured the ethos of the regime at midcentury: the spirit of the revolution would be channeled, in theory, into the institutional apparatus of the state.

If the New Deal meant little to Southern rural workers in the 1950s, *la revolución institucional* meant much to those Southern rural workers who were also Mexican citizens. A typical bracero in 1950s Arkansas was reared during the populist land redistributions and oil nationalization of the 1930s and educated, if only for a few years, in schools that had become deliberate parts of the nationalist project.[32] He came of age in the 1940s, a decade marked by uneven economic expansion and the growth of the state apparatus, and signed on to the bracero program, which promised to be an engine of both.[33] Braceros brought these expectations of modernity and first-class citizenship with them to Arkansas. They knew their contracts required planters to provide food and breaks in transit from the border, meet minimum housing requirements, bring them to the doctor when sick, cover them with medical insurance, and pay them a minimum salary notwithstanding bad weather or illness. Caballero Calderón, Salas Ochoa, and the other braceros who escaped the fire on Scott's farm therefore believed they were on solid ground in demanding that Scott cover their losses from the blaze.

Like countless other groups of braceros, those on Scott's farm struck on their own but also activated the citizenship rights their state had promised them. The Mexican government's efforts at cross-class nation building extended beyond its physical borders through the paternalistic function of *protección*, protection of emigrants, at its consulates in the United States. Beginning immediately with their arrival to Arkansas in 1948, braceros began lodging complaints with the nearest Mexican consulates in New Orleans and San Antonio. Before long, the Mexican Secretariat of Foreign Relations (Secretaría de Relaciones Exteriores, or SRE) opened a consulate in Memphis specifically to oversee the Delta's bracero contracts.[34] Complaints from workers to the Memphis consul arrived via both phone and letter and represented not just individual workers but also groups.[35]

The consul whom SRE sent to Memphis, Ángel Cano del Castillo, rapidly developed a reputation among planters and braceros for his willingness to take up even the smallest of workers' petitions, and some braceros went to extreme lengths to call their plight to his attention. While some braceros could simply write the consulate and receive responses care of the farms where they were employed, others had to circumvent planters' attempts to monitor their phone conversations.[36] In another case, one hundred Mexican men set out for a hundred-mile walk to see the consulate in Memphis when they refused the bad food and low salaries on Terry Jamison's plantation; forty-nine made it while the other fifty-one got stranded along the way.[37] These men trudged for hours through the chilly Arkansas fall because they believed they could find meaningful help in their country's Memphis outpost.[38] Far more than their counterparts decades earlier in the Mississippi Delta, these men believed that as full citizens in a modern nation, Mexico, they were due better wages, working, and living conditions in the United States; they hoped and expected that Mexican consular representatives would use their political power to enforce their contracts.

Cross-Border Liberalism and the Fate of the New Deal

In this moment of expanding national states, braceros' choice to work through the Mexican federal government touched a nerve in rural Arkansas. Planters there had successfully resisted the incursion of New Deal legislation and federal oversight into their labor relationships. They had crushed the STFU, which in 1934 organized across race lines to demand "decent contracts and higher wages," organizing rights, improved housing conditions, and overall security—in other words, many of the rights that had been granted to industrial workers over the previous two decades.[39] Now to planters' chagrin, Mexican braceros were lodging demands notably similar to those of displaced black and white cotton workers. Between 1948 and 1953, braceros filed at least four hundred complaints to their consulate. Each complaint represented an average of two to three men, with some representing dozens of braceros. About a third focused on unpaid wages, with transportation, lodging, discrimination (usually wage discrimination), and medical care each representing a significant share as well.[40] Mexican workers were petitioning, in effect, for economic security. Miguel Santiago complained that he had been forced to pay for his own medicine, when it should have been the farmer's responsibility.[41] Braceros demanded that Byron Landres pay them for the days of work they lost when the labor contractor's truck broke down on its way to Arkansas. Others demanded pay, as stipulated in the bracero contract, when poor weather made it impossible to pick cotton.[42] In all, braceros advocated for shifting the burden of risk from workers to employers.

These demands emerged from a liberal worldview deeply opposed to planters'—a view in which states and employers, not workers, absorbed the economic risks of markets, weather, and other unforeseen factors such as a fire in worker housing. When Esteban Saldaña convinced his fellow braceros to go on strike because a poor cotton crop made it impossible to earn decent wages, he framed the struggle as a "fight for our rights."[43] A local U.S. Labor Department official, who, like many of his counterparts, was more sympathetic to employers than laborers, acknowledged this liberal worldview in a private conversation in 1953 with Arkansas's conservative segregationist Democratic representative E. C. Gathings. Decrying Consul Cano's "megalomaniac" actions on behalf of Mexican workers, the official noted that neither drought nor economic conditions would sway the consul into accepting less for Mexican workers. "Cano takes the position that these things have no bearing," he complained. "He says we gamble on the weather."[44] The question of who would "gamble" on unforeseen circumstances struck at the heart of the New Deal reforms and welfare capitalism that urban industrial workers had already begun to enjoy.

Although Southern planters had thus far resisted U.S. government attempts to bring a minimum wage to agriculture, they proved unable to defeat the Mexican government's advocacy: in 1952–1953, Mexicans became the first agricultural workers in Arkansas to earn a minimum wage. Bracero agreements stated that braceros should be paid the local prevailing wage or an amount "necessary to cover their living needs," whichever was higher. But during the early 1950s, consulates also set a floor for the bracero wage scale: $0.50 per hour or $2.50 per hundred pounds of cotton.[45] During the 1953–1954 picking season, farm jobs in other bracero-receiving areas had prevailing wages as low as $0.45–$0.60 per hour in Texas and as high as $1–$1.25 per hour in Oregon. In Arkansas, however, prevailing hourly wages were $0.30–$0.40.[46] Only in Arkansas was the prevailing hourly wage substantially below the bracero program's $0.50 floor. Thus, only in Arkansas did the Mexican government effectively set a minimum wage for its emigrant workers.

The minimum wage for Mexicans threatened the economic advantage over all cotton laborers that Arkansas planters had fought so hard to maintain.[47] Farmer Earl Beck Jr. worried, "If we would all start paying 50 cents an hour to the Mexicans our common day labor would expect the same, no matter if they are worth it or not."[48] The head of the Parkin Farmers' Association declared, "I do not believe that our farmers or our government should be put in the position so that Mexico can dictate the wage for our farm workers."[49] A Mississippi Delta official, testifying before Congress in 1950, expressed farmers' fundamental concern: that organized labor would say: "All right, you have entered into an agreement with the Mexican Government to furnish certain facilities, bedding, housing, insurance, a guaranty of minimum work hours. . . . We feel that we want that for our domestic workers as well."[50] Planters had recruited braceros specifically to keep labor costs down, yet now they faced the prospect that

Mexican government intervention would erode the regulation-free work environment they had so desperately fought to maintain while giving new inspiration to domestic workers in search of better conditions.

In taking on the Southern planter class, consular officials sought to bolster their image as champions of their countrymen in the United States. To retain legitimacy as Mexicans' representatives and stave off independent strikes, consular officials would have to deliver on at least some of their promises, and evidence suggests that they did. No matter, it seemed, was too small to merit "protection" and attention from Consul Cano and his office's bureaucrats. The office regularly collected unpaid wages in amounts as low as $1—the equivalent of two to three hours of work—per bracero and distributed them via check to braceros' homes in rural Mexico.[51] Consul Cano demanded a $2.50 refund from the farmer R. S. Bretherick for braceros who were inappropriately charged for their kitchen utensils.[52] He followed up on bounced checks.[53] He contacted insurance companies directly to ensure they made good on their bracero policies.[54] By the early 1950s, Arkansas planters had experienced confrontations with share-croppers, the departure of unsatisfied workers, and even organized labor strikes.[55] This was the first time they had to answer to any government for the routine abuse and theft to which they had long subjected their workers.

Although interventions on small matters provided a constant nuisance to farmers, the consulate's most significant tool for battle was the threat of blacklisting, which could threaten farmers' labor source, often after the crop had been planted. At various points, entire states, including Texas and Idaho, were prohibited from employing braceros because of widespread discrimination.[56] But historians have noted that the Mexican government's bargaining power in the bracero program slipped away after 1948, in part because the U.S. government undermined it by allowing undocumented workers to enter the country.[57] In 1949, the Mexican government lost the right to blacklist entire areas and could blacklist only individual employers. Yet while farmers in the Southwest had easier recourse to Tejano or undocumented labor, the threat of blacklisting remained strong in Arkansas and other states far from the border through 1954, when the Mexican government relinquished the right to unilaterally blacklist altogether.[58]

The Mexican consulate in Memphis did not always succeed in blacklisting employers, but it succeeded often enough to scare planters into compliance. Cano refused to renew contracts for employers that had matters such as unpaid wages pending with the consulate.[59] Longview Farms' bracero request in 1950 was rejected as a result of contract noncompliance the year before.[60] John B. Luckie owed back wages to braceros from 1951, and he remained unable to contract for at least the following five years because he had refused to pay up.[61] The consulate's threat of blacklisting in Arkansas posed a real threat to planters' access to Mexican workers.

Those planters had fought off U.S. federal intervention into the labor conditions on their farms for decades, only to face this intervention from a different federal government during the bracero program. When J. S. Cecil found himself on the ineligible list, he threw up his hands and declared that he did not want any more Mexican workers anyway.[62] But consular interventions and contractual obligations notwithstanding, most farmers desperately wanted to continue employing Mexicans, and they fought hard to do so. They made their case to Representative Gathings, Senators John McClellan and J. William Fulbright, the Mexican embassy in Washington, the consul himself, or USES representatives. Leo Powell tried to circumvent his blacklist status by contracting braceros under his father's name.[63] Convinced that the only real problem with the bracero arrangement was Consul Cano's "personality problem," planters conspired with Gathings and Fulbright to have Cano removed from his post. They portrayed Cano as an outside agitator, suggesting that braceros themselves had no problem with their living and working conditions in Arkansas. A. H. Barnhill, for example, complained that "it was not until after they talked to the consul that they complained of the blankets being wet."[64] His comment, of course, ignored the fact that bracero complaints brought Cano to his farm in the first place.

The case of the fire on Scott's farm exemplifies these dynamics. The workers first approached Consul Cano to enlist his help in recovering the property that had incinerated that October night. In talking with the workers, Cano discovered other potential violations of the bracero contract on the farm. He arranged to meet the petitioning braceros, Scott, and USES representative Roy Bronander at the Arkansas State Employment Office in Pine Bluff several days later.[65]

At the meeting, Cano demanded that Scott reimburse the braceros for their losses. But Bronander told Scott the fire had been an act of God for which he bore no responsibility. Unsurprisingly, Scott refused to pay.[66] Interviews with braceros revealed other alleged violations of the bracero contract. Braceros said they had no access to toilets, water, or clothes-washing facilities, as well as inadequate mattresses and cooking supplies. They had not been given required breaks on the drive from the border, and they were not being paid the prevailing wage of the area.

With the men still on strike, Bronander prevailed upon Cano to instruct them to return to work immediately; in exchange, Scott would agree to correct the violations within five days. The consul eventually acquiesced, assuring workers that he would refer the matter of fire damages to his consulting attorney for a civil suit and would visit the farm in five days to inspect its conditions. Incensed at Scott's unwillingness to reimburse them for the fire damages, eight workers asked to return to Mexico, five requested a transfer to another employer, and nineteen decided to remain on the farm.[67] Those who returned to Mexico would petition Mexico's secretary of labor two weeks later from their homes in Tuitán, Durango, expressing their dissatisfaction with Consul Cano's apparent inability to successfully recover their losses from the fire.[68]

When Cano and Bronander met up at Scott's farm in England, Arkansas, five days later, they found conditions as abject as braceros had described. In one worker's house, only four of nine men had proper beds; the others slept on mattresses on the floor. Cooking stoves lay amid the sleeping quarters. The house had no screens on doors or windows, no facilities for washing clothes, and no toilets. Because of a broken water pump, the men had to carry any water they needed up from a nearby creek. There was only one pot and one pan for eighteen men. Cano concluded that the men's living conditions clearly violated the terms of the bracero contract.[69]

Yet on the matter of wages, it seemed, the bracero program had pushed Scott to pay all of his workers more—exactly as cotton farmers had feared. Interviews with braceros Juan Gonzáles, Bonifacio Reyes, and Blás Bétanqur revealed that the men were paid $2.50 per hundred pounds of cotton—the lowest permissible wage under the bracero contract. Yet because of Arkansas's uniquely low wages, the bracero minimum wage effectively created a new earnings floor for all of Scott's workers. African Americans Ruth Malvin, Charlie Lewis, Manuel Whitehead, Eli Jackson, J. H. Howell, and J. Modlin told Cano and Bronander that they had been earning $2.00 per hundred pounds of cotton until the day braceros arrived, when their rate was raised to $2.50.[70] These U.S. citizen workers had not benefited from the New Deal but had gotten a raise thanks to *la revolución institucional*.

As the story shows, the Mexican government's "protection" of Mexican workers more effectively promoted the New Deal's ideals in rural Arkansas than did New Dealers themselves. Like Bronander, local representatives of the U.S. Labor Department on the ground in Arkansas were generally sympathetic to farmers, not workers.[71] Liberal federal bureaucrats in Washington, DC, were still more than a decade away from forcing any type of labor regulation on the white Southern planters who, in the 1950s, remained key constituents in the Democratic Party.

Mexican citizens and the Mexican state, in contrast, did succeed in exerting some of the authority accorded to them in the bracero contract. Notwithstanding evidence of wage compliance, Consul Cano sought to blacklist Scott for his myriad violations while Bronander resisted the idea. The matter was elevated to the Mexican embassy in Washington, DC, which resolved it four months later, in early 1953. An embassy official and a DC-based U.S. Labor Department official agreed that although Scott could be given the benefit of the doubt on several of the accusations against him, there was no reasonable explanation for the lack of toilet and bathing facilities. Hence, they blacklisted Scott from future bracero contracting. To be removed from the list, Scott would have to submit his farm to an inspection by both U.S. and Mexican officials.[72] He and planters like him had long held a monopoly on rights in the employer-employee relationship. Now, the advocacy of Mexican citizens to their government had brought two states to bear on regulating the farmer's labor practices.

Although no government directly forced Scott to raise his black workers' wages to parity with Mexicans', he did so nonetheless because he knew that domestic workers' expectations would be raised by the bracero rates. Given African Americans' increased mobility in the postwar period, outrage at this injustice could well have caused the loss of Scott's black labor force altogether. In 1954, for example, African American truck drivers in Memphis complained to Memphis's black community leader George W. Lee that Mexicans were earning more than blacks for cotton labor in the Arkansas Delta. Lee lodged a formal protest with Memphis's Republican congressman Carroll Reece, claiming that African American laborers were paid $0.30 per hour for cotton chopping while Mexicans were paid $0.50.[73] On July 14, 1954, Reece staged a huge picnic in Memphis's Lincoln Park for the workers to present an "appreciation petition" to himself and Reece for their attempts to bring blacks' wages to parity with Mexicans'. Drawing on these workers' immediate personal and family histories of rural labor, the petition decried foreigners' superior treatment over those whose "fore-parents have toiled in the hot and chilly rains from season to season to plant, cultivate and harvest cotton." More than one thousand black workers ate barbecue and watermelon, singing songs and playing games with their children before piling into crew leaders' buses to go register to vote.[74]

As newly urban African Americans couched their protests in the language and symbols of emancipation and citizenship, rural white wage laborers embraced the populist rhetoric of the STFU in demanding the same rights as braceros. One man wrote his congressman in 1961: "Why should the Mexicans that are brought into Arkansas for farm work be treated better than a United States Citizen? . . . His living quarters must meet specifications. His electricity, gas, dishes, bedding, etc. are furnished. There is a minimum wage paid him, if weather does not permit him to work. . . . I would rather be a citizen of Mexico, so I could be sent here to work on their kind of terms." Unlike industrial workers who had similar guarantees, he contended, American agricultural workers were the "lost sheep of the employment world."[75] For poor white and black workers in the mid-South, not only distant factory workers but also nearby braceros provided concrete evidence that greater employment security and higher wages should be basic conditions of modern life and citizenship.

The Fall of *La revolución institucional*

By the late 1950s, the Mexican government's reduced authority in binational contracts led the Memphis consulate to lose its effectiveness alongside its counterparts elsewhere in the United States. Braceros' working conditions fell with it. The state's loss of authority abroad foreshadowed its loss of authority at home over the following decade. The bracero program ended in 1964, further limiting the Mexican federal government's role in the lives of its emigrants. And in any case, the so-called golden age of Mexican liberal nationalism was coming to an end, giving way to the neoliberal governing ideology that came to dominate the Mexican political scene in the 1980s. To date, the period of the late 1940s through mid-1950s in areas far from the border, particularly Arkansas, represents a high point in the Mexican government's effectiveness as a protector of its emigrant citizens' labor rights. The Deep South's Mexican agricultural workers experienced their state's new neoliberal order more than a decade ahead of their nonmigrant counterparts, though with no fancy ideology yet attached to it.

Mexican immigrants who migrated to the Deep South during the 1970s–1990s came of age during and after the decline of the Mexican state's economic and rhetorical support for social justice and the poor.[76] PRI leaders increasingly used violence on their own people over the course of the

1960s, culminating in the massacre of student protesters in Mexico City's Tlatelolco district in 1968. The massacre highlighted the state's loss of control over the narrative of Mexican political development, exposing severe internal fissures both nationally and internationally.[77] The economic crisis of the 1980s, known as Mexico's "lost decade," cemented the loss of public faith in the PRI while depriving the state of the resources needed to fund its huge apparatus. It also accelerated the ruling party's withdrawal from the policies of economic protectionism and state intervention in the economy. By 1992, two-thirds of rural Mexicans were laborers, not landowners.[78] Presidents and party leaders were promoting the notion that Mexican nationalism and sovereignty would be best advanced not through cross-class solidarity, but by ensuring Mexico's competitiveness in the global market.[79]

Developments in Mexico not only shaped Mexican immigrants' expectations of citizenship and labor; they also neutralized what had once been their most important ally in the Deep South: Mexican consulates. The rise of undocumented immigration eliminated Mexican bureaucrats' erstwhile role as intermediaries with the power to cut off the labor supply from uncooperative farmers. Although Mexico opened a consulate in Atlanta during the late 1970s, it dealt with business and trade matters, not migrant protection in its early years.[80] Even once the Atlanta consular staff began visiting migrant work sites in the mid-1980s, they involved themselves only in individuals' legal matters, mostly supporting criminal defendants or workers trying to collect unpaid wages.[81] The consular corps' retreat from its onetime role as defender of Mexicans' collective rights in the Deep South reflected the new emphasis on individual over group claims in Mexican political discourse, as well as a lack of sufficient budget and personnel to meaningfully complete the work of *protección*.[82]

From the perspectives of migrants, the disaffection was mutual. Having lived through "the end of faith in the Leviathan" of the Mexican state, the Deep South's Mexican immigrants mistrusted and evaded consular officials rather than turning to them for support.[83] When Mexican officials visited Cedartown, Georgia, in 1985, for example, Mexican workers at a meatpacking plant reported that they had not "been harassed by any group or person in this town"—a finding belied by anti-Mexican violence there just two years earlier.[84] Similarly, when Mexican officials responded to a newspaper article about anti-Mexican discrimination in Gainesville, Georgia, they were told by immigrants there that "at the moment they did not have any problem with authorities or civilians in this community."[85]

While Mexican immigrants three decades before walked dozens of miles and risked employer retribution to involve consuls in their struggles, by the 1980s they no longer believed that Mexican citizenship gave them, poor emigrants, the ability to make claims on the Mexican state.

Conclusion

From the Depression through the civil rights movement, the New Deal and U.S. federal government had little to offer the Deep South's Mexican migrants not because they were foreigners or because they labored in the U.S. South, but because they were agricultural workers. In contrast, the rise and fall of *la revolución institucional*—the political, economic, and cultural power of Mexican liberal nationalism—structured the expectations and political possibilities of Mexican workers there from the 1920s through 1990s. The two countries' visions of strong modern states providing economic security for their citizens developed in sustained conversation with each other. Unlike its U.S. counterpart, the more inclusive Mexican ideology offered real inspiration to Mexican agricultural workers in the Deep South, as well as real leverage in this area far from the Mexico-U.S. border.

As the Mexican state consolidated rule in the 1920s and 1930s, its consulate in New Orleans responded with limited resources and efficacy to the concerns of Mexican migrants in the Mississippi Delta. But when state-managed bracero migrants arrived to the Arkansas Delta in 1948, those workers reimported the New Deal, bringing the heightened expectations and robust political resources of *la revolución institucional*. While Mexicans in the U.S. Southwest found their leverage reduced by farmers' access to undocumented workers, the lack of such options in the Arkansas Delta empowered both braceros and their consul to demand compliance with the broad guarantees in the bracero contract. From 1948–1954, this power forced Arkansas planters to submit to government oversight of their labor conditions and offer agricultural workers a minimum wage for the first time in the area's history.

The current abject circumstances of Mexican and other Latino farmworkers in the Deep South therefore cannot be explained as simply a Juan Crow system that rose in the 1980s to replace Jim Crow's labor arrangements. Indeed, Mexicans worked in the Deep South throughout the Jim Crow period. Their experiences and effects, however, were not always predictable. For a brief but important period in the postwar years, braceros brought Mexican liberalism to Arkansas, indirectly securing higher wages for some white and black workers.

Along with other chapters in this volume, the rise and fall of the Mexican New Deal in the U.S. South reminds us that the histories of liberalism and neoliberalism are more complex than previously appreciated. For one, liberal ideas and policies moved around the world, entering the United States in unexpected ways. Because of historical contingencies, the Mexican version of liberalism commanded greater authority in the U.S. South than elsewhere. A more complex view of liberalism also invites a more expansive understanding of neoliberalism. While material and rhetorical bonds between citizens and the state may have risen and then fallen from 1930 to 1980 for the white middle class, other groups in the United States experienced these shifts on different timelines.[86] For most agricultural workers, the liberal moment barely came at all, but some Mexican agricultural workers did experience it the 1940s and 1950s. Rather than the Reagan revolution, the weakening of the bracero agreement in 1954, followed by the decline of Mexican state authority in the 1960s, prompted the actual fall of Mexican workers' New Deal order in the Deep South.

Notes

1. List of Losses—Coy Scott Farm, folder TM-10-30, Archive of the Secretariat of Foreign Relations, Mexico City (Archivo Histórico de la Secretaría de Relaciones Exteriores, AHSRE).

2. Facts in the Case of Coy Scott, folder TM-10-30, AHSRE.

3. Kenneth Finegold and Theda Skocpol, *State and Party in America's New Deal* (Madison: University of Wisconsin Press, 1995), 143.

4. Cindy Hahamovitch, *The Fruits of Their Labor: Atlantic Coast Farmworkers and the Making of Migrant Poverty, 1870–1945* (Chapel Hill: University of North Carolina Press, 1997).

5. Nan Elizabeth Woodruff, *American Congo: The African American Freedom Struggle in the Delta* (Chapel Hill: University of North Carolina Press, 2012).

6. Woodruff, *American Congo*; James C. Cobb, *The Most Southern Place on Earth: The Mississippi Delta and the Roots of Regional Identity* (New York: Oxford University Press, 1992).

7. Mary E. Odem and Elaine Lacy, eds., *Latino Immigrants and the Transformation of the U.S. South* (Athens: University of Georgia Press, 2009).

8. Robert Lovato, "Juan Crow in Georgia," *Nation*, May 26, 2008; Angela Stuesse and Laura E. Helton, "Low-Wage Legacies, Race, and the Golden Chicken in Mississippi: Where Contemporary Immigration Meets African American La-

bor History," *Southern Spaces* (2013), http://southernspaces.org/2013/low-wage-leg
acies-race-and-golden-chicken-mississippi.

9. Quoted in Moon-Ho Jung, *Coolies and Cane: Race, Labor, and Sugar in the Age of Emancipation* (Baltimore: Johns Hopkins University Press, 2006), 78.

10. James W. Loewen, *The Mississippi Chinese: Between Black and White* (Cambridge, MA: Harvard University Press, 1971).

11. Cobb, *Most Southern Place*, 110–11; Ernesto R. Milani, "Peonage at Sunnyside and the Reaction of the Italian Government," *Arkansas Historical Quarterly* 50, no. 1 (1991): 30–39; Robert L. Brandfon, "The End of Immigration to the Cotton Fields," *Mississippi Valley Historical Review* 50, no. 4 (1964): 591–611.

12. Rowland T. Berthoff, "Southern Attitudes toward Immigration 1865–1914," *Journal of Southern History* 17, no. 3 (1951): 328–60; Brandfon, "End of Immigration"; Jung, *Coolies and Cane.*

13. Devra Weber, *Dark Sweat, White Gold: California Farm Workers, Cotton, and the New Deal* (Berkeley: University of California Press, 1994); John Weber, *From South Texas to the Nation: The Exploitation of Mexican Labor in the Twentieth Century* (Chapel Hill: University of North Carolina Press, 2015); David Montejano, *Anglos and Mexicans in the Making of Texas, 1836–1986* (Austin: University of Texas Press, 1987); and Neil Foley, *The White Scourge: Mexicans, Blacks, and Poor Whites in Texas Cotton Culture* (Berkeley: University of California Press, 1997).

14. Sarah E. Cornell, "Americans in the U.S. South and Mexico: A Transnational History of Race, Slavery, and Freedom, 1810–1910" (PhD diss., New York University, 2008), 262–68.

15. Bureau of the Census Department of Commerce, ed., *Thirteenth Census of the United States Taken in the Year 1910* (Washington, DC: Government Printing Office, 1913), 1044–59.

16. Pete Daniel, *Breaking the Land: The Transformation of Cotton, Tobacco, and Rice Cultures since 1880* (Urbana: University of Illinois Press, 1985), 9.

17. Woodruff, *American Congo*, 41–49; James R. Grossman, *Land of Hope: Chicago, Black Southerners, and the Great Migration* (Chicago: University of Chicago Press, 1989), 38–59.

18. Woodruff, *American Congo*, 61–62.

19. "Plan to Bring in Mexican Laborers," *Arkansas Gazette*, August 11 1918. I am grateful to Story Matkin-Rawn for sending me this primary source.

20. Fernando Saúl Alanís Enciso, *El primer programa bracero y el gobierno de México, 1917–1918* (San Luis Potosí, Mexico: El Colegio de San Luis, 1999).

21. Enciso, *El primer programa bracero*, 35–38; and Dennis Nodín Valdés, *Al Norte: Agricultural Workers in the Great Lakes Region, 1917–1970* (Austin: University of Texas Press, 1991), 9–11.

22. Julie M. Weise, *Corazón de Dixie: Mexicanos in the U.S. South since 1910* (Chapel Hill: University of North Carolina Press, 2015), 51–81.

23. Weise, *Corazón de Dixie.*

24. Kitty Calavita, *Inside the State: The Bracero Program, Immigration and the INS* (New York: Routledge, 1992); and Deborah Cohen, *Braceros: Migrant Citizens and Transnational Subjects in the Postwar United States and Mexico* (Chapel Hill: University of North Carolina Press, 2011).

25. Ana Elizabeth Rosas, *Abrazando el Espíritu: Bracero Families Confront the US-Mexico Border* (Berkeley: University of California Press, 2014); and Mireya Loza, *Defiant Braceros: How Migrant Workers Fought for Racial, Sexual, and Political Freedom* (Chapel Hill: University of North Carolina Press, 2016).

26. Calavita, *Inside the State*; Cohen, *Braceros*; Rosas, *Abrazando el Espíritu*; Ernesto Galarza, *Merchants of Labor: The Mexican Bracero Story* (Charlotte, NC: McNally & Loftin, 1964); and Erasmo Gamboa, *Mexican Labor and World War II: Braceros in the Pacific Northwest, 1942–1947* (Austin: University of Texas Press, 1990).

27. This extrapolates from Holley's calculation that 251,298 braceros worked in Arkansas between 1953 and 1965, and uses his figures for braceros as a part of the overall cotton labor force during those years. Donald Holley, *The Second Great Emancipation: The Mechanical Cotton Picker, Black Migration, and How They Shaped the Modern South* (Fayetteville: University of Arkansas Press, 2000), 152.

28. Deborah Cohen, "Caught in the Middle: The Mexican State's Relationship with the United States and Its Own Citizen-Workers, 1942–1954," *Journal of American Ethnic History* 20, no. 3 (2001): 110–32; Calavita, *Inside the State*, 27–28; Manuel T. García y Griego, *The Importation of Mexican Contract Laborers to the United States, 1942–1964: Antecedents, Operation, and Legacy* (La Jolla: Program in United States–Mexican Studies, University of California, San Diego, 1981).

29. Mario Jimenez Sifuentez, *Of Forests and Fields: Mexican Labor in the Pacific Northwest* (New Brunswick, NJ: Rutgers University Press, 2016); Weise, *Corazón de Dixie*, 82–119; Gamboa, *Mexican Labor and World War II*.

30. On the limits of "free" labor in the absence of citizenship rights, see Woodruff, *American Congo*, 3–4.

31. Mauricio Tenorio Trillo, "The Cosmopolitan Mexican Summer, 1920–1949," *Latin American Research Review* 32, no. 3 (1997): 224–42; Helen Delpar, *The Enormous Vogue of Things Mexican: Cultural Relations between the United States and Mexico, 1920–1935* (Tuscaloosa: University of Alabama Press, 1992); Carlos Kevin Blanton, *George I. Sánchez: The Long Fight for Mexican American Integration* (New Haven, CT: Yale University Press, 2014); Ruben Flores, *Backroads Pragmatists: Mexico's Melting Pot and Civil Rights in the United States* (Philadelphia: University of Pennsylvania Press, 2014); and Tore C. Olsson, *Agrarian Crossings: Reformers and the Remaking of the U.S. and Mexican Countryside* (Princeton, NJ: Princeton University Press, 2017).

32. Vaughan, *Cultural Politics in Revolution*.

33. Cohen, *Braceros*.

34. Report about the Protection Case of the Mexican Workers of the Area of Pine Bluff, Arkansas, November 22, 1948, folder 1453/3, Archive of the Embassy of Mexico in the United States (AEMEUA).

35. Rafael Jiménez Castro, Consul in New Orleans, to Consul General of Mexico, San Antonio, October 29, 1949, folder 1453/3, AEMEUA.

36. See, for example, Cano del Castillo to Casildo Caldera Hurtado c/o Crain Company, Wilson Arkansas, September 19, 1952, folder TM-10-25, AHSRE; and Report of Consul Angel Cano del Castillo about the official commission that was conferred in Pine Bluff, Arkansas, November 15, 1948, folder 1453/3, AEMEUA.

37. AP, "Triste odisea de cien pizcadores mexicanos," *La Prensa*, November 24 1951.

38. Based on local weather data for November 23, 1951, from the National Climatic Data Center, http://www.ncdc.noaa.gov.

39. Howard Kester, *Revolt among the Sharecroppers* (New York: Covici Friede Publishers, 1936), 72.

40. This analysis extrapolates from a careful analysis of thirty-nine out of the ninety-six folders in Mexico's Foreign Relations archive relating to Arkansas employers, dated 1948–1953.

41. A. Cano to Ed McDonald, September 22, 1953, folder TM-10-22, AHSRE.

42. A. Cano to Ed McDonald, October 20, 1953, folder TM-23-15, AHSRE.

43. Esteban Saldaña, interview with Myrna Parra-Mantilla, Bracero Archive Item #49, http://braceroarchive.org/items/show/49.

44. Conversation between Mr. P. M. Kenefick, Mr. Holly, and Mr. Gathings, July 28, 1953, folder 4155, box 272—Farm Labor—Mexican, E. C. Gathings Papers, Arkansas State University, Blytheville (ECG).

45. Robert C. Goodwin, director, U.S. Department of Labor Bureau of Employment Security, to Hon. E. C. Gathings, April 21, 1952, folder 4153, box 272—Farm Labor—Mexican, ECG.

46. Rocco Siciliano, assistant secretary of labor, to E. C. Gathings, March 31, 1955, folder 4464, box 298—Foreign Agricultural Labor, ECG.

47. On Florida planters' opposition to minimum wage for domestic workers, see Cindy Hahamovitch, *No Man's Land: Jamaican Guestworkers in America and the Global History of Deportable Labor* (Princeton, NJ: Princeton University Press, 2011), 46 (Kindle ed.).

48. Earl C. Beck Jr. to E. C. Gathings, April 4, 1952, folder 4153, box 272—Farm Labor—Mexican, ECG.

49. E. D. McKnight, Parkin Farmer's Association, to Don Larin, March 14, 1952, folder 4153, box 272—Farm Labor—Mexican, ECG.

50. Testimony of J. C. Baird, president of the Delta Council, October 2, before the House Committee on Agriculture, *Farm Labor Investigation: Hearings*, 1950.

51. See, for example, the entire folder TM-9-19, AHSRE.

52. A. Cano del Castillo to W. B. McFarland, March 13, 1952, folder TM-6-3, AHSRE.

53. Cano del Castillo to McDonald, March 14, 1952, folder TM-24-31, AHSRE.

54. A. Cano del Castillo to Ed McDonald, December 18, 1952, folder TM-11-29, AHSRE.

55. Woodruff, *American Congo*.

56. Gamboa, *Mexican Labor and World War II*, 113; Galarza, *Merchants of Labor*, 77.

57. Cohen, "Caught in the Middle."

58. Mae M. Ngai, *Impossible Subjects: Illegal Aliens and the Making of Modern America* (Princeton, NJ: Princeton University Press, 2004), 146. Gamboa, in *Mexican Labor and World War II*, and Sifuentez, in *Of Forests and Fields*, observe a similar phenomenon in the case of the Pacific Northwest.

59. A. Cano del Castillo to Ed McDonald, November 6, 1952, folder TM-6-3; A. Cano to M. W. McFarland, U.S. Department of Labor, Dallas, June 16, 1952, folder TM-24-31, AHSRE.

60. Telegram from J. W. Fulbright to Gov. Homer Adkins, September 20, 1950, Homer Adkins Papers, Arkansas State Archives, Little Rock.

61. Arturo Garza Cantú, vice consul in Memphis, to Embassy of Mexico, Washington, DC, May 9, 1956, folder TM-67-20, AHSRE.

62. Paul Kenefick to Rafael Aveleyra, consul general of Mexico, Washington, DC, August 15, 1952, folder TM-23-16, AHSRE.

63. A. Cano to Ed McDonald, September 8, 1953, folder Leo Powell, AHSRE.

64. A. H. Barnhill to Ed McDonald, May 13, 1953, folder 4463, box 298—Foreign Agricultural Labor, ECG.

65. Joint Investigation Report, folder TM-10-30, AHSRE.

66. Facts in the Case of Coy Scott, folder TM-10-30, AHSRE.

67. Facts in the Case of Coy Scott.

68. Al C. Ministro de Trabajo y Prevención Social, October 27, 1952, folder TM-11-22, AHSRE.

69. Joint Investigation Report.

70. Joint Investigation Report.

71. For an example of the efforts of DC bureaucrats, see Paul M. Kenefick, special assistant to the secretary of labor, to Senor Hector Blanco-Melo, Mexican Embassy, September 18, 1952, folder TM-11-26, AHSRE. On long-standing patterns of local federal employees beholden to local power structures thwarting DC-initiated liberal initiatives in the South, see Pete Daniel, *The Shadow of Slavery: Peonage in the South, 1901–1969* (Urbana: University of Illinois Press, 1972), 149–66.

72. Joint Decision in Re: Coy Scott, February 25, 1953, folder TM-11-22, AHSRE.

73. "Probe Bias in Cotton Labor Wages," *Tri-State Defender* (*Memphis*), July 17, 1954. Thanks to Story Matkin-Rawn for leading me to this article.

74. "Cotton Workers Express Gratitude for Petition During Picnic Here," *Memphis World*, July 30, 1954.

75. W. J. Stoddard, Brookland, Arkansas, to E. C. Gathings, April 10, 1961, folder 4136, box 271—Farm Labor and Foreign Agricultural Labor, ECG.

76. Michael W. Foley, "Agenda for Mobilization: The Agrarian Question and Popular Mobilization in Contemporary Mexico," *Latin American Research Review* 26, no. 2 (1991).

77. Eric Zolov, *Refried Elvis: The Rise of the Mexican Counterculture* (Berkeley: University of California Press, 1999); and Sergio Aguayo, *1968: Los archivos de la violencia* (Mexico City: Editorial Grijalbo, 1998).

78. Michael W. Foley, "Privatizing the Countryside: The Mexican Peasant Movement and Neoliberal Reform," *Latin American Perspectives* 22, no. 1 (1995): 59–76.

79. Gavin O'Toole, "A New Nationalism for a New Era: The Political Ideology of Mexican Neoliberalism," *Bulletin of Latin American Research* 22, no. 3 (2003): 269–90.

80. Héctor Mena, former consul of Mexico in Atlanta, telephone interview with the author, January 29, 2008.

81. Visits to Work Sites, 1986, AHSRE IV-432-3 1ª parte; "Opinion" of Consul Luisa Virginia Junco, September 8, 1987, AHSRE IV-432-3 8ª parte; "Opinion" of Minister Luisa Virginia Junco, Consul of Mexico in Atlanta, August 25, 1986, AHSRE IV-343-2 2ª parte.

82. "Opinion" of Minister Luisa Virginia Junco, consul of Mexico in Atlanta, July 31, 1986, AHSRE IV-343-2 2ª parte; O'Toole, *New Nationalism for a New Era*.

83. "Opinion" of Junco.

84. Teodoro Alonso to Luisa Virginia Junco, February 21, 1985, folder IV-343-1 1ª parte, AHSRE.

85. "Opinion"—attachment to letter 874, June 1, 1987, folder IV-432-3 6ª parte, AHSRE.

86. Steve Fraser and Gary Gerstle, *The Rise and Fall of the New Deal Order, 1930–1980* (Princeton, NJ: Princeton University Press, 1989).

PART II

Crisis and Continuity

CHAPTER SIX

The Short End of Both Sticks

Property Assessments and Black Taxpayer Disadvantage in Urban America

Andrew W. Kahrl

In 2013, the city of Detroit filed for bankruptcy, the largest city to do so and the largest municipal filing of its kind in U.S. history. In the years that followed, as the city presided over draconian cuts to its budget and pension plans, it also searched for new revenue sources and aggressively pursued uncollected debts. It sold off public lands and other assets to private investors. It increased parking violations in the city's downtown by 450 percent. It cut off water services to residents who had failed to pay their bills. And it foreclosed on the homes of residents who had fallen behind on their property taxes. Between 2011 and 2015, Wayne County's treasurer foreclosed on one of every four properties in Detroit for non-payment of taxes, the highest property-tax foreclosure rate in any U.S. city since the Great Depression. Austerity-minded officials and longtime critics of the Motor City's black political leadership celebrated the mass evictions of so-called tax deadbeats as a welcome sign that the city was finally getting its fiscal house in order and enforcing citizens' compliance with the law.[1]

But as hundreds of thousands of Detroit families faced eviction over unpaid property-tax debts, critics began to question the basis of those property-tax obligations. They soon discovered that, while the Great Recession sent property values in this and other metropolitan housing markets plummeting, it did not result in a commensurate readjustment in the assessed values used to determine property taxes. Under Michigan state law, the assessed value of a property cannot be more than 50 percent of its market value. In Detroit in 2010, assessments were, on average, 7.3 times higher than the legal limit. In 2015, they remained 2.1 times higher than the legal limit. The lower the value of the property, the higher the disparity. That, combined with the persistence of racial segregation in housing markets and the market penalty inflicted on black neighborhoods, meant that African American homeowners and renters were forced to pay higher property taxes and bore the brunt of the city's aggressive tax foreclosure program.[2]

In its rush to collect revenue, the county indiscriminately foreclosed and auctioned off homes owned by its poorest and most vulnerable residents. For example, a disabled African American retiree purchased a home in Detroit for $2,500 in 2012 and lost it to tax foreclosure in 2017. This, despite being eligible for a tax exemption based on his income, and despite the home's being appraised by the city as worth $49,824, nearly twenty times its market value. "This whole mess makes me feel like I was stuck up and robbed," he later commented. He was not alone. By one estimate, more than one hundred thousand Detroit families have lost their homes to tax foreclosures based on unconstitutional overassessments.[3]

While Detroiters suffered, local officials, creditors, and bond markets celebrated. Since 2008, the imposition of higher interest rates on unpaid taxes and foreclosure and auctioning of tax-delinquent properties has generated more than $421 million in revenue for Wayne County and has played a critical role in erasing a $22.5 million deficit. More than merely relying on citizens' misfortunes, the systematic overassessment of property (in particular, in poor and minority neighborhoods) indicates the role local governments can play in creating those misfortunes.[4] Law professor Bernadette Atuahene, who uncovered the problem and has since led the fight against tax foreclosures, labels Detroit's revenue-generating scheme a form of "stategraft," defined as the expropriation of property by state agents in violation of state laws and in the service of the state's financial interests.[5] Others characterize Detroit's efforts to balance its budget through water shutoffs and tax foreclosures targeting the city's poor, all the while offering generous tax breaks to lure businesses to and spur development in its downtown, as a quintessentially neoliberal approach to urban governance.[6] The current crisis facing homeowners in Detroit also sheds light on a powerful if often invisible instrument of white privilege and black disadvantage in twentieth- and twenty-first-century America— property assessments—one whose history forces us to question just how "neo" many of the ideas and practices associated with neoliberalism are.

The overassessment of African American property owners is almost as old as African American property ownership in America. As N. D. B. Connolly's chapter in this volume demonstrates, African Americans' relationship to both property and taxes is long and complicated. As black men and women struggled to build a land base in the post-Emancipation South, local white assessors routinely—and systematically—overassessed the value of black-owned property, forcing disfranchised black populations to pay more in taxes for fewer and far inferior public services. When African Americans migrated to northern cities during the first half of the twentieth century, discriminatory modes of property taxation followed them there.

Biased assessments played an instrumental role in the uneven development of American cities from the 1950s through the 1970s. Although discriminatory assessments were as much the product of bureaucratic inaction as the deliberate actions of racist officials, they still increased the cost of living and further decreased the value of property in black neighborhoods in cities across the country. They made overtaxed homeowners more vulnerable to tax delinquency and to the loss of their home to tax foreclosure. They led to property abandonment, sped neighborhood deterioration, and stymied attempts at recovery and revitalization. And yet, despite the patent unfairness of assessments, its negative impact on black families' struggles to acquire property and build wealth, and its corrosive effects on black neighborhoods as a whole, racist property assessments remained a peripheral civil rights issue, capable of generating sporadic instances of heated outrage but unable to generate any mass movements for reform. Black taxpayers' struggle to be heard stands in stark contrast to white suburban homeowners, who during these same years led successful tax revolts that resulted in immediate—and often dramatic—tax reductions and tight constraints on future increases, and fueled the rise of a conservative anti-tax revolution that would profoundly influence tax policy and politics at the federal, state, and local level for decades to come. Scholarship on taxpayer politics in modern America similarly privileges white taxpayers' interests and influence to the virtual exclusion of African Americans, who are invariably cast as the object of white taxpayers' ire, never as taxpayers in their own right.[7]

African Americans' experience as taxpayers does more than deepen our understanding of how local governments administered racial privileges and disadvantages. It also reveals deep and enduring ties linking America's Jim Crow past to its neoliberal present. In cities today, critics invoke the term *neoliberalism* to describe the underlying interests behind

tax policies favoring the wealthy and serving the interests of land speculators and corporate investors. But as this chapter shows, many of the
features of urban governance that critics today describe as neoliberal are
rooted in the administrative practices and prerogatives of the Jim Crow
state, then bloomed during the apex of postwar liberalism—a period and
a politics often framed as the counterpart to our neoliberal present—
serving as instruments of racial segregation, white middle-class homeowner advantage, and corporate capital accumulation.[8]

*   *   *

Biased assessments helped build and populate the post–World War II
American suburb. Developers bargained with local tax assessors to keep
property assessments artificially low so as to stimulate home sales and
increase corporate profits. County and municipal officials, likewise, attracted homebuyers and kept voters happy with low assessments. In his
book *The Permanent Tax Revolt*, the political scientist Isaac William Martin argues that low property taxes in the form of fractional assessments
became a pervasive feature of postwar suburban housing markets. For
white suburban homeowners, the material benefits of low assessments
were considerable and contributed in no small measure to white wealth
accumulation in the postwar era. Martin argues that the "hidden social
policy" of fractional assessments provided "more benefits than any other
social policy in America except for . . . Social Security and Medicare."[9]
It wasn't just homeowners who enjoyed artificially low property assessments. Suburbs also manipulated property assessments to lure businesses
and industry. As the authors of a 1958 article, "Local Tax Competition
within Metropolitan Areas," in the *Journal of Tax Policy* noted, when it
came to providing tax favors to lure businesses, "property assessments
offer the greatest leeway."[10]

Urban governments also embraced competitive underassessments, but
they often did so from a position of weakness. Determined to stop the
exodus of white people and jobs-producing industries from the central
city, urban governments during these decades manipulated property assessments to influence business locational decisions and convince white
middle-class homeowners to stay. As fiscally distressed cities faced the
prospect of "white flight," white homeowners who still lived in the central city enjoyed outsized influence over local tax administrative practices.
Big-city assessors lived in constant fear of "alienating . . . middle-class

homeowners and voters," noted the economists James Fuerst and Andrew Ditton.[11] A 1973 study by the New York Commission of Investigation reported that the undervaluation of single-family homes in New York City "is apparently a traditional and deliberate decision on the part of various city administrators to deter middle-income families from leaving the city for the suburbs."[12]

Corruption and malfeasance saturated the assessment process. Assessors' offices and appeals boards routinely took bribes from major property owners and businesses in exchange for drastic reductions on property assessments, or exchanged artificially low assessments for certain neighborhoods for votes, or, more often, did both simultaneously.[13] In Gary, Indiana, U.S. Steel, the city's largest industry and largest owner of taxable property, used bribes to obtain obscenely low property assessments, which, by one estimate, reduced the industrial behemoth's annual tax bill to the city by more than $225 million. "Tax assessors [in Gary] retire as wealthy men," one local official remarked, "because they are paid off." The city, meanwhile, struggled to provide the most basic of services to its residents. Starved for funds, Gary taxed property at a rate 50 percent higher than the statewide average, while subtly shifting the tax burden to the city's most disadvantaged residents.[14] As one economist found, homes in the city's black neighborhoods received assessments 10 percent higher than homes in affluent white neighborhoods, and black-owned businesses (as well as white non-Gary residents who owned businesses in the city) were also being assessed at higher rates than white-owned businesses. What had long been dismissed as "ghetto folklore" was being substantiated with hard data. Black voters took notice.[15]

In 1967, Richard Hatcher was elected mayor of Gary, the first African American to hold the office in the city's history and the first elected to a midsized American city in the nation's history. Hatcher had made tax equity the central plank of his campaign, promising that, if elected, he would force corporations to pay their share, relieve the burden on homeowners, and expand social services. But in this and other cities, assessors' offices operated independent of city government, even as they played a formative role in determining cities' fortunes. Under Indiana law, assessors were elected at the township level and answered only to the state Board of Tax Commissioners. The year before he ran for mayor, Hatcher managed an insurgent black candidate's campaign for Calumet Township assessor, and he succeeded in winning a majority of Gary voters, but not enough to overcome votes for incumbent assessor Tom Fadell in the remainder of the township.[16] Hatcher's inability to influence the one office with direct power to increase local revenue would come to define the limits of black power in the city. After entering the mayor's office, Hatcher attempted to access U.S. Steel's corporate records, citing a state law that empowered municipalities to examine (but not change) assessments, in the hopes that the airing of the facts would force the assessor's office to take action. In response, U.S. Steel filed a temporary injunction to prevent the city's controller from accessing its corporate records and also launched a public relations campaign to sow fears among its shrinking workforce of further job losses and possible relocation if it was forced to pay higher taxes.[17]

Powerless to force an intransigent, corrupted assessor's office to do its job, and prevented by the courts from accessing the facts needed to apply political pressure, Hatcher's administration was instead forced to enact severe cuts to the very services he promised to expand. Seeking to reduce operating expenses by $3.1 million, he slashed the budgets for schools, fire, and police, and laid off scores of city employees. He gutted the city's recreation department, laying off twenty-nine full-time employees and eliminating 90 percent of the summer recreation program. And he cut half of the city health department's budget. But the crisis only worsened. Two months into the following school term, the city faced the prospect of having to close its schools for lack of funds. Tax reformers struggled in vain to direct public attention and outrage at the untaxed corporations responsible for the urban fiscal crisis. Companies like U.S. Steel, consumer and taxpayer advocates Ralph Nader and Jonathan Rowe argued, are "literally pilfering billions of dollars out of schools, out of streets and courts and parks and libraries and other services that civilized people need. [They are] taking billions of dollars from the pockets of the small taxpayers that have to make up the difference." As the city's white population shrank, it was African Americans living in the city's poorer neighborhoods who were forced bear the heaviest costs. A separate study found that both residential and commercial and industrial properties in Gary worth less than $20,000 were assessed at a higher percentage of their market value than citywide averages.[18]

As tax reformers tried to connect the dots linking fraudulently low assessments to budget crises and rising property taxes on those who could least afford it, assessors' offices used their expertise as a shield from scrutiny. Called to testify before a U.S. Senate subcommittee in 1972, Calumet Township assessor Tom Fadell evaded answering a series of pointed

questions from senators on allegations of discriminatory assessment practices by referencing formulas and manuals known and understood only
by industry professionals.[19] Snowing his questioners with a flurry of bu-
reaucratese was a winning strategy.[20] As an exacerbated Nader and Rowe
explained to congressional lawmakers, "If what happens daily hundreds
of times, in the administration of the property tax, were to happen in
plain view, on the street, we would call it unarmed robbery. . . . But it does
not happen in the street. It happens in the dull world of assessment rolls
and depreciation formulas and obscure laws and corporate accounting
offices . . . so this crime goes undetected."[21]

In Gary, the crime was detected but remained unproven. After years
of battling U.S. Steel and the Calumet Township assessor's office in court,
the Hatcher administration quietly dropped its lawsuit. As Gary's fiscal
crisis worsened, critics blamed Hatcher for the city's woes and disparaged
his administration as incompetent, a common charge leveled at African
American mayors, many of whom had entered office at the very moment
when their cities' tax bases were being decimated by suburbanization,
deindustrialization, and corporate relocation.[22]

Local assessors and their corporate benefactors had good reason to
stymie attempts at greater transparency and accountability. In cities across
the United States, political firestorms erupted following the release of studies finding rampant inaccuracies in local assessment practices. Throughout the 1960s and 1970s, locally based research teams, investigative journalists, grassroots organizations, and in some cases public officials pored
over assessment rolls and produced dozens of studies and reports. All
found that, when it came to property taxes, the poor pay more. In Pittsburgh, researchers found that the city's assessment method "systematically underestimate[d] high-value properties."[23] In New York, the Citizens
Housing and Planning Council found "all types of residential properties
in low-income areas are over-assessed compared to the same types of
residential properties in higher-income areas of the city,"[24] and the New
York Public Interest Research Group similarly found an "ominous pattern of discrimination against poor and low value homes," which resulted
in economically distressed neighborhoods taxed at over two and one-half
times the rate of stable neighborhoods.[25] In a 1973 report to Congress,
the Department of Housing and Urban Development concluded, "All evidence indicates that the poorer neighborhoods of many cities are being
forced to subsidize heavily, through tax payments, the special tax concessions granted to residents of upward transitional neighborhoods where

revitalization is strongest, capital appreciation most likely, and residents most affluent."[26]

Many of these studies also found that not all low-income neighborhoods were overtaxed equally. In Boston, Harvard law professor Oliver Oldman and economist Henry Aaron reported that property assessments in the city's minority neighborhoods were on average 70 percent higher than the rest of the city.[27] In Milwaukee, a 1974 State Department of Revenue report showed that homeowners on the city's heavily black north side were paying as much as $200 more each year in property taxes than owners of property with the same market value on the city's all-white south side.[28] In Atlanta, where the state of Georgia mandated that local assessors assess property at 40 percent of its appraisal, a study done in 1974 found that residents of affluent neighborhoods on the city's north side enjoyed assessment ratios as low as 26.4 percent, whereas heavily black neighborhoods on the south side tended to be assessed well above 40 percent.[29] In 1975 the *Miami Herald* published a study showing that three predominantly African American subdivisions in Miami-Dade County were assessed at levels well above the county average and far in excess of comparable white residential subdivisions, which tended to receive assessments below the county average.[30]

When confronted with charges of discriminatory taxation, local officials invariably blamed assessment-to-sales ratio disparities on what they euphemistically referred to as "assessment lag." Because reassessment occurred infrequently, defenders argued, any changes in market values in the interim inevitably benefited owners of appreciating real estate and disadvantaged those in depreciating markets.[31] The problem was not racist tax assessors; it was black owners and occupants, whose infiltration of urban neighborhoods sparked a white exodus and sent property values plummeting. In short, don't blame us; blame the victim. Or, if you like, blame the racist logic of the real estate market, or decades of federal housing policies and mortgage lending practices that had placed a stigma on blackness and consigned African Americans to depressed neighborhoods.

But while assessment lag sounded like a plausible explanation, it often failed to withstand scrutiny. Districtwide reassessments, critics noted, often did little to close the gap between wealthier and poorer neighborhoods. Assessors' offices were notorious for simply copying the previous year's figures and calling it a day.[32] The only adjustments, it seemed, came to those taxpayers who had the time, knowledge, and resources to file an appeal, which were often so complex and cumbersome they necessitated a tax attorney to navigate and tended to be used only by high-income property owners.

Castigating assessors as lazy and derelict in their duties, as many critics at the time did, might have fit neatly into an emerging argument in the 1970s that the nation's mounting problems stemmed from bureaucratic incompetence, one which executives in the private, for-profit tax administration services industry were quick to embrace and trumpet.[33] But it often failed to consider how these instances of incompetent mismanagement were, as one tax-policy scholar remarked, "the result of quite purposive behavior."[34] Some tax-policy experts posited that assessors used the powers of their office to affect (as opposed to merely administer) tax policy. In their study of assessment inequities in Boston, Oldman and Aaron concluded that the high assessment ratios in low-income minority neighborhoods could be due only to the conscious bias of assessors, who, they surmised, believed that residents of these neighborhoods received proportionately more benefits from local government than residents of higher-income neighborhoods. By overassessing the value of these properties, assessors sought to align individuals' tax contributions with their tax benefits and, in effect, transform the property tax from a proportional excise tax into a user charge.[35] The 1973 Department of Housing and Urban Development study similarly speculated that the overassessment of properties in "blighted" neighborhoods could be due to "a conscious effort to overtax those landlords and tenants with the greatest need for local public services."[36] Other studies of tax administrative practices arrived at similar conclusions.[37] On rare occasions, local officials copped to the charge. In Baltimore, an African American columnist for the *Baltimore Afro-American* quoted unnamed public officials who "admitted they sock it to low-income areas as a means of collecting taxes from them to offset what they can't fork over because of meager incomes."[38]

Two distinct elements of the postwar metropolis combined to generate discriminatory assessments: the practice of competitive underassessments that pitted cities and suburbs against each other in a fight for middle-class homeowners and businesses and industry, and the racist dual housing market that kept African Americans locked in urban ghettos. Tax-policy expert Diane Paul commented, "If [the] goal [of the assessor] is to maximize revenue, then discrimination against blacks . . . is rational."[39] But it was the subtlety of the practice—and the numerous difficulties an average citizen faced in challenging an unfair assessment, much less overturning a racist system—which help explain its endurance. Throughout the decade, tax-policy experts and grassroots organizations expressed frustration that, despite the large body of evidence, assessment discrimination failed to generate enough outrage and indignation among urban minority populations to affect tax policy and administration.[40] This was by design. The use of fractional assessments made inaccuracies harder for the average homeowner to detect, as the assessment was already well below the property's value. Even if they believed they were being overtaxed, few victims had the time and resources needed to challenge an assessment.[41] Most appeals were filed on higher-value properties in underassessed neighborhoods and, as a result, tended to exacerbate existing disparities. For African American tenants, who paid their property taxes in the form of rent to landlords, overassessments were entirely invisible.

*   *   *

The problem of property taxation often seemed one step removed from the main problems affecting disadvantaged urban populations, too abstract and technical to arouse a mass movement. Pollution, in contrast, was one of those issues galvanizing grassroots action. In Chicago, the Campaign against Pollution (CAP) tried to demonstrate the relation between the two. Launched by community organizer Saul Alinsky, CAP targeted the industries responsible for the city's air pollution problem, which had reached a critical stage by the summer of 1969, when columnist Mike Royko dubbed the thick, dark clouds wafting from the steel mills and power utilities "a blanket of floating filth." In the course of investigation, CAP found that, not only were city and county officials not enforcing existing environmental regulations; the assessor's office was awarding polluters generous tax breaks in the form of artificially low assessments. CAP found that U.S. Steel's South Works plant alone received a $12 million annual tax break from Cook County. In total, CAP estimated that the county lost more than $100 million each year to favorable underassessments awarded to steel mills, power utilities, banks, and race tracks, among other beneficiaries. The losers, it stressed in campaign materials, were the city's schools, parks, hospitals, junior colleges, sanitary districts, and forest preserves, which were "being starved of cash," and "ordinary homeowners," who were "being victimized by an increasingly onerous property tax burden."[42]

Seeking to engage citizens in the fight, CAP distributed "taxpayer reassessment forms" in low-income neighborhoods urging homeowners to file appeals with the assessor's office for a 73 percent reduction in their assessments, so as "to equalize all assessments with U.S. Steel's tax break." To further its "property-taxpayers' counter-offensive," in 1972 CAP released the findings of a study conducted by the young economist Arthur Lyons on assessment ratios in two South Side neighborhoods: one predominantly black and rental properties (South Shore), the other overwhelmingly (if tenuously) white and owner occupied (Beverly). Lyons found that properties in both neighborhoods received assessments 33 percent above average. At the time of the study, South Shore was more than 85 percent black, up from less than 5 percent in 1960. Ironically, many of the whites who had fled South Shore moved to Beverly, which by the early 1970s was fighting to preserve racial segregation in its housing markets. Black home buyers in Beverly had been subject to incessant harassment, vandalism, and fire bombings. The area's well-organized local planning association, meanwhile, worked to ensure that the area "remain[ed] predominantly white" by targeting blockbusters and panic peddlers.[43]

The findings inflamed white Beverly residents' anxieties even as it brought them into a temporary alliance with blacks in South Shore. Following the report's release, Beverly residents formed the group Fair Assessments for Beverly and staged a march and protest outside the office of their local alderman. Later, they joined with South Shore residents in protests outside the office of the state's attorney Bernard Carey, demanding that he order the county to conduct a reassessment. For Beverly residents, it was the shock that their neighborhood could be subject to unfavorable treatment, and fear that it could spark a white exodus, that compelled many to protest. For the city's black residents, the report gave additional weight to long-standing grievances over the city's uneven distribution of local services and history of forced displacement of black residents. In the severely depressed and predominantly black neighborhood of Lawndale—which, despite property values in a free fall, had seen its property assessments rise during the 1960s—protesters hanged Cook County assessor P. J. "Parky" Cullerton in effigy. Resident Anna Moore, whose property tax on her two-flat had risen sharply in previous years, remarked: "I wouldn't mind paying if we got any kind of decent service from the city. But there's poor police protection. The street lights don't work half the time. The streets never get repaired, and the garbage pickup is a laugh." "If Cullerton can give special tax breaks to downtown interests and friends of City Hall," Monroe Lollar, chairman of the Lawndale Peoples Planning and Action Committee (LPPAC) asked reporters, "why can't he give them to

this community?" Referring to residents' past experiences with urban renewal and slum clearance, LPPAC chairman Lollar told reporters: "We
have been 'urbaned' out of our communities, only to look back and see our
former communities 'developed' without us. We're now being 'taxed' out."[44]

These echoed concerns being aired in overtaxed black neighborhoods
in other cities. In Philadelphia, the writer Gerald Horne commented, "It
has been an open scandal . . . that the [local assessor's office] tends to tax
property in 'certain neighborhoods' higher than others. Property owners,
unable to pay soaring tax bills, sell their homes for a song often to those
with close connection to [the assessor's office], who then re-sell it at a
dramatic profit—often to young white professionals." Horne's contention
seemed substantiated by the numbers of black homeowners in the city
who reported sharp increases in property assessments, followed by a flood
of speculators seeking to buy up properties in their neighborhoods.[45]

CAP, which had commissioned the study, hoped to use its findings to
unite white and black homeowners in a shared fight against corporate fa-
voritism. In press releases and campaign materials, CAP chairman Paul
Booth stressed the relationship between air pollution, property value depreciation, corporate profits, and taxpayer hardship. While "the property
of hundreds of thousands of citizens of the south side has been devalued
by U.S. Steel's bombardment of our neighborhoods with over 60,000 tons
of dirt, year after year," these same neighborhoods, Booth told reporters, "are subsidizing the beneficiaries of illegal tax breaks such as United
States Steel, the First National Bank, Arlington Park Race Track and the
Woodfield Mall Shopping Center. These big businesses are all assessed at
a lower percentage of value than South Shore homes." CAP's campaign
forced the assessor's office to grant 27 percent and 33 percent reductions
on property assessments in South Shore and Beverly, respectively, and
commission an independent study of the county's assessment practices.[46]

The tax reductions quelled one incipient tax revolt on Chicago's South
Side. After achieving its tax reductions, the group Fair Assessments for
Beverly disbanded, homeowner politics reoriented around limiting the
influx of black homeowners, and any sense of shared interests among
whites in Beverly with the poor, overtaxed tenants in South Shore faded.[47]
But among black Chicagoans, the findings raised more questions about
the prevalence of unequal assessments and the extent of black taxpayer
disadvantage. The author of the CAP study shared these concerns. Following his findings of overassessments in two South Side neighborhoods
in 1972, economist Arthur Lyons directed a team of graduate students

at the University of Illinois at Chicago Circle's (UIC) School of Urban Sciences on a more extensive study of assessment ratios in the city's white and black neighborhoods. The team examined the sales prices and assessments of nearly four thousand properties in six predominantly white and six predominantly black neighborhoods across Cook County. The team discovered that, almost without exception, property in African American neighborhoods was overassessed relative to property in white neighborhoods, with race the key determinant.

Many of the UIC students' findings confirmed previous studies: homes in wealthy neighborhoods tended to receive the lowest assessments relative to property value, whereas property in poor neighborhoods the highest; small homes were assessed at a higher rate than larger, more expensive homes. But their study also found that homes in black neighborhoods sometimes paid three times the amount in property taxes than comparable homes in white neighborhoods. While poorer white neighborhoods were overtaxed relative to upper-end white neighborhoods, they were undertaxed compared to all African American neighborhoods, regardless of class composition and neighborhood condition. Politics, the report strongly implied, was a key factor in assessment levels. Of the twelve neighborhoods studied, the one that enjoyed the lowest assessments was none other than the working-class white Irish Catholic South Side neighborhood Bridgeport, home to the late Mayor Richard J. Daley and the nucleus of the local Democratic Party machine.[48]

In April 1979, the city's two major daily newspapers began running front-page stories reporting the study's findings. Black Chicagoans were outraged but not surprised. For decades, the Daley machine had routinely discriminated against the city's black neighborhoods in the distribution of municipal services. The report's release came just months after Mayor Michael Bilandic, who had assumed the office following Boss Daley's death in 1976, had notoriously closed several Chicago Transportation Authority (CTA) "L" stations, all in black neighborhoods, in the midst of a crippling blizzard, a decision that led black voters to overwhelmingly support his opponent in the February 1977 primary, Jane Byrne, providing the decisive margin in her victory.[49] Many black Chicagoans had long believed that their neighborhoods were being forced to pay more for less in return. The Lyons report offered confirmation. "We were not totally shocked to hear this," state senator Harold Washington said of the report's findings. "It's something that's been known on the South and West Sides for a long time. But none with the credibility of [Lyons's team] has documented the issue before."[50] "The black community of Evanston has long suspected that we pay a color tax for our property," Evanston alderman Edna Summers commented.[51] "I've known for a long time that blacks get the short end of both sticks," NAACP South Side chapter president Frank Williams added. "People call up all the time and say their taxes are high," state representative Raymond W. Ewell told a reporter. "But people always say that. . . . But this is the first time we've had a comprehensive report," he continued.[52]

The report's stark findings, the publicity it received, and previous campaigns against inequitable assessments laid the groundwork for a black tax revolt in Chicago. "I have never yet known an issue which has aroused such explosive concern in my community," Harold Washington commented. "We're playing with dynamite."[53] Throughout the spring of 1979, civil rights and community organizations staged protests and launched petitions calling on the governor to order the assessor's office to reassess black neighborhoods. Washington, for one, saw it as an opportunity to educate and organize. He and Art Lyons held miniseminars in church basements, where Lyons explained the mechanics of property taxation, the study's findings, and its implications. Other organizations staged workshops that instructed homeowners on how to file an appeal. Operation PUSH's vice president George E. Riddick demanded that the county postpone its upcoming tax sale until the disparities uncovered in the report were resolved.

In calling for the postponement of the upcoming tax sale, Riddick connected overtaxation to one of the most notorious—and devastating—forms of economic predation taking place in the city's lower-income neighborhoods throughout the postwar decades: tax lien investing. A close-knit class of investors annually purchased liens on thousands of tax-delinquent properties across the city, which entitled them to saddle homeowners with crippling debts and, should they fail to settle their debts, claim title to their homes for the mere cost of a single unpaid tax bill. The lucrative practice disproportionately victimized the poor, the elderly, and the overtaxed; in other words, those homeowners who were most likely to miss a tax payment due to oversight or economic hardship. Not only did overassessments drain the savings of hard-pressed working families, drive down the value of black-owned property, and contribute to neighborhood decline. They also, Riddick argued, set in motion "a chain of events which takes property away from poor owners and transfers it to tax speculators who reap large profits from reselling it for many times what they paid for it."[54] "Taxing Black homeowners higher than Whites," Harold Washington speculated, "could be seen as part of an overall plan to debilitate the Black community and bleed them dry, force them to give up prime land so they can bring in commercial property and middle income people to populate these sections."[55] Such words resonated with black Chicagoans, who had experienced firsthand the expropriation of black property and disintegration of black neighborhoods under urban renewal in the 1940s and 1950s, and who understood the city's concerted efforts to facilitate the gentrification of older neighborhoods as another form of "Negro removal."

On the floor of the state senate in Springfield and on the streets of Chicago, Washington led the fight against what he labeled the "black tax." Along with state senator Richard Newhouse, he publicly called on U.S. attorney Thomas Sullivan to launch an investigation into possible federal civil rights violations by the county assessor's office.[56] On May 18, 1979, he led a contingent of more than one hundred protesters from eleven community groups from the South and West Sides on a march on the assessor's office in downtown Chicago.[57] He also led a delegation of black senators in Springfield that called on the state's Department of Local Government Affairs to investigate the report's findings and hold hearings. He sponsored a Senate bill that would give the state authority to order, supervise, and direct county reassessments if it determined that a local assessor's board was not in compliance with the law. Speaking from the Senate floor, the senator thundered, "In Cook County there's been a pall casted on the assessor's office . . . [and] a lot of people in Cook County . . . are very much disturbed about whether or not they're being . . . overtaxed because they happen to live in a black or a poor neighborhood." The public's trust in their government, he reminded colleagues, was at stake: "If you're dealing with taxpayers and people's money and property, you've got to be cleaner than a houndstooth. There can't be even any reasonable suspicions arouse as to whether or not you're being fair."[58]

In June 1979, Washington announced the formation of the Black Taxpayers' Federation, a network of community organizers from twenty-one of the city's neighborhoods, as well as plans to file a class-action lawsuit on behalf of black property owners in Cook County. "Black taxpayers in Cook County," he told the pool of reporters assembled at the Hyatt Regency Hotel, "have lost tens of millions of dollars through discriminatory taxes. We intend to stop this practice . . . [and] file a class action lawsuit requesting that the millions of dollars in over assessed discriminatory real estate taxes be return [sic] to the black property owners of Cook County. It is our purpose," he stressed, "to pay our fair share . . . and our fair share only."[59]

For Washington, the surge of outrage emanating from these two separate and distinct segments of black Chicago also presented an opportunity. For decades, blacks on the South and West Sides had been riven by
political factions and divided in the face of the city's all-powerful Democratic machine. The black tax study sampled from African American
neighborhoods on both the South and West Sides and showed that, regardless of geography, black taxpayers were uniformly assessed unfairly.
The Black Taxpayers' Federation deliberately sought to bring together
community organizations from both sections of the city and forge a coalition that could unite the city's African American population around a
common set of issues. One of the federation's founding members, Arvis
Averette, who also served as one of Washington's key political advisers,
argues that Washington's outspoken leadership in fighting discriminatory
taxation in 1979 laid the groundwork for his successful run for mayor in
1983, when he became the first African American elected to the office in
the city's history.[60]

As a coalition of black taxpayers began to take shape, Cook County's newly elected assessor Thomas Hynes worked to contain the fallout.
Hynes attacked Lyons's character, questioned his motives, and called his
research techniques faulty. He publicly labeled him a "rabble-rouser" and
"activist" academic.[61] At a press conference on May 8, 1979, with Lyons
in attendance, Hynes called the report "inaccurate, unreliable, and invalid."[62] He argued that any research carried out by graduate students
should not be taken seriously, even as he could offer no specific examples
of what the report got wrong, or how its methodologies were faulty. His
office dismissed accusations of racism as absurd. A top staffer told reporters, "The assessments are done by computer, and the computer is literally
color-blind."[63] Case closed. Those claiming that there's a so-called black
tax were trafficking in conspiracy theories. And because those critics were
ill informed, county officials told the public, any proposed reforms they
advocated would invariably harm you, the (nonblack) taxpayer. It was
a message tailored to appeal to white suburban voters, many of whom
viewed urban minorities strictly as tax recipients (not taxpayers), scoffed
at claims of institutional racism (especially those issued by outspoken
black politicians), and equated progressive tax reform with tax hikes and
increased aid for the "undeserving poor."

Middle-class white suburban homeowners and residents of urban white
ethnic neighborhoods had good reason to be leery of black taxpayers' calls
for assessment reform. They were, after all, the primary beneficiaries of

discriminatory assessment practices. Writing of proposed assessment reforms in 1970s Illinois, the urban policy scholar Brian J. L. Berry noted, "Black homeowners . . . had the most to gain . . . whereas nonblack owners of the smallest oldest homes (the embattled blue-collar white ethnics) had the most to lose."[64] Ironically, the revelations of discriminatory overtaxation of urban neighborhoods and media coverage of the protests that followed alerted many white homeowners to tax privileges many had taken for granted, and which calls for tax fairness and greater oversight and accountability threatened. Even as he pushed for reform, Washington acknowledged this political reality. To a senate colleague's argument that assessment reform threatened to raise taxes on other homeowners, Washington responded: "All you're saying is that you've been unjustly enriched with our money, and you don't want to put it back. . . . In plain simple English[,] if your taxes are lower, because mine are higher, then you unjustly enriched. I don't expect you to give it up willingly, no I expect you to go kicking, screaming and yelling, into the twentieth century, but you're going there one way or the other."[65]

The white beneficiaries of low assessments were, by then, already in a fighting mood. Two years earlier, a modest reform to Cook County's assessment procedures sparked tax revolts in the county's predominantly white northern suburbs. In response to CAP's reports on assessment inequities and campaign for tax fairness, the assessor's office announced in 1973 that it would no longer assess the value of homes according to replacement cost. Critics charged that this approach, which ignored a property's location (and thus the main factor in determining its market value), constituted a "fraudulent uniformity" that invariably disadvantaged low-income and declining neighborhoods.[66] It also, of course, greatly advantaged property owners in appreciating markets, where even a cheaply built home could command top dollar. Just how great those tax benefits had been became evident in the summer of 1977, when homeowners in the county's north quadrant received their new assessments. Many saw their property's assessment jump by 50 percent, and some by as much as 100 percent and higher. Homeowners were shocked and outraged. In the days that followed, one journalist described, "Hundreds of people came to hastily arranged protest meetings, [and] exchanged horror stories of whopping tax increases." Aggrieved taxpayers joined newly formed anti-tax organizations like the National Taxpayers' Union of Illinois, whose pamphlets and letterhead sported the coiled snake and the words, "Don't Tread on Me." At boisterous meetings, speakers denounced the tax reforms as fascist, tyrannical, and the like. "This is a Nazi method, not an American one," a speaker at a North Shore protest meeting said of the new assessment procedures.[67]

This mirrored the response to property-tax reforms among middle-class white homeowners elsewhere. Nationwide, progressive and good government tax reformers had spent the decade fighting to bring a level of professionalism and accountability to local assessors' offices and to institute tax administrative procedures that were fair, equitable, and transparent. They forced state legislatures to pass tax-reform bills that standardized the appraisal of real estate, empowered and required state tax commissions to enforce common standards across jurisdictions, removed the discretionary powers of assessors, and required them to pass competency tests and meet professional qualifications to hold the position. States consolidated jurisdictions that had previously served as little more than tax havens and established mechanisms for the timely reappraisal of property to reflect changes in the market.[68] As Isaac William Martin points out, these reforms were meant to ensure that tax bills reflected the actual value of property "rather than the social status or political party of the taxpayer."[69] But in so doing, new assessment procedures threatened to remove hidden, often unacknowledged privileges from middle-class white homeowners at a time when wages were stagnant and the cost of living on the rise, as was the case in California, the seedbed of the late 1970s tax revolt. After the state standardized assessment ratios in 1967, property owners in appreciating markets began receiving tax bills double or triple prereform bills. Conversely, owners of property in low-income and minority neighborhoods saw their tax bills remain stagnant or lowered to reflect drops in value that prereform assessors had quite deliberately ignored.[70]

During these same years, a resurgent right was exploiting white taxpayers' racial anxieties for political gain. On the stump, presidential candidate Ronald Reagan told stories of a "Chicago welfare queen" who "used 80 names, 30 addresses, 15 telephone numbers to collect food stamps, Social Security, veterans' benefits for four nonexistent deceased veteran husbands, as well as welfare" to delegitimize blacks' claims on the state; to reinforce the age-old myth that poor people, especially poor black people, don't pay taxes; and to build support for new, more regressive tax policies.[71] Cities, meanwhile, increasingly adopted neoliberal models of local taxation, characterized by tax breaks, concessions, and nonenforcement for corporations and developers, as well as a benefits-received principle, in which levels of services correspond with individuals' tax contributions, for everyone else. This not only led cities like Chicago to adopt a host of new revenue-collection schemes designed to shift the tax burden to the poor; it also helped rationalize long-standing practices that discriminated against minority neighborhoods. While it aggressively pursued sources of revenue in the city's poorer neighborhoods, Chicago continued to look the other way at rampant corporate tax avoidance.[72]

In 1981, inequitable assessment practices gained protection from legal challenge when the U.S. Supreme Court ruled, in *FAIR v. McNary*, that federal courts lacked the jurisdiction to hear cases brought under section 1983 of the Civil Rights Act challenging the administration of state and local taxes. The Court based its decision on the doctrine of comity, which held that the federal courts should not interfere with state tax systems, as well as the 1937 Tax Injunction Act, which denied taxpayers the right to contest state and local taxes in federal court so long as a "plain, speedy and efficient remedy" was available in state court. The *FAIR* decision, one legal scholar wrote, "opened the door to all types of discriminatory state tax practices."[73]

In this political and legal environment, aggrieved African American taxpayers struggled to be heard and could gain only the most minor concessions. In Chicago, Cook County assessor Thomas Hynes established a commission to investigate evidence of racial bias in the county's assessment practices. He named Leon Finney, an African American former community organizer turned Democratic Party machine insider, as the committee's chairman and enlisted the participation of the Chicago Urban League. Six months later, the commission released a report claiming that it found "no evidence of racial discrimination" and chalked up racial disparities to "bugs" in the computing system used to calculate assessments. Because it could find no evidence of bias by the assessor's office or the explicit use of race in determining assessment levels, the committee concluded that racism played no role.[74] In a press conference following the report's release, Finney stated unequivocally that there was "no discrimination against black homeowners." For public officials and local media, Finney's endorsement of the report offered all the confirmation needed to conclude that the "black tax" was indeed a myth. The following day, the front page of the *Chicago Sun-Times* carried the headline "No Racial Bias in Tax Process." Case closed.

Privately, Washington fumed at the cynical appointment of Finney, who had years earlier given up community organizing work in favor of

patronage positions inside the city's Democratic Party machinery, to provide cover for institutional racism inside the assessor's office. Publicly,
he stated that he still stood "solidly behind the Lyons report." Lyons,
meanwhile, assailed the biased, unscientific nature of the study, and noted
that it "contain[ed] not one single shred of evidence which in any way
call[ed] into question, or can call into question, our finding[s]." Others
noted that the Finney committee's finding that upward of 40 percent of
Chicago neighborhoods suffered from assessment regressivity was damn-
ing enough. As the *Chicago Defender* remarked, "If you're paying more
than you should, it doesn't help one bit to be cheerfully informed that it's
not your race but your pocketbook that makes the difference—not when
you know darn well that your color has a lot to do with the state of your
pocketbook in the first place."[75]

After months of organizing and campaigning against the "black tax,"
Washington quietly dropped the issue. That fall, he won a seat in Congress
representing Chicago's South Side. Two years later, Washington returned
to Chicago to run for mayor, where he beat incumbent Jane Byrne in a bitterly fought Democratic primary, and he later prevailed over Republican
candidate Bernard Epton, who had mounted an openly racist campaign,
in the general election. During his term in office, Washington struggled
to bring a measure of fairness and equity to taxes and urban finance. But
with Cook County assessor Thomas Hynes aligned with his opponents on
city council, Washington could exert little influence over assessment administration. As it suffered massive job losses from corporate and industrial relocation to neighboring suburbs, Cook County instead focused on
lowering assessments on commercial and industrial properties.[76] Months
after winning reelection and after having claimed victory in the protracted
"council wars" that engulfed his first term, Washington died unexpectedly
on November 25, 1987. Two years later, Richard M. Daley assumed the
office once held by his father. Over the following two decades, the second
Mayor Daley aggressively remade the city into what historian Andrew J.
Diamond has called a "poster child" for neoliberal urban governance.[77]
Property-tax policy and administration played a key role in that process.
Under Daley and his successor, Mayor Rahm Emanuel, Chicago has used
property-tax breaks, abatements, and subsidies to spur real estate development and gentrification in the city's neighborhoods and to facilitate
private capital accumulation in its downtown. As it generously dispensed
tax breaks and benefits in the Loop and the predominantly white, upper-
middle-class neighborhoods on its North Side, the city grew increasingly
reliant on fines, fees, and user charges, disproportionately targeting the

city's poor, for revenue, while the assessor's office continued to serve as a virtually invisible force in the production of the city's glaring inequities. Invisible, that is, until the summer of 2017.

*　*　*

To many younger readers, the news came as a shock. To most older, long-time residents of Chicago's African American neighborhoods, the report in the *Chicago Tribune* on June 17, 2017, finding wild inaccuracies in assess-ment rates benefitting wealthier, whiter parts of the city, and disadvantaging poorer, blacker ones, was too familiar. After analyzing more than one hundred million property-tax records from 2003 through 2015, the *Tribune* found a pattern of over- and underassessment that mapped neatly onto the city's race and class-segregated landscape. While the city's young, upper-middle-class, and predominantly white neighborhoods received a tax break in the form of lower assessments, its poorer, heavily black and brown neighborhoods on the West Side got hammered. While homes in the poor, heavily industrial south suburbs tended to be overassessed, luxury homes on the North Shore in Wilmette and Winnetka were undervalued, some, it found, by as much as one-half market value. The effective tax rate in North Lawndale, one of the city's most severely depressed neighbor-hoods, was two times that of the Gold Coast or Lincoln Park, two of the city's hottest markets. It cited examples of homes in poorer, heavily minor-ity neighborhoods purchased for $75,000, only to be assessed at more than twice that amount, and of homes worth upward of $1.5 million that were assessed at less than $800,000. As University of Chicago urban policy profes-sor Christopher Berry explained, "It's a textbook example of institutional racism."[78]

The standard response from this and other assessors' offices to such reports is that aggrieved homeowners should appeal, as is their right un-der law. This was what the Cook County assessor's office said to critics in the 1970s, and today. But as was the case then, the *Tribune* found that the appeals process remained so poorly understood and hard for the aver-age taxpayer to navigate that it exacerbated inequities between wealthier and poorer neighborhoods. Wealthier neighborhoods, it found, appeal at much higher rates and are more likely to receive significant assessment reductions, even though their homes tended to be underassessed to begin with. The study found that the assessor's office violated state-mandated standards on accuracy and uniformity every year between 2009 and 2015, and that both measures got worse, not better, after the appeals process.

In this neoliberal house of mirrors, even laws and procedures claiming to protect the poor and disadvantaged from abuse work, in practice, to the advantage of developers, corporations, and wealthier homeowners.[79]

In contrast to the 1970s, when Chicago's and other assessors' offices were firmly under the control of white men and closely aligned with white business and homeowner interests, in today's neoliberal city, the architects and administrators of discriminatory local tax laws and procedures often hail from minority communities, rose to power by appealing to minority voters, and, when under attack, used their minority status to deflect charges of racism and resist reform. After the *Tribune* story broke, Cook County assessor Joseph Berrios claimed his Latino heritage and childhood spent in the Cabrini-Green housing project as defense against accusations of racially biased assessments.[80]

But in both Chicago and Detroit, this neoliberal model for resisting democratic reform and demobilizing grassroots insurgencies is under attack. Following the *Tribune* report, a multiracial and ethnic group of community organizations staged protests outside Berrios's office. Organizers of the rally rejected local officials' calls for another study, dismissed Berrios's cynical attempt at identity politics, and demanded tax refunds for victims and an overhaul to a system that, as Clem Balanoff, of the group Our Revolution, told a reporter, "transfers money from poor and minority communities into the hands of the wealthy."[81] In the wake of the city's tax foreclosure crisis, activists in Detroit have employed a variety of strategies to protect homeowners and mobilize citizens. Local hip-hop artist Will See recorded the protest rap, "Take Tha House Back," calling on Detroiters to take direct action against tax foreclosures. The city's United Community Housing Coalition has provided direct assistance to homeowners in danger of losing their homes while organizing educational and outreach efforts across Wayne County. Armed with the findings of law professor Bernadette Atuahene, the grassroots Coalition to End Unconstitutional Tax Foreclosures has staged dozens of protests outside county offices and the homes of county officials; recorded short videos for the public explaining, in practical terms, the issue and the stakes; and filed legal challenges seeking to end what it alleges are illegal assessments, secure compensation for families who lost their homes to tax foreclosures, and place a moratorium on county tax auctions.[82]

In launching campaigns against discriminatory taxation, today's activists are fighting to overturn an enduring feature of urban fiscal policy and administration, one whose power is derived through the denial of its existence. As this look inside big-city assessors' offices across the country during the age of urban crisis and suburban growth reveals, these and other obscure, opaque, and local administrative practices and procedures have and continue to play an important, if often invisible, role in distributing white racial privilege and black disadvantage, and, more critically, in manufacturing a culture of political quiescence in which neoliberal polices could flourish.

Notes

1. "Parking Tix: War on Poor," *Michigan Citizen*, August 17, 2014, A1, A4; "Nearly 18K at Risk as Detroit Water Shutoffs Begin," *Detroit News*, April 19, 2017, http://www.detroitnews.com/story/news/local/detroit-city/2017/04/19/water-shutoffs-begin-detroit/100661242/; and Laura Gottesdiener, "Detroit Just Had the Single Largest Tax Foreclosure in American History," *Mother Jones*, April 21, 2015, http://www.motherjones.com/politics/2015/04/low-income-black-and-elderly-residents-detroit-isnt-city-rise-one-under-siege. On the causes and consequences of Detroit's bankruptcy filing, see Wallace C. Turbeville, *The Detroit Bankruptcy* (New York: Demos, November 2013), http://www.demos.org/sites/default/files/publications/Detroit_Bankruptcy-Demos.pdf; and Saqib Bhatti, "Why Chicago Won't Go Bankrupt—and Detroit Didn't Have To," *In These Times*, June 22, 2015, http://inthesetimes.com/article/18096/a_scam_in_two_cities. On the formulation of state legislation aimed at incentivizing private investment in tax delinquent properties in Michigan, see Joshua M. Akers, "Making Markets: Think Tank Legislation and Private Property in Detroit," *Urban Geography* 34, no. 8 (2013): 1070–95.

2. Bernadette Atuahene, "Detroit's Tax Foreclosure Indefensible," *Detroit Free Press*, September 1, 2016, http://www.freep.com/story/opinion/contributors/2016/09/01/detroits-tax-foreclosures-indefensible/89717644/; and Atuahene, "Racial Discrimination and Detroit's Tax Foreclosure Crisis," ACLU Michigan, June 8, 2017, http://www.aclumich.org/article/guest-blog-racial-discrimination-and-detroits-tax-foreclosure-crisis.

3. Bernadette Atuahene, "Don't Let Detroit's Revival Rest on an Injustice," *New York Times*, July 22, 2017, https://www.nytimes.com/2017/07/22/opinion/sunday/dont-let-detroits-revival-rest-on-an-injustice.html?_r=0.

4. Joel Kurth, "Sorry We Foreclosed Your Home: But Thanks for Fixing Our Budget," *Bridge*, June 6, 2017, http://www.bridgemi.com/detroit-journalism-cooperative/sorry-we-foreclosed-your-home-thanks-fixing-our-budget.

5. Bernadette Atuahene and Timothy Hodge, "Stategraft" (working paper, Chicago-Kent College of Law, January 2018), http://bernadetteatuahene.com/files/2016/08/Stategraft.pdf.

6. Josiah Rector, "Neoliberalism's Deadly Experiment," *Jacobin*, October 21, 2016, https://www.jacobinmag.com/2016/10/water-detroit-flint-emergency-management-lead-snyder-privatization/; Dianne Feeley, "A Hurricane without Water:

Detroit's Foreclosure Disaster," *Black Agenda Report*, June 3, 2015, https://www
.blackagendareport.com/detroit_foreclosure-disaster.

7. On the more chronicled, predominantly white-led tax revolts of the 1970s and
1980s, see Robert Kuttner, *Revolt of the Haves: Tax Rebellions and Hard Times*
(New York: Simon and Schuster, 1980); David O. Sears and Jack Citrin, *Tax Revolt:
Something for Nothing in California* (Cambridge, MA: Harvard University Press,
1982); Bruce J. Schulman, *The Seventies: The Great Shift in American Culture, Society, and Politics* (Cambridge, MA: Da Capo, 2001), esp. chap. 8; Robert O. Self,
American Babylon: Race and the Struggle for Postwar Oakland (Princeton, NJ:
Princeton University Press, 2003), esp. chap. 8; Isaac William Martin, *The Permanent Tax Revolt: How Property Tax Transformed American Politics* (Stanford, CA:
Stanford University Press, 2008); and Lily Geismer, *Don't Blame Us: Suburban Liberals and the Transformation of the Democratic Party* (Princeton, NJ: Princeton University Press, 2015), esp. chap. 10.

8. On the long history of urban fiscal policies and growth strategies associated
with neoliberalism, see Andrew J. Diamond, *Chicago on the Make: Power and Inequality in a Modern City* (Berkeley: University of California Press, 2017).

9. Martin, *Permanent Tax Revolt*, 8, 10.

10. In the article, the author Mabel Walker mentioned that numerous tax officials she interviewed indicated that these practices were common but none admitted to doing it themselves. Mabel Walker, "Local Tax Competition within Metropolitan Areas," *Tax Policy* 25 (July 1958): 3–8, quote on 5.

11. James Fuerst and Andrew Ditton, "Reducing Property Taxes: An Evaluation
of a Collective Action," *Land Economics* 51 (February 1975): 94–97, quote on 97.

12. See Diane B. Paul, *The Politics of the Property Tax* (Washington, DC: Lexington Books, 1975), 27.

13. See Kuttner, *Revolt of the Haves*, esp. 125–28.

14. See George Crile, "A Tax Assessor Has Many Friends," *Harper's*, November 1972, 102–4, 106–11; "Fiscal Feud: Homeowners Challenge Business Tax
Breaks in Some Communities," *Wall Street Journal*, April 5, 1971.

15. "Gary, Indiana Property Assessments," 1971, folder 11, box 87, Business
and Professional People for the Public Interest, University of Illinois at Chicago
(UIC) Special Collections; and Larry Silverman, "Preliminary Memo on Lake
County Tax Crisis," June 13, 1971, folder 13, box 87, UIC Special Collections.

16. J. Phillip Thompson III, *Double Trouble: Black Mayors, Black Communities,
and the Call for a Deep Democracy* (New York: Oxford University Press, 2006), 212–13.

17. Edward Greer, *Big Steel: Black Politics and Corporate Power in Gary, In-
diana* (New York: Monthly Review Press, 1979), 169; Charles Howard Levine,
*Community Conflict and Mayoral Leadership: A Theoretical Examination with
Applications to Black Mayoral Leadership in Gary, Indiana, and Cleveland, Ohio*
(Bloomington: Indiana University Press, 1971), 201n39; "Gary, Indiana Property
Assessments," 1971, folder 11, box 87, Business and Professional People for the
Public Interest, UIC Special Collections.

18. "Gary, Indiana Property Assessments"; Silverman, "Preliminary Memo on Lake County Tax Crisis"; Ralph Nader and Jonathan Rowe, Statement before the Senate Subcommittee on Intergovernmental Relations, May 9, 1972, folder 5, box 2, Paul Booth (CAP), Chicago History Museum Research Center; "Impact and Administration of the Property Tax," U.S. Senate, 92nd Cong., 2nd sess., June 26, 1972, p. 99.

19. Tom Fadell, Testimony before Senate Subcommittee on Intergovernmental Relations, June 26, 1972, *Congressional Record*, 92nd Cong., 2nd sess., p. 129.

20. "In a democracy," historian Richard White observed, "boredom works for bureaucracies and corporations as smell works for a skunk. It keeps danger away. Power does not have to be exercised behind the scenes. It can be open. The audience is asleep." Richard White, *The Organic Machine: The Remaking of the Columbia River* (New York: Hill and Wang, 1995), 64.

21. Nader and Rowe, Statement before the Senate Subcommittee on Intergovernmental Relations.

22. Robert A. Catlin, *Racial Politics and Urban Planning: Gary, Indiana, 1980–1989* (Lexington: University Press of Kentucky, 1993); S. Paul O'Hara, *Gary: The Most American of All American Cities* (Bloomington: Indiana University Press, 2011). On racially laden attacks on African American elected officials during this period, see George Derek Musgrove, *Rumor, Repression, and Racial Politics: How the Harassment of Black Elected Officials Shaped Post-Civil Rights America* (Athens: University of Georgia Press, 2012).

23. Robert Carbone and Reinhard S. Lai, "Assessment of Urban Residential Properties: An Empirical Study of Pittsburgh," *Journal of Environmental Systems* 4, no. 3 (1974): 207–16.

24. Emanuel Tobier, *Aspects of the New York City Property Market: A Study of Trends in Market Values, Assessments, Effective Tax Rates and Property Tax Delinquency*, December (New York: Citizens Housing and Planning Council of New York, 1975), vi.

25. Frank Domurad, David Fleischer, Gene Russianoff, and Loretta Simon, *City of Unequal Neighbors: A Study of Residential Property Tax Assessments in New York City*, New York Public Interest Research Group Report (Albany: New York Public Interest Research Group, 1981), iii.

26. George E. Peterson, Arthur P. Solomon, Hadi Madjid, and William C. Apgar Jr., *Property Taxes, Housing, and the Cities* (Lexington, MA: Lexington Books, 1973), 88.

27. Oliver Oldman and Henry Aaron, "Assessment-Sales Ratios under the Boston Property Tax," *National Tax Journal* 18 (March 1965): 36.

28. "Northside Property Assessed Higher," *Milwaukee Star*, June 6, 1974, 1.

29. Research Atlanta, *Property Tax Administration within Fulton County, Part I: Property Tax Assessment*, March (Atlanta: Research Atlanta, 1974); "NAACP Suit Attacks Inequity in County's Tax Assessments," *Atlanta Daily World*, February 9, 1975.

30. "Miami Probe: Whites Seen Paying Less in Property Tax," *Baltimore Afro-American*, March 1, 1975.

31. State laws on periodic reassessments varied wildly, with some states requiring local governments to update their assessment rolls biennially or quadrennially, and others (e.g., Cook County) conducting reassessments in a different quadrant of the taxing district each year (resulting in each property being reassessed each four years), while others (e.g., New Jersey) placing no requirements on when local governments had to reassess property values.

32. In Mississippi, two investigators for the Emergency Land Fund studying the impact of property taxes on the poor, remarked: "In most cases . . . there is little time left to keep abreast of current trends in the land market. It's just easier to copy last year's mistakes, and of course, last year's mistakes become this year's injustices." See Barbara Phillips and Joseph Huttie, *Mississippi Property Tax: Special Burden for the Poor* (New York: Black Economic Research Center, 1973), 16. A 1970 issue of *Property Tax Newsletter* included "An Ode to the Assessor," which read: "To find a value good and true, / Here are three things for you to do: / Consider your replacement cost, / Determine value that is lost; / Analyze your sales to see / What market value really should be; / Now if these suggestions are not clear, / Copy the figures you used last year." See *Property Tax Newsletter*, October 1970, 3. See also Martin, *Permanent Tax Revolt*, 7.

33. See "Cole-Layer-Trumble To Be Investigated," *People and Taxes*, April 1976, 2.

34. Martin A. Levin, "Urban Politics and Political Economy: The Politics of the Property Tax," *Policy Sciences* 9 (April 1978): 240.

35. Oldman and Aaron, "Assessment-Sales Ratios under the Boston Property Tax," 36.

36. Arthur D. Little, *A Study of Property Taxes and Urban Blight: Prepared for the U.S. Department of Housing and Urban Development* (Washington, DC: Government Printing Office, 1973).

37. John C. Hilke, "Determinants of Property Assessment Differentials with Emphasis on Delaware County, Pennsylvania" (Swarthmore, PA: National Science Foundation and Swarthmore College, 1973).

38. Val Hymes, "Ghetto Tax Used by Cities to Gouge Poor, Aid Flight," *Baltimore Afro-American*, April 28, 1973.

39. Paul, *Politics of the Property Tax*, 43, 45.

40. See Paul, *Politics of the Property Tax*, 70.

41. Paul, *Politics of the Property Tax*, 38.

42. Sanford D. Horwitt, *Let Them Call Me Rebel: Saul Alinsky—His Life and Legacy* (New York: Knopf, 1989), 531–32; U.S. "Steal" Rally, April 20, 1971, folder 6, box 1, Paul Booth (CAP), Chicago History Museum Research Center; Campaign against Pollution—Where We Stand on the Big Business Property Tax Scandals, April 1971, Chicago History Museum Research Center.

43. Campaign against Pollution—Where We Stand on the Big Business Property Tax Scandals; U.S. "Steal" Rally; CAP Yearly Report—Second Half of 1972, folder 2, box 1, Citizen Action Program (CAP) Records, UIC Special Collections; "CAP Again," *People and Taxes*, 4; James Fuerst and Andrew Ditton, "Reducing Property Taxes: An Evaluation of a Collective Action," *Land Economics* 51 (February 1975): 94–97; Stuart Greene, "Beverly—The Small Town in the Big City," *Chicago Tribune*, February 15, 1968; "Resurgent Beverly Won't Fold Up," *Chicago Tribune*, April 10, 1977; Constance Lauerman, "Beverly Hills Strives for Stability," *Chicago Tribune*, November 30, 1972; "Beverly Challenges Conventional Patterns, but Race Remains a Crucial Issue," *Chicago Tribune*, June 9, 1974; Robert McClory, "Fear Beverly May Become All Black," *Chicago Defender*, April 21, 1973.

44. "Residents Form Tax Protest Unit," *Chicago Tribune*, November 20, 1972; "Carey Meets with Taxpayers," *Chicago Tribune*, December 6, 1972; "Blacks Hang Cullerton in Effigy," *Chicago Defender*, May 9, 1972.

45. Gerald Horne, "Whither Black Political Power," *Pittsburgh Courier*, March 21, 1981; "Poor Forced Out Again," *Philadelphia Tribune*, March 13, 1979; and "Land Developers Find the Elderly Easy Prey," *Philadelphia Tribune*, January 18, 1980.

46. "Blacks Hang Cullerton in Effigy"; "Pay Off P.J. Day," July 15, 1971, folder 2, box 2, Paul Booth (CAP); "CAP to 'Visit' Cullerton Today," *Chicago Defender*, December 5, 1972, 2; Richard J. Kissel (supervisor), *Report on the Assessment Practices in Cook County (Illinois Department of Local Government Affairs)*, October (Springfield: Illinois Department of Local Government Affairs, 1972).

47. "But Race Remains Crucial Issue," *Chicago Tribune*, June 9, 1974; "Racial 'Steering' Suit Filed," *Chicago Tribune*, November 10, 1983.

48. Fred Bremer, Ed Dolan, Thelma Karson, Toni Mahan, Larry Wenderski, and Arthur Lyons, *Relative Tax Burdens in Black and White Neighborhoods of Cook County* (Chicago: School of Urban Social Sciences, University of Illinois Chicago Circle, April 24, 1979). A similar study of race and housing in Chicago released in 1979 also found that neighborhoods represented by aldermen who were aligned with the Daley machine tended to receive lower assessments than other parts of the city. See Brian J. L. Berry, *The Open Housing Question: Race and Housing in Chicago, 1966–1976* (Cambridge, MA: Ballinger, 1979), 496.

49. Diamond, *Chicago on the Make*, 250.

50. "Schedule Public Hearings: Plan to Investigate Overassessment of Black-Owned Homes," *Chicago Defender*, April 17, 1979.

51. Roy Harvey, "Residents of Evanston, Englewood Unite in Drive," *Chicago Defender*, May 5, 1979, folder 7, box 13, Illinois State Senate Records, 1976–1980, Harold Washington Archives and Collections, Pre-Mayoral Records, Special Collections and Preservation Division, Chicago Public Library.

52. "Black Leaders Seek Probe of Cook Assessor," *Chicago Sun-Times*, April 17, 1979.

53. "Probe to Precede Tax Reassessments," *Chicago Defender*, May 16, 1979.

54. Ed McManus, "PUSH Asks Tax Sale Delay," *Chicago Tribune*, May 6, 1979.

55. "Black Taxpayers Revolt: Charge Assessor Discriminates," *Keep Strong*, September 1979, 23–24. On predatory tax buying in 1970s Chicago, see also Andrew W. Kahrl, "Capitalizing on the Urban Fiscal Crisis: Predatory Tax Buyers in 1970s Chicago," *Journal of Urban History* 44 (May 2018): 382–401.

56. "Black Senators Seek Study of Alleged Property Tax Bias," *Chicago Tribune*, April 20, 1979, D4.

57. Ed McManus, "Property Tax Assessment Fraud in Cook County," *Illinois Issues* 6 (December 1980): 9–12.

58. Illinois State Senate, Transcript of Debates, May 1979, folder 10, box 4, Harold Washington Archives and Collections, Pre-Mayoral Records, Illinois State Senate Records, 1976–1980, Chicago Public Library.

59. "Sen. Washington Forms Black Taxpayers Coalition," *Chicago Weekend*, June 22, 1979; and Pierre Guilmant, "Tax Payer's Federation: Another Crisis Group?" *Chicago Defender*, August 16, 1979.

60. Arvis Averette, interviewed by author, May 12, 2015.

61. Ed McManus, "Discrimination in Property Assessment: Human or Computer Bias?" *Illinois Issues*, August 1979.

62. Thomas C. Hynes, Statement of Cook County Assessor Thomas C. Hynes on May 7, 1979, regarding the Report "Relative Tax Burdens in Black and White Neighborhoods of Cook County," May 7, 1979, Cook County Black-White Assessment Study (1979) folder, Arthur Lyons Personal Papers, Center for Economic and Policy Analysis, Chicago.

63. Ed McManus, "Property Tax Rate Higher in Black Areas, Study Says," *Chicago Tribune*, April 14, 1979, S1.

64. Berry, *Open Housing Question*, 497.

65. Illinois State Senate, Transcripts of Debates, June 1979, folder 12, box 4, Harold Washington Archives and Collections, Pre-Mayoral Records, Illinois State Senate Records, 1976–1980.

66. Kissel Report, 253.

67. Dona P. Gerson, "Tax Revolt in Cook County: Inflation of Property Values Combined with Increased Tax Levies," *Illinois Issues*, January 1978, 4–7.

68. See Jonathan Rowe, "Property Taxes: Increasing Action . . . as Outrage over Inequities Grows," *People and Taxes*, March 1975, 8, 9; and Joshua Mound, " 'Take the Rich off Welfare': Rising Taxes, Glaring Loopholes, and the Temporary Triumph of Left-Leaning Tax Populism," paper presented at Business History Conference, Columbus, OH, March 2013.

69. Martin, *Permanent Tax Revolt*, 12–13.

70. See Martin, *Permanent Tax Revolt*; Kuttner, *Revolt of the Haves*; Schulman, *The Seventies*, esp. 207–16; and Self, *American Babylon*, esp. 282–86.

71. Josh Levin, "She Used 80 Names: The Real Story of Linda Taylor, America's Original Welfare Queen," *Slate*, December 19, 2013, http://www.slate.com /articles/news_and_politics/history/2013/12/linda_taylor_welfare_queen_ronald _reagan_made_her_a_notorious_american_villain.html.

72. Corporate property-tax avoidance grew over the 1970s. By 1979, Cook County collected only 60 percent of all property taxes on corporations, annually costing Chicago's city schools an estimated $75 million in revenue. See Gregory Squires, Larry Bennett, Kathleen McCourt, and Phillip Nyden, *Chicago: Race, Class, and the Response to Urban Decline* (Philadelphia: Temple University Press, 1987), 136.

73. *Fair Assessment in Real Estate Association v. McNary*, 454 U.S. 100 (1981); Michael J. Bednarz, "Comity Bars Federal Damages for Section 1984 Discriminatory State Tax Assessments," *Boston University Journal of Tax Law* 1 (1983): 147–65.

74. "Panel Finds No Bias in Assessments," *Chicago Tribune*, January 9, 1980.

75. Averette interview; "Panel Finds No Bias in Assessments"; Arthur Lyons, "Some Questions Raised by 'A Report to the Assessor on Assessment Practices & Procedures for Residential Properties in Cook County,'" January 17, 1980, folder 6, box 9, Harold Washington Archives and Collections, Pre-Mayoral Records, Illinois State Senate Records, 1976–1980; editorial, "Black Homeowners," *Chicago Defender*, January 16, 1980.

76. "Change in Tax Breaks Likely," *Chicago Tribune*, June 27, 1984.

77. Diamond, *Chicago on the Make*, 264.

78. See "An Unfair Burden," *Chicago Tribune*, June 7, 2017, http://apps.chicago tribune.com/news/watchdog/cook-county-property-tax-divide/; and "An Era of Errors," *Chicago Tribune*, June 8, 2017, http://apps.chicagotribune.com/news/watch dog/cook-county-property-tax-divide/houlihan.html.

79. "The Problem with Appeals," *Chicago Tribune*, June 8, 2017, http://apps .chicagotribune.com/news/watchdog/cook-county-property-tax-divide/appeals.html.

80. "What It'll Take to Root Out Discriminatory Property Taxes in Cook County," *Chicago Reporter*, August 3, 2017, http://chicagoreporter.com/what-itll-take -to-root-out-discriminatory-property-taxes-in-cook-county/.

81. "What It'll Take."

82. Will See, "Take Tha House Back," 2016, http://genius.com/Will-see-take -tha-house-back-lyrics; Jerry Paffendorf, "We Can Do Something to Stop Tax Foreclosures," *Detroit Free Press*, July 7, 2017, http://www.freep.com/story/opinion /contributors/2017/07/07/opinion-we-can-do-something-stop-tax-foreclosures/457081001/; Atuahene, "Racial Discrimination and Detroit's Tax Foreclosure Crisis." See also Atuahene's website, at http://bernadetteatuahene.com/detroit/.

CHAPTER SEVEN

Clearing the Air and Counting Costs

Shimp v. New Jersey Bell *and the Tragedy of Workplace Smoking*

Sarah E. Milov

In February 1976, Donna Shimp addressed a formal thank-you note to Luther Terry, the former surgeon general of the United States. Shimp was a white forty-four-year-old customer service representative at the Millville offices of New Jersey Bell Telephone. She suffered from an "acute sensitivity" to tobacco smoke and was suing her longtime employer for failing to provide a safe work environment by not banning smoking in her presence. Terry, who was the first surgeon general to declare cigarette smoking a health hazard, had agreed to serve as an expert on Shimp's behalf. A New Jersey Superior Court judge, Philip Gruccio, would begin hearing Shimp's case in the spring. Shimp informed Terry that her case would especially need his expert opinion that "the presence of tobacco smoke in the work place can be a health hazard to a significant number of workers as well as a source of minor irritation to an even greater number of workers."[1] Terry's statement, Shimp hoped, would carry great weight in what was the first lawsuit brought by an employee against an employer's smoking policies.

Decided in December 1976, *Shimp v. New Jersey Bell* was the culmination of more than eighteen months of acrimony among Shimp, her employer, her coworkers, and her union, the Communications Workers of America (CWA). The decision, suggesting that employers' common-law obligation to maintain a safe and healthy work environment extended to the regulation of cigarette smoke, was first of its kind in the United States.

As such, it introduced smoking as a significant workplace issue: whose preferences would rule the air at work—smokers or nonsmokers, employees or employers?

When he received Donna Shimp's letter, Terry was enjoying an active retirement from public life. From his home in Philadelphia, he was on the faculty at the University of Pennsylvania Medical School, and he maintained close connections with the "health voluntaries"—the Heart Association, the Cancer Society, and the Lung Association.[2] As the first surgeon general to take a stand against tobacco, Terry was a public relations boon to these organizations. He was widely known for overseeing the landmark 1964 *Report on Smoking and Health*, the first government document linking cigarettes with heart and lung disease in men. The report was medically conservative in its own time, which was a result of its drafting by a committee partially made up of doctors acceptable to the tobacco industry. Yet Terry became strongly associated with the report's most lasting legacy: federal regulation of tobacco and the establishment of smoking as a public health hazard.

Upon leaving public office, Terry had grown sick of the halting incrementalism that had marked recent efforts to regulate tobacco in the name of public health. In the ten years since he stepped down as surgeon general, few public health measures had passed Congress: a strengthening of the wording of the cigarette warning label (1971), the extension of a health warning to print and mail advertising (1972), a ban on television advertising voluntarily agreed to by the tobacco companies after the application of the fairness doctrine enabled antismoking groups to get free anti-tobacco messages on the air (1970). Administrative agencies, notably the Interstate Commerce Committee (ICC) and the Civil Aeronautics Board (CAB), had done the most to regulate public space in the name of public health. Both agencies required the segregation of smokers and nonsmokers on common carriers by 1973. This rulemaking reflected and reinforced the increasing salience of claims for "nonsmokers' rights"—or the "right" of nonsmokers to be free of air contaminated by tobacco smoke in public places. Entrepreneurial public-interest lawyers and grassroots antismoking groups, foremost among them a group called Group Against Smoking Pollution (GASP), pressed brashly and publicly for clear air on behalf of nonsmoking Americans. Nonsmokers, these activists pointed out, constituted a numerical majority that needed only to be awakened to harness its full political power. As one activist put it, "We like to think that every non-smoker is a potential GASPer."[3]

To awaken the political sensibilities of silently suffering nonsmokers,

nonsmokers' rights activists became as visible as possible. They held ral-
lies; they cultivated a humorous political aesthetic, courting and evading
confrontation ("Yes, I mind if you smoke," "Don't blow smoke on my but-
ton," "Kiss a nonsmoker: taste the difference"). And they sued. Action
on Smoking and Health (ASH) had, by the early 1970s, emerged as the
legal arm of the antismoking movement, suing administrative agencies and
prodding the Department of Health, Education, and Welfare and the
National Institutes of Health to issue long-promised reports on smoking
and health. At the grassroots level, GASP petitioned, postered, pestered,
and pressured local governments and businesses to curtail or ban smoking
in public spaces. Terry occasionally attended events sponsored by local
GASP chapters. He gave the keynote address at a Philadelphia nonsmokers rally proclaiming a "Declaration of Independence from Smoking" in
January 1974, joined on the stage by local dentists, nurses, and "other community leaders."[4]

This burgeoning network of grassroots, legal, and medical activists
brought Shimp and Terry together. *Shimp* was a breakthrough for activists
who sought to expand the physical spaces in which smoke-free air could
be claimed as a right. Activists had long sought to awaken less vocal or liti-
gious nonsmokers to the possibility of a world where their desires, and not
those of smokers, would govern space. The workplace represented a particularly significant gain for activists because, unlike going to a restaurant
or a movie theater, going to work was not a purely voluntary activity. And
it certainly was not leisure. Thus, workplace smoking restrictions helped
create a *right* to smoke-free air in compulsory situations. And, by corollary,
they suggested that smoking was a privilege that could be enjoyed only in
designated leisure spaces.

Smoking was far from the only issue changing the American workplace in the 1970s. Many Americans found themselves confronting novel
situations at work: historic numbers of women in the workforce, increasing
mechanization and reliance on technology, the implementation of affirmative action policies that boosted numbers of African Americans at federally contracted jobs. Donna Shimp's own employer, New Jersey Bell, was a
component of AT&T, the nation's largest private employer and the largest
employer of American women. And it was no stranger to these demands
for inclusion, signing a series of consent decrees during the 1970s requiring
an end to discriminatory hiring, pay, and promotion practices.[5] Ideas about
acceptable workplace behavior changed as civil rights law opened new
opportunities for redress. Smoking on the job was but one of many extra-
curricular customs whose reevaluation activists forced during the 1970s.

Three interrelated dynamics shaped the struggle for nonsmokers' rights at work: the rise of "rights" as a tool for making political claims, the erosion of the political power of unions, and the increasing salience of cost arguments in regulating employee behavior. Activists like Donna Shimp challenged one vision of postwar liberalism—one in which unions were entrusted and authorized to bargain for workers' entitlements, to determine who and what was acceptable on the shop floor.[6] By seeking relief in the courts, Shimp challenged the legitimacy of collective decision making—a reminder that industrial democracy was not just about wages and hours but also about protecting cherished visions of workplace behavior and culture.

In challenging the collective bargaining agreements that governed workplace smoking policy, Shimp drew on another aspect of the liberal tradition—one particularly attentive to the rights, particularly the bodily rights, of individuals. Nonsmokers argued that they should not be forced to breathe in the pollution of somebody else's habit—an argument that would have been familiar in its contours, if not its specifics, to nineteenth-century liberals. Donna Shimp used the language of rights to endow her demands with political authority and joined thousands of other rights claimants across the country who found the courts, rather than the legislative or administrative branches, receptive to their demands.[7] Advocacy for nonsmokers arose from the same participatory impulses that animated social movements of the 1960s and 1970s—and in the same idiom of individual rights. This rights-based model of citizenship posed a potent challenge to the economic collectivism that sustained labor's political and organizational power—not mention to the white, male culture that predominated at all but a handful of public and service-sector unions.[8]

Creating the expectation of smoke-free air at work did not represent the straightforward triumph of the individual vision of liberalism over the pluralist vision. Rights did not trump solidaristic obligations. Individuals did not win over collectivities—although it would be easy to shoehorn the advent of smoking bans into a narrative that labor's indifference, if not hostility, toward the rights revolutions of the 1960s and 1970s hastened the decline of labor's political power and with it the New Deal order.[9] The story of *Shimp v. New Jersey Bell* suggests a far more dynamic and unpredictable vision of liberalism than "rise and fall" narratives permit. The New Deal order created imaginative possibilities, legal and administrative levers, and ways of envisioning a citizen's relationship to the state and the state's obligations to citizens that made it possible for lawyers and activists to argue that existing institutions did not represent the broad public interest. Demands for greater citizen participation in the distant and sclerotic decision-making structures of American life—administrative agencies, unions, corporations, and universities—animated civil rights, feminist, student, and environmental activism in the 1960s and 1970s.[10] Nonsmokers and other public-interest activists of the era took aim at different targets, but they were fighting the same political order that seemed about as chauvinistic and entitled as a worker blowing smoke in the face of a nonsmoking colleague. The battle for nonsmokers' rights at the workplace testifies not to the waning of the New Deal order, but to the ways that law, administration, and ideas about health and the environment had expanded the realm of the contestable.

With Shimp's victory in court, the individual's right to work in an environment free of tobacco smoke could arguably supersede a union's right to bargain over smoking. But the rights claims of antismoking activists like Donna Shimp did not clear the smoke-filled rooms of American offices or factories: arguments about smoking's cost did. Liberalism in the 1970s afforded antismoking activists a vocabulary and an institutional apparatus that allowed them to mount a critique of smokers' atmospheric hegemony. But smoking at work and opposition to smoking at work were both legacies of the New Deal order—the former guarded by labor unions, the latter by advocacy on behalf of previously unrepresented constituencies.

This chapter first lays out the particulars of Shimp's case, embedding her story in the rise of public-interest lawyering. It then discusses Shimp's struggle against her union, which viewed workplace smoking as a right to be guarded, not chiseled down. This was a stance wholeheartedly exploited by the tobacco industry's posture as a friend to the workingman—who smoked more than any other demographic group. Thus, as labor unions embraced tobacco, nonsmokers found management to be a receptive audience for arguments couched in terms of economics: smokers were expensive, accident-prone, unproductive. As one insurance executive explained, workplace smoking restrictions reflected the fact that "smokers use more company time to smoke, and are gone from their offices more frequently."[11] At work, the rights talk of liberalism was simultaneously the cost talk of managerialism.

"Like a Piece of Meat Thrust into a Smoke-House for Curing"[12]

In 1961, at age twenty-nine, Donna Shimp began her career at the New Jersey Bell Telephone Company at an office in Salem. The office was not far from her home in rural southwestern New Jersey, on the Delaware River. In 1975, the company's Salem office closed, and Shimp was transferred sixteen miles southeast to the company's new Bridgeton facility—a low-slung, solid-looking brick building with few windows. Shimp's coworkers at Bridgeton smoked heavily, and the smoky air made Shimp nauseated, caused rashes on her face, and resulted in several episodes of intense eye irritation, redness, tearing, and swelling. Because of her sensitivity to smoke, Shimp had a long-standing prescription for antiemetic drugs, which she took daily to ward off the nausea that overtook her around tobacco. Shortly after arriving at Bridgeton, she began wearing a gas mask to work—the "Gasfoe" model manufactured by the Mine Safety Appliance Company of Pittsburgh.[13] She would lower but not remove it when she spoke with customers on the phone or in person. She later marveled that the company allowed her to wear a gas mask in front of customers.

In the Bridgeton office, seven of the thirteen employees smoked on the job, and there was no prohibition on customer smoking in the offices. Relative to other Bell offices, Bridgeton was especially smoky. More than half of Bridgeton employees smoked, whereas only an estimated 30 percent of all company employees smoked, as documents from the *Shimp* trial later revealed. Office managers did not attempt to segregate smokers and nonsmokers spatially in Shimp's office, believing it would interfere with her duties as a service representative. The only way to make her working environment better, Shimp thought, would be to find a doctor able to certify the necessity of smoke abatement in the office, rather than one who would prescribe an individualized palliative. The office needed the prescription, not her. Shimp found somatic and psychic validation from an allergist who recommended that the office open its air-circulating vents. This seemingly basic remedy had not been attempted by Bell because it made the office drafty. The company honored the doctor's request for exactly one afternoon. The experiment in industrial hygiene was aborted after coworkers complained about the cold. As if to put an exclamation point on the smokers' reconquest of space, Bridgeton's union steward closed the open window by Shimp's desk that same afternoon.

In April 1975, Shimp was finally examined by the company doctor who told her that "it was a disgrace for any employee to have to work in such an atmosphere."[14] He ordered that she go home on paid leave until her supervisors could find a way to accommodate her need for a smoke-free work environment. Shimp believed that she'd be at home for just a few days. But days turned into months. During this extended leave—the

duration of which must have signaled the depths of her employer's unwillingness to implement a nonsmoking policy—Shimp became an activist.
She immersed herself in anti-tobacco research and politics. She established contact with ASH, which provided her with pro bono advice; she
got in touch with the recently formed New Jersey GASP, a thread on a
national web of locally focused antismoking advocacy.[15] And she began
learning more about the state of the field of tobacco research.

Anti-tobacco Science

In 1971, Jesse Steinfeld, Nixon's surgeon general, made headlines by announcing that it was "time . . . [to] interpret the Bill of Rights for the non-
smoker as well as the smoker."[16] The following year's *Report on Smoking
and Health* gave substance to this proclamation, becoming the first of the
surgeon general's *Reports* to examine the issue of passive smoking. Citing recent studies of people and animals exposed to tobacco smoke, the
report concluded that smoking affected nonsmokers in three major ways.
The mechanism of exposure was the emission of dangerous compounds
in "sidestream smoke"—smoke from the burning end of the cigarette.
First, sidestream smoke contributed to nonsmokers' acute discomfort—
producing a range of symptoms, including nosebleeds, eye irritation, elevated heart rates, increased respiratory illness, giant hives, gastrointestinal
symptoms, and migraine headache.[17]

By elaborating on the serious ways in which a term as fuzzy as *discomfort* presented itself clinically, the report helped to legitimize the physical
(rather than emotional) plight of nonsmokers. For women, this sense of
scientific validation may have been particularly important. Women's physical pain was still easy to dismiss as unreal—merely a result of feminine
sensitivity, or a somaticizing of schoolmarmish moral judgments. The gendering of nonsmoking had a basis in empirical fact. In 1975, 39 percent
of American men and 29 percent of American women smoked. There
was also a class dimension to the practice. In government surveys, more
than 50 percent of blue-collar men and 39 percent of blue-collar women
smoked.[18] On the job, the masculine toughness of the Marlboro man was
more apt to look like a male worker, senior to and better paid than his female colleagues, who resented deferring to the physical sensitivities of coworkers. Describing nonsmokers' rights activists as "modern day Carrie
Nations," tobacco forces subtly tied femaleness to the worst of all social

CLEARING THE AIR AND COUNTING COSTS 225

regulatory excesses: Prohibition.[19] In imparting the authority and dispassion of science, the report also imparted the authority of men.

The report also summarized recent discoveries about the composition of sidestream smoke, namely that it contained a great deal of carbon monoxide and oxides of nitrogen, the latter of which was associated with pulmonary dysfunction, and the former with oxygen deprivation. Indeed, studies of sidestream smoke exposure under laboratory conditions found that even short-term carbon monoxide exposure could produce an atmosphere that "exceeded the legal limits for maximum air pollution" in several localities, and induce changes in the body such that carbon monoxide in nonsmokers' blood exceeded the threshold values established by the Occupational Safety and Health Administration (OSHA). By noting environmental and industrial regulation of the poisons contained in tobacco smoke, the report highlighted a gap in governmental oversight of tobacco. It did not, however, suggest what should be done about that fact.

Finally, the report cited suggestive, if not definitive, animal studies demonstrating that secondhand smoke impaired cardiac and pulmonary function in dogs and rats. Its final sentence read like an invitation for further inquiry. "The extent of the contributions of [smoke particulate matter] to illness in humans exposed to . . . an atmosphere contaminated with tobacco smoke is not presently known."[20] The report formed the basis for understanding nonsmokers in new ways: as clinical patients, as research subjects, as victims, and as a class of people on whose behalf government should regulate. Together, the language of atmospheric contamination (so resonant with the environmentalist discourse of the time), the observation that other agencies were already regulating the same harmful byproducts of tobacco smoke, and the elevation of somatic discomfort to clinically recognizable symptoms provided cultural, legal, and scientific justification for nonsmokers' rights.

At home in Salem, Shimp wrote to the New Jersey Department of Health, New Jersey Department of Labor, county health departments, the Public Health Service, the Environmental Protection Agency (EPA), as well as Action on Smoking and Health and the health voluntaries. From each, she requested more information and assistance on how to bolster the case against workplace smoking. The responses she received suggested that she was in uncharted legal territory. ASH and the voluntaries contacted Bell on her behalf, offering advice to the company on how to implement a nonsmoking policy in the workplace. The Departments of Health and Labor told her there were no laws covering tobacco smoke in work environments, unless it was a question of fire safety. The Clean Air Act authorized the EPA to monitor the quality of ambient air outside buildings or vehicles. Administrative agencies supplied Shimp with information, but not relief.

The recent establishment of OSHA and the EPA provided antismoking activists with a new vocabulary for claiming rights—the right to "clean air," the right to be free of smoke "pollution"—and also the technical standards to quantify harm from ambient tobacco smoke. But both agencies lacked the authority to regulate the harms that agency expertise helped identify. The limits of agency authority were precisely what spurred public-interest lawyers like John Banzhaf and Ralph Nader, as well as new environmental organizations like the Environmental Defense Fund and the National Resources Defense Council to initiate litigation against the government. "Federal administrative agencies," according to the environmental historian Paul Sabin, "had not fulfilled the promise of the New Deal."[21] And yet for nonsmokers, these agencies—their technical capacity and legal authority to define air pollution thresholds in certain contexts—were terra firma, solid ground to build a case for clear air.

In June 1975, more than five hundred physicians, government officials, economists, activists, and public health officials from more than fifty countries descended on New York City's posh Waldorf Astoria hotel for the Third World Conference on Smoking and Health. Sponsored by the American Cancer Society and the National Cancer Institute, the conference presented an opportunity for tobacco activists to learn and share technical medical research, educational initiatives, policy, and social action that could reduce the social and economic cost of tobacco. The event was a living encyclopedia of those engaged in anti-tobacco science and activism. For the first time, the conference had a panel devoted to nonsmokers' rights, in addition to other panels on general research reviews, smoking and pregnancy, smoking and cardiovascular disease, antismoking education for children and adults, and cessation methods. A representative from nearly every agency Shimp had ever contacted attended the conference, and she pored over its voluminous proceedings. Within a week, she had prepared a recommendation for the implementation of a nonsmoking policy at New Jersey Bell, which she hand delivered to the company's president (or at least his secretary) and board of directors.

Shimp's plan was "to have smoking in the work areas of the business offices banned in the same manner that it is in the central offices, switchboards, and . . . public offices." She cited "data on passive inhalation" presented at the "Third World Council on Smoking and Health" [*sic*] to support the contention that "passive inhalation of smoke . . . is injurious to the health of everyone." She leaned hard upon the 1972 surgeon general's report in claiming nonsmokers' rights, although she noted that OSHA did not yet have legislative authority to regulate smoke as an occupational safety hazard. Her claim for "rights" rested largely on the fact that medical authorities, including prominent ones in government, had begun to focus on secondhand smoke as part of a larger public health agenda. Without a regulatory shepherd, nonsmokers' rights, Shimp realized, would not carry the day at Bell. In addition, much of the analysis in Shimp's short proposal focused on the "cost-factors" of workplace smoking. A no-smoking policy would not cost money and would save the company even more. The Lung Association had even offered to provide cessation clinics and antismoking programming for free.

And smoking employees were costly employees. Citing the Public Health Service, Shimp pointed out that smokers "spend over a third . . . as much time away from their jobs because of illness than do persons who have never smoked cigarettes." If Bell would not act on behalf of nonsmokers, it could act on behalf of its bottom line and wring greater productivity out of its smoking employees by encouraging them to quit.[22]

The Legal Department responded to Shimp's proposal with the blunt and factual statement that "there is not now any specific law or regulation which could compel the Company to prohibit smoking in its Commercial business offices." Bell's general counsel cited fear of unrest that might follow a unilateral smoke policy change without prior bargaining with the Communications Workers of America. For Bell to single-handedly impose a smoking policy would violate the collective bargaining agreement between the company and its largest union. Bell was unwilling to take such a risk. By inviting judicial compulsion, Bell exacerbated conflict between Shimp and her union, which jealously guarded the collective bargaining agreement from court interference.

Union Troubles

In her proposal, Shimp insisted that "employees deserve the same protection afforded the machinery so vital to our communications network, as the human body cannot be duplicated." Bell, it seems, took at least this part of Shimp's proposal seriously. In early July Shimp's supervisor offered her a solution: a demotion to the nonsmoking position of switchboard operator. Had not Shimp herself pointed out that these employees, by virtue of their proximity to valuable equipment, enjoyed a smoke-free work environment? The CWA seemed to think that this was a reasonable offer—despite the fact that Shimp would lose pay, work longer and less predictable hours, and lose seniority and thus become easier to fire, and despite the fact that labor representation was intended to protect individual workers from corporate bullying in the face of worker grievance.

From the moment her union steward slammed down her open window at Bridgeton, Shimp would spend as much time fighting her union as Bell. When Shimp began working at Bell, all offices were smoke free. But in the mid-1960s, the Communications Workers of America had bargained and won the privilege of smoking on the job. With less than ten years of advocacy supporting the concept of nonsmokers' rights, smoking as a health and safety issue looked far less substantial to union officials than did smoking as a worker autonomy issue—particularly in a sector where rapid technological changes threatened to eliminate entire classes of jobs and introduce numbing, machine-centered routines into others.[23] For the CWA, and for many other unions, the right to smoke at work was an index of labor power itself.[24] At Bell, the smoking policy had been set during the collective bargaining process. To accommodate Donna Shimp would mean subverting the very source of the union's authority. And as an act, smoking underscored worker autonomy. It was valuable to employees precisely because it was not productive, because it carved out a routine enjoyed either in solitude or in fellowship that afforded absolutely no economic benefit to Bell Telephone.

Shimp not only had been a member of the CWA but also had served for many years in positions of leadership, first as an office steward, and then as a steward for her district. CWA officials informed her that she had no grounds for a grievance until she lost pay or was fired. The steward at her office in Bridgton refused to offer her assistance in initiating a grievance procedure. When Shimp turned to the sympathetic vice president of her local to represent her in a grievance proceeding, the president of the local intervened to stop it. In July 1975, Shimp had a face-to-face a meeting with the president, who, between puffs, informed her that her grievance would be heard only upon court order. Shimp appealed to the president of the national Communications Workers of America. Through a spokesman she was told that the union would continue to uphold the right of the smoker to smoke anytime, anywhere.[25] Because of union ambivalence toward antismoking—ambivalence that stemmed from a genuine desire to protect the collective bargaining process and the autonomy of union members—nonsmokers' rights activists pursued arguments intended to appeal to management.[26]

The tobacco industry and organized labor had a long, complicated, and frequently acrimonious history, as before World War II Southern to-bacco companies had resisted unionization by exploiting the racialized division of labor that prevailed at factories.[27] However, the *Shimp* case bolstered Big Tobacco's ties with organized labor. Tobacco company ex-ecutives were deeply concerned about the rise of the nonsmokers' rights movement because it subverted the individual choice argument central to tobacco's defense. The Tobacco Workers International Union (TWIU), which represented workers in cigarette manufacturing plants, had long been involved in pro-tobacco politics, lobbying alongside the Tobacco In-stitute against tax increases or increased federal oversight.[28] The TWIU, like the CWA, was an affiliate of the AFL-CIO. Beginning in the 1970s, the Tobacco Institute began to suggest that occupational hazards, and not cigarettes, were to blame for worker health problems. An AFL-CIO News article ghostwritten by the Tobacco Institute argued that "in por-traying smoking as the cause of all health problems, the anti-smoking lobby is unwittingly helping industry escape responsibility for cleaning up the job environment."[29] To consider tobacco smoke an occupational disease, or even a social problem, would be to "delay cleaning up the work environment."

In forming an alliance with labor unions, the Tobacco Institute skill-fully exploited the political salience of occupational hazards in the decade following the establishment of OSHA. As titles like *Work Is Dangerous to Your Health* (1970) and *Expendable Americans: The Incredible Story of How Tens of Thousands of American Men and Women Die Each Year of Preventable Industrial Disease* (1974) attest, the decade witnessed rev-elations about the obscene hazards that Americans encountered on the job. Historians Gerald Markowitz and David Rosner have demonstrated that during the 1970s greater awareness of the risks posed by low-level long-term exposure to lead meant that a wide swath of the American workforce—brass founders, brick makers, cable makers, and even dental technicians—faced the prospect of renal, neurological, and reproductive damage because of occupational exposures.[30] Meanwhile, suits brought against asbestos manufacturers illustrated the deadly toll that the flame

retardant took on the workers who produced it.[31] In a historical irony resulting from a cynical attempt to mitigate corporate liability, the Johns-
Manville Corporation instituted one of the first and most far-reaching
corporate smoking bans in 1976. While the deadly properties of asbestos
had been known for decades, epidemiologists in the late 1960s and early
1970s were only discovering the terrifying synergistic effects between asbestos inhalation and cigarette smoking. Asbestos workers who smoked
had a ninetyfold greater risk of dying of lung cancer than people who neither smoked nor worked around asbestos.[32] The American Lung Association and Donna Shimp praised Johns-Manville for its foresight just as the
company was drowning in the deluge of toxic torts brought by employees
who suffered from asbestos-related lung disease.[33]

Unions, however, were skeptical of the J-M smoking ban, which they
viewed as a threat to collective bargaining and implied that workers themselves were to blame for illnesses contracted on the job. The International
Association of Machinists, which represented asbestos workers at plants
in Dallas and Boston, sued the company over its smoking ban. Unions did
not dispute the terrifying epidemiology that underlay the decision; rather,
they fought the policy on the grounds that the bans violated collective
bargaining agreements. While the arbitrator in the Boston case upheld
the company's decision, the Dallas ban was declared invalid. J-M then
filed suit precisely on the grounds that nonsmokers' rights advocates like
Shimp were trying to fortify: that common law supported an employer's
efforts to eliminate threats to worker health. In 1980, the Fifth Circuit
Court of Appeals affirmed the arbitrator's decision—a win for the strategic power of organized labor and the sanctity of the collective bargaining agreement, which, the court ruled, "denied the company the right" to
discharge workers who continued to smoke. It is hard to imagine a victory
more pyrrhic than the defense of a protective bargaining agreement that
protected a worker prerogative to exponentially increase his or her risk
of contracting lung cancer.

The Short Trial

In late July 1975, Donna Shimp was reassigned to a new office at Millville,
forty-five minutes southeast of her home. Shimp was optimistic about the
transfer: only one employee in the office smoked, and her doctor's request
to keep her as far as possible from the smoking employee was honored for

a few months. After October, the manager at Millville stopped adhering to the medical request, and an air-circulating machine that Shimp had requested to use was turned off because coworkers complained of the chilly air as the temperatures fell. When Shimp turned the fan back on, she was threatened with suspension. In her fall performance review, her ratings had fallen. She suspected that the company and the union were conspiring to fire her.

It's not surprising that Shimp sued Bell Telephone. Multiple forces pointed toward the courtroom as the only place where Donna Shimp's grievance could be resolved. Allies within the nonsmokers' rights movement viewed legal action as an important tool to change the regulation of space. Founded by John Banzhaf, a feisty young lawyer with a penchant for publicity, ASH was quick to offer assistance in a legal battle. Regulatory agencies had told Shimp that workplace smoking fell outside of their purview; her company told her that they would reconsider their smoking policy only on court order; the CWA made it clear that the union viewed workplace smoking as a right, not a threat to workers.

These forces all pointed toward legal action, but contingency played an important part in the outcome of the *Shimp* case. As she was searching for more scientific information on smoking, a desperate phone call to a reference librarian at Rutgers connected Shimp with Alfred Blumrosen, a professor of employment and labor law. Blumrosen had returned to teaching at Rutgers after spending much of the 1960s in public service in the Johnson administration. Active in the creation of the Equal Employment Opportunity Commission, and later counsel to the agency, Blumrosen was a consistent advocate of the federal government's power to intervene in workplaces to affirmatively address racial discrimination in employment. At the agency, he supported the use of private suits to initiate agency enforcement.[34] Public-interest law, particularly surrounding questions of consumer protection, the environment, and poverty, reflected the contradictions of American liberalism in the 1970s: a skepticism toward government that nonetheless sought social change through more representation within the state and a critique of "the system" articulated with law, the idiom of power.[35]

Blumrosen was part of a broader cohort of law professors who had begun to use law school classrooms as incubators of social activism.[36] At Yale Law School, students of Charles Reich, whose surprise bestseller *The Greening of America* combined environmental critique with a celebration of the counterculture, started their own environmental groups. Ralph

Nader, who did more than any single figure of the era to invigorate the idea
of the public interest and participatory administration of the law, launched
generations of college students into consumer activism through the establishment of campus chapters of the Public Interest Research Group
(PIRG). At George Washington University National Law Center, students
in John Banzhaf's Unfair Trade Practices course filed petitions with administrative agencies and courts, some demanding agency action on public smoking.[37] Despite the fact that lawsuits were the preferred weapon for
many public-interest lawyers, their use of courts did not represent a return
to a prelapsarian innocence of administration. Public-interest suits were
intended to compel administrative agencies to enforce existing laws. As
Banzhaf put it, "A great many problems can be solved within the system."[38]

The explosion in public-interest law was less a revolt against the New
Deal than an exploration of the possibilities of the legal system to advocate
for traditionally excluded constituencies. Frankly inspired by the ways in
which the NAACP and the American Civil Liberties Union had taken on
the government, public-interest lawyers of the 1970s viewed the courts as
one way of making sure government, in the form of administrative agencies, protected this more expansive notion of the public.[39] Just two years
earlier, students in Blumrosen's seminar on administrative law had spent
the semester focusing on the failures of OSHA and the possibilities for judicial rulings to be used as the basis of injunctive relief for individual workers.[40] Secondhand smoke was not among the occupational hazards studied.
Shimp had a real-world need for the legal theory developed in class, and,
luckily for her, Blumrosen prepared Shimp's case pro bono.

Nothing about the procedure of the Shimp case was routine. On the
strength of Shimp's medical affidavits, the New Jersey superior court issued an injunction against smoking in the work area at the Millville office
in the spring of 1976. When a return court date was set, Bell filed no response to Shimp's charges, suggesting that the company indeed wanted
a court to force its hand to act. In lieu of oral testimony, attorneys submitted only written affidavits. There would be no courtroom showdown.
But on the basis of the judge's earlier injunction, it seemed likely that the
expert testimony provided by Shimp would carry great weight.

Indeed, when Judge Philip Gruccio handed down his final opinion
in December 1976, he cited not only the 1964 and 1972 surgeon general
reports but also the affidavits of the surgeons general who issued them:
Drs. Luther Terry and Jesse Steinfeld. For Shimp, the American medical
bureaucracy was anything but cold and distant. Terry and Steinfeld intervened personally and directly on her behalf. "The evidence is clear and

overwhelming," Gruccio wrote, drawing on Terry's opinion that "passive smoking in the workplace can be injurious to the health of a significant percentage of the population." But Gruccio was also moved by Bell's existing policies to prevent damage to machinery—the same observation that had occasioned the offer of demotion to the position of switchboard operator. "The company already has in effect a rule that cigarettes may not be smoked around the telephone equipment," Gruccio wrote. "A company which has demonstrated such concern for mechanical components should have at least as much concern for human beings."[41] And so by court order, Bell was required to banish smoking to the lunchroom in whichever offices Shimp worked. The order applied only to Donna Shimp. It did not change overall company policy. Bell did not appeal the decision.

The Virtues of Nonsmoking Employees

The validation of Donna Shimp's right to clean air did not cause a chain reaction. In 1985, only 25 percent of American workers enjoyed smoke-free air at work.[42] *Shimp* is less significant as a precedent than as a prism, reflecting currents in the nonsmokers' rights movement while changing the shape of future confrontations. Forceful, energetic, articulate, but also matronly in a way that suggested a kind of measured reluctance to enter the fray, Shimp became a national and, later, international symbol of nonsmoking advocacy, especially in the workplace.[43] After the trial, Shimp published a how-to manual for workers suffering from ambient tobacco smoke. It contained all the legal materials from her trail, as well as a directory of antismoking groups and physicians. Distributed through Lung Associations, *Clearing the Air at Work* helped make visible not only the legal remedies available to workers but also the large network of authorities that were on their side, ready to help. After its publication, several individuals wrote to Luther Terry requesting his expert opinion to present to their bosses, or for affidavits for legal proceedings. The response was uniformly positive, and Terry frequently suggested that sufferers seek additional support from other experts, including Dr. Jesse Steinfeld, Nixon's surgeon general who had been ousted for his strong statements on behalf of nonsmokers.[44] Well before Surgeon General C. Everett Koop released *Health Consequences of Involuntary Smoking* in 1986, high-ranking public health officials had been willing, even eager, to advocate directly on behalf of individual workers who sought assistance in legal battles with their employers. Nonsmoking workers had not found relief in the administrative agencies most equipped to oversee air quality and workplace safety; they looked instead toward the Office of the Surgeon General for assistance, validation, and authority. It is ironic that personal interventions by former surgeons general on behalf of nonsmokers grew in importance at the very same moment as many Americans decried the bloated impersonality of the government bureaucracy.

While still maintaining her job at Bell and her membership in the CWA, Shimp founded a nonprofit consultancy called Environmental Improvement Associates (EIA) in 1978. EIA was a two-person operation that Shimp and her husband, Ben, ran out of their home. Its purpose was to advocate for workplace smoking restrictions and to consult with businesses about how to go about implementing a policy. EIA's well-connected advisory board was a testament to Donna Shimp's historical place in anti-tobacco advocacy. It included Terry and Banzhaf, as well as Robert Drinan, the Jesuit priest and liberal Massachusetts congressman, and Dr. Samuel Epstein, a world-renowned expert on environmental and occupational disease for his theory of widespread environmental carcinogens.[45] Naturally, Shimp first offered EIA's services to New Jersey Bell with a Smokefree Day at Work program she had created. Unsurprisingly, the company declined her offer.[46] Other firms were more receptive to EIA's advice. In 1978 Chase Manhattan Bank, Mobil Oil, Campbell Soup, the Communications Workers of America, the International Brotherhood of Electrical Workers, the Pennsylvania, New Jersey, Florida, and Philadelphia Departments of Health, and the Washington, Florida, South Carolina, and Nebraska Lung Associations had purchased the Smokefree Day at Work kits that New Jersey Bell had turned down. On top of that, individual employees at TransWorld Airlines, New York Telephone, DuPont, the *New York Times*, ABC-TV, the University of California, Los Angeles, and MIT, as well as employees working within several branches of the mammoth Bell System, contacted EIA for smoke-free literature, even though their workplaces declined participation in Smokefree Day.[47] Awareness of the workplace smoking issue was rising. But in the corporate setting—conceived of as a change in personnel policy potentially requiring the assistance of consultants, cessation classes for employees, incentivized quit programs, or, at the very least, new signage alerting employees to the policy—it became unmoored from the rights-based language that prevailed in the courtroom.

After *Shimp*, arguments for nonsmokers' rights increasingly centered on the cost—both economic and moral—not just of smoking but of smokers. To some degree, Shimp invited this reframing, particularly in appeals to companies that lacked unionized employees. In an era of declining union density—in 1982 only 22 percent of the labor force was unionized, as opposed to 30 percent in 1964—arguments that would have been familiar to early twentieth-century managers became more common. For example, in *Clearing the Air*, Shimp applauded a time and motion study conducted by a pool equipment manufacturer in Clifton, New Jersey. The results of the study showed that smokers were between 2 percent and 10 percent less efficient than nonsmokers—reason enough for company stockholders to pay a 2 percent bonus to nonsmoking employees. Merle Norman Cosmetics went smoke free voluntarily in 1976, estimating that the company would save thousands in lower absenteeism and higher productivity. Talk of the pecuniary benefits of nonsmoking employees easily shaded into language of their moral attributes as well. As Shimp explained, "An increasing number of employers are growing enthused about the virtues of nonsmoking employees."[48] Just as some labor unions had feared—a fear stoked by the tobacco industry's dire warnings about the creation of "second-class citizenship"—smokers began to be viewed with suspicion by employers. "Can You Afford to Hire Smokers" queried a 1981 article in a management journal. After a decade of energy shocks and in the midst of a recession, the answer was no.[49]

In its quest to catalyze the implementation of smoke-free policies, EIA frequently embraced this economizing and moralizing approach. The ammunition against workplace smoking supplied by EIA was powerful: 399 million workdays were lost annually by American smokers and non-smokers as a result of smoking; smokers were involved in twice as many accidents as nonsmokers; smokers were at greater risk for industrial poisoning because of the synergistic effects of chemical compounds and cigarette smoke; smokers wasted 2 percent to 10 percent of the day "just in the mechanics of smoking"; smokers damaged equipment and upholstery; smokers cost more in housekeeping and utilities; and, should these rank-and-file concerns fail to persuade management, "smoking executives are more susceptible to coronary or other crippling disease in their most productive years, and the cost of replacement is very high."[50] Nonsmoking policies were good for the bottom line because smokers as a class of people engaged in unproductive and destructive work practices.

A decade later, opponents of smoking in the workplace had grown even more strident in their indictment of smokers. In 1989, John Banzhaf, director of ASH, authored a letter to the *Washington Post* arguing that differential insurance rates for smokers and nonsmokers, which some insurance companies initiated in 1984, "insure that the majority are not forced to subsidize the self-indulgences of the minority."[51] Moralizing characterizations of smokers stood uneasily next to the science that increasingly focused on causal pathways of nicotine addiction. Ironically, Big Tobacco, which had long maintained that smoking was an individual choice and an American freedom, embraced the position that collective decision making by unions, and not management policies, should control the workplace environment—so long as collective rights were smokers' rights.

Despite the antiregulatory filigree embroidering the vocabulary of modern conservatism, the most salient divides in the smoking issue have never been partisan. Through the strategies pursued by labor unions, Big Tobacco, and the nonsmokers' rights movement, smoking came to mean the freedom of working-class people—imagined as male for reasons associated with both the demographics of smoking and the cultural associations of the working class—to assert their autonomy, satisfy their desires, guard the authority of the union to determine which behaviors and practices were acceptable at work and which were not. Such moral and physical satisfactions took on additional meaning in the 1970s as deindustrialization, the feminization of the labor force, and mechanization eroded the political power of unions and the cultural authority of men.

The yawning gulf in rates of cigarette use between blue- and white-collar workers stands as a grim index of the achievement of the nonsmokers' rights movement. In 2011, a third of blue-collar and service workers were smokers, compared to a fifth of white-collar workers. Nonsmokers in the construction, service, hospitality and manufacturing industries are still more likely to work in smoky environments.[52] This means that even working-class people who do not smoke are at greater risk for diseases related to secondhand smoke—including lung cancer—than are white-collar Americans. That these same people are routinely derided for making bad health, parenting, and financial decisions—even as cigarette taxes push regressively higher across the United States—stands as a testament to the tragic slide from nonsmokers' rights to smokers' costs.

Notes

1. Donna Shimp to Luther Terry, February 6, 1976, folder 1, box 7, Luther L. Terry Papers, National Library of Medicine (NLM), Bethesda, MD.

2. He chaired the Interagency Council on Smoking and Health, a consortium of private- and public-sector health associations, from 1967 to 1969.

3. "A Long Burn over Smokers' Rights," *Washington Post*, June 28, 1977.

4. "Non Smokers Rally" leaflet, folder 39, box 3, Terry Papers; "Congress to Adopt Bill of Rights for Nonsmokers," folder 7, box 6, Terry Papers.

5. For more on the investigation, suit, and consent decree at AT&T, see Marjorie Stockford, *The Bellwomen: The Story of the Landmark AT&T Sex Discrimination Case* (New Brunswick, NJ: Rutgers University Press, 2004); Lois Herr, *Women, Power and AT&T: Winning Rights in the Workplace* (Boston: Northeastern University Press, 2003); Phyllis Wallace, *Equal Employment Opportunity and the AT&T Case* (Cambridge, MA: MIT Press, 1976). Venus Green, *Race on the Line: Gender, Labor, and Technology in the Bell System* (Durham, NC: Duke University Press, 2001), 229–48; and Nancy MacLean, *Freedom Is Not Enough: The Opening of the American Workplace* (New York: Russell Sage Foundation; Cambridge, MA: Harvard University Press, 2006), 131–33.

6. The literature on labor's role in forging postwar liberalism is voluminous. Nelson Lichtenstein, *State of the Union: A Century of American Labor* (Princeton, NJ: Princeton University Press, 2002) provides an introduction. Nancy MacLean's *Freedom Is Not Enough* is the seminal account of the struggle by civil rights activists and feminists for access and equality at work. For an account of the racial and economic contradictions of postwar liberalism, see Reuel Schiller, *Forging Rivals: Race, Class, Law, and the Collapse of Postwar Liberalism* (New York: Cambridge University Press, 2015); Paul Frymer, *Black and Blue: African Americans, the Labor Movement, and the Decline of the Democratic Party* (Princeton, NJ: Princeton University Press, 2009). For a cultural account of the role of "identity politics" in dissolving the class solidarism of labor, see Jefferson Cowie and Nick Salvatore, "The Long Exception: Rethinking the Place of the New Deal in American History." *International Labor and Working-Class History*, no. 74 (2008): 3–32.

7. Laura Kalman, *The Strange Career of Legal Liberalism* (New Haven, CT: Yale University Press, 1996); Reuel Schiller, "Enlarging the Administrative Polity: Administrative Law and the Changing Definition of Pluralism, 1945–1970," *Vanderbilt Law Review* 53 (2000) 1389–1453; Alice Kessler-Harris, *In Pursuit of Equity: Women, Men, and the Quest for Economic Citizenship* (New York: Oxford University Press, 2006), 239–89; and Nancy MacLean, *Freedom Is Not Enough*.

8. Gregory Wood's *Clearing the Air: The Rise and Fall of Smoking in the Workplace* (Ithaca, NY: Cornell University Press, 2016) is the only social history of smoking at work and in the lives of working people. Wood sees the prevalence of indoor smoking as a barometer of the strength of organized labor in the postwar United States. Ruth Milkman, *On Gender, Labor, and Inequality* (Urbana: University of Illinois Press, 2016), 171–80. On the language of individual rights in the earlier era, see Karen M. Tani, *States of Dependency: Welfare, Rights, and American Governance, 1935–1972* (New York: Cambridge University Press, 2016).

9. Lichtenstein, *State of the Union*, 165–72.

10. Schiller, "Enlarging the Administrative Polity," 1410–14; and Paul Sabin, "Environmental Law and the End of the New Deal Order," *Law and History Review* 33 (2015): 965–1003.

11. Association Management Success Smoking Policies Survey 1987, Tobacco Institute, https://www.industrydocumentslibrary.ucsf.edu/tobacco/docs/shgg0140.

12. Mary Gibson, *To Breathe Freely: Risk, Consent, and Air* (Totowa, NJ: Rowman & Allanheld, 1985), 13.

13. Donna Shimp, Alfred Blumrosen, and Stuart B. Finifter, *How to Protect Your Health at Work: A Complete Guide for Making the Workplace Safe* (Salem, NJ: Environmental Improvement Associates, 1976), 18.

14. Shimp, Blumrosen, and Finifter, *How to Protect Your Health*, 67.

15. For more on citizen activism, particularly in the fields of health and the environment in the 1970s, see Christopher Sellers, *Crabgrass Crucible: Suburban Nature and the Rise of Environmentalism in Twentieth Century America* (Chapel Hill: University of North Carolina Press, 2013); and James Longhurst, *Citizen Environmentalists* (Medford, MA: Tufts University Press, 2010).

16. See, for instance, Constance Nathanson, *Disease Prevention as Social Change: The State, Society and Public Health* (New York: Russell Sage Foundation, 2007), 118.

17. *The Health Consequences of Smoking; a Report of the Surgeon General* (Washington, DC: U.S. Public Health Service, 1972), 121–31.

18. Office on Smoking and Health, U.S. Public Health Service, *Smoking and Health: A Report of the Surgeon General—Appendix: Cigarette Smoking in the United States, 1950–1978*, A-10, https://profiles.nlm.nih.gov/ps/access/nnbcph.pdf. Gender discrepancies in smoking prevalence were consistent regardless of occupational type, although men and women clerical workers smoked at the closest rates: 40 percent and 34 percent, respectively.

19. W. D. Hobbs, October 16, 1976, Lorillard Records, https://www.industrydocumentslibrary.ucsf.edu/tobacco/docs/gmgh0126.

20. *Health Consequences of Smoking*, 131.

21. Sabin, "Environmental Law and the End of the New Deal Order," 984.

22. Shimp, Blumrosen, and Finifter, *How to Protect Your Health*, 92–95.

23. Sally L. Hacker, "Sex Stratification, Technology and Organizational Change: A Longitudinal Case Study of AT&T," *Social Problems* 26, no. 5 (June 1, 1979): 539–57.

24. Wood, *Clearing the Air*, 125.

25. Shimp, Blumrosen, and Finifter, *How to Protect Your Health*, 110.

26. More than twenty years after Shimp's lawsuit, public health organizations still puzzled over how best to communicate with labor unions. See "Finding Common Ground: how Public Health Can Work with Organized Labor to Protect Workers from ETS," *Journal of Public Health Policy* 18, no. 4 (1997): 453–64; "Labor Positions on Worksite TC Policies: A Review of Arbitration Cases," *Journal of Public Health Policy* 18, no. 4 (1997): 433–52. "Hospitality Workers' Attitudes

and Exposure to Secondhand Smoke, Hazardous Chemicals, and Working Conditions," *Public Health Reports* 122, no. 5 (2007): 670–78.

27. Robert Korstad, *Civil Rights Unionism: Tobacco Workers and the Struggle for Democracy in the Mid-Twentieth Century South* (Chapel Hill: University of North Carolina Press, 2003); Bruce Kaufman, *Challenge and Change: The History of the Tobacco Workers International Union* (Kensington, MD: Bakery, Confectionery, and Tobacco Workers International Union, 1986).

28. Rene Rondou/Tobacco Workers International, January 10, 1976, Brown & Williamson, http://industrydocuments.library.ucsf.edu/tobacco/docs/prfx0057.

29. Tobacco Workers International Union, February 19, 1975, Tobacco Institute, http://industrydocuments.library.ucsf.edu/tobacco/docs/mmxy0146.

30. Gerald E. Markowitz, *Deceit and Denial: The Deadly Politics of Industrial Pollution* (Berkeley: University of California Press, 2002).

31. Markowitz, *Deceit and Denial*; Gerald Markowitz and David Rosner, " 'Unleashed on an Unsuspecting World': The Asbestos Information Association and Its Role in Perpetuating a National Epidemic," *American Journal of Public Health* 106 (2016): 834.

32. Irving J. Selikoff, E. Cuyler Hamond, and Jacob Churg, "Asbestos Exposure, Smoking and Neoplasia," *Journal of the American Medical Association* (1968): 106–12; Robert L. Rabin, "A Sociolegal History of the Tobacco Tort Litigation," *Stanford Law Review* 44, no. 4 (1992): 860–65; John A. Jenkins, *The Litigators: Inside the Powerful World of America's High Stakes Trial Lawyers* (New York: St. Martin's Press, 1989), 119.

33. "Johns-Manville Says No Smoking," *American Lung Association Bulletin*, July 1978, folder 20, carton 2, Shimp Papers, Tobacco Control Archives, University of California–San Francisco (UCSF).

34. For more on Blumrosen's encouragement of private litigation during his time at the EEOC, see Quinn Mulroy, "Public Regulation through Private Litigation: The Regulatory Power of Private Lawsuits and the American Bureaucracy" (PhD diss., Columbia University, 2012).

35. Sabin, "Environmental Law and the End of the New Deal Order," 969.

36. Winton D. Woods and Clark Derrick. "Introduction," *Arizona Law Review* 13, no. 4 (1971): 797–800; Edgar S. Cahn and Jean Camper Cahn, "Power to the People or the Profession? The Public Interest in Public Interest Law," *Yale Law Journal* 79, no. 5 (1970): 1005–48; Gordon Harrison and Sanford Jaffe, "Public Interest Law Firms: New Voices for New Constituencies," *American Bar Association Journal* 58, no. 5 (1972): 459–67; and Schiller, "Enlarging the Administrative Polity," 1414.

37. "John Banzhaf, the So-Called 'Nader of the Tobacco Industry,' " *Washington Post*, March 15, 1970; "Group Will Spur Suits against Cigarette Makers," *New York Times*, January 29, 1969; and "Tobacco Men Bar Evasion of TV Ad Ban," *New York Times*, January 9, 1971.

38. "John Banzhaf, the So-Called 'Nader.'"

39. Sabin, "Environmental Law and the End of the New Deal Order"; Schiller, "Enlarging the Administrative Polity."

40. Shimp, Blumrosen, and Finifter, *How to Protect Your Health*, 37–38; Alfred Blumrosen, Donald Ackerman, Julie Kligerman, and Peter VanSchaick, "Injunctions against Occupational Hazards: The Right to Work under Safe Conditions," *California Law Review* 42, no. 3 (1976): 702–31.

41. *Shimp v. New Jersey Bell Tel. Co.*, 368 A.2d 408 (N.J. Super. Ct. 1976).

42. William N. Evans, Matthew C. Farrelly, and Edward Montgomery, "Do Workplace Smoking Bans Reduce Smoking?" *American Economic Review* 89 (1999): 728–47.

43. See, for example, "Japanese Colleagues," folder 2, box 6, Shimp Papers, UCSF.

44. Luther Terry to Paula L. Carey, October 27, 1977, folder 40, box 3, Terry Papers; and Luther Terry to June Mercer, July 22, 1980, folder 43, box 3, Terry Papers.

45. Samuel S. Epstein *The Politics of Cancer* (Garden City, NY: Anchor Press, 1979).

46. John Kingsbury to Donna Shimp, December 15, 1977; "To All Personnel Vice Presidents," October 15, 1979, box 1, folder 1, Shimp Papers.

47. Smokefree Day at Work, January 11, 1978, folder 41, box 1, Shimp Papers.

48. Shimp, Blumrosen, and Finifter, *How to Protect Your Health*, 3.

49. W. L. Weis, "Can You Afford to Hire Smokers?" *Personnel Administrator* 26, no. 5 (May 1981): 71–73, 75–78.

50. Shimp, Blumrosen, and Finifter, *How to Protect Your Health*, 3.

51. "Making the Self-Indulgent Pay," *Washington Post*, February 18, 1989.

52. Kaori Fujishiro, Karen D. Hinckley Stukovsky, Ana Diez Roux, Paul Landsbergis, and Cecil Burchfiel, "Occupational Gradients in Smoking Behavior and Exposure to Workplace Environmental Tobacco Smoke: The Multi-Ethnic Study of Atherosclerosis (MESA)," *Journal of Occupational and Environmental Medicine* 54, no. 2 (2012): 136–45; and Public Health Law Center, "Blue Collar Workers and Tobacco," October 2011, http://www.publichealthlawcenter.org/sites/default/files/Blue%20Collar%20Workers%20and%20Tobacco.pdf.

CHAPTER EIGHT

Glocal America

The Politics of Scale in the 1970s

Suleiman Osman

On January 1976, at a meeting of the World Affairs Council of Philadelphia honoring the nation's bicentennial, Henry Steele Commager presented his "Declaration of Interdependence." Most in the audience were likely amused by his wordplay. Decades before scholars popularized the term *globalization*, *interdependence* had become a hot buzzword in the 1970s among economists and political scientists. The timing of the document however was provocative. In a year commemorating the formation of the United States, the historian declared the nation-state obsolete. On an increasingly interconnected planet, economic and environmental issues transcended outdated national borders. "WE AFFIRM that the resources of the globe are finite, not infinite, that they are the heritage of no one nation or generation, but of all peoples, nations and of posterity. . . . WE AFFIRM that the economy of all nations is a seamless web, and that no one nation can any longer effectively maintain its processes of production and monetary systems without recognizing the necessity for collaborative regulation by international authorities." Rejecting "little plans" and "chauvinistic nationalism," the declaration ended with a call for global governance through a stronger United Nations and World Court. The reaction from the public was enthusiastic. One hundred and twenty-six senators and congressmen subsequently signed the declaration. The Minnesota state legislature endorsed the declaration and even voted to have UN flag fly over its state capitol.[1]

While Commager pushed audiences to think more globally, elsewhere the People's Bicentennial Commission (PBC) championed the decentralization of power from the national government to local communities. Founded by former antiwar activists in 1971, the New Left–inspired group challenged official plans for the bicentennial that, in the commission's view, had become commercialized and politically vapid. Instead, the PBC hoped that through protest, guerrilla theater and publications they could reintroduce the public to the radical and leftist roots of the American Revolution. Along with distributing a newsletter titled *Common Sense*, PBC members carried muskets and wore three-cornered hats. In one well-publicized event, the group tossed oil barrels into Boston Harbor to re-enact a Boston "Oil Party." In 1975, the PBC issued its "Declaration of Economic Independence." Big business and the federal government had become modern-day versions of Tories and King George III, funneling money to a small elite and controlling the lives of citizens. The declaration called for "decentralized economic enterprises, with ownership and control being shared jointly by the workers in the plants and by the local communities in which they operate."[2]

The PBC was one of many groups pressing for the decentralization of the bicentennial festivities. Federal officials in the late 1960s had originally proposed a massive expo in Philadelphia, along with centralized celebrations in other major cities. Mayors eagerly awaited an influx of federal money to help develop tourist facilities in struggling downtowns. But in the 1970s few Americans had a taste for large-scale plans. Neighborhood groups fought with mayors over redevelopment schemes. Protesters demanded more citizen participation. Women, African Americans, and Puerto Rican and Native American groups pushed for a more inclusive and less sanitized rendering of U.S. history. In Boston, a small group of white antibusing activists set off a bomb at Plymouth Rock and threatened more attacks against historical sites during the celebration unless school integration plans were halted. Hampered by protests and budget shortfalls, the federal American Revolution Bicentennial Administration abandoned ideas for a central event and devolved planning and funding to local communities, nonprofits, and private corporations. The result on July 4 was a highly decentralized celebration consisting of more than sixty-six thousand local events.[3]

These new globalist and localist political impulses ran squarely against the hopes of Gerald Ford that the bicentennial revive the public's collective faith in the American nation-state. "I see this Bicentennial of 1976 as a rebirth," Ford declared standing on a train platform aside an "American Freedom Train" set to ride from Alexandria, Virginia, throughout the country. "We must renew ourselves as a people and rededicate this Nation to the principles of two centuries ago," he reemphasized a few months later in a speech to a crowd in Boston. "We must revitalize the pride in America. . . . Perhaps national unity is an impossible dream. . . . we have suffered great internal turmoil and torment in recent years."[4]

But in his nostalgia for the imagined national consensus of the past, Ford misinterpreted the decade's seemingly fractious politics. The participants in the bicentennial's sixty-six thousand minicelebrations were enormously prideful and full of a sense of political renewal. But they were mobilizing around a new politics of scale. In a decade of growing skepticism about the nation-state, a diverse array of Americans developed new and stronger supranational and subnational political identities. Environmentalists hung photos of planet Earth on their walls and claimed that "small is beautiful." The women's movement strove for "global sisterhood" and founded thousands of fiercely autonomous women's centers, health clinics, bookstores, and communal living spaces. African American activists reembraced an older internationalist black identity and strove for neighborhood power and community control. Architects championed both local "human scale" architecture and global "human rights." The United States in the 1970s, to use a term developed by geographers, was *glocalizing*. Or as the popular phrase at the time went, Americans were "thinking globally and acting locally."

This chapter is a call for political historians to think more about scale. Despite the recent "spatial turn" in the field, political historians have yet to draw from a sophisticated body of theoretical work developed by geographers and environmental historians about the social construction of scale—theoretical tools of great potential value for political historians of the modern United States. Integrating scale more fully into the analysis would help historians of the 1970s, in particular, avoid several declension frameworks that are common in the field. They can also help historians be more precise with scalar language and avoid using terms like *local* or *global* in ways that are fixed, essentialist, or normative.

With this conceptual framework in place, the chapter makes three historical arguments about scale in the 1970s: (1) the decade is a key political turning point that provides a bridge between the social movements of the 1960s and the conservative or "neoliberal" political culture of the 1980s; (2) rather than a fracture of postwar liberal consensus or a shift "rightward," the decade saw a new "politics of scale" in which a variety of groups embraced new subnational and supranational political identities that sought alternatives to the nation-state and do not easily fit into categories of "left" or "right"; and (3) the "neoliberal" political order that historians argue coalesced in the 1980s had complex origins in an array of "glocal" antistatist and anticorporate impulses on both the left and right in the previous decade.

To make this historical and historiographical intervention, the chapter locates four nonscalar declension frameworks that historians have developed to interpret the political culture of the 1970s: red-blue, whole-unwhole, happy-unhappy, and pre-post. The four titles are offered solely as a conceptual tool and are not meant to oversimplify, caricature, or debunk very sophisticated scholarship. The chapter then demonstrates how concepts from scalar theory such as politics of scale and scale jumping can bolster each framework and help orient them away from slipping into declension narratives. The chapter then concludes with an illustrative discussion of glocalization, the politics of scale, and the emergence of neoliberalism during the 1970s.

Scholarship on the 1970s has blossomed in the past decade. No longer considered a dull interlude between the dynamic social movements of the 1960s and conservative counterrevolution of the 1980s, the 1970s—since the publishing of Bruce Schulman's seminal book—is now recognized as the "big bang" moment during which New Deal liberalism transformed into new political, economic, and social configurations. Yet despite the growing enthusiasm for studying the decade, historians have struggled to find a unifying framework that makes sense of its politics. Unlike the more legible 1960s and 1980s, the 1970s offered few clear story lines, strong international engagements, or compelling national figures for historians, points out Thomas Borstelmann. Like the sixty-six thousand events of the bicentennial, the decade was incoherent and fragmented.[5]

Perhaps because of the decade's illegibility, historians often take a bleak view of the 1970s. Declension narratives abound. Economic crisis ended decades of unprecedented growth and prosperity. Vietnam and the oil crisis challenged American hegemony abroad. The New Deal liberal order ruptured along race and class lines. Disgruntled white ethnics, evangelical Christians, and Southern suburbanites coalesced into a powerful new right that attacked the women's movement and dismantled federal attempts to address racial inequality. Exasperated African American and other minority activists turned from hopeful protest to black power realpolitik and the thankless task of governing economically devastated cities. The student movement become increasingly radical and violent, and eventually dissolved. Former activists became young urban professionals or retreated to narcissistic New Age communes. The nation was increasingly divided, disinterested, and depressed.

For many historians, nothing captured the decade's bleakness more than the glum and lackluster 1976 bicentennial celebration. "There was this sort of dismal quality pervading the celebration of the bicentennial," explains Bruce Schulman. "There was a widespread sense the best days were in the past." "Instead of being a celebration of 200 years of government policy and U.S. independence, it became a sort of party that was full of cynicism and disgust," agrees Peter Carroll. Where one hundred years earlier participants in centennial celebrations reveled in the nation's promise, the 1976 bicentennial, concludes David Frum, "was really something of a bust."[6]

Many political historians analyzing the 1970s adopt what Matthew Lassiter calls a "red-blue" approach. Drawing largely on the results of elections and shifting party affiliations, "red-blue" historians attempt to place the historical era on a spectrum from left to right. For most of these scholars, the 1970s was the moment when the nation abandoned the centrist politics of postwar liberalism and "turned rightward." After decades of work by grassroots activists and conservative intellectuals, the new right of the 1970s finally stitched together Southern white suburbanites, working-class Northern white ethnics, and Christian evangelicals into a powerful political force. Other "red-blue" historians, in contrast, point to the 1970s as the high-water mark of the radical left. Abandoning the cautious liberalism of the previous decade, the women's, prison rights, gay, black power, and other liberation movements entered full bloom and offered truly transformative critiques of technocracy, capitalism, incarceration, and patriarchy. By the middle of the decade, the radical left shifted to formal politics and won significant victories in Gary, Indiana; Washington DC; San Francisco, Berkeley, and Santa Monica, California; and Burlington, Vermont.[7]

"Red-blue" approaches work well and illustrate the sharp divides of American politics in bold and familiar hues. But as Lassiter, Brian Balogh and other historians have pointed out, the framework risks setting up too neat an opposition between reified political binaries: public versus private, federal versus local, regulation versus deregulation. Clear and important ideological differences certainly existed. But when one looks closer at the politics of the 1970s, the distinction between left and right in many areas becomes murky. "Ideas slipped across the conventional divisions of politics, often incongruously and unpredictably," writes Daniel Rodgers. As historians have shown, for example, many of the most potent critiques of "big government" in the 1970s emerged from the left. Ralph Nader and consumer rights activists were among the first champions of deregulation. Charter schools later associated with conservative policy makers had origins in the decade's countercultural alternative school movement. African American activists in the 1970s were among the most influential advocates of devolving political power to local communities. As a result, center cities experimented with decentralization initiatives during the decade at much higher rate than suburbs and rural areas. Enterprise zones were initially the brainchild of 1970s British anarchist planners. With which hue should historians paint community development corporations? What about the embrace of postmodern architecture and waterfront festival marketplaces by city growth machines? Or the politics of self-help that undergirded the do-it-yourself aesthetic of early hip-hop and punk culture? Rather than oscillating like a pendulum, the politics of the 1970s was a strange mix of conflict and consensus. "In the late seventies, the people of the United States were moving vigorously to the Left, the Right and the Center, all at the same time," wrote Michael Harrington about the era's ideological incoherence.[8]

To better grapple with this complexity, some historians have developed more holistic frameworks. Rather than pointing left or right, whole-unwhole frameworks argue that the country in the 1970s shifted from whole to fragmented. Universalist modernism and technocratic consensus politics of Cold War liberalism gave way to a politics that celebrated homeownership, individual autonomy, the free market, ethnic identity, and personal self-fulfillment. "E pluribus plures" writes Bruce Schulman playfully about a society that had come to emphasize diversity and cultural pluralism over integration. The 1970s commenced an "era of disaggregation, a great age of fracture," writes Daniel Rodgers in his award-winning book. "The fracture of the social—though it took different terms and operated through different analytical languages—was, in the end, as much a product of left-leaning intellectuals as it was of the new intellectual right." Gary Gerstle and Steve Fraser put it more bluntly. In the 1970s, New Deal liberalism "disintegrated."[9]

The interdisciplinary breadth and depth of these works is remarkable. Yet even with their rich complexity, whole-unwhole frameworks still can hint at declension. Although most of the scholars do emphasize that the country has never been "whole," the notion of national rupture can still be misinterpreted as normative. Furthermore, too strong an emphasis on fragmentation overlooks the strong supranational political and cultural identities that simultaneously emerged in 1970s America. The decade of disintegration was also the era of the human rights movement, the growth of international nongovernmental organizations, and the environmentalist movement. Just as splitting entails both a widening and a shrinking of space, Americans' fractured sense of nationhood sparked both more local and more global imaginaries. "The 1970s global human rights imagination," explains Mark Philip Bradley of this shift, was a transnational movement that shared a planetary vision and yet played out on the ground in unstable and contested "local vernaculars." To avoid allowing categories like "whole" and "unwhole" from slipping into normativity, it could be helpful to think additionally about shifting political scales.[10]

A third popular declension framework focuses on affect. Rather than a shift from whole to not whole, or from center to left and right, these happy-sad frameworks point to a change in national mood. Americans in the 1970s according to some scholars felt alternatively a collective "malaise," "disenchantment," "irony," "boredom," and "rage." Certainly many commentators in the 1970s pointed to a dour mood that pervaded the public. "A central fact," the Harris polling company concluded in 1976, "is that in our nation, our people, disaffection and disenchantment abound at every turn. *That disaffection has now reached majority proportions.*" Yet by focusing uncritically on the national scale, many happy-sad frameworks risk painting with too thick a psychological brush. Did all groups in the nation share the same mood as baby-boomer white men in the 1970s? What about the euphoria experienced by African Americans after electing the first black mayors like Maynard Jackson? Or the liberating feeling young women activists may have had participating for the first time in a consciousness-raising group? Or the numinous awe felt by a Southern Walmart worker becoming a born-again Christian?[11]

One should not, of course, dismiss the history of emotions. In recent years the humanities have taken an "affective turn," and political historians of the 1970s have begun to draw from a sophisticated body of affect theory to unpack the complex relationship between feelings and politics.[12] But as Daniel Rogers points out, historians still need to pay attention to different scales of emotions. The history of "national moods" too often relies on easy pop psychology and sweeping generalizations. "The notion of a national mood or psyche is the illusion of writers and journalists hard-pressed by a deadline," warns Rodgers. "To imagine a national mood across a society as diverse as the United States is to fall into the language of partisans of time rather than to explain it."[13]

The pre-post framework is the most theoretical of the four. Developed by geographers and other social scientists, pre-post terminology has recently been embraced by the burgeoning subfield of the history of capitalism. According to this framework, the 1973–1974 fiscal crisis was a watershed moment in which the American New Deal liberal state transformed to a society of "posts": post-Keynesian, post-Fordist, postmodern, postindustrial, and postmaterialist. Centralized planning, large assembly-line factories, mass consumer culture, and mass-produced suburbs gave way to devolution, decentralized planning, flexible accumulation, segmented consumer markets, and privatization. The material-based blue-collar politics that undergirded New Deal liberalism was supplanted by postmaterialist "new social movements" led by white-collar workers and college students that focused on lifestyle choices. A modernist faith in scientific expertise and centralized planning shifted to a postmodernist skepticism about metanarratives and progress, reflected in a postmodern architecture that celebrated quirkiness, historicity, and playful references to the past. Cold War liberalism gave way to *neoliberalism*—a term well developed by social scientists that historians are only recently beginning to embrace.[14]

A revived interest in political economy, class, and capitalism is long overdue. But historians of the 1970s are right to be wary of adopting too schematic an approach. The prefix *post* suggests too clean a break from the past. Historians should continue to emphasize continuities and the slow evolution of "long" social movements and ideas. Whether in Sunbelt suburbs, urban gentrifying districts, or countercultural communes, the politics of white-collar communities was not simply "postmaterialist." As the editors of this volume point out, the concerns of women, African Americans, Native Americans, tech workers, and environmentalists in the 1970s were in fact quite concrete. The biggest hurdle is the term *neoliberalism*, which is protean and still needs to be historicized. Archival research on the actual development of "neoliberal" policy on the local level in the 1970s is growing but remains scant.[15]

What if one were to think of the political culture of the 1970s not in terms of national polarization or fragmentation but in terms of a shifting politics of scale?

The spatial turn in U.S. political history is now several decades old.

Historians have developed a sophisticated literature about "place" and "space," borrowing from geography a rich vocabulary about mental mapping, Lefebvrian spatial trialectics, and public and private spheres. Political historians of the 1970s use the term *spatial turn* most often to refer to three specific trends in the field. For some, "turning to the spatial" means paying more attention to environmentalism and the role of the natural or built environment in political movements. For others, it means a greater emphasis on local place identity and the ways battles over neighborhoods, towns and homes shaped race conflict and hindered broader political coalitions. To others, the spatial turn is cartographical and refers to a more rigorous use of GPS and mapping technology by historians. All are welcome developments.[16]

While well attuned to place and space, political historians along the spatial turn have not yet dedicated enough attention to scale. Despite pleas from environmental historians like Richard White for more engagement with geographic theory, many historians still use terms like *local*, *regional*, *national*, and *global* as if they were natural and fixed. Debates about scale are limited largely to temporal disputes about periodization or epistemological arguments among local, national, and transnational historians about what spatial scale best reveals historical truths. Different scales go in and out of style. Years ago community studies and microhistory were fashionable. In recent years, the arrival of big data, GIS maps, and the internet have sparked a rush to bigger and bigger scales of history.[17]

This is not to suggest that political history has been "nonscalar." Because the United States is a federal system, political historians have long examined the shifting power relationship between different levels of government. In recent years, for example, there has been a revival of interest in exploring how tensions between national and local political cultures shaped the growth of an idiosyncratic American nation-state that was both "weaker" and "stronger" than its European counterparts. Scholarship about the competing drives toward administrative centralization and localism in the nineteenth century is particularly strong.[18] But with scale relatively undertheorized, too many accounts still present a single Russian doll of nested administrative levels that are tacitly hierarchical and normative.

Historians thus often infuse the scales of federalism with unacknowledged cultural value. Some in Weberian fashion champion the struggles of small communities and grassroots politics against the inexorable expansion of modern development and centralized planning. More often political historians adopt the motto "the bigger, the better." Larger scales appear as more real (or less invented), as well as more powerful and just. Historians of the New Deal often describe a reactionary and anachronistic localism that persisted as hindrance to the more progressive national scale of the emerging social democratic state. Transnational approaches often not only seek to move beyond but also critique the scale of the nation-state. Historians have argued, for example, that by embracing a national identity, African American racial liberals during the Cold War abandoned what could have been a truer "global vision." The goal here is not to caricature this enormously sophisticated scholarship. By drawing attention to the social construction of scale, this chapter instead echoes calls by Brent Cebul, Karen Tani, and Mason Williams to "de-essentialize federalism," and treat federalism as relational, culturally constructed and historically contingent rather than fixed, hierarchical, and normative.[19]

Geographers have since the 1990s developed sophisticated theories of scale that could be drawn on by political historians. Scale is no longer understood as an ontologically given and politically neutral framework for understanding the world. Instead, geographers argue that scale is socially produced, culturally imagined, and politically contested. Rather than a single Russian doll of nested and fixed levels from global to the local, multiple scales coexist in space that form a scaffolding of overlapping and competing categories. Scale is also a process in a constant state of change. Marxist geographers emphasize the way capitalism reshapes scale. Others point to a more quotidian process in which scale is "continually forged and remade through everyday habits, routines, practices, negotiations, experiments, conflicts and struggles." Feminist geographers have examined the way scale is gendered and have even developed models of horizontal rather than vertical scalar thinking. More work is needed linking critical race theory and scale.[20]

The geographer Neil Smith's concept of a politics of scale can be particularly useful for political historians. Smith argues that scale is constantly produced, negotiated, and reproduced in a highly contested political process. Capitalism in his view causes periodic "scalar crises," which render older scalar arrangements obsolete. State, business leaders, and organized labor in response continually grapple to find "scalar fixes." Countries might empower new global institutions like the International Monetary Fund. Cities might try to brand themselves as locally distinct. But while primarily drawing from Marxist political economy, Smith also emphasizes that social movements and everyday citizens have agency to contest and change scalar arrangements. In a process he calls "jumping scale," political groups continually shift scales to challenge existing power relations. A social movement might adopt nationalist symbols, assert its global reach, or call itself "neighborhood based" for example. Jumping scale also occurs in the cultural realm. Just as important as political and economic institutions are the changing "scalar imaginaries" of everyday citizens.[21]

Although much of it remains theoretical and is at times jargony, scalar theory can help historians of the 1970s eschew declension narratives by examining how scalar categories were formed, dismantled, and reformed. To avoid reifying the salient divisions between left and right, red-blue historians can also analyze how both adopted similar local and global scalar language for different purposes. For whole-unwhole historians, the concept of jumping scale can help avoid positioning the national scalar level as more "complete" than more fragmented local or diffuse global ones. Happy-sad historians can break new ground by forging new connections between scalar theory and affect theory. How have the scales of emotion changed over time? What emotions did the local, national, and global produce in the 1970s, ranging from patriotism to empathy, malaise, comfort, boredom, alienation, nostalgia, and rage? Mark Bradley's terrific work, for example, describes the way a new "global affect and feeling" of the human rights movement shifted the "affective bonds" of individual, nation-state, and global community in new and important ways. Michael Foley, in contrast, convincingly shows how the "local," home, and even individual body produced a new "existential and emotional" politics.[22]

Scalar theory can also help pre-post historians make sense of the murky origins of neoliberalism in the 1970s. Geographers have devoted particular attention to "scaling" the watershed decade. The rise of multinational corporations, the collapse of Bretton Woods, inflation and the energy crisis, argue Neil Brenner and others, sparked a paradigm-shifting scalar crisis for the post-1945 Westphalian system of self-contained Keynesian social democratic nation-states. The United States, West Germany, and other advanced-industrial nations as a result began a process that Erik Swyngedouw calls "glocalization." Nation-states "hollowed out" with financial capital and economic power scaling upward to the supranational level and the regulatory and redistributive functions of the state devolving to local governments, nonprofits, and private institutions. The nation-state did not disappear. But a new neoliberal order emerged with scalar arrangements that were both more globalized and localized.[23]

Glocalization may make jargon-averse historians cringe. But the notion that political actors in the 1970s jumped scale from national to supra and subnational configurations is useful and is supported by two bodies of seemingly divergent scholarship about the 1970s: diplomatic, global, and international historians who analyze the history of globalization, and urban historians who examine the plethora of localist and neighborhood-based African American, Latino, Native American, LGBT, environmentalist, and women's protest in cities and suburbs of the 1970s.

For historians like Daniel Sargent and Akira Iriye who study the history of globalization, the 1970s was the decade in which Americans developed a new "global consciousness" that transcended the borders of the nation-state. During the early postwar era, the United States had developed an unprecedentedly strong sense of national identity. While on the ground deep political and racial fissures existed, the dominant political culture coalesced around what Wendy Wall refers to as a new and imagined "politics of consensus." The New Deal, Fair Deal, and Great Society expanded and strengthened the federal government. Immigration was curtailed by restriction. Internal migration and mass consumer culture blurred regional distinctions. Universities founded new American studies departments that celebrated the nation's exceptionalism. While McCarthyism silenced radical internationalist voices, mainstream branches of the civil rights movement of the 1950s and 1960s strategically rallied behind national symbols to push federal courts and Congress to dismantle state and local laws supporting white supremacy. In foreign policy, Cold War liberals envisioned a Westphalian world order of sovereign social democratic nation-states. Modernization theory, Keynesian economics, and military aid would help newly independent African and Asian states maintain their sovereignty from Soviet influence and internal unrest.[24]

In the 1970s, according to these historians, the national boundaries, both institutional and symbolic, that held together this fragile Westphalian world order began to break down. The Bretton Woods system of fixed exchange rates collapsed. In 1973, the Organization of Petroleum Exporting Countries (OPEC) organized an oil embargo that forced everyday Americans to think for the first time about transnational flows of energy, natural resources, capital, and pollution. In the Global South, civil war and autocratic leadership ravaged newly independent postcolonial nations. Television brought the first images of humanitarian disasters in places like Bangladesh into American homes. As multinational corporations grew during the decade from a handful to nearly nine hundred, industry left devastated Rust

Belt cities for distant parts of the world. Just as satellites projected the first pictures of the planet Earth, the problems facing the United States suddenly seemed global in size. Many Americans of a variety of political leanings increasingly came to the shared conclusion that the national government was not up to the task of solving them.[25]

As a result, many Americans began to participate in what Akira Iriye calls a new "global civil community." In 1974–1975, a study by the Chicago Council on Foreign Relations found that 70 percent of Americans supported "fostering international coordination to solve common problems such as food, inflation, and energy." Many helped support an explosion of new international nongovernmental organizations (NGOs). Humanitarian groups like Oxfam America multiplied and expanded at an astonishing rate. A new "human rights movement" drew a groundswell of support from both secular leftists and evangelical Christians. By the late 1970s both Jimmy Carter and Ronald Reagan made "human rights" central parts of their foreign-policy programs. New environmentalist international NGOs like Friends of the Earth pushed Americans to think in planetary terms about pollution, endangered species, and population growth. During what the United Nations called "the International Decade for Women," the women's movement began a decade-long struggle to organize at the global level. At international conferences on women's issues in Mexico City and Copenhagen, as well as parallel meetings, women activists debated the possibilities and limits of organizing around the concept of global sisterhood.[26]

Whether Greenpeace boats speeding through territorial waters or Doctors without Borders medics shuttling into disaster areas without official approval, this new globalism reflected a growing disenchantment with the nation-state. "Globalism imparted an antistatist accent," explains Daniel Sargent. "Human rights [was] a suitable moral vocabulary for a world in which the vectors of interdependence seemed to be erasing the barriers of territorial sovereignty."[27]

While diplomatic and international historians describe a "shock of the global," urban historians, in contrast, point to an era of increased localism. Disenchanted with the national government and large corporations, Americans around the country echoed the words of best-selling author and "Buddhist economist" E. F. Schumacher: "Small is beautiful." "The idea that big is bad and that there is something good to smallness is something the country has come to accept much more today than it did ten years ago," explained pollster and Carter administration adviser Patrick

Cadell in 1977. "We are indeed in the grips of a mass movement toward decentralization," explained African American journalist Ellis Cose. "A new wind blows across the political horizon, a wind created by thousands of politicians and public figures calling for a return of power to 'the people.'" Rather than "New Federalists" or "New Populists," Cose argued that these "New Fed-upists" came from across the political spectrum. But they shared "one central proposition: that society has become too centralized, too impersonal, that big government and big business have not only made people less human, but made them less capable of meeting their most basic needs."[28]

Like the new globalism of the human rights movement, the new localism of the 1970s was strikingly diverse and cut across deep and salient race, class, and political divides. In center cities, a "neighborhood movement" spearheaded by African American and Latino activists led grassroots campaigns to fight redlining by banks, gain neighborhood control over school systems, and rehabilitate dilapidated housing. In areas ranging from New York City's gentrifying brownstone districts to rural Vermont, young, white college graduates moved "back to the land" and "back to the city," and experimented with communal living arrangements. African American, Latino, and white "activist-entrepreneurs" opened thousands of radical bookstores, head shops, and natural food groceries. By 1980, seventy-one million Americans belonged to a cooperative of some sort, including more than ten thousand food cooperatives. A do-it-yourself industry increased by 200 percent from 1974 to 1977, creating a $16.5 billion annual business. Radical feminist groups ranging from the Boston Women's Health Book Collective to the Combahee River Collective created hundreds of autonomous women's centers, bookstores, medical clinics, domestic violence shelters, and cooperative day-care facilities. Native American activists seized and occupied federal land to protest for greater tribal sovereignty and self-determination. Eclectic coalitions of slow-growth activists around the country fought the expansion of nuclear plants, airport runways, and new highways. Conservative activists from Kanawha, West Virginia, to East Boston, Massachusetts, mobilized around a more reactionary version of localism, leading drives to protect local schools from "anti-Christian" textbooks and federally mandated busing programs. Both the left and right grasped for new words to describe their disenchantment with large institutions: community control, empowerment, self-determination, devolution, decentralization, autonomy, home rule, privatization, and even more troublingly secession.[29]

Echoing the Black Panther Huey Newton's 1970 call for "intercommunal-ism," or the New Republic of Africa's call for an autonomous black nation in the rural South, most groups articulated a "glocal" mix of global and local political language. In his award-winning *Nation of Neighborhoods*, Benja-min Looker captures this strange and contradictory web of global and local-ist antistatist political ideas in the 1970s that ran from the counterculture to black nationalism to the new right. In 1980, John McClaughry, a Republi-can speechwriter and self-declared "Jeffersonian Republican," sent his boss and presidential candidate Ronald Reagan a copy of the "back-to-the-land" magazine *Mother Earth News*. The chief architect of Richard Nixon's 1968 "black capitalism" proposals, McClaughry spent the 1970s in the Vermont countryside where, inspired by E. F. Schumacher's *Small Is Beautiful*, he founded a libertarian research institute and dedicated himself to creating a "human-scale" society. "Note the Reagan themes: self-reliance, indepen-dence, etc.," he wrote about the counterculture magazine. "There is much gold to be mined by reaching out to people who read this stuff."[30]

A complete history of scale and neoliberalization is too ambitious for a chapter this length. The chapter is thus more of a call for more historical work on the process of glocalization that roots the history of neoliberal policy and thought in an array of ideologies, political movements, and pol-icy experiments to the ground. Rather than a coherent national strategy driven by neoconservative think tanks, right-wingers in the federal gov-ernment, and Wall Street executives, "neoliberalization" in its embryonic stage was a distinctly unsystematic and uneven process that unfolded in individual localities in different ways. In response to a scalar crisis caused by the collapse of a global financial order, domestic fiscal austerity, and the retrenchment of an increasingly inert federal government, a variety of grassroots groups launched a hodgepodge of local ad hoc "self-help" ex-periments and global advocacy campaigns that were only later institution-alized into new public-private partnerships. Some of these initial makeshift experiments were simply pragmatic. Others were the expression of a new and diverse antistatism emerging on the left and right that viewed the federal government as bureaucratic, technocratic, destructive, and "out of scale." Some policy experiments were the brainchild of free-market and public-choice theorists. Others represented a range of anarchist, coun-tercultural, black nationalist, Chicano, pastoral, indigenous, feminist, and queer ideas about space and autonomy. The murky roots of neoliberalism can be found not only in Mount Pelerin, Switzerland, but also in the natural food stores of Austin and San Francisco.[31]

The history of neoliberalism in the 1980s is thus less a story of revolution than *interpretatio neoliberali*—the successful opening of a new and peculiar ideological umbrella that creatively recast local self-help initiatives and global NGOs as exemplars of good governance and free-market economics. Even with his call to "make America great again" and repudiation of the radical social movements of previous decades, Reagan's election did not signal a return to an older politics of scale and resurgence of nationalism. Rather, with his desire to dismantle the national social democratic state, his push for open trade accompanied by a militarized defense of human rights, and his eagerness to devolve social services to self-help groups and local governments, Reagan's neoliberalism was in practice a hypertrophy of 1970s glocalization.

The chapter in conclusion thus remains more of a historiographical suggestion. Historians should pay more attention to scale. The goal has not been to drown the differences between political groups in a sea of relativist jargon. While less normative, scalar analysis can and must also remain critical. Local, regional, national, and global scales have always been constructed for a variety of political purposes. Localism in the 1970s was in some hands progressive and humanizing. In other hands, it was reactionary, violent, and racist. Globalism signaled for some activists on the left a more radical planetary politics. It was also the language used by new multinational corporations.[32] But scale also acknowledges uncomfortable shared language. This can help historians to make sense of the strangeness of the 1970s and its legacy.

Notes

1. For an analysis of Commager, the bicentennial and "interdependence," see Daniel Sargent, *A Superpower Transformed: The Remaking of American Foreign Relations in the 1970s* (New York: Oxford University Press, 2014), 165–66; Henry Steele Commager, "A Declaration of Independence," October 1974, http://www.onthecom mons.org/magazine/declaration-interdependence; Peter G. Peterson, "Preparing for the Future," *New York Times*, January 4, 1974, 29.

2. Christopher Capozzola, "'It Makes You Want to Believe in the Country': Celebrating the Bicentennial in an Age of Limits," in *America in the Seventies*, ed. Beth Bailey and David Farber (Lawrence: University Press of Kansas, 2004), 36–37; Robert Reinhold, "Radical Group Presses New Bicentennial View," *New York Times*, January 18, 1976, 38; and Emma E. Fullen, "A Revolutionary View of the Bicentennial," *Los Angeles Times*, October 28, 1975, A7.

3. Capozzola, "It Makes You Want," 31–39; John E. Bodnar, *Remaking America: Public Memory, Commemoration and Patriotism in the Twentieth Century* (Princeton, NJ: Princeton University Press, 1992), 226–44.

4. Capozzola, "It Makes You Want"; Margot Hornblower, "Ford Talks about Train for Freedom," *Washington Post*, December 20, 1974, C1; Gerald Ford, "Presidential Remarks to for American Freedom Train Certification," December 19, 1974, and Ford, "Address at the Old North Church," April 18, 1975, Boston, https://www.fordlibrarymuseum.gov/library/document/0122/1252286.pdf.

5. "Big bang" is from Bruce Schulman and Julian Zelizer, *Rightward Bound: Making America Conservative in the 1970s* (Cambridge, MA: Harvard University Press, 2008), 2; Thomas Borstelmann, *The 1970s: A New Global History from Civil Rights to Economic Inequality* (Princeton, NJ: Princeton University Press, 2012), 3.

6. Quoted in Steve Hockensmith, "The Silly Patriots Games of '76," *Chicago Tribune*, July 1, 2001.

7. Matthew Lassiter, "Political History beyond the Red Blue Divide," *Journal of American History* 98, no. 3 (December 2001): 760–64; Brian Balogh, *The Associational State: American Governance in the Twentieth Century* (Philadelphia: University of Pennsylvania Press, 2015), 3–4; Schulman and Zelizer, *Rightward Bound*; Laura Kalman, *Right Star Rising: A New Politics* (New York: W. W. Norton, 2010); Daniel Berger, ed., *The Hidden 1970s: Histories of Radicalism* (New Brunswick, NJ: Rutgers University Press, 2010); Stephen Tuck, "Reconsidering the 1970s— The 1960s to a Disco Beat?" *Journal of Contemporary History* 43, no. 4 (October 2008): 617–20.

8. Daniel Rodgers, *Age of Fracture* (Cambridge, MA: Belknap Press of Harvard University Press, 2011), 8, 18; Harrington quoted in Jefferson Cowie, *Stayin' Alive: The 1970s and the Last Days of the Working Class* (New York: New Press, 2011), 3.

9. Rodgers, *Age of Fracture*, 8; Bruce J. Schulman, *The Seventies: The Great Shift in American Culture, Society, and Politics* (Cambridge, MA: Da Capo, 2001); Gary Gerstle and Steve Fraser, *The Rise and Fall of the New Deal Order, 1930– 1980* (Princeton, NJ: Princeton University Press, 1989), ix.

10. Mark Philip Bradley, *The World Reimagined: Americans and Human Rights in the Twentieth Century* (New York: Cambridge University Press, 2016), 155.

11. Philip Jenkins, *Decade of Nightmares: The End of the Sixties and the Making of Eighties America* (New York: Oxford University Press, 2008); William Graebner, "America's *Poseidon Adventure*: A Nation in Existential Despair," in Bailey and Farber, *America in the Seventies*, 158–59; Kirkpatrick Sale, *Human Scale* (New York: Coward, McCann & Geoghegan, 1980), 25; Borstelmann, *The 1970s*, 10–11.

12. Susan J. Matt, "Current Emotion Research in History; or, Doing History from the Inside Out," *Emotion Review* 3, no. 1 (January 2011): 117–24; Ruth Leys, "The Turn to Affect: A Critique," *Critical Inquiry* 37, no. 3 (Spring 2011): 434–72; Barbara H. Rosenwein, "Worrying about Emotions in History," *American Historical Review* 107, no. 3 (June 2002): 821–45. For an introduction to seminal writings in affect theory by Brian Massumi, Sara Ahmed, Lauren Berlant, and others, see Melissa Greg and Gregory Seigworth, eds., *The Affect Theory Reader* (Durham, NC: Duke University Press, 2010); Michael Stewart Foley, "'Everyone Was

Pounding on Us': Front Porch Politics and the American Farm Crisis of the 1970s and 1980s," *Journal of Historical Sociology* 28 (2015): 104–24.

13. Rodgers, *Age of Fracture*, 6.

14. Rodgers, *Age of Fracture*, 8–9; Jason Hackworth, *The Neoliberal City: Governance Ideology and Development in American Urbanism* (Ithaca, NY: Cornell University Press, 2007); David Harvey, *A Brief History of Neoliberalism* (New York: Oxford University Press, 2007); and Jamie Peck, *Constructions of Neoliberal Reason* (New York: Oxford University Press, 2013).

15. Cebul, Geismer, and Williams, introduction to this book; for a history of neoliberalization on the ground in New York City, see Benjamin Holtzman, "Crisis and Confidence: Reimagining New York City in the Late Twentieth Century" (PhD diss., Brown University, 2016). For a transnational analysis of neoliberalization in the United States and the United Kingdom, see Timothy P. R. Weaver, *Blazing the Neoliberal Trail: Urban Political Development in the United States and United Kingdom* (Philadelphia: University of Pennsylvania Press, 2015).

16. Ralph Kingston, "Mind over Matter: History and the Spatial Turn," *Cultural and Social History* 7, no. 1 (2010): 111–21; for an alternative argument that urban geographers and sociologists who have developed a rich vocabulary about space need to dedicate equal attention to time, see Suleiman Osman, "What Time Is Gentrification?" *City & Community* 15 (2016): 215–19.

17. Richard White, "The Nationalization of Nature," *Journal of American History* 86, no. 3 (1999): 976–86; "AHR Conversation: How Size Matters: The Question of Scale in History," *American Historical Review* 118, no. 5 (2013): 1431–72.

18. Bruce Schulman, in *Making the American Century: Essays in the Political Culture of Twentieth Century America*, ed. Bruce Schulman (New York: Oxford University Press, 2014), 2; Thomas Sugrue, "All Politics Is Local: The Persistence of Localism in Twentieth-Century America," in *The Democratic Experiment: New Directions in American Political History*, ed. Meg Jacobs, William Novak, Julian Zelizer (Princeton, NJ: Princeton University Press, 2003), 301–26; Nikhil Singh, *Black Is a Country: Race and the Unfinished Struggle for Democracy* (Cambridge, MA: Harvard University Press, 2004).

19. Daniel Immerwahr refers to this common historical narrative of local place crushed by modernization as "Modernization Comes to Town"; Daniel Immerwahr, *Thinking Small: The United States and the Lure of Community Development* (Cambridge, MA: Harvard University Press, 2015), 5–7; Brent Cebul, Karen Tani, and Mason B. Williams, "Clio and the Compound Republic," *Publius* 47, no. 2 (2017): 235–59; Heather Gerken, "A New Progressive Federalism," *Democracy: A Journal of Ideas*, no. 24 (Spring 2012), https://democracyjournal.org/magazine/24/a-new-progressive-federalism/.

20. Neil Brenner, *New State Spaces: Urban Governance and the Rescaling of Statehood* (Oxford: Oxford University Press, 2004); Sallie Marston, "The Social Construction of Scale," *Progress in Human Geography* 24, no. 2 (2000): 219–42;

Roger Keil and Rianne Mahon, *Leviathan Undone? Towards a Political Economy of Scale* (Vancouver: University of British Columbia Press, 2010).

21. Neil Smith, "Remaking Scale: Competition and Cooperation in Pre-National and Post-National Europe," in *State/Space: A Reader*, ed. Neil Brenner, Bob Jessop, Martin Jones, and Gordon MacCleod (Malden, MA: Wiley-Blackwell, 2003), 225–38; Neil Smith, "Geography, Difference and the Politics of Scale," in *Postmodernism and the Social Sciences* (London: Macmillan, 1992), 57–79.

22. Bradley, *World Reimagined*, 7–8, 131.

23. Erik Swyngedouw, "Globalisation or 'Glocalisation'? Networks, Territories and Rescaling," *Cambridge Review of International Affairs* 17, no. 1 (2004): 25–48; Swyngedouw, "Neither Global nor Local: 'Glocalisation' and the Politics of Scale," in *Spaces of Globalization: Reasserting the Power of the Local* (New York: Guilford Press, 1997), 137–66.

24. Akira Iriye, *Global Community: The Role of International Organizations in the Making of the Contemporary World* (Berkeley: University of California Press, 2002); Sargent, *Superpower Transformed*, 22–25; Gary Gerstle, *Liberty and Coercion: The Paradox of American Governance from the Founding to the Present* (Princeton, NJ: Princeton University Press, 2015), 287–88, 308–9; Adam Green, *Selling the Race: Culture, Community and Black Chicago* (Chicago: University of Chicago Press, 2007); Singh, *Black Is a Country*, 3, 86–87.

25. Sargent, *Superpower Transformed*, 74–75; Iriye, *Global Community*, 127–28; Bradley, *World Reimagined*, 131–37; Singh, *Black Is a Country*, 53–54; Meg Jacobs, *Panic at the Pump: The Energy Crisis and the Transformation of American Politics in the 1970s* (New York: Hill and Wang, 2016).

26. Sargent, *Superpower Transformed*, 38, 128–29, 166; Iriye, *Global Community*, 129–46; Estelle Freedman, *No Turning Back: The History of Feminism and the Future of Women* (New York: Random House, 2007), 108–12; Joyce Ocelott, *International Women's Year: The Greatest Consciousness-Raising Event in History* (New York: Oxford University Press, 2017).

27. Daniel Sargent, "Oasis in the Desert? America's Human Rights Rediscovery," in *The Breakthrough: Human Rights in the 1970s*, ed. Jan Eckel and Samuel Moyn (Philadelphia: University of Pennsylvania Press, 2014), 136–37; Bradley, *World Reimagined*, 137–50.

28. Niall Ferguson, Charles S. Maier, Erez Mandela, and Daniel J. Sargent, eds., *The Shock of the Global: The 1970s in Perspective* (Cambridge, MA: Belknap Press of Harvard University Press, 2010); E. F. Schumacher, *Small Is Beautiful: Economics as If People Mattered* (New York: Harper & Row, 1973); Sale, *Human Scale*, 45; Ellis Cose, *Decentralizing Energy Decisions: The Rebirth of Community Power* (Boulder, CO: Westview Press, 1983), 2–3.

29. Benjamin Looker, *A Nation of Neighborhoods: Imagining Cities, Communities, and Democracy in Postwar America* (Chicago: University of Chicago Press, 2015), 231–59; Sale, *Human Scale*, 45–46; Michael Foley, *Front Porch Politics:*

The Forgotten Heyday of American Activism in the 1970s and 1980s (New York: Hill and Wang, 2013); Daphne Spain, *Constructive Feminism Women's Spaces and Women's Rights in the American City* (Ithaca, NY: Cornell University Press, 2016); Joshua Clark Davis, *From Head Shops to Whole Foods: The Rise and Fall of Activist Entrepreneurs* (New York: Columbia University Press, 2017); Borstelmann, *The 1970s*, 99–101; Carol Mason, *Reading Appalachia from Left to Right: Conservatives and the 1974 Kanawha County Textbook Controversy* (Ithaca, NY: Cornell University Press, 2011); Ronald Formisano, *Boston against Busing: Race, Class and Ethnicity in the 1960s and 1970s* (Durham: University of North Carolina Press, 2004). Daniel Rodgers describes a "contagion of metaphors" in *Age of Fracture*, 10–11.

30. For an analysis of the delocalization and relocalization of American evangelical Christianity in the 1970s, see Andrew Preston, "Universal Nationalism: Christian America's Response to the Years of Upheaval," in Ferguson et al., *The Shock of the Global*, 306–8. For an analysis of Newton's global-localist "intercommunalism," see Immerwahr, *Thinking Small*, 158–59; Russell Rickford; "'We Can't Grow Food on All This Concrete': The Land Question, Agrarianism, and Black Nationalist Thought in the Late 1960s and 1970s," *Journal of American History* 103, no. 4 (March 2017): 956–80; Benjamin Looker, *Nation of Neighborhoods*, 330–31.

31. For the distinction between "neoliberalism by design" and "neoliberalism by default," see Weaver, *Blazing the Neoliberal Trail*, 18; also Tracy Neumann, *Remaking the Rust Belt: The Postindustrial Transformation of North America* (Philadelphia: University of Pennsylvania Press, 2016), 58–59; for an exploration of the ways neoliberalism was both by default and design in New York City, see Holtzman, "Crisis and Confidence"; for the example of public-private parks, see Holtzman, "Crisis and Confidence"; see also Osman, "We Are Doing It Ourselves: The Unexpected Origins of New York City's Public-Private Parks during the Fiscal Crisis," *Journal of Planning History* 16, no. 2 (2017): 162–74.

32. James Holston and Arjun Appadurai, "Cities and Citizenship," in Brenner et al., *State/Space: A Reader*, 298–99.

CHAPTER NINE

The Government Alone Cannot Do the Total Job

The Possibilities and Perils of Religious Organizations in Public-Private Refugee Care

Melissa May Borja

O n an October morning in 1979, a minister, a rabbi, and a pair of priests went to the White House. Although they appeared on behalf of different religious communities, they shared one mission: convincing President Jimmy Carter to lead a robust American response to the refugee crisis in Southeast Asia. Five days earlier, the International Red Cross (IRC) and the United Nations had appealed to the world to aid the millions of Cambodians who had fled to Thailand after suffering under the brutal Pol Pot regime. The minister, rabbi, and priests—each of whom represented organizations that had long histories of involvement in refugee relief—agreed with the UN and the IRC that the humanitarian situation was dire. When President Carter appeared in the White House briefing room early that afternoon, the religious leaders appeared to have succeeded in their mission to persuade him to take action. Drawing parallels between America's moral failures during the Holocaust and the consequences of indifference to the Cambodia crisis, President Carter declared that Americans "must act swiftly to save the men, women, and children who are our brothers and sisters in God's family."[1]

President Carter not only described Cambodian refugees in religious terms—as fellow members of "God's family"—but also prescribed a religious response. He urged Congress to appropriate an additional $20 million to support relief efforts, and he outlined plans for providing additional

funds to UNICEF, the IRC, and other refugee assistance programs. He
then praised the commitment by religious groups and private charities to
"match the government effort" and called for local religious congregations to contribute as well. "I ask specifically that every Saturday and Sunday in the month of November, up until Thanksgiving, be set aside as days
for Americans in their synagogues and churches, and otherwise, to give
generously to help alleviate this suffering," he said.[2]

The minister, rabbi, and priests who appeared with President Carter
echoed his message of public-private, interreligious compassion. Like
President Carter, they emphasized that the responsibility for generosity in
the face of the Cambodian refugee crisis must be shared by both government and religious communities. "I think one of the best things that came
out of this morning's conference is the way the private sector is really
working with government," Rabbi Bernard Mandelbaum observed. He
and other faith leaders celebrated refugee care as an expression of the benevolent religious pluralism that characterized a unified America. Father
Theodore Hesburgh emphasized the same theme of cooperation. "I think
it says something about America of 1979 when so many different religious
groups, often in conflict in the past, stand together as brothers and sisters
representing about 150 million Americans and are willing to pool their
efforts, their enthusiasm, commitment and zeal to do something about
this horrendous situation," he said.[3] In a country where the relationship
between church and state was often contentious, and where interactions
between religious groups had historically been hostile, concern for Cambodian refugees united Christians and Jews, public and private agencies,
and church and state.

This chapter explores how federal, state, and local governments worked
with religious organizations to aid and resettle Southeast Asian refugees
in the late 1970s. It makes two arguments. First, American refugee care is
not only a public-private enterprise but also a church-state enterprise. In
both humanitarian relief overseas and resettlement services at home, the
U.S. government has depended on religious organizations to implement
its refugee program. By delegating work to religious institutions, federal,
state, and local governments have been able to expand capacity and provide refugees with aid and assistance that they would not have had the resources to offer otherwise.

Second, this chapter argues that this governing capacity has been
bought at the cost of a new set of challenges, especially concerning matters
of accountability, religious pluralism, and religious freedom. Importantly,

the organizations that partner with government to provide refugee care are not just private, but often religious, and working with religious organizations is different from working with secular private organizations. In particular, partnering with religious organizations has made it more important, and also more complex, for governments to maintain accountability among the broad set of private actors that provide humanitarian aid and social services. In the case of refugee care, the most prominent groups involved in refugee care have been the professionalized voluntary agencies that operate national and regional offices. In addition, the American refugee system also depends on the involvement of local congregations and faith-based charities that are powered by a corps of enthusiastic church volunteers who have often pursued their work as religious service, not as work delegated to them by the government. Given these circumstances, governments and voluntary agencies have made efforts to manage the religiousness of these organizations, and, in general, voluntary agencies have strived to serve their clients in a religiously neutral manner. However, the congregation-based volunteers doing most of the day-to-day work of resettling refugees have not always been experienced or effective at honoring commitments to religious freedom and putting ideals of religious pluralism into practice. As a result, refugees who have received these services have sometimes experienced pressures for religious conformity and change.

As many scholars in this volume and elsewhere have shown, the U.S. government frequently relies on private institutions to expand capacity and get things done. William Novak described this phenomenon as "public-private governance," and Martha Minow and Jody Freeman called it "government by contract."[4] The overlap of public and private is perhaps the most distinctive feature of American government, to the point that political historians have described the United States as an "associational state," a "subsidiarist state," and a "Rube Goldberg State" in which the dizzying number of institutions and complex chains of delegation make the entire system seem like a confusing and often puzzling contraption.[5]

Public-private cooperation has been particularly important in efforts to care for vulnerable populations and provide for the social welfare. Social service provision within the United States involves a mixed economy of government and voluntary agencies, and though government social welfare programs expanded and coincided with some reduction in the involvement of voluntary agencies in the 1930s, the role of private organizations generally increased throughout the twentieth century.[6] Government and private organizations have also worked together to alleviate suffering around the globe. From feeding the hungry to caring for orphaned children, private agencies have played a central role in providing relief and assistance during international humanitarian crises.[7] As scholars like David Harvey have pointed out, public-private partnerships have been one of the defining features of neoliberalism, which has been associated with the withdrawal of state support for social welfare provision and the reduction of a social safety net.[8] In these circumstances, private organizations do work that government might otherwise do and play a primary role in aiding poor and marginalized people.

But if public-private governance has been the subject of a large and exciting body of research, the dynamics of specifically public-religious governance have received less attention. Bruce Nichols, Sara Fieldston, and others have written about the involvement of religious organizations in global relief work.[9] There have also been studies about the provision of public funds for domestic religious social service programs. Much of this scholarship has focused on issues related to Charitable Choice laws and "faith-based initiatives," which sparked controversy in the 1990s and early 2000s. Focused on contemporary public policy debates, the analytical frame of this body of work reveals how the advent of Charitable Choice and faith-based initiatives are perceived as part and parcel of the rise of the Religious Right and the political influence of American evangelicals at the end of the twentieth century.[10] Axel Schäfer has offered the most complex portrait of religious organizations and their relationship with government by placing Charitable Choice and faith-based initiatives in broader historical context. Throughout the second half of the twentieth century, he writes, evangelicals "made access to funds and the preservation of their faith-based practices within a system of state subsidies the linchpin of their new attitude" about the relationship between church and state. Charitable Choice and faith-based initiatives were thus the culmination of several decades of evangelical cooperation with government.[11]

Yet serious consideration of religious organizations still remains largely absent in the rich body of research about the history of public-private governance. Indeed, religious voluntary agencies, charities, and churches have played major roles in domestic social service provision and international humanitarian care throughout American history. And even in the scholarship that does exist on this topic, important questions remain unexplored. To begin, there is a need to better understand how these partnerships functioned on the ground. How have government and religious groups actually worked together, and how have these partnerships operated in different settings? What types of work have federal, state, and local governments delegated to religious groups? How have religious groups carried out this work, and how have governments maintained accountability?

In addition, scholars must consider a broader range of religious actors. Most of the existing scholarship has focused on evangelicals, a reflection of the contemporary fascination with the Religious Right and faith-based initiatives, but scholars have not fully considered the perspective of religious groups beyond evangelicals in these church-state partnerships. Catholics, mainline Protestants, and Jews all worked with government well before evangelicals did. What has been their experience? Just as important, how have religious minorities—Muslims, Buddhists, and Hindus, for example—experienced these partnerships?

Engaging in the perspectives of religious minorities is particularly important, given recent changes in religious demographics. During the same period that the Religious Right gained prominence, immigrants from Asia, Africa, and Latin America arrived in the United States in significant numbers and introduced unprecedented religious diversity. This new religious pluralism has changed many aspects of American public life, from public education to the military. Less is known, though, about how religious pluralism has complicated the long-standing practice of government contracting out work to religious organizations. These organizations have historically been staffed by Christians and Jews who have primarily served fellow Christians and Jews. However, the organizations now serve an increasingly multireligious population, as religious minorities comprise not only a growing share of the American population but also a growing share of the population that receives and provides social services. In this changing context, to what degree have religious organizations upheld commitments to religious freedom and religious pluralism? Most of the discussion about contracting out government work to religious organizations has centered on protecting the religious freedom of Christian service providers—but what has been done to protect the religious freedoms of Muslim, Hindu, and Buddhist service recipients?

Finally, we need a better understanding of the distinctly religious dimensions of these church-state partnerships. In studying government partnerships with faith-based organizations, scholars need to see these organizations not merely as another type of private entity but as religious entities. By making religion a focus of analysis, scholars will better understand how belief, practice, and identity shapes why religious groups pursue partnerships with government and, just as important, how they do their work. Moreover, viewing these organizations as religious institutions sheds light on the religious repercussions of these church-state partnerships. What impact have church-state partnerships had on religious life? The sociologist Robert Wuthnow likened his work on the restructuring of American religious life to an environmental impact study.[12] A similar approach would be useful for understanding partnerships between government and religion. When government delegated public work to faith-based institutions, what was the "environmental" impact on American religion?

By focusing on the cooperative effort between government and religious organizations to aid and resettle Southeast Asian refugees, this chapter tells a larger story that addresses these questions. Indeed, exploring refugee resettlement illuminates the involvement of religious groups in humanitarian care and social service provision and highlights an overlooked player in "public-private governance."[13] Like Schäfer's work, this chapter calls attention to the fact that the U.S. government has a long history of contracting out work to religious groups, which have worked with government even before World War II. However, while Schäfer showed how evangelicals took advantage of the state, this chapter suggests that the opposite was also true: the state took advantage of religious organizations. Refugee resettlement has been consistently underfunded in the United States, with religious institutions carrying a disproportionately heavy burden. Especially in the era of neoliberalism, voluntary agencies have performed a heavier load of work with fewer resources and support from government.

Finally, this chapter sheds light on the complications that can arise when government relies on religious voluntary agencies and congregations. Government often treated religious organizations like other private organizations with which it had contracts. In so doing, it ignored these organizations' most unique feature: they were religious organizations, with religious purposes and religious people carrying out its work. Stories shared by both resettlement workers and refugees during the years of Southeast Asian refugee resettlement make clear that many people who implemented the federal refugee program considered resettlement to be a religious ministry. This approach was particularly salient at the local level, where resettlement was carried out by patently religious institutions—congregations—and where religious commitment shaped the provision of care.[14] Even though both government and religious groups promised to provide resettlement services in a religiously neutral fashion, it was sometimes hard to do so. Ultimately, Southeast Asian refugee resettlement reveals that in public-private and church-state collaborations, it can be difficult to ensure accountability, and religious freedom can be compromised when the sacred and the secular overlap.

Expanding Capacity through Partnerships with Religious Organizations

Voluntary agencies, especially religious voluntary agencies, have been central to American refugee care throughout the twentieth century. Beginning in the late 1930s, voluntary agencies first worked with the federal government to provide aid to refugees overseas. During World War II, the War Relief Control Board united the efforts of the voluntary agencies and the federal government to assist war victims abroad. The public-private approach to refugee care became more established and expansive after 1945, when President Harry Truman signed an executive order that allowed refugees admitted to the United States to be sponsored not only by individuals but also by humanitarian organizations. This executive order allowed voluntary agencies to play a prominent role in both international refugee relief and domestic refugee resettlement throughout the Cold War. When two hundred thousand European refugees arrived in the United States under the Displaced Persons Act of 1948, the federal government covered the cost of transatlantic transportation, while the voluntary agencies cared for refugees upon their arrival. When thirty-five thousand Hungarian refugees arrived in the United States after the Hungarian uprising in 1956, the federal government began to give payments—about $40 per refugee—directly to the voluntary agencies to cover the cost of resettlement. When one hundred thousand Cubans fled to the United States in 1959 and 1960, the federal government's commitment to refugee care increased substantially. Shortly after the authorization of the Cuban Refugee Program, Congress passed the Migration and Refugee Assistance Act of 1962, which appropriated funds to assist Cuban refugees. But while the federal government spent $260 million on refugee assistance between 1961 and 1967, the government's refugee program still operated through the voluntary agencies and through the states.[15] As Naomi and Norman Zucker argued, voluntary agencies provided services that "range from governmental and quasi-governmental to purely private aid activities" and connect "the refugee to the various public and private bureaucracies." In short, voluntary agencies were "integral to the formulation and execution of refugee policy in general."[16]

When the United States faced the question of how to resettle Southeast Asian refugees after the Vietnam War, turning to voluntary agencies appeared to be the most expedient and effective response to the demanding humanitarian crisis. In 1981 researchers for the Bureau of Refugee Programs at the Department of State wrote a report about voluntary agencies, also known as "volags," and listed several reasons the government relied on private voluntary agencies for resettlement:

(1) The volags are <u>there</u> and likely to stay, providing capacities and continuity lacking in public agencies.
(2) They are more flexible in size and in function than units of government.
(3) They bring private resources to bear, as governmental agencies cannot.
(4) They attract, and keep, dedicated staff people.
(5) They avoid a potential bias towards welfare, which might be found in the human resources agencies.
(6) They are knowledgeable about, and sensitive to, ethnic differences and the special problems of refugees.[17]

More than anything, voluntary agencies provided government an opportunity to expand its capacity in a resettlement effort of unprecedented scale. Providing relief and resettlement services to one million Southeast Asian refugees uprooted by war and genocide was a task that was, in the words of one Catholic Charities official, "beyond the ability of our government to solve."[18] Stanley Breen of the American Refugee Committee echoed this sentiment. "The government alone cannot do the total job," he said, "and the private sector including the voluntary agencies, the churches, and the business community will really get the job done with the proper support of government services that are needed."[19] Voluntary agencies were not alone in understanding that the support of religious groups was essential for the success of the refugee program; government officials knew this, too. In the early days of Southeast Asian refugee resettlement, members of Congress asked direct questions about the breadth of religious support. "Every church group in the United States is with us," assured L. Dean Brown, ambassador and director of the Interagency Task Force during one congressional hearing. "That is marvelous," responded Representative Hamilton Fish.[20]

Religious voluntary agencies worked with government at all stages of the resettlement process. Overseas, voluntary agencies were critical to relief efforts in the refugee camps. About two-thirds of the voluntary agencies operating in the refugee camps in Thailand were religious agencies.[21]

These religious charities were typically affiliated with Christian denominations and staffed by missionaries dispatched by churches across the globe. Although the agencies came from numerous countries and represented a wide array of religious groups, they were all an essential part of the global response to the humanitarian crisis and were responsible for a wide array of services. These religious voluntary agencies provided refugees with food, shelter, medical care, educational programming, and agricultural support. In addition, they helped screen, interview, and prepare refugees for third-country resettlement.

The activities at Ban Vinai refugee camp in Thailand, for example, demonstrate how religious organizations were responsible for much of the refugee relief effort. The Christian and Missionary Alliance ran a handicraft sales program, a small pig-raising project, and a rice mill. Catholic Relief Services operated an in-hospital patient feeding program and a sewing and tailoring school. Finally, World Vision, an evangelical Christian organization, was one of the lead agencies and oversaw relief and emergency supplies, educational and vocational training, English-language instruction, agriculture projects to support home gardens, camp development and maintenance, and family development programs. Most important, World Vision was in charge of medical care in the camp. With the American Refugee Committee and the Free Finnish Mission second to them, World Vision provided all of the inpatient and outpatient services for the tens of thousands of Hmong refugees at Ban Vinai.[22]

After refugees left the overseas camps to be resettled in the United States, they continued to rely on voluntary agencies, which received grants from the federal government to provide resettlement services. Southeast Asian refugees were first admitted and resettled under the Indochinese Migration and Refugee Assistance Act of 1975. Later, Congress passed the Refugee Act of 1980, which sought to fix the inefficiencies in the resettlement program, created admission procedures that facilitated the efficient resettlement of refugees, and provided funding for refugee resettlement programs.[23] Although the Refugee Act of 1980 brought major changes to the refugee resettlement system, it also kept much of the same basic approach to refugee care. In particular, refugee resettlement remained a cooperative enterprise in which government relied heavily on voluntary agencies for the day-to-day implementation of resettlement policy. To resettle Southeast Asian refugees, voluntary agencies received a per capita government grant, which ranged from $300 to $500, to provide initial reception and placement services for refugees. In addition, they received grants from the newly formed Office of Refugee Resettlement, under the

Department of Health, Education, and Welfare, to provide long-term programs to assist refugees' integration, such as English as a second language (ESL) classes, job training, and mental health programs.[24] In short, the government refugee resettlement program was carried out through the voluntary agencies. As Ingrid Walter, director of Lutheran Immigration and Refugee Service, put it, resettlement involved essentially "servicing their communities with Lutheran agencies, with government monies."[25]

Among the private voluntary agencies that had contracts with the federal government for resettlement work, religious voluntary agencies were the most prominent and numerous, and they were responsible for the lion's share of refugee cases. Although some nonreligious agencies participated in Southeast Asian refugee resettlement, Christian organizations—the United States Catholic Conference (USCC), the Lutheran Immigration and Refugee Service (LIRS), World Relief, Church World Service (CWS)— resettled the majority of Southeast Asian refugees. According to the annual reports from the Office of Refugee Resettlement, church-affiliated voluntary agencies resettled most refugees in the first two decades after the passage of the 1980 Refugee Act. A large percentage of resettled refugees found help through the USCC alone, which was the largest of the nine agencies that held contracts with the federal government to resettle Southeast Asian refugees. LIRS and CWS, a Protestant Christian agency associated with the National Council of Churches, also assisted a large number of refugees. World Relief, a Christian voluntary agency associated with the National Association of Evangelicals, began to resettle refugees in 1979 and reflected the growing interest of conservative religious groups in joint enterprises with government. Together, these four Christian voluntary agencies resettled roughly two-thirds of the Southeast Asian refugees who arrived in 1981, which was approximately the peak of Southeast Asian refugee resettlement.[26]

Church-state collaboration characterized refugee care at the state level, too. In Minnesota, for example, the regional and local affiliates of the voluntary agencies partnered with state governments to coordinate refugee services. The 1979 official Minnesota "State Plan for Refugees," which each state was required to produce in order to receive funding from the Department of Health and Human Services, described how government and voluntary agencies shared the work of resettlement:

> To accomplish effective resettlement, the public and private agencies have cooperated closely. The private agencies' unique domain is to secure sponsors and bring the refugees to this country. Because federal funding for resettlement has

gone through the public welfare system and because the welfare system is that which is equipped to deal with the range of services required, the state agency is responsible for the coordination and provision of services after the refugees arrive. Together, the state and voluntary agencies form a consortium to provide services and to respond to the ever changing parameters of the refugee program.[27]

In Minnesota, the government and voluntary agencies determined that it was most efficient to assign each agency one area of follow-up services in which to specialize. In that state's system, the International Institute (the local affiliate of the American Council of Nationalities Service) offered English-language instruction, Catholic Charities (the local affiliate of the USCC) provided employment counseling and job training, and Lutheran Social Service (the local affiliate of LIRS) focused on health and social adjustment services.[28] The creators of this plan hoped that these arrangements would streamline the refugee assistance system and improve the quality of services.

At the local level, voluntary agencies turned to perhaps the most valuable — and most overlooked — source of support: congregations. Voluntary agencies, in an effort to expand their capacity and to widen the scope of their services, delegated critical responsibilities to local churches and synagogues, which were recruited to serve as "sponsors" that housed, clothed, fed, and assisted refugees throughout the first few weeks after arrival. Local churches thus functioned as extensions of the voluntary agencies and were integral to the resettlement of Southeast Asian refugees in the congregational sponsorship system. Just as the State Department formed cooperative agreements with voluntary agencies for the administration of reception and placement services, the voluntary agencies delegated essential tasks to local congregations through the "moral commitment" of sponsorship. The terms of sponsorship agreements changed over time and varied across agencies, but most resembled this agreement from CWS:

[Name of Congregation or Sponsoring Unit] hereby agree to assist a refugee family with their resettlement in the United States. In agreeing to assist the family, the congregation assures Church World Service that it will help them become self-supporting in the shortest possible time after their arrival in the community and will assist them in the following ways:

1. Meet the family at the airport upon arrival.
2. Arrange for temporary housing.

3. Assist with food, clothing, housewares, basic furniture, etc.

4. Assist in finding employment for the breadwinner.

5. Help the refugee and his family become oriented in the community.

6. Assist in enrolling in English classes.[29]

The national voluntary agencies considered congregational support a fundamental component of their system of resettlement. "The labors of love, the common sense and the dedication of thousands of Lutherans is the most important single resource of the resettlement program," declared officials at LIRS. According to the Lutheran plan, congregations were "the primary working unit in the resettlement process," whereas the national offices and local affiliates existed primarily to "support congregations, sponsors and refugees," by coordinating services, providing information, and procuring new sponsors.[30] Although the Protestant voluntary agencies were most likely to rely on the congregational sponsorship model of resettlement, Catholics used this approach, too.[31] "Basically the best resettlement it appears to us is a group resettlement approach where community, a church, a parish assumes the responsibility for a family," said John McCarthy of the USCC during a 1975 testimony before Congress.[32] Mark Franken, who served as executive director for the same Catholic voluntary agency, described the local parish as "the key ingredient in the Catholic network."[33]

From initial reception and placement services to long-term programs to assist refugees in attaining self-sufficiency, local congregations offered a rich reserve of enthusiastic volunteers and financial support. Churches carried much of the cost of resettlement, did most of the daily work of caring for refugees, and were refugees' first point of contact for assistance. Fong Her, a Hmong refugee from Laos, was sponsored by a congregation in St. Paul, Minnesota, and was amazed by the church's generosity:

When we got to Saint Paul, it was May the 9th, 1980. It was still cold that year. We don't have any coats, they passed us coats for that spring. A church sponsored us—it's a church it's not a family—that meant they had more funds to receive us at that time. We had a house ready to move in when we got here. We had food in the refrigerator. We had a lot of food . . . It was a church that sponsored us, not a family that meant we had everything ready when we got here.[34]

Government and voluntary agency officials, recognizing that congregational sponsorship marshaled abundant resources to support refugees, actively supported the recruitment of churches to assume this role. For example, Albert and Gretchen Quie, governor and first lady of Minnesota, appeared in two television commercials in which they urged the public to volunteer to sponsor refugees and offer a "warm welcome that makes people feel at home in Minnesota."[35] These sponsorship recruitment efforts by government, voluntary agencies, and churches resulted in an outpouring of public support. In the first seven years after the fall of Saigon, forty-five Catholic parishes in the Twin Cities and southern Minnesota sponsored Southeast Asian refugee families. Several dozen Protestant and Jewish congregations also sponsored refugees. Religious organizations outside of congregations—monastic communities, women's circles, and college campus fellowships, for example—supported resettlement. Even a local nursing home was eager to support resettlement efforts. Residents at the Oak Terrace Nursing Home offered one of their facility's vacant buildings to "be made available as a Christian Connection Center" that could function as "a temporary resettlement center for the Indochinese refugees who are being sponsored by the members of the churches."[36]

Overall, voluntary agencies and religious organizations have shouldered most of the cost and performed most of the labor of aiding refugees. This was true in the 1970s, when Indochinese refugees were first resettled. A report on the activities of the Bethlehem Lutheran Church in Minneapolis, Minnesota, presented at congressional hearings in 1976, highlight how congregations valuably supplemented government resettlement efforts. Although the government granted voluntary agencies $500 per refugee, the true cost was much higher. Accounting for the cost of housing, utilities, home furnishings, clothing, professional support, and more, LIRS found that it actually cost Bethlehem Lutheran Church $5,601 to resettle a Vietnamese refugee family. Bethlehem Lutheran Church's generous resettlement project was primarily possible through donations of money, material goods, and volunteered time by members of the congregation.[37]

In the decades since the resettlement of Southeast Asian refugees, government dependence on religious groups has only grown. Government investment in refugee resettlement has declined in recent years, meaning private agencies, especially religious agencies, have been responsible for bearing more of the burden. A 2008 study conducted by LIRS found that the State Department funded only 39 percent of the actual cost of resettling a refugee, while private giving covered the remaining 61 percent.[38] "Failing to adequately fund the costs associated with the system places a significant amount of stress on the resettlement agencies' ability to do their job effectively," argued Todd Scribner and Anastasia Brown of the U.S. Conference of Catholic Bishops. Such reduced funding, they said, "could in the long-term undermine the capacity of the system to continue functioning at a high level."[39] In these circumstances, voluntary agencies, especially religious groups, have picked up the slack and have continued to fill the yawning gap between the rising cost of resettlement and the declining availability of government resources.

Managing Religion in Religious Refugee Care

The religious voluntary agencies that resettled Southeast Asians consistently framed refugee work as a ministry of Christian charity and love. Across the denominational spectrum, the Christian voluntary agencies recruited church sponsors by presenting resettlement work as religious work. For example, CWS described churches as "avenues of God's love to refugees" and described sponsorship as a chance to serve Jesus. "Jesus, Who was Himself a refugee, said that by helping refugees we are really helping Him," read a CWS flyer.[40] Episcopal Migration Ministries declared that "welcoming strangers is a response to our Christian imperative to care for those in need."[41] A LIRS pamphlet described resettlement as "a face-to-face ministry."[42]

Indeed, the church volunteers who answered the call to aid refugees possessed unparalleled passion for refugee service, work they imbued with deep moral meaning. Their motivations varied. Some church volunteers saw resettlement work as an act of penance for America's sins during the Vietnam War. "It may sound improbable at first that sponsoring a refugee will earn you God's forgiveness," argued Joseph Aurele-Plourde in the *Catholic Bulletin*. "But we do have some sins to be forgiven as a nation. We ought to help the refugees now so we'll have the forgiveness of God to help us through troubles we may have in the future."[43] Other church volunteers saw resettlement as a missionary project. "I never thought that God would pick up a whole people and move them to our country so we could do missions with them," said Pearl Jones, whose Baptist congregation resettled several Hmong families.[44] For her, "sharing the Gospel with these people [was] of the uppermost."[45]

Most church volunteers chose to contribute to resettlement because it was a chance to adhere to the golden rule and live out biblical teach-ings to feed the hungry, clothe the naked, serve the poor, and welcome the stranger, responsibilities articulated in the twenty-fifth chapter of the Gospel of Matthew. Matthew 25—which includes the verse "I was a stranger and you welcomed me"—was a common reason that church volunteers offered as an explanation for their volunteer work. "Welcoming was probably the biggest motivation," said Dorothy Knight, who said that her commitment to refugees arose from the call to "love thy neighbor."[46] Church committees dedicated to organizing refugee sponsorship projects even named themselves "Matthew 25" committees, in honor of this chapter in the Bible.[47]

Importantly, congregations pursued refugee work as religious work, sometimes without acknowledging any connection to the government refugee program at all. Kathy Vellenga, for example, organized a church sponsorship of a Hmong refugee family, the Vangs, in 1976. In one report to her congregation, she noted that the Vangs were "very appreciative of all the hands of friendship and the financial aid" but "were surprised that all the money comes from people in the churches and none from the government."[48] Later, she wrote: "It is difficult for them to understand that after all they risked and lost for the U.S.A. during the war that it is the church not the government that provides sponsorship for them now."[49] Both Vellenga and the Vang family saw resettlement as a church effort, not a government program. However, her words failed to acknowledge the fact that congregations were doing work delegated to them by the voluntary agencies, which in turn were doing work financed in part by government. In other words, congregations were so far removed from government in the complex bureaucratic apparatus of refugee resettlement that church volunteers did not easily recognize their work as having anything to do with government.

Religious commitments animated the Christian refugee care offered by Kathy Vellenga, Dorothy Knight, and Pearl Jones, as it had other Christian church volunteers involved in refugee resettlement throughout the twentieth century. However, Southeast Asian refugee resettlement brought new religious circumstances and challenges. In contrast to previous refugee populations aided by Christian and Jewish voluntary agencies, refugees from Vietnam, Cambodia, and Laos were nonwhite and often non-Christian, and religious voluntary agencies were no longer settling people who belonged to their own religion. Ingrid Walter of LIRS recalled that, before the 1970s, "refugees registered pretty much along the line of their confession or their religion. Catholics went to the Catholic agencies. Lutherans came to the Lutheran agency, et cetera."[50] But the 1970s was "the first time that the Lutheran churches knowingly sponsored a refugee group which had had no previous, what should I say, connections with the Lutheran faith. It was a group of refugees rather than Lutheran refugees."[51] Although some people, like Walters, were optimistic about the ability of voluntary agencies to overcome differences of religion, race, and culture, not everybody was so optimistic. "Many problems will arise because of the new influx of people to America," said the pastor at Christ Lutheran Church in St. Paul. In his view, the "new people coming from different cultures and backgrounds" would be "a new minority group in America." He asked, somewhat gloomily, "How will these new immigrants be accepted?"[52]

Given these circumstances, both government and voluntary agencies attempted to manage the religiousness of refugee care. Governments expected that the voluntary agencies serve refugees without discrimination, and the religious voluntary agencies committed to providing refugee care in a religiously neutral and pluralistic manner. The professionalized staff of the voluntary agencies, for example, made the effort to refrain from openly religious activities. "Because you're receiving public funds and other sources of funding outside of your own religious community . . . there are certainly restrictions and so on in terms of promoting your own religion or requiring people to participate in services of your own religion," said Tom Kosel, who worked for Catholic Charities in Minnesota. "Those kinds of restrictions have to be followed. At Catholic Charities, you come in for services; you don't have to start the day praying or something. Some other agencies that provide services require their participants to be part of religious ceremonies or services. That's not something done at Catholic Charities or Lutheran Social Service, to my knowledge. It could be an optional thing in some circumstances, but, by and large, the promoting of a particular religious belief isn't done."[53]

However, in a system with a long chain of delegation, accountability was difficult to maintain at the local level, where patently religious institutions— congregations—played a major role. Governments and voluntary agencies needed to handle congregations carefully, especially because sponsoring churches were responsible for most of the day-to-day tasks of resettlement and had the closest contact with refugees. The professionalized staff of the voluntary agencies attempted to manage the religiousness of refugee resettlement efforts through a series of orientations and pamphlets, which often gave unclear, even conflicting advice. On one level, the voluntary agencies urged congregations to respect refugees' religions, in part because the religious disruption might hinder successful resettlement. "Great care should be taken to refrain from showing disdain or disrespect for the refugees' religious beliefs and convictions," said World Relief.[54] LIRS stated that "respecting [refugees] as human beings means respecting their beliefs as well" and reminded sponsors that "the purpose of sponsorship is not to gain new members or convert refugees to Christianity or to Lutheranism."[55] CWS argued that respecting refugees' religions was important because religion is "a fundamental part of one's identity." CWS leaders warned against "rushed or pressured religious changes or 'conversions,'" because, in their view, these religious experiences would be "disastrous both psychologically and emotionally for refugees." The CWS manual explained: "Religious beliefs and traditions may be one of the elements of their heritage that refugees have not lost in their flight. Abruptly relinquishing these beliefs adds one more loss to their already overflowing burden of losses and grief and thus further complicates their adjustment, mental health and ultimate integration."[56]

At the same time that they intended resettlement to be a pluralistic, religiously neutral enterprise, the voluntary agencies acknowledged that congregational sponsorship presented special opportunities for Christian missionary outreach. LIRS told sponsors that "it is natural for you to want to share with the refugees what is important to you and what you believe is beneficial."[57] A pamphlet from World Relief declared that "demonstrating how the love of Christ has motivated Christians and the Church to reach out to them in love is the most effective witness."[58] The "heartbeat" of World Relief's refugee work was, in fact, securing "places for people whose lives will be changed by Jesus Christ."[59] Voluntary agencies even gave practical support for congregations interested in sharing the Gospel with refugees. CWS distributed Lao, Vietnamese, and Khmer translations of the Bible.[60] LIRS budgeted $25,000 to create "Christian education materials" to be used for "encounter sessions" during which Lutheran church volunteers could discuss their faith with refugees curious about Christianity.[61]

Trying to balance the desire of church sponsors to share their Christian faith and the commitment to respecting refugees' religions, the voluntary agencies attempted to guide churches in the proper way to handle religion with refugees. First, there was the question of whether refugees should go to church with their congregational sponsors. The voluntary agencies saw church participation as an opportunity for valuable social connection that was critical to refugee adjustment. World Relief advised that "sponsors should feel free to invite their refugees to go to church with them," as one of the basic tasks of resettlement was "inclusion in spiritual experiences through church and church-related activities."[62] In the same vein, LIRS said that refugees must be "welcome to participate in church activities and services."[63] The Lutheran manual stated that refugees benefited from fellowship and community, and even for non-Christian refugees, "invitations to church activities may, in fact, be welcome" because they "will appreciate being related to a family of persons who are concerned about them." However, the voluntary agencies advised strongly against pressuring refugees to go to church. LIRS cautioned that the decision to attend Sunday worship services with their church sponsors must be a "choice."[64] Likewise, World Relief stated that "refugees must not be coerced or placed under obligation to accept" invitations to participate in Sunday worship services.[65] In addition, the voluntary agencies encouraged church sponsors to separate religious and nonreligious resettlement activities. LIRS manuals advised church sponsors to "keep religious instruction and English-as-a-Second-Language training distinct" because, even though "teaching the Christian faith and English at the same time may seem to be a good idea," "to overemphasize religious instruction at the expense of language training is also unfair."[66] Overall, the resettlement manuals reveal one fundamental problem: the voluntary agencies asked church volunteers to draw a boundary between religious and nonreligious work, which was hardly an easy task for people who understood the work of caring for the poor and welcoming the stranger to be a fundamentally Christian calling.

In practice, maintaining accountability and overseeing congregations proved logistically difficult. Congregations often had a lot of autonomy, and voluntary and government agencies had limited resources to manage them. Tom Kosel recalled the difficulty of ensuring that congregations carry out sponsorship properly. "When a volag [voluntary agency] is getting in contact with a particular congregation there, there is supposed to be some good orientation process, and you go in to have meetings with the parish leadership, and you explain the ins and outs of proper resettlement," he said. "To my knowledge, that's what's done, but that doesn't mean that there wouldn't still be individuals in congregations that either don't get that message or don't follow that message very closely. So you're dealing with individuals here that you can't always be on top of [in] all situations."[67]

The difficulty of separating religious from nonreligious work, the challenge of putting ideals of pluralism into practice, and the perils of delegating public work to private religious agencies become particularly clear when refugees, church volunteers, and voluntary agency officials shared stories of their resettlement experiences. In these circumstances, refugees sometimes experienced pressures for religious conformity, despite sincere efforts by government and religious voluntary agencies to resettle refugees in a religiously neutral and pluralistic way.

Some of the concerns about religious pressure came from voluntary agency officials and church volunteers. Tom Kosel recalled such an instance when Lutheran, Baptist, Methodist, and Catholic churches worked together to sponsor a large Vietnamese family that was Catholic. "One of the churches was, in effect, trying to 'convert' the people to their religion, and they would actually pick them up, eight o'clock in the morning on Sunday, drive them over to their church, and have them attend their services, and then take them back home, and then, of course, being very practicing Catholics, [the refugees] would then come to the Catholic church," he said. "And I didn't hear about that, or I wasn't aware of that, until quite a long time into it, but it was one of those things that has to be carefully watched when you're dealing with congregations and refugees— that there's a respect for refugees' current religious beliefs. And we aren't here to change their beliefs; we're just here to help them."[68]

The issue of religious pressure is even clearer in refugees' stories. To be sure, almost universally refugees expressed gratitude for the help that they received from the churches that sponsored them. Timothy Vang, a Hmong refugee from Laos, appreciated the help he received from the church that sponsored his family to resettle in Green Bay, Wisconsin. "We were so lucky!" he said. "The church helped us in everything." He found his church sponsor to be so generous that he remarked, "I feel bad for the other families that did not have good sponsors like us."[69]

At the same time, many refugees shared stories of feeling uncomfortable about attending church with their sponsors. Mai Vang Thao, for example, was resettled by a church in Minnesota. Although she practiced indigenous Hmong religion, she went to church for seven or eight years after her first arrival in the United States. It was not her preference, though. "We did not like Christianity," she said, "and we did not like to go to church." The only reason she went was because she was sponsored by a church. "When we arrived in this country, the Americans took us to church," she said, "so we went."[70] Soua Lo, another Hmong woman, had a similar story. "From January until April, we were there in Pittsburgh, and we went to a Catholic church because we felt like we had to, because we were sponsored by a Catholic church, and so we felt obligated to go," she said. In her view, participating in the church of her sponsors was not a choice. "We knew that it was different from what we believed, and that it's different from what we are used to in Laos, but we just know we had to do something in ways that we just didn't know," she said.[71] Refugee resettlement by churches in some cases had a large influence over the religious lives of refugees, who sometimes changed their religion entirely because of their experiences with their church sponsors. "After the church helped us, we decided—the whole family decided—to be baptized," said Kia Vue, a Hmong woman resettled by a Catholic parish in Oklahoma. When asked why she made this decision, she explained simply, "Because this church has helped us."[72]

Concerned about refugees' stories of religious pressure, voluntary agency officials and church volunteers continued to emphasize the importance of respecting refugees' religion. Some sponsoring congregations followed through with this commitment by actively supporting refugees' religious practices. Two Lutheran congregations in Oregon, for example, arranged for a Buddhist monk to visit refugee families.[73] Similarly, Mark Franken recalled how Catholic Charities in Ohio made arrangements for a Buddhist monk from Washington to visit Vietnamese families in Columbus.[74] Religious leaders also criticized the aggressive evangelism of churches and faith-based voluntary agencies and urged them not to pressure refugees. "What's important is to offer the friendship and support," said Ellen Erickson, director of the refugee resettlement programs at Lutheran Social Service in Minnesota: "What you need to caution them [the churches] is that there's not a price tag on your help."[75]

In the end, though, pluralistic refugee resettlement was difficult to achieve. While delegating resettlement responsibilities to local congregations allowed voluntary agencies to expand their capacity and to serve a larger number of refugees, the involvement of openly religious institutions undermined the goal of implementing a policy of religious neutrality. On the ground, the people who had the most contact with refugees—volunteers from sponsoring congregations—also had limited and conflicting guidance about how to manage religion in their resettlement work. They also had a tremendous amount of freedom and autonomy, without much oversight from the professionalized voluntary agencies and government agencies. While these volunteers had a keen interest in engaging in people from different cultural and religious backgrounds, they had limited experience in how to put ideals of religious pluralism into practice.

Conclusion

When President Carter met with Catholic, Protestant, and Jewish leaders to discuss aid to Cambodian refugees, he urged American churches and

synagogues to "match the government effort" by taking up an extra collection for refugees at their worship services. When he described refugees as "brothers and sisters in God's family," he was speaking directly to
the American religious public. These were the very people who had been
at the front lines of the American response to refugee crises throughout
the twentieth century. He was making a moral appeal to mobilize what
he knew was a powerful reserve of manpower and material resources.
Moreover, he was continuing a strategy of governance that had proved
successful in administrations before his own: borrowing capacity through
partnerships with religious communities.

Refugee care in the United States is a public-private, church-state
endeavor, and religious organizations have played a critical role in implementing American refugee policy. The task of resettling one million Vietnamese,
Cambodian, Lao, and Hmong refugees was an unprecedented undertak-
ing, one too big for public agencies to handle alone, particularly in the late
1970s as the United States was also confronting a recession and substantial budgetary shortcomings. As Carter himself put in his 1978 State of the
Union address: "Government cannot eliminate poverty or provide a boun-
tiful economy or reduce inflation or save our cities or cure illiteracy or provide energy. And government cannot mandate goodness. Only a true partnership between government and the people can ever hope to reach these
goals."[76] The federal government thus depended on religious organizations
at all levels of refugee care: from relief efforts abroad to national, state, and
local resettlement programs. Religious voluntary agencies, congregations,
and charities responded to the Southeast Asian refugee crisis with enthusiasm and generosity, as they had so many times before, and this was, in part,
why using religious organizations to administer American refugee care was
an expedient approach. The United States could make the claim that its
government was committed to providing humanitarian aid and honoring
the loyalty of its Cold War allies, and by relying on private religious groups
to shoulder most of the burden of paying for and carrying out refugee
resettlement, the government could fulfill its promises with relatively small
public investment.

However, there were hidden costs to this arrangement that were not
immediately apparent to the government officials who planned resettlement.
Government resettlement planners tended to see religious voluntary agencies as just another type of private charity. What they failed to understand
is that these organizations were, first and foremost, religious organizations.
Stories shared by people who participated in Southeast Asian refugee
resettlement offers rich empirical evidence of the deeply religious character

of faith-based refugee work. For many people who did the ground-level work of refugee resettlement, refugee care was not a government responsibility but a religious responsibility rooted in biblical principles. These religious commitments clearly shaped the services that the voluntary agencies, sponsoring congregations, and church volunteers provided.

This situation might not have produced any problems had it not overlapped with an important change in American life: the religious diversification of American society, a matter generally overlooked in the scholarship on government-subsidized religious charity. Unprecedented religious diversity changed the setting in which both governments and religious organizations operated. In Southeast Asian refugee resettlement, religious organizations made some sincere efforts to adapt to new circumstances of religious pluralism. However, the enduring religious missionary impulse at the center of Christian refugee care existed in tension with the new imperative to "respect refugees' religions." Despite attempts by government and voluntary agencies to manage the religiousness of refugee care, congregations did not always fulfill their promise to offer their assistance in a religiously neutral manner, at least from the viewpoint of refugees themselves. Delegating work to religious organizations thus had a noticeable religious impact on the non-Christian refugees who received care from faith-based voluntary agencies and churches.

The accounts of resettlement shared by Southeast Asian refugees undercut much of the current narrative surrounding government partnerships with religious institutions. Most of the contemporary public policy discussion focuses on fears that the religious freedom of Christian service providers might be compromised when church and state cooperate. However, the history of Southeast Asian refugee resettlement demonstrates that partnerships between religious organizations and government affected religious minorities—in this case, Buddhist, animist, and ancestor-worshipping people—more than anybody. Ultimately, this story reveals the unique and often unexpected challenges that can arise when government leans heavily on private charity and religious benevolence.

Notes

1. "Organizational Files: Correspondence and Miscellanea, 1979–1980," box 1, American Refugee Committee Papers, Minnesota Historical Society, St. Paul.

2. "Organizational Files: Correspondence and Miscellanea, 1979–1980," box 1, American Refugee Committee Papers.

3. "Organizational Files: Correspondence and Miscellanea, 1979–1980," box 1, American Refugee Committee Papers.

4. William Novak, "Public-Private Governance: A Historical Introduction," in *Government by Contract: Outsourcing and American Democracy*, ed. Martha Minow and Jody Freeman (Cambridge, MA: Harvard University Press, 2009), 23–40; and Jody Freeman and Martha Minow, eds., *Government by Contract: Outsourcing and American Democracy* (Cambridge, MA: Harvard University Press, 2009).

5. Brian Balogh, *The Associational State: American Governance in the Twentieth Century* (Philadelphia: University of Pennsylvania Press, 2015); Axel R. Schäfer, *Piety and Public Funding: Evangelicals and the State in Modern America* (Philadelphia: University of Pennsylvania Press, 2012); Elisabeth Clemens, "Lineages of the Rube Goldberg State: Building and Blurring Public Programs, 1900–1940," in *Rethinking Political Institutions: The Art of the State*, ed. Ian Shapiro, Stephen Skowronek, and Daniel Galvin (New York: New York University Press, 2006), 380–443.

6. Elisabeth Clemens and Doug Guthrie, eds., *Politics and Partnerships: The Role of Voluntary Agencies in America's Political Past and Present* (Chicago: University of Chicago Press, 2011).

7. Stephen R. Porter, *Benevolent Empire: U.S. Power, Humanitarianism, and the World's Dispossessed* (Philadelphia: University of Pennsylvania Press, 2016); Sara Fieldston, *Raising the World: Child Welfare in the American Century* (Cambridge, MA: Harvard University Press, 2015).

8. David Harvey, *A Brief History of Neoliberalism* (New York: Oxford University Press, 2005), 76–78.

9. Fieldston, *Raising the World*; Scott Flipse, "To Save 'Free Vietnam' and Lose Our Souls: The Missionary Impulse, Voluntary Agencies, and Protestant Dissent against the War, 1965–1971," in *The Foreign Missionary Enterprise at Home: Explorations in North American Cultural History*, ed. Grant Wacker and Daniel Bays (Tuscaloosa: University of Alabama Press, 2003), 206–22; Scott Flipse, "The Latest Casualty of War: Catholic Relief Services, Humanitarianism, and the War in Vietnam, 1967–1968," *Peace & Change* 27, no. 2 (2002): 245–70; J. Bruce Nichols, *The Uneasy Alliance: Religion, Refugee Work, and U.S. Foreign Policy* (New York: Oxford University Press, 1988).

10. For a discussion of contemporary public policy debates about government funding for faith-based social service provision, see Robert Wuthnow, *Saving America? Faith-Based Services and the Future of Civil Society* (Princeton, NJ: Princeton University Press, 2004); Ram Cnaan, *The Invisible Caring Hand: American Congregations and the Provision of Welfare* (New York: New York University Press, 2002); E. J Dionne and Ming Hsu Chen, eds., *Sacred Places, Civic Purposes: Should Government Help Faith-Based Charity?* (Washington, DC: Brookings Institution Press, 2001); Ram Cnaan, *The Newer Deal: Social Work and Religion in Partnership* (New York: Columbia University Press, 1999).

11. Schäfer, *Piety and Public Funding*, 5.

12. Robert Wuthnow, *The Restructuring of American Religion: Society and Faith since World War II*, Studies on Church and State (Princeton, NJ: Princeton University Press, 1988), 8.

13. Several scholars have studied the involvement of religious institutions in refugee resettlement. See Porter, *Benevolent Empire*; Stephen Porter, "Defining Public Responsibility in a Global Age: Refugees, NGOs, and the American State" (PhD diss., University of Chicago, 2009); Carl Bon Tempo, *Americans at the Gate: The United States and Refugees during the Cold War* (Princeton, NJ: Princeton University Press, 2008); Stephanie Nawyn, "Welcoming the Stranger: Constructing an Interfaith Ethic of Refuge," in *Religion and Social Justice for Immigrants*, ed. P. Hondagneu-Sotelo (New Brunswick, NJ: Rutgers University Press, 2007), 141–56; Stephanie Nawyn, "Making a Place to Call Home: Refugee Resettlement Organizations, Religion, and the State" (PhD diss., University of Southern California, 2006); Stephanie Nawyn, "Faithfully Providing Refuge: The Role of Religious Organizations in Refugee Assistance and Advocacy," University of California–San Diego, Center for Comparative Immigration Studies, 2005.

14. Several scholars have studied the involvement of churches in congregational refugee sponsorship. See Nicole Ives, Jill Witmer Sinha, and Ram Cnaan, "Who Is Welcoming the Stranger? Exploring Faith-Based Service Provision to Refugees in Philadelphia," *Journal of Religion and Spirituality in Social Work: Social Thought* 29, no. 1 (2010): 71–89; Mary Pipher, *The Middle of Everywhere: The World's Refugees Come to Our Town* (New York: Harcourt, 2002); Helen Fein, *Congregational Sponsors of Indochinese Refugees in the United States, 1979–1981: Helping beyond Borders* (Rutherford, NJ: Fairleigh Dickinson University Press, 1987).

15. Anastasia Brown and Todd Scribner, "Unfulfilled Promises, Future Possibilities: The Refugee Resettlement System in the United States," *Journal on Migration and Human Security* 2, no. 2 (2014): 103–6. See also Porter, *Benevolent Empire*; Bon Tempo, *Americans at the Gate*; Gil Loescher and John Scanlan, *Calculated Kindness: Refugees and America's Half-Open Door, 1945 to the Present* (New York: Free Press, 1986).

16. Norman Zucker and Naomi Zucker, *The Guarded Gate: The Reality of American Refugee Policy* (San Diego, CA: Harcourt Brace Jovanovich, 1987), 121–22.

17. David North, Lawrence Lewin, and Jennifer Wagner, *Kaleidoscope: The Resettlement of Refugees in the United States by the Voluntary Agencies* (Washington, DC: New TransCentury Foundation, 1982), 21–22.

18. "More Church Involvement Urged in Refugee Programs," *Stockton Record*, October 17, 1980.

19. "Correspondence by Name, 1979–1981," box 2, American Refugee Committee Papers.

20. Refugees from Indochina, May 5, Hearings before the Subcommittee on Immigration, Citizenship, and International Law of the Committee on the Judiciary, 94th Congress.

21. CCSDPT, *The Committee for Coordination of Services to Displaced Persons in Thailand (CCSDPT) Handbook: Refugee Services in Thailand* (Bangkok: Craftsmen Press, 1982).

22. "Orientation Manual," box 4, American Refugee Committee Papers.

23. Nichols, *Uneasy Alliance*, 112–16. For discussion of Southeast Asian refugee admissions policy, see Bon Tempo, *Americans at the Gate*; Loescher and Scanlan, *Calculated Kindness*. For discussion of Southeast Asian refugee experiences under these policies, see Eric Tang, *Unsettled: Cambodian Refugees in the New York City Hyperghetto* (Philadelphia: Temple University Press, 2015); Steven Gold, *Refugee Communities: A Comparative Field Study* (Newbury Park, CA: Sage Publications, 1992); Aihwa Ong, *Buddha Is Hiding: Refugees, Citizenship, the New America* (Berkeley: University of California Press, 2003).

24. North, Lewin, and Wagner, *Kaleidoscope*, 3–17.

25. Oral history interview with Ingrid Walter, transcript, 59, Evangelical Lutheran Church of America Archive, Elk Grove, IL.

26. North, Lewin, and Wagner, *Kaleidoscope*, 27.

27. State Plan for Refugees 1979, Governor's Refugee Resettlement Office, 1976–1977, Minnesota Department of Public Welfare, Refugee Program Office Records, Minnesota Historical Society, State Archives.

28. Bruce Downing, *Hmong Resettlement Study Site Report: Minneapolis–St. Paul* (Minneapolis: Southeast Asian Studies Project, Center for Urban and Regional Affairs, University of Minnesota, 1984), 7.

29. Church World Service Agreement Sponsor Form, Pamphlets Relating to Refugee Relief and Assistance in Minnesota and the United States, Minnesota Historical Society Pamphlet Collection, Minnesota Historical Society, St. Paul.

30. Standing Committee, Protocol, Minutes, August 9, 1976, Lutheran Council in the U.S.A., Department of Immigration and Refugee Service, Record Group 10/1, Evangelical Lutheran Church in America Archive.

31. North, Lewin, and Wagner, *Kaleidoscope*, 33.

32. Refugees from Indochina, Hearings before the Subcommittee on Immigration, Citizenship, and International Law of the Committee on the Judiciary, 94th Congress, 370.

33. Mark Franken, interview by the author, October 19, 2006, Washington, DC, transcript, 5.

34. Fong Her, interview by Peter Chou Vang, Hmong Oral History Project, Concordia University.

35. Albert Quie, *Sponsor a Refugee*, videotape, 1978, Minnesota Governor Audio-Visual Materials, 1978–1983, Minnesota Historical Society, St. Paul.

36. Oak Terrace Resettlement Plan, Minnesota Department of Public Welfare, Refugee Program Office Records, Minnesota Historical Society, State Archives, St. Paul.

37. Refugees from Indochina, Hearings Before the Subcommittee on Immigration, Citizenship, and International Law of the Committee on the Judiciary, 94th Congress, 325–28.

38. Lutheran Immigration and Refugee Service, "The Real Cost of Welcome: A Financial Analysis of Local Refugee Reception" (Baltimore, 2009), 8.

39. Brown and Scribner, "Unfulfilled Promises, Future Possibilities," 111.

40. Folder 35, box 2, Refugee Studies Center, University of Minnesota Records, General/Multiethnic Collection, Immigration History Research Center, University of Minnesota, Minneapolis.

41. Pamphlets Relating to Refugee Relief and Assistance in Minnesota and the United States, Minnesota Historical Society Pamphlet Collection.

42. Lutheran Council in the U.S.A., Department of Immigration and Refugee Service, Record Group 10/3, Evangelical Church in America Archive.

43. Bernard Casserly, "Welcome 'Boat People,'" *Catholic Bulletin*, July 6, 1979.

44. Pearl Jones, interview by the author, August 29, 2012, White Bear Lake, MN, digital recording at pt. 8. Name has been changed at the request of the interview narrator.

45. Jones interview, digital recording at pt. 11.

46. Dorothy Knight, interview by the author, August 6, 2012, St. Paul, MN, digital recording at pt. 13.

47. Jeanne Luxem, "Gospel Verse Puts Parishes into Action," September 7, 1979, *Catholic Bulletin Magazine*.

48. Dayton Parish News of Dayton Avenue Presbyterian Church, March 1976, Minnesota Historical Society, St. Paul, MN.

49. Dayton Parish News of Dayton Avenue Presbyterian Church, September 1976, Minnesota Historical Society, St. Paul, MN.

50. Ingrid Walter, interview, transcript, 28.

51. Walter interview, 30.

52. *Christ Lutheran Bulletin*, May 3, 1975, Minnesota Historical Society, St. Paul, MN.

53. Tom Kosel, interview by the author, June 23, 2011, St. Paul, MN, digital recording at 1:49:35–1:51:23.

54. Folder 56, box 3, Refugee Studies Center, University of Minnesota Records, General/Multiethnic Collection, Immigration History Research Center, University of Minnesota, Minneapolis, MN.

55. Lutheran Immigration and Refugee Services, *Face to Face: The Ministry of Refugee Resettlement*, Lutheran Council in the U.S.A., Department of Immigration and Refugee Service, Lutheran Immigration and Refugee Services Assorted Publications, Evangelical Church in America Archive, Elk Grove, IL.

56. Church World Service, *Manual for Refugee Sponsorship*, Church World Service Records, Presbyterian Historical Society, Philadelphia, PA. In Canada, the Mennonite voluntary agency adopted a similar approach, although Mennonite congregational sponsors had different beliefs about how to share Christianity with church-sponsored Hmong refugees. Voluntary agency officials insisted on

not taking advantage of refugees' vulnerability, but sponsors objected to this approach, considering it "negative spiritually." See Daphne Winland, "The Role of Religious Affiliation in Refugee Resettlement: The Case of the Hmong," *Canadian Ethnic Studies/Études ethniques au Canada* 24, no. 1 (1992): 102.

57. Lutheran Immigration and Refugee Services, *Face to Face: The Ministry of Refugee Resettlement*, Lutheran Council in the U.S.A., Department of Immigration and Refugee Service, Lutheran Immigration and Refugee Services Assorted Publications, Evangelical Church in America Archive, Elk Grove, IL.

58. Folder 56, box 3, Refugee Studies Center, University of Minnesota Records, General/Multiethnic Collection, Immigration History Research Center, University of Minnesota, Minneapolis, MN.

59. Organizational Files: Correspondences and Miscellanea, 1979–1980, box 1, American Refugee Committee Records.

60. Church World Service, *Manual for Refugee Sponsorship*, Church World Service Records, Presbyterian Historical Society, Philadelphia, PA.

61. Standing Committee, Protocol, Minutes, March 29–30, 1976, Lutheran Council in the U.S.A., Department of Immigration and Refugee Service, Record Group 10/1, Evangelical Church in America Archive.

62. Folder 56, box 3, Refugee Studies Center, University of Minnesota Records, General/Multiethnic Collection, Immigration History Research Center, University of Minnesota, Minneapolis.

63. Standing Committee, Protocol, Minutes, January 8–9, 1976, Lutheran Council in the U.S.A., Dept. of Immigration and Refugee Service, Record Group 10/1, Evangelical Church in America Archive.

64. Lutheran Immigration and Refugee Services, *Face to Face: The Ministry of Refugee Resettlement*, Lutheran Council in the U.S.A., Department of Immigration and Refugee Service, Lutheran Immigration and Refugee Services Assorted Publications, Evangelical Church in America Archive.

65. Folder 56, box 3, Refugee Studies Center, University of Minnesota Records, General/Multiethnic Collection, Immigration History Research Center, University of Minnesota Minneapolis.

66. Lutheran Immigration and Refugee Services, *Face to Face: The Ministry of Refugee Resettlement*, Lutheran Council in the U.S.A., Department of Immigration and Refugee Service, Lutheran Immigration and Refugee Services Assorted Publications, Evangelical Church in America Archive.

67. Tom Kosel, interview, digital recording at 9:20–10:10.

68. Ibid.

69. Timothy Vang, interview by the author, September 20, 2012, Maplewood, MN, digital recording at pt. 3.

70. Mai Vang Thao, OH 86.2, Oral History Interviews of the Hmong Women's Action Team Oral History Project (Hmoob Thaj Yeeb Oral History Project) 1999–2000, Minnesota Historical Society, transcript, 11.

71. Soua Lo and Shong Yang, interview by the author, translated by Maile Vue, August 6, 2012, St. Paul, MN, digital recording at pt. 15.

72. Kia Vue, interview by the author, translated by Maile Vue, September 8, 2012, St. Paul, MN, digital recording at pt. 7. For more discussion of how refugee resettlement produced religious changes among Southeast Asian refugees, see Daphne Winland, "Revisiting a Case Study of Hmong Refugees and Ontario Mennonites," *Journal of Mennonite History* 24 (2006): 169–76; Ong, *Buddha Is Hiding*; Lillian Faderman, *I Begin My Life All Over: The Hmong and the American Immigrant Experience* (Boston: Beacon Press, 1999); Anne Fadiman, *The Spirit Catches You and You Fall Down: A Hmong Child, Her American Doctors, and the Collision of Two Cultures* (New York: Farrar, Straus & Giroux, 1998); Daphne Winland, "Christianity and Community: Conversion and Adaptation among Hmong Refugee Women," *Canadian Journal of Sociology/Cahiers canadiens de sociologie* 19, no. 1 (Winter 1994): 21–45; Winland, "Role of Religious Affiliation in Refugee Resettlement."

73. Refugees from Indochina, Hearings before the Subcommittee on Immigration, Citizenship, and International Law of the Committee on the Judiciary, 94th Congress, 323.

74. Mark Franken, interview, transcript, 11.

75. Ellen Erickson, quoted in Wendy Tai, "Unsettling influences," *Minneapolis Star-Tribune*, February 8, 1993.

76. Jimmy Carter: "The State of the Union Address Delivered before a Joint Session of the Congress," January 19, 1978, American Presidency Project, http://www.presidency.ucsb.edu/ws/?pid=30856.

CHAPTER TEN

A Carceral Empire

Placing the Political History of U.S. Prisons and Policing in the World

Stuart Schrader

In 1972, faced with an apparent increase in crime, New York governor Nelson A. Rockefeller sent the magazine publisher and department-store president William Fine to Japan for a weekend. The governor wanted him to figure out why levels of drug use were so low there. Fine's own son had struggled with addiction, which spurred his interest in the topic. In the often-cited account of this trip, Fine "came away with the apparent secret to the Japanese success against drugs—life sentences for pushers." His investigation inspired Rockefeller, but not before the businessman had also informed California's governor at the time, Ronald Reagan, of his discovery. As the Republican Party drifted rightward, Fine's discovery stoked Rockefeller's competition with Reagan over who was tougher on crime and forced him to take immediate action. Japan provided a model for new laws—which included, in the governor's words, "stern measures," like life sentences, for "all pushers" of dangerous drugs regardless of age, as well as for people convicted of committing violent crimes while under the influence—that would in time be replicated in almost every U.S. state. This is at least the way scholars of the carceral state have usually narrated the story of Fine's journey and its effect.[1]

The Rockefeller drug laws have figured prominently in the growing literature on the carceral state. They symbolize at least three key shifts, typically explained through reference to localized and punctual swings in the electorate, a crime crisis, or elite political ambitions. First, the laws repudiated rehabilitation-oriented programming for addicts in favor of incarceration for "pushers." Second, they became a foundation for a nationally prominent Republican official to espouse his toughness in the fight against crime, reorienting priorities for both parties, especially at the state level. Third, they initiated a racially selective form of punishment by imposing much harsher penalties for possession of types of drugs that tended to be concentrated in black urban neighborhoods rather than in white suburbs or college dorms. Yet these three shifts all look different when Rockefeller's trajectory is placed "in the world" and when the peculiar story of Japan's influence on him is situated in the broader sweep of U.S. foreign policy.

Rather than novel innovations, with this perspectival shift, the transformations the Rockefeller laws symbolize begin to look more like continuities with modes of governing overseas—and the carceral state like the outgrowth and consequence of state building beyond borders. First, the shift to rehabilitation instead of strict punishment that peaked during the 1960s becomes a deviation from a more consistently punitive orientation that U.S. officials recommended in other countries as part of a suite of security-conscious, anticommunist development repertoires. Although other countries developed therapeutic approaches for addicts, U.S. officials consistently downplayed their relevance by focusing on drug producers and distributors. Rockefeller ignored what Fine told him about therapeutic measures for addicts, focusing only on Japan's coercive measures for dealers, which abrogated what Fine called "human rights." A message like this was already on offer from a wider panoply of law-enforcement professionals, security specialists, and international institutions that advocated and shaped intensely punitive capacities across the foreign-domestic divide.

Second, Rockefeller himself was a denizen of the foreign-policy establishment long before he entered the governor's mansion, specializing on Latin America. In that role, he maintained contact with this more hidden echelon of security officials. His turn toward "law and order" politics as governor built on his consistent and long-standing advocacy for robust security spending. Sections of Rockefeller's 1969 report on hemispheric relations prefigured his own arguments for what was at stake in crafting more punitive policy in New York, by pointing to the pervasiveness of "fear," the severity of threats to "freedom," and the urgency of acting to bolster the resources devoted to security in the face of political opposition that did not take threats seriously.[2] Yet these arguments were already common among experienced security actors. Their ideas were an underappreciated driver of the growth of the carceral state, shaping elected officials' attitudes.

Low- and midlevel security officials not only honed practical repertoires of enforcing social order. Through their experience of constructing a global anticrime, countersubversion, and narcotics-control apparatus, they also developed personal preferences for security-based solutions to social problems, as well as institutional cohesion to issue legitimate demands for these approaches. In the fallout from the debacle of the U.S. war in Vietnam, and after the upheavals of the 1960s, they turned their attention homeward. In turn, these figures' ideological and practical focus on security, to the detriment of other social or political values, was consonant with long-standing foreign-policy demands that came from elites, including Rockefeller. The carceral state inherited and bolstered this commitment to security first.

Third, in Japan, as elsewhere, drug-control policies can be seen as shaped by U.S. policy makers, stamped with U.S. racial thinking of the 1940s. The model policies that inspired Rockefeller originated in the postwar U.S. occupation. Accompanying strict controls on marijuana and opium was leniency on amphetamines. This disparity represented the congruence of exported U.S. racial ideologies with Japanese xenophobia. Occupation officials' failure to appreciate the widespread use of amphetamines among Japanese war veterans and among the malnourished amid postwar food shortages paralleled domestic U.S. attitudes at the time: speed was not considered much of a problem because its users tended to be white, whereas heroin was thought to be a black and Chinese problem and marijuana a black problem. For Japanese officials, opium was thought a Chinese problem and speed not much of a problem because it was the drug of choice among Japanese nationals. The result was that Japanese lawmakers later felt they had to play catch-up to an epidemic, leading to harsh penalties that captured the attention of Albany. Fine presented this drug-control regime to Rockefeller as having the air of technical rationality and dispassionate confrontation with an otherwise intractable social problem. Transplanted to New York, its predicted racially invidious outcomes could be narrated as regrettable and accidental results of an otherwise neutral program. But U.S. influence on postwar Japan baked racial inequality into its drug laws. Such inequality was not new in New York in the years after the successes of the civil rights movement.

To center the carceral state in U.S. political history is now imperative. But the aperture must also be widened to help understand the carceral state's nascence, persistence, and effects. As currently written, scholarship examining the political history of the U.S. carceral state remains domestically oriented, analyzing institutional and political histories in isolation from the broader domains of foreign-policy formation, cross-border political advocacy, and globetrotting technical expertise in which they were historically enmeshed. This chapter seeks to overcome the carceral state literature's methodological nationalism by suggesting avenues of analysis that emphasize its relationships with the national security state and U.S. empire.[3] It advocates a reconfigured approach to political history that transcends national borders. Actions overseas, particularly under the voracious demand of security, profoundly affected domestic state formation and reshaped domestic politics by creating and sustaining political agendas among actors traditionally excluded from political history, as well as among leading figures whose biographies must be reevaluated as straddling the foreign-domestic divide.

New Historiographies of the Carceral State

The burgeoning historical literature on the carceral state is among the most vibrant and politically urgent subfields of study among historians and historically minded social scientists today.[4] Carceral state historians are also rethinking periodizations and political divisions that have long characterized the historiography of U.S. politics by paying close attention to bipartisan initiatives and coalitions, as well as shared political idioms—and to the centrality of race, gender, and sexuality to cause and effect alike. With a keen appreciation of politics beyond the ballot box, the literature often tends toward the elusive synthesis of social history with more elite-based histories of policy and state action.[5] This literature is also frequently open to influence from social science—or it is emerging in other fields, such as American political development, American studies, geography, and law and society.

Many historians have investigated the carceral state because of the highly racialized and gendered character of incarceration in the United States. Nearly one-third of black men (and one-sixth of Latino men) are likely to be sent to jail or prison in their lifetime.[6] The country's overall level of incarceration grew by 500 percent in the three decades after 1973, but in relative and absolute terms, a disparity in incarceration between white and black populations emerged and increased dramatically from 1970 through the 1990s.[7] The disparity remains high, although it is leveling somewhat. The result of this social reality has led the historical study of the carceral state to emerge largely within African American history.

Scholars of the carceral state have built on and overlapped with the fundamental reshaping of the historiography of black freedom struggles over the past two decades. This work discarded the declensionist narrative of virtuous integration-oriented Southern civil rights activism followed by rebellious and violent separatism-oriented Northern radicalism.[8] In this scholarship, blame no longer falls on Black Power militants for alienating white moderates and fracturing racially integrated coalitions. New scholarship focuses on everyday and grassroots activists, many of whom encountered police repression or were jailed or incarcerated as a result of their activism (as were major figures like Martin Luther King Jr.). Political organizing by imprisoned people themselves is increasingly entering the historical narrative of the "long civil rights movement."[9] How policing and incarceration as tools of repression have shaped wider political horizons is a key concern. The forerunners to the academic history of the carceral state were black freedom movement voices inside and outside the academy, inside and outside prison, inside and outside the United States. With more direct terminology, though, they tended to refer to it simply as repression. Further, from the outset of the New Deal through Reagan's ascendancy, black movement voices consistently issued demands for democratic inclusion from the streets to ballot boxes to union halls to workplaces, critiques of U.S. empire and its domestic reverberations, and prescient analyses of carceral forms of governance. Historians therefore need to specify what exactly rose and declined, and for whom, with the New Deal order—and what role prisons and punitive crime policy played in the shattering of that order.[10]

Analysis of the carceral state has also been shaped by contention over the legacies of the 1960s. Older literature claimed that dissatisfaction with the War on Poverty and practical manifestations of racial desegregation ushered in demands for law and order.[11] Field-defining new works rebut this argument about a right-wing backlash leading to law-and-order politics.[12] Before racial desegregation had become the law of the land, elites deployed talk of crime threats and demanded muscular law enforcement to resist it.[13] Further, liberal procedural reforms, consonant with New Deal credos, empowered and enlarged apparatuses of policing, punishment, and civic exclusion. The long-accepted causal linkage between the rise of the carceral state and the electoral success of the new right has been revised.[14] The carceral state was a liberal project, too: "Crime policy and carceral expansion were not reactions against civil rights; they were the progeny of civil rights as lawmakers defined them."[15] Elected officials then pushed to find consensus. Liberal leaders in the 1970s like Senator Edward Kennedy hoped to, in an aide's words, "depoliticize the crime debate and develop the kind of bipartisanship that was the hallmark of post–World War II foreign policy."[16] Rising conservative congressman Newt Gingrich, in turn, demanded a World War II–like mobilization of state capacities against drugs in the 1980s.[17] A commitment to aggressive foreign policy modeled bipartisanship. The carceral state realized bipartisanship's promise at home.

Imperial Formations

The undertheorized treatment of Fine's trip to Japan is symptomatic of the carceral state literature's unrealized promise and foreshortened geographical horizons. Of foundations and paradigms in American studies, Amy Kaplan trenchantly observed that "imperialism has been simultaneously formative and disavowed."[18] The same is true in American carceral state historiography. Many works in this literature gesture toward a consideration of the world beyond U.S. borders—and of the consequential U.S. entanglement with it.[19] But methodological nationalism is pervasive. The common units of analysis are either a single state or the contiguous forty-eight states, rather than these plus the U.S. territorial empire including, for example, Guam and Puerto Rico, much less the globe-spanning archipelago of military bases and black sites, or the many informal arenas of imperial control and influence that jurisdictionally have belonged to other sovereignties. To put it bluntly, a literature that has as its focus the apparent transformation of U.S. policy and political proclivities toward harsh, coercive, and punitive state violence has avoided consideration of the ways prior and concomitant U.S. state action around the globe that is harsh, coercive, punitive, and violent might have shaped, conditioned, and determined that transformation.[20]

The history of the carceral state, therefore, must be reconceptualized. This essential phenomenon in postwar U.S. history was not a purely domestic affair. It was entangled with the wider world, conditioned by U.S. foreign relations and the national security state. The way historians write its history should be reformatted in theoretical, methodological, and empirical dimensions to account for deep and abiding relationships between what are improperly perceived as two separate spheres, the carceral state and U.S. empire. Scholars have begun to pay close attention to "the resources, the discourses, and the expertise political elites employ to promote certain policies" that led to the carceral state.[21] Indeed, these have all been shaped by the imperial. Key figures developed technical implements and political resources to "govern through crime" overseas before and while they did so at home.[22]

A reconfigured historiography of the carceral state must conceive this governing assemblage—and its racially unequal characteristics—as effects of the imperial, not merely as coincidental to it. This reconfiguration can help elucidate who the political actors were behind the rise of the carceral state and how they gained legitimacy, developed their worldviews, and crafted their technical expertise. With "the imperial," building on the definitional work of historian Paul Kramer, I am emphasizing the long-term outcome or effect of asymmetries of power concretized through the attempt, if not the actuality, of U.S. actors to dominate multiple scales and terrains of political struggle, constraining possibilities of resistance or rejection.[23] The national security state has been its most prominent vehicle. The imperial is a mode of hierarchical, disciplining, and frequently violent state power that operates across borders and at multiple geographic scales simultaneously.

In the postwar period, U.S. imperial formation has relied on a normative discourse of formal equality while exceptionalizing racial and gender difference across these scales as threats posed to this formal equality. So, too, has carceral state formation. Yet is the carceral merely one tool in the multifaceted repertoire of the imperial? Dylan Rodríguez has argued that the "prison regime" is excessive to the state, that it "possesses and constitutes the state" rather than the state marking the limits of the prison regime or the carceral.[24] This uncoupling is useful and suggests a further refinement: the imperial, which is also exorbitant to the state yet distinctly tethered to it, possesses and constitutes the carceral. To see the carceral as not simply tool but also governmental effect of the imperial poses dramatically different questions for historians and political challenges for all those who wish to see the end of the carceral state in the near term, rather than the mere reconfiguration of some carceral capacities.[25] It places the burden on historians to explain which aspects of the carceral state are unrelated to the imperial, as some may be, rather than presuming from the outset that they are unrelated unless otherwise specified.

The political and institutional infrastructure, as well as the biographies of key figures, behind the carceral state must be placed "in the world." The coalitions that came together to support the expansion of harsh and punitive state policy rehearsed and refined their messages and their techniques at scales larger than the beat, the precinct, the district, or even the nation-state. They envisioned and enacted security at regional, hemispheric, and global scales. The roots of these efforts extend to the early moments of the Cold War, when leaders first began to cobble together the national security state. This perspective reconsiders not only the geographies of U.S. state power in the twentieth century but also commonplace periodizations, including the breakdown of the New Deal order and its replacement with a new social order and the collapse of a liberal consensus and the rise of the new right. Less pivotal was the rise of the New Deal political coalition of Southern and Northern Democrats than the bipartisan marshaling of state capacities for warfare in World War II, which included the mass internment of 120,000 Japanese Americans in prison camps, along with other wartime detentions. These capacities then transformed into a steady-state infrastructure of both defensive and offensive war making spurred by bipolar rivalry, accompanied by implements of counterrevolution to be deployed in the developing world. The national security state produced and enveloped a range of institutions, as well as actors who became committed to its maintenance. This commitment inflected and shaped adjacent and even unrelated political domains by reorienting priorities.

In this light, there were strong continuities across familiar moments of transformation. The fall of the New Deal order by the 1980s was not accompanied by a collapse in the bipartisan commitment to putting security first, nor did actors with this outlook, first incubated in the New Deal, retreat.[26] If anything, that fall unleashed this commitment, and the carceral state is proof. Analysis of the political constituency of the carceral state should be reoriented away from revanchist white voters and conservative black elites, as in the current literature. Many people who became increasingly organized institutionally as the managers and executors of punishment self-interestedly advocated for more punitive forms of governance and the redirection of state expenditures toward courts, police, and prisons. Law-enforcement professional organizations gained coherence, autonomy, and institutional legitimacy as they engaged with national security objectives and their members traveled, researched, and consulted around the globe. The global fight against communism provided their idiom, threat inflation their vocabulary. Professional organizations gained the wherewithal to coordinate political campaigns that held security as a primary objective because members once divided sectionally could agree on an objective and an organizing principle that conflated threats of crime and political radicalism. Imperial excursions glued them together.

Welfare and Warfare

To understand how the carceral state emerged, some historians are already breaking out of topical boxes and inherited periodizations by highlighting the interpenetration of penal and welfare policies. Lyndon Johnson's Wars on Poverty and Crime actually were intertwined, and to attribute one to the left and the other to the right is unsupportable. The Johnson administration initiated legislative pushes to extend civil rights and remediate poverty simultaneously with others designed to bolster carceral capacities. Further, these wars both targeted the same populations: largely segregated and impoverished African Americans, and in particular, "juveniles." Surveillance was a key feature of programs that were intended to create economic opportunities because of the sense that a criminal propensity would be unleashed among those who failed economic and social uplift schemes. Moreover, officials justified spending on welfare by calling attention to its effects on crime control, which slid easily into earmarking funds from welfare appropriations (from, for example, the Model Cities program) for "new precincts, police-training centers, service bureaus for adjudicated youth, probation and legal services, and police-community relations programs."[27] Many of the features of the carceral state's professionalization efforts for law enforcement, selective targeting of populations, and inflexible penalization of relatively minor offense (lest they lead to greater ones) were already present in the very social welfare programming that scholars had long contrasted to more coercive forms of governance. Rather than the state shrinking in this period, as neoliberal ideology would have it, state capacities underwent a process of "carceralization."[28]

The carceralization process worked through, and heightened, forms of inequality. The rhetoric of criminality that attended to supposed welfare cheating furthered the entanglement of carceral and welfare apparatuses and enhanced racial, gender, and sexual hierarchies. As a result, "contestation and crises" of welfare "set the stage for expansion in the penal system."[29] Rather than simply an entwinement of the two at the carceral state's genesis, the two coexisted and shared "governing rationales." Ultimately, however, the penal apparatus "supplanted" the welfare apparatus, as "responsibility for handling specific social problems was transferred from welfare programs to law enforcement."[30] This crisis-induced commingling was a characteristic feature of counterinsurgency campaigns across the globe during the Cold War and into the present. Thus, historians track tentative, contingent, and uncoordinated enlargements of carceral capacities in and through the reconfiguration of welfare capacities. These birthed what in retrospect we can understand as the carceral state.

Canonical divisions that often structure historical research and even historical archives, like civilian versus military, eroded in the early moments of the carceralization process. Welfare programs at home came to rely on the military both for its comparatively vast budgets and its normative culture. Leaders in the military and welfare apparatuses saw in each other solutions to crises, but this collaboration, in turn, was contested. For the military, to join recruitment with welfarist programming could solve insufficiencies of recruitment. For welfare programs, the Pentagon could supplement inadequate resources. Although Defense Secretary Robert S. McNamara wanted a greater role for the Pentagon in welfare programming during the 1960s, protests limited the types of assistance provided.[31] McNamara and Daniel P. Moynihan, on behalf of the Department of Labor, collaborated to invent manpower programs to help make poor, unemployed, and unsatisfactorily educated black men eligible for induction into the military. In turn, municipal officials who saw such young men as a potential security problem were happy to call on the Pentagon.

Outside Baltimore, for example, a naval base provided the venue for a welfare-oriented youth camp called Camp Concern. It removed predominantly black young men from the city's streets during summer months when municipal officials anticipated unrest after 1968. Although Camp Concern provided recreational activities and square meals, campers' days were strictly regimented and their actions monitored. When the camp eventually relocated to a Baltimore park during the 1970s, a barbed-wire fence surrounded it and nighttime guards stood watch. Critics at the time claimed the camp inveigled poor kids: a chance to breathe fresh air was actually an attempt to convince them to enlist in the military. These experiences not only normalized confinement and military-influenced discipline; they held them as rewards, as an escape from putatively degraded, unhealthy, and unsafe urban life.[32] Further, McNamara instituted a program called Project Transition to assist chiefly African American veterans returning from the U.S. war in Vietnam in becoming police officers (or other civil-service careers). The academic history of the program remains to be written. How war experiences in Vietnam affected these men as police officers is an open question.[33] To put the Pentagon at the center of this warfare-welfare-carceral effort sheds new light on periodization and state transformations after the 1970s.[34]

Imperial Institutions

If postwar approaches to identifying and solving social problems never maintained a rigid divide between the carceral and the welfarist, then an appreciation of this cross-fertilization should only encourage further widening of the geographic aperture. What Elizabeth Hinton calls the "fusion of social services and law enforcement measures" extended beyond borders to the practices of international development.[35] Many experts of both punishment and welfare trafficked models and ideas between foreign and domestic domains, iteratively and recursively testing and rehearsing tactics.[36] When U.S. officials overseas confronted intractable problems, they summoned advice from domestic agencies whose leadership eagerly obliged. Experts mobilized notions of delinquency and criminal propensity previously tested in African American neighborhoods as they surveyed developing countries. South Vietnam was a key node in this circulation, where Pentagon resources were abundant, but many other locales mattered, too. The imperial skein was in part composed of these transitory, often crisis-induced interactions across borders. It hid in dozens of Rolodexes, each name in them associated with a lesson learned, a technique refined, a hypothesis taken as proven right. From these experiences emerged the security-first consensus that would guide the reconfiguration of governance that the carceral state embodies.

The attempt to achieve law and order suffused overseas work by the U.S. government and its proxies both in advance of the concept's popularity at home and after it became predominant in political discourse. The reason is that law-enforcement experts themselves were important advocates of a turn toward this type of discourse. Bolstered politically, they transformed discourse into practice. It is therefore important, in the analysis of the carceral state, to pay attention to various law-enforcement and criminal-justice constituencies as pushing for policies that would enlarge carceral capacities. They had a clear self-interest in such enlargement and must not be treated as neutral recipients of political preferences independent from or exogenous to them but rather as sculptors of political preferences themselves. Not simply the work of political elites, law-enforcement professionals engaged in this consequential activity. Though not typically included in social history, cops were historical actors whose preferences and demands should be taken seriously, particularly because elites heeded them.

The development and dissemination of law-enforcement and criminological expertise at home and abroad entrenched crime as the primary object of state intervention. In turn, this expertise was self-justifying. As security concerns trumped other governing concerns—or redefined social goods through reference to security—the necessity of a well-resourced professional penal apparatus became the sine qua non of governance. The institutions responsible often relied on extraterritorial experience, and individuals proved their mettle and savvy through reference to this experience. These included research firms and their funders, fraternal organizations, security contractors, and specific agencies tasked with law-enforcement cooperation and assistance across borders, in addition to agencies like the Secret Service, Marshals Service, Bureau of Narcotics and Dangerous Drug and then Drug Enforcement Administration, Federal Bureau of Investigation (FBI), Customs Service, Border Patrol, and others that actually engaged in extraterritorial law enforcement. Further, new federal and state funding enabled coordination in training exercises and planning for emergency situations among police, National Guard, and army units. Further research should examine the effects of this commingling at an everyday level on the political attitudes and professional outlooks of these officers. Separately, suprastate organizations like the United Nations played a valuable role in legitimizing the political focus on narcotics and juvenile delinquency, for example. Interpol, in addition, is a key, understudied institution that enabled U.S. intervention in transnational crime control in the guise of multilateralism. Far removed from the ken of voters, these institutions nevertheless offered a sense of coherent mission to actors interacting with them.

Institutional networks in law enforcement developed wide scopes and scales of reach. Their influences on practice as well as political discourse were self-reinforcing. Police legitimacy during the tumultuous postwar years, for instance, turned on the widespread applicability of expert and reformist practices. The magazine *Police* was geared toward rank-and-file officers, and it carried, during the 1960s, several articles that were intended to inform police about how the U.S. government was using police assistance overseas to achieve broader geopolitical goals. These articles were also tools to recruit officers who might be seeking adventure. They could become public safety advisors, whom the Agency for International Development (AID) was sending around the globe. One such 1966 article detailed police assistance to Brazil, titled "The Agency for International Development Helps Brazilians Fight War on Crime."[37] Now, it is true that President Lyndon Johnson had used the phrase "war on crime" to describe his efforts, including the 1965 Law Enforcement Assistance Act. But the phrase did not yet have the political purchase it would obtain in the coming months and years, first as Republicans won a significant number of seats in Congress in the midterm election six months later, and second as Richard Nixon campaigned for and won the White House two and half years later. This AID-produced article emblematized how security experts proactively used the very political vocabulary by which their own activities achieved legitimacy. The article applied the term *war on crime* to overseas work to make it more legible. And it tethered overseas work, which was at its core concerned with preventing or halting political subversion, to the shifting domestic political consensus. AID staff signaled how this war would be waged using the same tools in Brazil as in U.S. cities and towns, developed by a single coterie of experts. This article and others like it narrated the implementation of what was thought to be a universally applicable model of professionalism that included high education standards for officers, the latest forensic laboratory equipment, and state-of-the-art training facilities. Police professionalization knew no territorial limits.

In turn, a variety of nonstate institutions acted as conduits of law-enforcement expertise and innovations across borders. The nexus of foundations, research firms, and think tanks has been fruitfully examined in both domestic and foreign dimensions. The management of poverty at home and the management of poverty overseas were, as scholars have shown, two areas in which intellectuals shaped policy and reconfigured the demands of social movements directly. The logical next step is to "follow the policy" itself across territories, places, and scales.[38] Following the policy does not mean assuming the policy remained unchanged as it traveled or that the vessels of its travel were even or static. How, for example, think tanks grew and transformed in the process of disseminating new ideas and policies of state coercion is an important phenomenon to examine. The RAND Corporation, the U.S. Army's Special Operations Research Office, the Bureau of Social Science Research, and American Institutes for Research all turned toward new audiences and new funders in the civilian sector as New Left critiques of university-military collaborations mounted.[39] Their findings

incrementally reshaped municipal, state, and federal criminal-justice institutions while also reconfiguring public conversations about crime. For instance, after one of its analysts leaked the Pentagon Papers, the embattled
RAND Corporation needed to mend its relationship with the national
security state while also covering its expenditures. The New York Police
Department (NYPD), which was in the midst of its own crises of legitimacy
and effectiveness, turned to RAND for help. RAND officials were happy
to work with the NYPD, devising new patrol guidance. The institutional
culture of the NYPD differed greatly from that of the military—the latter
lacks a collective bargaining agreement, to start—which made this collaboration difficult at first. In time, the NYPD came to accommodate the
data-driven approach RAND advocated on the basis of its past military
experience. Today's NYPD is synonymous with data-driven approaches to
policing. The legitimacy of these approaches is in part conferred by the
imprimatur of well-regarded research firms. These firms' institutional and
intellectual history, in relation to the carceral state, should be central to
future research.

Beginning in the aftermath of the U.S. war in Vietnam, the private security sector boomed. It is another difficult-to-access but crucial area for
future research. These contractors, some of which predated the U.S. war
in Vietnam, would employ many veterans of U.S. imperial ventures and
operate in the interstices of the national security state. The domains of
military contracting, engineering and construction, private security, and
private detention and incarceration have become incestuous. The corporations maintain political clout. Their leaders as well as their low-rung employees have lived transnational lives.

Beyond these institutions, long-standing fraternal and professional organizations like the International Association of Chiefs of Police (IACP),
as well as newer ones like the International Corrections and Prisons Association, merit examination. In particular, they have shaped political decisions and exemplified the organizational heft that came from coordination
and alignment with the national security state. A former high-ranking FBI
agent and close ally of J. Edgar Hoover, the virulently anticommunist Quinn
Tamm was the IACP's executive director during the Johnson administration.
While other police executives voiced skepticism, Tamm and his colleagues
were early advocates of the 1965 Law Enforcement Assistance Act, which
scholars have argued set into motion the construction of the carceral state.
Engrained habits of threat inflation, rehearsed in the fight against communism, proved useful in convincing legislators of the necessity of expanding

penal capacities. One IACP leader testified before Congress in hearings on the legislation that became the 1965 act: "It is not a question of whether you *should* act but rather it is a question as to the price in lives, property loss, and freedom should you *fail* to act."[40] Such apocalyptic language, honed in prior denunciations of communism, was these cops' specialty. Elected officials believed them. Soon Tamm built on this advocacy to put the IACP's weight behind that legislation's expansion into the 1968 Omnibus Crime Control and Safe Streets Act. Johnson, in turn, used the IACP to bolster support for federal action. The experience of the IACP with the national security state was complicated; around the time Tamm became the organization's leader, a canceled contract relating to overseas police assistance left him sour. But that hiccup emboldened him to argue more forcefully on the organization's behalf and to issue demands on the federal government to heed the authority of police chiefs and to ensure that federal dollars flowed to them. Security first was a realizable goal, and if the chiefs were empowered, they could achieve it.

Imperial Itineraries

A biographical approach to the history of the carceral state is another promising pathway out from methodological nationalism. Attention to individuals at multiple levels is necessary to break free from the political-methodological containers that have framed the subfield of U.S. history, separating elite from everyday actors. As a rough guideline, low-ranking figures were responsible for reproducing and transposing the cultural ways of the imperial; mid-ranking ones for producing and circulating the practical expertise of security; and the high-ranking ones for the policies and legislative transformations that integrated the imperial and carceral. Each level contributed in different ways to reorienting state priorities.

At the lowest level were those soldiers, military police officers, public safety advisors, and others who left their overseas deployments to fashion the growing carceral state. They were assisted by initiatives like Project Transition and institutions like the IACP, as well as by informal networks and fraternal connections that then became the basis for political organizing and appeals. Many officials shuttled back and forth between domestic and foreign employment in the service of law enforcement. The federal government occasionally sent big-city cops and firefighters with the necessary foreign language skills overseas for short periods beginning in the 1950s as consultants and evaluators. CIA brass did not like having to justify such junkets to municipal chiefs who had to approve leaves-of-absence for their officers.[41] As a result, overseas police assistance became formalized. Officers then became professional advisers and trainers, employed after 1962 by AID. Some of these overseas public safety advisors who had been police officers or prison guards returned to those professions after retiring from AID. The relationships forged through overseas deployment helped them to find work stateside, or overseas again. Further, the fraternity among these veterans became a political organizing vehicle. They also mobilized their identity as veterans of overseas service to make their voices heard in professional publications and at conferences like the IACP's annual meeting, where law enforcement's state of the art is ritually crafted and shared. A gritty loyalty to security or law and order, rather than to the state per se, would be honed among such figures in this period, setting the stage for their continual demands on the state to advance their projects. In the professional policing literature from the 1960s into the 1970s, many of the most fervent calls for putting security first emanated from figures with overseas experience and imperial trajectories.

At higher ranks were leaders of law-enforcement agencies, criminology professors, and high-profile experts who developed doctrines and routines of forensics, policing, and incarceration. Some of AID's public safety advisors were such experts, but this type of international expertise predated AID's police-assistance program and then outlived it. Many of these personal stories have been barely told, and beyond the technical advances they made, their contributions to state building should be assessed. For example, the director of the Federal Bureau of Prisons from 1937 to 1964, James V. Bennett, participated in numerous international meetings. A keen student of Soviet incarceration practices, he also believed in the tactical necessity of some forms of racial segregation in prisons.[42] Bennett and his Bureau of Prisons colleagues also worked overseas, conducting, for instance, reviews of penitentiaries in Guatemala, Thailand, and Brazil.[43] In those countries, they insisted that insufficient attention had been paid to prisons as an integral part of the overall criminal-justice system. Their recommendations were frequently couched in terms of aligning foreign practice with domestic U.S. practice, and they sought test cases that would prove the applicability of their proposals to even more locales. In Thailand, Bennett recommended reforms to alleviate overcrowding, which could improve conditions in prisons, but he also recommended the introduction of probation as one method. In this way, by assuming the universality of U.S. penal practices, his consulting work introduced new forms of punishment overseas.[44] The same year Bennett traveled to Guatemala, he successfully advocated domestically for what was later termed "truth in sentencing," reducing federal sentencing disparities based on judges' discretion. Overseas, as in the United States, he believed that those who worked in the prison system should have a stronger say in who got locked up and for how long. Even as Bennett did not zealously recommend harsh and lengthy prison sentences, he was a consummate state builder, interested in expanding bureaucracies and delegating greater oversight to technicians rather than elected or appointed officials. He rehearsed this orientation overseas. Studies of law-enforcement leaders like him, O. W. Wilson, August Vollmer, Harry Anslinger, and even J. Edgar Hoover could reveal new connections across borders while also demonstrating that state-building pushes originated within the bureaucracies themselves, rather than with, for example, elected officials' campaign promises.

The histories of schools of criminology and the discipline itself should become part of the analysis of the carceral state, as these were the venues for the production and reproduction of carceral knowledge that crossed borders. Schools of criminology were crucial for creating an independent institutional identity for law enforcement, as well as fraternal connections among practitioners. For example, Vollmer's School of Criminology in Berkeley attracted many students from overseas who then became assets and proxies of U.S. security forces during World War II and throughout the Cold War.[45] Michigan State University professors supported the regime of Ngô Đình Diệm in South Vietnam, including through police training. After, some continued to teach in its School of Police Administration and Public Safety, which in 1970 changed its name to the School of Criminal Justice. These professors' links to the national security state was fodder for a scandal during the 1960s, one of the initial bursts of criticism from the New Left of such university entanglements.[46] The School of Criminal Justice only grew in size and influence after the scandal. It seems that weathering public criticism actually helped build institutional knowledge and cohesion, even as individual figures suffered.

Finally, Nelson A. Rockefeller represents the top echelon of state officials whose imperial lives shaped their development of the carceral state. At the outset, I argued that Japan's drug laws took shape within a U.S. imperial crucible. Rockefeller did not draw on a separate example of carceral success in creating his own drug laws but was actually drawing on the imperial experience of the United States itself. The peculiarities of Japan's drug laws dated to the U.S. postwar occupation, reflecting the contours of the racialized viewpoints of U.S. officials. What Rockefeller's friend Fine discovered—Japan's willingness to sacrifice individual "human rights" in the quest for collective security—was a microcosm of the sacrifices and abridgments of other sovereignties U.S. hegemony demanded.[47] This experience sheds light on the deep, border-crossing roots of the carceral state: security first was a racialized U.S. political disposition that shaped Japanese drug policy under the occupation, with long-lasting consequences.

Rockefeller, in fact, was already a key player in the development of the infrastructure of that political disposition well before his January 1973 unveiling of the new laws that drew on it.[48] Although a Republican, he had served in President Franklin Delano Roosevelt's administration as the coordinator of inter-American affairs, a role that entailed coordinating propaganda with intelligence gathering during World War II, predominantly focused on Nazi connections in Latin America. He worked with the FBI and the predecessor to the Central Intelligence Agency.[49] He then became assistant secretary of state for Latin America. During this early postwar period, a dominant issue for U.S. policy toward Latin America was the control of the supply of drugs.[50] Rockefeller could not have avoided it. His Office of Inter-American Affairs, in turn, was a predecessor to the International Cooperation Administration, which became AID; these later agencies globalized the meshed concerns with security and development that grew out of U.S. efforts in Latin America that Rockefeller and his colleagues oversaw.

During this period, Rockefeller maintained a keen interest in the status of U.S. influence over the hemisphere. He foregrounded security issues over others, a frame of mind for policy that his drug laws would recapitulate. One of the U.S. government's key achievements concerning Latin America while he was assistant secretary was the Treaty of Chapultepec, which, in the name of hemispheric security, reiterated the Monroe doctrine. Even before World War II had ended, Rockefeller raised the specter of Soviet aggression to justify the treaty, transposing the risk of Nazi influence already under investigation through his outfit's efforts, in collaboration with the FBI. Then, in negotiations around self-defense provisions in the Charter of the United Nations, Rockefeller argued for an interpretation of articles 51 and 52 as preserving the Monroe doctrine. Some Latin American countries, which had been working for decades to remove the Monroe doctrine from international agreements, could interpret this move only

as a neo-imperial affront.[51] During the Truman and Eisenhower administrations, Rockefeller, mostly in advisory capacities, helped shape foreign
assistance in the realms of military and economic development aid, tethering them ever more tightly to each other. As a biographer notes, "Rockefeller remained an advocate of virtually unhampered defense outlays"
his entire life.[52] He maintained intimacy with the national security state.
When the rebellion in the Attica State Prison broke out, this governor
was unavailable to his staff because he was in Washington, DC, attending
a meeting of Nixon's Foreign Intelligence Advisory Board.[53]

In 1969, Rockefeller had a directly formative experience for his approach
to the carceral. As discussed by Micol Seigel, Rockefeller's disastrous "fact-
finding" visit on President Nixon's behalf to a restive Latin America shaped
his response to the Attica rebellion two years later. Rockefeller faced violent protests in Colombia, Ecuador, and Honduras, and his visits to Chile,
Peru, and Venezuela were canceled out of fear of similar protests. Bombings targeted symbols of U.S. power in the hemisphere, with those specifically linked to Rockefeller bearing the brunt of protesters' ire. Rockefeller
was surprised. He felt his contributions to the region should have earned
him plaudits. Also galling were connections he discovered between New
York and some of the countries where protests erupted. As he would with
Japan, based on Fine's research, he drew analogies: in Rockefeller's words,
"resentment from local groups" in the Dominican Republic was reminis-
cent of his "problems with a proposed State Office Building in Harlem."
But as with Japan, there were also material connections across borders: in
this case, radicals who traveled between New York and Jamaica learned
some of their methods stateside and then deployed them on the island, according to the prime minister.[54]

Rockefeller conflated these various forms of often legal political protest
with crime. After the rebellion in Attica, which Rockefeller ordered vio-
lently crushed, causing the deaths of more than thirty prisoners, he framed
his decisions to act so aggressively in terms of the Cold War perils of the
prairie-fire spread of rebellion. Rockefeller declared, "I've observed both
at home and abroad how both subversive and revolutionary forces have
abused the rights and responsibilities of free people and taken advantage
of them." He interpreted Attica through the lens of a global power struggle,
seeing it as a localized face parallel to what he had encountered during
his sojourn across Latin America. Further, racial anxieties underpinned the
conflation of crime with dissidence. Rockefeller's application of the word
revolutionary removed race from the security vocabulary while nevertheless

reinscribing racial meaning.[55] Rockefeller's drug laws also disavowed racism while reinscribing racial hierarchies, with their focus on drugs known to be prevalent in black urban neighborhoods.[56] And, as Seigel argues, the conflation of political dissidence with crime that Rockefeller and others proffered ultimately underwrote New York's shift away from rehabilitation, on the principle that political dissidents avowedly would refuse rehabilitation. This shift, Michael Fortner concludes, was the crucial policy pivot the new drug laws made manifest. Seen in this light, though, it was a pivot on the scale of the hemisphere, if not the globe.

The title of the governor's often-cited biography, *The Imperial Rockefeller*, describes not simply his stint as governor of the Empire State but indeed his lifelong commitment to the use of the coercive power of the state to maintain group-differentiated hierarchical relations. Rockefeller did become more punitive, less open to negotiation, and "bitter" and "retributive" after his 1969 journey to Latin America, as shown in his response to the rebellion in Attica and his subsequent drug laws.[57] But even this personal shift must be set against a broader set of paternalistic policies he championed that were aggressive and domineering, especially in Latin America.[58] In other words, it was not only a shift of mentality, or a shift of partisan politics, that explains Rockefeller's supposed punitive turn. Rather, his approach to crime in New York was in many respects continuous with his antecedent approach to the world beyond U.S. borders. The imperial encaged him.

Conclusion

The political history of the carceral state is powerful and growing, but as long as it remains inwardly focused, it will remain incomplete. Because this work is new, the scholarship is malleable and should be remolded. The existing literature does at times gesture toward a consideration of the imperial—of the entanglement of the national security state and the carceral state—but has for the most part not followed through on this inclination. To put the history of the U.S. carceral state "in the world" is the most important step for its scholars to take, particularly as they have begun to chart bipartisan initiatives, ideological consensus, and even liberal leadership, rather than only conservative revanchism, in both foreign and domestic policies of coercion in the postwar period. I have suggested some avenues of research and specified how a transnational approach can proceed on theoretical, methodological, and empirical axes. This effort aligns with trends seen in other aspects of the history of the United States and other imperial formations. Growing attention to state- and county-level penal initiatives should not insulate scholarship from a concern with policy constructed through institutional entanglements with the wider world.[59]

Rather than treating the carceral state of the United States only as something historians should compare to prison systems of other nations, historians must be alert to the comparisons and connections historical actors themselves have made and practically implemented. It is imperative to consider the effects of imperial state building on the transformations of governance over the past four decades. The "carceral continuum" today extends from police shootings of fleeing crime suspects in U.S. suburbs to drone strikes on terrorism suspects identified by "signature" behaviors, which, according to the Department of Justice, share a legal justification.[60] As Alfred McCoy has pointed out, the Philippines, Vietnam, and Indonesia each found itself in the grips of what was effectively a "police state" after the termination of colonial rule by the United States, France, and the Netherlands, respectively.[61] Yet neither France nor the Netherlands today incarcerates people on the scale of the United States. The difference is found in the imperial experience of the United States in the postwar period, characterized by the efflorescence of the national security state, which bequeathed ideological, institutional, and individual foundations of a mutated police state at home that we now call the carceral state.

Since 1945, there has never been a match between U.S. capabilities of global military dominance and the actual extent of U.S. economic interests overseas. Instead, there is a profound mismatch, leading to the extension of security practices abroad far in excess of the economic necessity of access to overseas markets for consumer goods, labor, or raw materials.[62] The national security state as such is analogous to the carceral state, whose capacities to encage or kill people far exceed any functional social, economic, political, or moral necessity. But we might also recognize that these two phenomena historically have not been mere analogues of each other but have been both sequential and consubstantial.

Yet today the carceral state is transforming. As soon as historians are at last putting their hands on it and detailing its contours, those very contours are shifting. The imperial, too, is modifying. But these shifts demand only more rigorous accounting and periodization. As the political consensus around imprisonment has begun to shift, with unexpected bipartisanship emerging, some are cautiously optimistic. Yet if political conversations around expenditures on imprisonment and policing remain distinct from those around expenditures on national security, optimism may be unwarranted. Firmly entrenched and bipartisan political constituencies formed through imperial histories are unlikely to give up easily on the carceral state's persistence. The future of the carceral state remains unknowable, even as its past is finally coming into view.

Notes

1. Michael Javen Fortner, *Black Silent Majority: The Rockefeller Drug Laws and the Politics of Punishment* (Cambridge, MA: Harvard University Press, 2015), 248; Julilly Kohler-Hausmann, "'The Attila the Hun Law': New York's Rockefeller Drug Laws and the Making of a Punitive State," *Journal of Social History* 44, no. 1 (2010): 71–95, 79; Julilly Kohler-Hausmann, *Getting Tough: Welfare and Imprisonment in 1970s America* (Princeton, NJ: Princeton University Press, 2017), 80–82; Joseph E. Persico, *The Imperial Rockefeller: A Biography of Nelson A. Rockefeller* (New York: Simon and Schuster, 1982), 144; "Excerpts from the Message by Governor Rockefeller on the State of the State," *New York Times*, January 4, 1973. The accuracy of Fine's summary of Japan's drug laws is questionable, as Kohler-Hausmann hints. Japan began to apply life sentences in 1963 solely for "trafficking (export or import) or manufacturing with the intent to sell" narcotics; H. Richard Friman, "The United States, Japan, and the International Drug Trade: Troubled Partnership" *Asian Survey* 31, no. 9 (1991): 875–90.

2. Nelson A. Rockefeller, *The Rockefeller Report on the Americas: The Official Report of a United States Presidential Mission for the Western Hemisphere* (Chicago: Quadrangle Books, 1969), 59–65; "Excerpts from the Message by Governor Rockefeller."

3. The national security state consists of the institutions created, realized, and fostered by the Truman administration's National Security Act, including, but not limited to, the Department of Defense, the National Security Council, the Central Intelligence Agency and other intelligence agencies, and police and military assistance programs to other countries coordinated by these agencies.

4. Key figures in this subfield, including Marie Gottschalk, Khalil Gibran Muhammad, and Heather Ann Thompson, participated in a major national research effort as members of the Committee on Causes and Consequences of High Rates of Incarceration, which resulted in a landmark study: Jeremy Travis, Bruce Western, Steve Redburn, eds., *The Growth of Incarceration in the United States: Exploring Causes and Consequence* (Washington, DC: National Academies Press, 2014).

5. Emerging research has been previewed recently in special, edited sections of history journals, including "Historians and the Carceral State" in *Journal of American History* (*JAH*) in 2015; "Urban America and the Carceral State" in

Journal of Urban History (*JUH*) in 2015 (that journal has a scheduled forthcoming special section specifically on urban policing); and "African Americans, Police Brutality, and the US Criminal Justice System: Historical Perspectives" and "Gendering the Carceral State: African American Women, History, and the Criminal Justice System" in *Journal of African American History* (*JAAH*) in 2013 and 2015, respectively; Kelly Lytle Hernández, Khalil Gibran Muhammad, and Heather Ann Thompson, "Introduction: Constructing the Carceral State," *JAH* 102, no. 1 (2015): 18–24; Heather Ann Thompson and Donna Murch, "Rethinking Urban America through the Lens of the Carceral State" *JUH* 41, no. 5 (2015): 751–55; Clarence Taylor, "Introduction: African Americans, Police Brutality, and the U.S. Criminal Justice System" *JAAH* 98, no. 2 (2013): 200–204; Kali N. Gross and Cheryl D. Hicks, "Introduction—Gendering the Carceral State: African American Women, History, and the Criminal Justice System" *JAAH* 100, no. 3 (2015): 357–65. In the field of U.S. history, the agenda-setting article was Heather Ann Thompson, "Why Mass Incarceration Matters: Rethinking Crisis, Decline, and Transformation in Postwar American History" *JAH* 97, no. 3 (2010): 703–34.

6. Marie Gottschalk, "Hiding in Plain Sight: American Politics and the Carceral State," *Annual Review of Political Science* 11 (2008): 235–60.

7. Travis, Western, and Redburn, *Growth of Incarceration*, 56–59.

8. This literature is vast. Important summaries are Jacquelyn Dowd Hall, "The Long Civil Rights Movement and the Political Uses of the Past" *JAH* 91, no. 4 (2005): 1233–63; Jeanne Theoharis, "Black Freedom Studies: Re-imagining and Redefining the Fundamentals," *History Compass* 4, no. 2 (2006): 348–67.

9. Dan Berger, *Captive Nation: Black Prison Organizing in the Civil Rights Era* (Chapel Hill: University of North Carolina Press, 2014); Michael Hames-García, *Fugitive Thought: Prison Movements, Race, and the Meaning of Justice* (Minneapolis: University of Minnesota Press, 2004); Dylan Rodríguez, *Forced Passages: Imprisoned Radical Intellectuals and the U.S. Prison Regime* (Minneapolis: University of Minnesota Press, 2006). On an earlier moment, see Christina Heatherton, "University of Radicalism: Ricardo Flores Magón and Leavenworth Penitentiary" *American Quarterly* 66, no. 3 (2014): 557–81. The resistance and rebellion of U.S. soldiers and sailors of color during the Cold War should be considered part of this history as well, particularly as many were incarcerated in military stockades; see, e.g., Wallace Terry II, "Bringing the War Home," *Black Scholar* 2, no. 3 (1970): 6–18.

10. Nikhil Pal Singh, *Black Is a Country: Race and the Unfinished Struggle for Democracy* (Cambridge, MA: Harvard University Press, 2004); Robert O. Self, "The Black Panther Party and the Long Civil Rights Era," in *In Search of the Black Panther Party: New Perspectives on a Revolutionary Movement*, ed. Jama Lazerow and Yohuru Williams (Durham, NC: Duke University Press, 2006), 15–55.

11. Malcolm Feeley and Austin D. Sarat, *The Policy Dilemma: Federal Crime Policy and the Law Enforcement Assistance Administration* (Minneapolis: University of Minnesota Press, 1980); Thomas E. Cronin, Tania Z. Cronin and Michael E.

Milakovich, *U.S. v. Crime in the Streets* (Bloomington: Indiana University Press, 1981).

12. Christian Parenti, *Lockdown America: Police and Prisons in the Age of Crisis* (New York: Verso, 1999); Marie Gottschalk, *The Prison and the Gallows: The Politics of Mass Incarceration in America* (New York: Cambridge University Press, 2006); Ruth Wilson Gilmore, *Golden Gulag: Prisons, Surplus, Crisis, and Opposition in Globalizing California* (Berkeley: University of California Press, 2007); Naomi Murakawa, *The First Civil Right: How Liberals Built Prison America* (New York: Oxford University Press, 2014); Vesla Weaver, "Frontlash: Race and the Development of Punitive Crime Policy" *Studies in American Political Development* 21, no. 2 (2007): 230–65.

13. Weaver, "Frontlash"; Elizabeth Hinton, *From the War on Poverty to the War on Crime: The Making of Mass Incarceration in America* (Cambridge, MA: Harvard University Press, 2016).

14. Murakawa, *First Civil Right*; Jordan T. Camp, *Incarcerating the Crisis: Freedom Struggles and the Rise of the Neoliberal State* (Berkeley: University of California Press, 2016). Among recent historical analyses of law and order, one stands out as supporting the backlash thesis: Michael W. Flamm, *Law and Order: Street Crime, Civil Unrest, and the Crisis of Liberalism in the 1960s* (New York: Columbia University Press, 2005). Earlier exponents tended to be veterans of 1960s politics, who used their past to bolster and give legitimacy to their analyses: e.g., Thomas Byrne Edsall and Mary Edsall, *Chain Reaction: The Impact of Race, Rights, and Taxes on American Politics* (New York: Norton, 1992).

15. Murakawa, *First Civil Right*, 4.

16. Ted Gest, *Crime and Politics: Big Government's Erratic Campaign for Law and Order* (New York: Oxford University Press, 2001), 33.

17. David Dagan and Steven Teles, *Prison Break: Why Conservatives Turned against Mass Incarceration* (New York: Oxford University Press, 2016), 63.

18. Amy Kaplan, "'Left Alone with America': The Absence of Empire in the Study of American Culture," in *Cultures of United States Imperialism*, ed. Amy Kaplan and Donald E. Pease (Durham, NC: Duke University Press, 1993), 3–21.

19. In particular, Fortner, *Black Silent Majority*, as mentioned, as well as Hinton, *From the War on Poverty to the War on Crime*, and Murakawa, *First Civil Right*, gesture toward such considerations.

20. There are exceptions: for example, Jordan T. Camp and Christina Heatherton, eds., *Policing the Planet: Why the Policing Crisis Led to Black Lives Matter* (New York: Verso, 2016); Kelly Lytle Hernández, *City of Inmates: Conquest, Rebellion, and the Rise of Human Caging in Los Angeles, 1771–1965* (Chapel Hill: University of North Carolina Press, 2017); Julilly Kohler-Hausmann, "Militarizing the Police: Officer Jon Burge, Torture, and War in the 'Urban Jungle,'" in *Challenging the Prison-Industrial Complex: Activism, Arts, and Educational Alternatives*, ed. Stephen John Hartnett (Chicago: University of Illinois Press, 2010),

43–71; Parenti, *Lockdown America*; Stuart Schrader, "American Streets, Foreign Territory: How Counterinsurgent Police Waged War on Crime" (PhD diss., New York University, 2015); Micol Seigel, "Objects of Police History" *JAH* 102, no. 1 (2015): 152–61; Tracy Tullis, "A Vietnam at Home: Policing the Ghettos in the Counterinsurgency Era" (PhD diss., New York University, 1999). Growing interest in deportation and migrant detention across the twentieth century intersects with this historiography. Because immigration offenses are federal, they shift the scale of analysis up from the states. The connections between the 1965 Immigration and Nationality Act and other concomitant and subsequent legislation leading to the carceral state compose a vital topic, but the vast increase in migrant detention occurred after the 1980s; Torrie Hester, "Deportability and the Carceral State" *JAH* 102, no. 1 (2015): 141–51; Kelly Lytle Hernández, *Migra! A History of the U.S. Border Patrol* (Berkeley: University of California Press, 2010). A promising approach that puts ongoing U.S. colonial relations front and center is Marisol LeBrón, "Violent Arrest: Punitive Governance and Neocolonial Crisis in Contemporary Puerto Rico" (PhD diss., New York University, 2014). Finally, military detention is another important line of inquiry: Michelle Brown, " 'Setting the Conditions' for Abu Ghraib: The Prison Nation Abroad" *American Quarterly* 57, no. 3 (2005): 973–97; James Forman Jr., "Exporting Harshness: How the War on Crime Helped Make the War on Terror Possible" *NYU Review of Law and Social Change* 33 (2009): 331–74; Avery Gordon, "Abu Ghraib: Imprisonment and the War on Terror" *Race & Class* 48, no. 1 (2006): 42–59; A. Naomi Paik, *Rightlessness: Testimony and Redress in U.S. Prison Camps since World War II* (Chapel Hill: University of North Carolina Press, 2016).

21. Gottschalk, *Prison and the Gallows*, 10.

22. Jonathan Simon, *Governing through Crime: How the War on Crime Transformed American Democracy and Created a Culture of Fear* (New York: Oxford University Press, 2007).

23. Paul Kramer, "Power and Connection: Imperial Histories of the United States in the World" *American Historical Review* 116, no. 5 (2011): 1348–91.

24. Rodríguez, *Forced Passages*, 43. He further remarks that "the specificity of the prison regime as a production of state power is its rigorous and extravagant marshaling of technologies of violence, domination, and subjection otherwise reserved for deployment in sites of declared (extradomestic) war or martial law" (44).

25. Historians of U.S. empire's domestic reverberations have examined prisons and policing as key sites, but the bulk of research has been focused on the early part of the twentieth century rather than the second half. See, for example, part 2 of the landmark collection edited by Alfred W. McCoy and Francisco A. Scarano, *Colonial Crucible: Empire in the Making of the Modern American State* (Madison: University of Wisconsin Press, 2009); Alfred W. McCoy, *Policing America's Empire: The United States, the Philippines, and the Rise of the Surveillance State* (Madison: University of Wisconsin Press, 2009).

26. Ira Katznelson fruitfully advocates analyzing the New Deal in terms of "security." Ira Katznelson, *Fear Itself: The New Deal and the Origins of Our Time* (New York: Liveright Publishing Corporation and W. W. Norton, 2013).

27. Elizabeth Hinton, "'A War within Our Own Boundaries': Lyndon Johnson's Great Society and the Rise of the Carceral State," *JAH* 102, no. 1 (2015): 100–112, 106.

28. Jamie Peck, "Geography and Public Policy: Mapping the Penal State," *Progress in Human Geography* 27, no. 2 (2003): 222–32; "Zombie Neoliberalism and the Ambidextrous State" *Theoretical Criminology* 14, no. 1 (2010): 104–10.

29. Julilly Kohler-Hausmann, "Welfare Crises, Penal Solutions, and the Origins of the 'Welfare Queen,'" *JUH* 41, no. 5 (2015): 756–71, 757.

30. Julilly Kohler-Hausmann, "Guns and Butter: The Welfare State, the Carceral State, and the Politics of Exclusion in the Postwar United States," *JAH* 102, no. 1 (2015): 87–99, 91.

31. Tullis, "Vietnam at Home," 239–84.

32. Leif Fredrickson, "The Riot Environment: Sanitation, Recreation and Pacification in the Wake of Baltimore's 1968 Riot," in *Baltimore Revisited: Rethinking and Remaking an American City*, ed. Nicole King and Kate Drabinski (New Brunswick, NJ: Rutgers University Press, forthcoming).

33. On the history of police torture in Chicago, orchestrated in part by veteran Jon Burge: Kohler-Hausmann, "Militarizing the Police."

34. See Jennifer Mittelstadt, *The Rise of the Military Welfare State* (Cambridge, MA: Harvard University Press, 2015).

35. Elizabeth Hinton, "Creating Crime: The Rise and Impact of National Juvenile Delinquency Programs in Black Urban Neighborhoods," *JUH* 41, no. 5 (2015): 808–24, 812.

36. The global dimensions of the War on Poverty have been explored in Francis J. Gavin and Mark Atwood Lawrence, eds., *Beyond the Cold War: Lyndon Johnson and the New Global Challenges of the 1960s* (New York: Oxford University Press, 2014), particularly the chapter by Sheyda Jahanbani; Alyosha Goldstein, *Poverty in Common: The Politics of Community Action during the American Century* (Durham, NC: Duke University Press, 2012); Jennifer S. Light, *From Warfare to Welfare: Defense Intellectuals and Urban Problems in Cold War America* (Baltimore: Johns Hopkins University Press, 2003); Amy C. Offner, *Sorting Out the Mixed Economy* (Princeton, NJ: Princeton University Press, forthcoming). The connections of these global dimensions to security practices are explored in: Daniel Immerwahr, *Thinking Small: The United States and the Lure of Community Development* (Cambridge, MA: Harvard University Press, 2015); Ananya Roy, Stuart Schrader, and Emma Shaw Crane, "Gray Areas: The War on Poverty at Home and Abroad," in *Territories of Poverty*, ed. Ananya Roy and Emma Shaw Crane (Athens: University of Georgia Press, 2015), 289–314; Roy, Schrader, and Shaw Crane, "'The Anti-Poverty Hoax': Development, Pacification, and the Making of Community in the Global 1960s," *Cities* 44 (2015): 139–45; Stuart Schrader, "To Secure the Global Great Society: Par-

ticipation in Pacification," *Humanity: An International Journal of Human Rights, Humanitarianism, and Development* 7, no. 2 (2016): 225–53.

37. "The Agency for International Development Helps Brazilians Fight War on Crime," *Police*, May–June 1966, 85–86.

38. Jaime Peck and Nik Theodore, "Follow the Policy: A Distended Case Approach," *Environment and Planning A* 44, no. 1 (2012): 21–30.

39. Joy Rohde, *Armed with Expertise: The Militarization of American Social Research during the Cold War* (Ithaca, NY: Cornell University Press, 2013); Duong Van Mai Elliott, *RAND in Southeast Asia: A History of the Vietnam War Era* (Santa Monica, CA: RAND, 2010).

40. George W. O'Connor, "IACP Testimony on H.R. 6508," *Police Chief*, August 1965, 22.

41. DCI Diary, Tuesday, August 15, 1950, CIA Records Search Tool, Document No. 5166d49399326091c6a604c4.

42. Scott H. Bennett, *Radical Pacifism: The War Resisters League and Gandhian Nonviolence in America, 1915–1963* (Syracuse, NY: Syracuse University Press, 2003), 125.

43. Technician Interview No. 50 [Description of Guatemalan Police Forces], September 25, 1962, Accession No. GU00095; Guatemala and the United States Collection, Digital National Security Archive.

44. James V. Bennett, *A Report on the Prisons of Thailand* (Washington, DC: International Cooperation Administration, October 26, 1960).

45. Frederic Wakeman Jr., "American Police Advisers and the Nationalist Chinese Secret Service, 1930–1937," *Modern China* 18, no. 2 (1992): 107–37.

46. John Ernst, *Forging a Fateful Alliance: Michigan State University and the Vietnam War* (East Lansing: Michigan State University Press, 1998).

47. Kohler-Hausmann, " 'Attila the Hun Law,' " 79.

48. Kohler-Hausmann insists that "politicians proactively and creatively used the spectacle of punishing policy . . . to mobilize support and reshape the political terrain." For her, the harsh new "policies were also performative and creative; they were instrumental in producing the 'common sense' and worldviews they purported to reflect" (73). Read this way, Rockefeller used the example of Japan to give legitimacy to a policy that did not need Japan's example per se. But it is important to note that the shaping of the political terrain, so to speak, occurred in Japan under U.S. auspices decades earlier, bequeathing the spectacle of punishment that Rockefeller then instrumentalized.

49. Thomas F. Troy, *Donovan and the CIA: A History of the Establishment of the Central Intelligence Agency* (Frederick, MD: Aletheia Books, 1981).

50. Suzanna Reiss, *We Sell Drugs: The Alchemy of US Empire* (Berkeley: University of California Press, 2014).

51. Christy Thornton, "Sovereignty and Solidarity: The Mexican Revolution and the Origins of the Postwar Order, 1919–1948" (PhD diss., New York University, 2015).

52. Perisco, *Imperial Rockefeller*, 47.

53. Heather Ann Thompson, *Blood in the Water: The Attica Prison Uprising of 1971 and Its Legacy* (New York: Pantheon Books, 2016), 61.

54. Micol Seigel, "Nelson Rockefeller in Latin America: Global Currents of US Prison Growth," *Comparative American Studies* 13, no. 3 (2015): 161–76, 167.

55. Seigel, "Nelson Rockefeller," 168, 170.

56. Fortner, *Black Silent Majority*. On the long history of less intense punishment for white, suburban drug users than black, urban drug users, see, Matthew D. Lassiter, "Impossible Criminals: The Suburban Imperatives of America's War on Drugs," *JAH* 102, no. 1 (2015): 126–40. Fortner treats the adoption of a harsh policy in New York as basically innocent of racism—Rockefeller was a racial liberal acting on demands made by a small coterie of elite black actors—to make a broader claim about how the rise of the carceral state is not attributable to white racism. Yet his insertion of Japan into the story troubles this racial innocence. U.S. promulgation of drug prohibition overseas, particularly in East Asia, was coiled around the global color line. Harry Anslinger, longtime leader of the Federal Bureau of Narcotics, was a vocal bigot. He attracted support for his abstemious positions through continual reference to racial stereotype and through the conflation of racialized foreign nationals with racialized domestic persons to manufacture a singular threat to white safety. Prior to the end of World War II, Japan bore the brunt of his xenophobic accusations of foreign-derived threat of addiction; after the war, China and Mexico became new sources of racialized threat. David Patrick Keys and John F. Galliher, *Confronting the Drug Control Establishment* (Albany: State University of New York Press, 1999), 130–32.

57. Seigel, "Nelson Rockefeller," 166.

58. Rockefeller was but one elite among many whose careers bridged criminal justice and foreign policy. The same was true of contemporaries Bayless A. Manning, Orville Schell Jr., and Harold "Ace" Tyler, who were all in various ways involved in debates around Rockefeller's drug laws.

59. John F. Pfaff, *Locked In: The True Causes of Mass Incarceration and How to Achieve Real Reform* (New York: Basic Books, 2017).

60. Nikhil Pal Singh, "The Whiteness of Police," *American Quarterly* 66, no. 4 (2014): 1091–99.

61. McCoy, *Policing America's Empire*, 538.

62. Perry Anderson, "Imperium," *New Left Review* 83 (2013): 5–111; Tom Reifer and Jamie Sudler, "The Interstate System," in *The Age of Transition: Trajectory of the World-System, 1945–2025*, ed. Terence K. Hopkins and Immanuel Wallerstein (Atlantic Highlands, NJ: Zed Books, 1996), 13–37.

CHAPTER ELEVEN

Fears of a Nanny State

*Centering Gender and Family in the Political
History of Regulation*

Rachel Louise Moran

During the 1970s, the Federal Trade Commission (FTC) became a
flash point for attacks against federal regulations meant to help
consumers and to protect children. In 1979, the agency proposed regulating junk-food advertisements during children's television programming,
an issue that quickly got dubbed "KidVid"—and which immediately ignited a political furor. "The FTC roamed far beyond congressional man-
dates with a shotgun attempt to regulate all kinds of business activities
that should not be the concern of the government," the *National Journal*
editorialized.[1] Another critic described the FTC's interest in limiting this
advertising as "the most radical agency initiative ever conceived."[2] Republican senator Alan Simpson criticized the FTC for "tossing about the
taxpayers' money."[3] Then he served up an epithet that had gained currency in Great Britain but had rarely been used in American politics: "I
think that most Americans feel that they are quite capable of raising their
own children," Simpson explained, "without some kind of all-seeing 'national nanny' such as the FTC interjecting its opinions."

The KidVid episode was only one of many conflicts over regulation in
the 1970s.[4] But it deserves particular attention because of the way it combined political anxieties about regulation with concerns over the relationship between state and family, and over personal and familial versus public
responsibility for health and well-being. The idea of American antistatism
and fears of "big government" are common in political history; historians

have cataloged U.S. resistance to public health measures, taxation, and regulation.[5] But scholars have only begun to appreciate the ways in which growing anxieties about unsupervised children and unhealthy eating were heightened by the specter of state intervention—and, in turn, how those anxieties gave rise to gendered languages like "the nanny state" that have been used to contest the boundaries of the state ever since.[6]

The nicknames that Americans have given the regulatory state can tell us a lot about U.S. politics at the moments they become popular. Not unlike the transnational nature of neoliberal politics, we imported the bully state, the Big Brother state, and the nanny state from England. The state has been father (paternalism), mother (maternalist state), teacher (national schoolmarm), officer (police state) and doctor (therapeutic state).[7] The FTC of the 1960s, which at that time was chided for its refusal to act on many cases, was called "the little old lady of Pennsylvania Avenue."[8] When it seemed to overreach in the late 1970s, the FTC became "the national nanny."

This language of the "nanny state" was popularized at a moment when Americans were politically obsessed with the family and evinced a growing anxiety over extrafamilial influences.[9] For many, the family and state were understood as oppositional forces, as private versus public. At the same time, this private realm functioned as the basis of all sorts of political claims making (e.g., children must be protected, families must be preserved). By the late 1970s, as the language of "family values" gained political traction, both major political parties emphasized the importance of the family unit to their approach. In the 1976 Republican Party platform, the GOP emphasized that "families—not government programs—are the best way to make sure our children are properly nurtured."[10] At the same time, the Democrats moved language about the well-being of "working families" into their platform.[11] Jimmy Carter decried "the steady erosion and weakening of our families" just as those on the far right did.[12] Robert Self describes this moment as one when the concept of the "family" had "suddenly and powerfully joined communism and civil rights as the battlegrounds on which conservatives would wage war against liberalism."[13] The reality was that the idea of "family" was a battleground for liberals and conservatives who worried about an erosion of parental influence over children, whether by government or by corporation.[14] Neoliberal understandings of the family seek to artificially separate it from the market, both devaluing maternal labor and decreasing or eliminating social welfare benefits for low-income families, especially families of color.[15] While social conservatives feared the moral changes in the family model, neo-liberals worried about the fiscal costs of such changes.[16] While social conservatives were most closely linked with the language of "family values," groups of all political stripes experimented with the political purchase of "family" in these decades.

When KidVid erupted, then, it was not simply a debate over the limits of regulation or the rights of consumers versus corporations; instead, it developed around questions of gender and the family. Senator Alan Simpson critiqued the FTC's "belief that it alone is capable of protecting children from their parents' supposed inability to resist their own children's unwise demands for various brands of cereals, soft drinks, candy, which would surely be purchased for them by their weak-willed and uninformed parents."[17] The FTC, he said, aspired to "be big mother" when it came to monitoring advertising. Uncertainty over the proper boundaries of the state manifested as feminized name-calling, be it with the state as a "nanny" or a "big mother." The regulatory state was imagined as female, both for those who supported its expansion as an extension of maternal power and for those who rejected it as a nanny encroaching on the private realm of the family.

Origins of the Debate

KidVid grew out of larger American concerns about domestic nutrition and the role of the state in addressing the problem. While anxieties over hunger dominated the late 1960s, by the late 1970s the attention was squarely on something called "overnutrition."[18] George McGovern became head of the Senate's Select Committee on Nutrition and Human Needs. From that position, he held a series of congressional hearings on potential food-related problems—sugar, obesity, heart disease. These efforts culminated in the 1977 report *Dietary Goals for the United States*, which recommended food labeling, rules for food advertising, and financial support for national nutrition education.[19] While McGovern's committee was disbanded shortly after issuing its report, worries about malnutrition remained prominent in political discussions of the period. During the late 1970s, for instance, the Food and Drug Administration challenged the sugar substitute saccharin.[20] In 1978, the House Subcommittee on Health and the Environment held preliminary hearings on nutrition labeling, centered on disclosing the sugar content of foods. When the committee met resistance, Representative Henry Waxman, a Democrat from California, said the labeling plan should please everyone at a moment when "we hear so much [complaining] that the Government tries to come in and make decisions for us described as a nanny role, or big brother role."[21] The government, he explained, was simply providing the information consumers needed to make their own decisions. In so doing, it was also reorienting corporations' historical place in the liberal imagination: from the helpful delivery of cheap calories to a threat to public health. Still, the labeling rules, like McGovern's dietary guidelines before them, angered well-organized industry groups like the National Dairy Council and the International Sugar Research Foundation. And the more such interventions were called nannying, the more Americans worried that they and their families were indeed being overregulated. This attempt at mandating nutrition labeling went nowhere during the 1970s.

While labeling floundered, other critics of the American diet turned their attention toward food advertising. It was a moment of "sucrophobia," according to historian Harvey Levenstein, with popular books attacking the "white plague" of sugar addiction.[22] Consumer politics were gaining strength in and out of government; federal employment related to consumer protections doubled over the course of the 1970s.[23] As early as 1975, the private Center for Science in the Public Interest (CSPI) attempted to control how sugary foods were sold to children. The CSPI had a loud voice in the fight, amid a larger context of advocacy group proliferation.[24] It unsuccessfully petitioned the Food and Drug Administration to make breakfast cereals list the amount of sugar in their products.[25] Then it focused its energies on the FTC. In 1977, CSPI dramatically sent 170 decayed teeth (and petitions signed by ten thousand health professionals) in a bag to the Federal Trade Commission, along with a request the FTC regulate the advertising of foods to children.[26] Specifically, CSPI wanted health warnings on food ads shown during children's programming for foods that contained more than 10 percent added sugar. Around the same time, a Boston-based parents group, Action for Children's Television, also asked the FTC to regulate candy advertisements.[27]

That antisugar activists turned to the FTC at this moment was no accident. The new FTC chairman, Michael Pertschuk, was a Carter appointee who had been vocal about his own activist approach.[28] Pertschuk was especially concerned about sugar and had gone as far as saying television advertising was making a "nation of sugar junkies."[29] While in charge of the FTC, Pertschuk pushed a regulatory agenda in a variety of arenas, and he attacked everything from deceptive acne medication ads to the taglines on Listerine and the prices of eyeglasses. "Pertschuk may be anathema to more American businessmen, large and small, than any other agency chief in Washington," one popular magazine wrote of him.[30] He made a natural ally for children's health and antisugar activists. More than that, he was explicitly on their side: he purportedly told his staff at the FTC that if they did not pursue KidVid, he might donate his salary to the American Dental Association.[31] Under Pertschuk, the FTC moved forward with its aims of making Americans healthier and better informed. Where some saw progress, though, others saw a growing nanny state.

Pertschuk and the FTC adopted a plan to regulate television advertising. In 1978, they initiated an investigation into the effects of advertising to children during children's television programming.[32] They called this investigation the Children's Advertising Rule, although it quickly gained the nickname "KidVid." Although there was initially bipartisan concern over child nutrition and advertising, the debate over what specifically should be done about these concerns was much more divisive.[33] Potential outcomes of these proceedings included banning all advertising to young children, banning advertising sugar to children, and requiring a balance in which all sugary foods that were advertised were paired with advertiser-funded health and nutrition public service announcements.[34] What followed was a multiyear debate over the limits of government bureaucracy and the role of parental control in such matters.

This battle over regulation must be understood as a contest over changing ideas of masculinity and femininity, of family, and of a changing economy. While the language of this regulatory debate is the earliest sustained debate over the nanny state in U.S. politics, with its explicit imagination of feminized roles and responsibilities, regulation had been coded as nonmasculine for much of the postwar era. In the 1960s, consumer protests—which did have origins in maternalist activism—were slurred as "girlcotts" and "big motherism,"[35] while the masculinity and heterosexuality of male regulatory leaders like Ralph Nader was questioned.[36] When General Motors paid investigators to get dirt on Nader, the investigators asked Nader's friends why he was not married and whether he had any "effeminate tendencies."[37] Meanwhile, AFL-CIO leaders complained that the Democratic Party "had been taken over by people . . . who look like Jills."[38] More generally, Americans imagined an interventionist "national nanny" as "making Americans weak, fat, and dependent on her bounty."[39] This was not only a description of overregulation; it was increasingly used to describe other moments of "big" government from social welfare programs to guidelines from the surgeon general. The nanny-state metaphor, then, both highlights and reifies the centrality of gendered ideas to debates about the state. At the core of the complaint is concern over the impingement of the masculine autonomy of the citizen. Liberalism was already coded as weak, dependent, and feminized, an idea that became only further entrenched by conservative opposition during the Carter years.[40] A *Wall Street Journal* piece from 1984, for instance, went so far as to describe Carter as "a 'woman' president."[41]

The language of the "family" began to dominate political rhetoric, but it was not simply divided along partisan lines. Patricia Strach, a political scientist who has examined family values language in modern America, argues that the growing obsession with the "family" in 1970s and 1980s politics changed the way many political issues were framed, especially issues about parental choice.[42] Both self-identified liberals and conservatives used this framing language in the 1970s. The KidVid debate quickly devolved into just such a battle over political framing, as those on both sides positioned themselves as the true crusaders for the American family.

Unfairness and Deception

Contemporary researchers demonstrated that television was a much greater part of the lives of 1970s children than of those in previous generations. As historian Warren J. Belasco phrased it, "parents needed children's television, counternutritional or not."[43] The parents who most needed it were those juggling dual-career households who were, as Belasco explained, needing television to do the "baby-sitting." The television "gets more of his time and attention than [a child's] parents or school teachers do," a critic wrote in 1970.[44] American children saw an average of twenty thousand advertisements a year in 1977. Seven thousand of those advertisements were for sugary foods.[45] Groups like the Center for Science in the Public Interest and Action for Children's Television argued that children, as a special class who lacked maturity and understanding, should not be advertised to the same way that adults could. This line of argument concluded that the FTC must issue special regulations to manage how sugary foods could be sold during children's television programming.

The idea the FTC should expand its regulatory powers into this realm turned out not only to be politically controversial but also logistically complicated. It was difficult to determine when programming was solely children's programming and when it had a more general audience, because there were no channels dedicated to children's entertainment. Even though Saturday-morning cartoons were the most decidedly aimed at children of all these programs, they reached children of many ages. The arguments the FTC and its allies used to describe why a five-year-old deserved special advertising regulations did not necessarily apply to a ten- or twelve-year-old.[46] Additionally, the FTC could not use its traditional regulatory approach of attacking deception. The FTC was not arguing that selling sugary snacks to children was deceptive or that advertisements for cereals were lying. Instead of calling the ads "deceptive," the FTC attempted to regulate them on the basis of the principle that advertising to children was "unfair" because children cannot appropriately assess an ad's truthfulness.[47] FTC chairman Pertschuk argued that advertisers "seize on the child's trust and exploit it as a weakness for their gain."[48] This was perhaps unfair behavior, but it did not meet the criteria for deception. The difference between calling cereal ads "deceptive" and "unfair" might sound small, but it had major implications for the FTC. While the KidVid case would be brought down by family and gender politics, it started off weak on a number of fronts.

Attacking unfairness was legally a power of the FTC's, but it was one it had rarely employed. Instead, the agency typically relied on regulating businesses and industries that actively deceived the public. While regulating deceptive advertising generally did not win the FTC friends in industry, the shift toward critiquing the whole notion of advertising to children as unfair appeared a far greater blow. The result was that the unfairness principle was almost instantly portrayed as FTC overreach, as a bureaucracy pulling extra powers out of its hat. As a representative from the National Retail Merchants Council explained to a congressional committee, "Instead of limiting its reach to practices that . . . resulted in demonstrable harm, the FTC was apparently trying to use its 'unfairness' authority as a tool for social reform."[49] In other words, the case exemplified the activist FTC that critics and corporations feared. As the KidVid case evolved, major media portrayed it as a fight over government-as-nanny. The "unfairness" principle, which was beyond the normal toolbox of the FTC— and even sounded whiny—did not help the agency's case that it was working within its legal authority to protect children's health.

Once the actual rulemaking proceedings for KidVid began, they were a drawn-out debacle. The hearings produced more than sixty thousand pages of commentary. Industry called over two hundred witnesses who insisted there was nothing "unfair" about advertising to children.[50] Then they filed private lawsuits. A federal judge ruled that FTC Chairman Michael Pertschuk could not participate in the hearings "because he was biased in favor of some sort of ban."[51] Experts ranging from advertisers to child psychologists to pediatricians testified about the effects of advertising, often providing deeply conflicting information. After a year of this, the FTC staff recommended the end of the KidVid project.

By the end, advertising was no more regulated and the FTC was severely damaged. The Senate voted to formally stop the hearings, and then a bitter Congress allowed the FTC's funding to lapse. Congress passed—and President Carter grudgingly signed—the Federal Trade Commission Improvements Act of 1980, which completely eliminated the language of "unfairness" as a basis for regulation. This legislation also allowed for a congressional veto on any perceived FTC overreach.[52] While Carter mostly supported the FTC, and would famously attack American consumption patterns in his "malaise" speech, Congress would not reauthorize FTC funding without these restrictions.[53] To save the regulatory agency, then, the Democratic president had to deeply curb that agency's power. The new FTC could attack only advertising that was "inherently misleading or deceptive."[54] This was a major blow to the agency. The wave of anti-regulation sentiment that followed accelerated the FTC's declining power and influence.

Once President Reagan took office in 1981, he replaced Chairman Pertschuk with James C. Miller, an economist who had spent the KidVid years codirecting the right-wing American Enterprise Institute's Center for the Study of Government Regulation. A legal assistant for one of the original plaintiffs, Boston's Action for Children's Television (ACT), told a reporter that "the Reagan administration's middle name is deregulation."[55] One industry representative, a lawyer for several large retail chains, happily testified in 1982: "We have not heard all morning any reference to the 'national nanny.' I think that there has been a change in attitude at the Commission."[56] He then reiterated that none of the removed regulatory powers should be restored to the FTC. While Congress had begun its attacks on the FTC several years earlier, the new administration reinforced the idea that the agency—and perhaps any overly regulatory agency—was trying to play the role of a "national nanny."

Stoning the National Nanny

In a 1982 book about his time as FTC chairman, Michael Pertschuk angrily recounts the KidVid story in a chapter titled "Stoning the National Nanny." In it, he begins by recalling that it was not some far-right agency that first publicly called the FTC a nanny. It was, instead, the relatively liberal *Washington Post*.[57] Pertschuk was surprised by the *Post's* 1979 editorial on the matter. "The editorial helped undermine the commission's political standing," he wrote. "It ceded to the opponents of such rule making the single most powerful political symbol upon which we had depended for our political shield against congressional interference—the defense of the family."[58] Ideas about regulation and the regulatory state were just as critical—and ultimately inseparable—from concurrent debates over middle-class women's work, the organization of the family, and changing ideas about child rearing. The fight over the FTC's ability to regulate advertising to children was really a fight over the gendering of regulation itself.

The origins of this language predate its popularity in U.S. politics by about ten years. The first use of the phrase "nanny state" to mean an overbearing or overregulating state is usually attributed to a 1965 article in the conservative British magazine the *Spectator*, although there are several references to nanny-like politicians and even the "nursemaid state" in earlier British publications.[59] In that 1965 instance, like in the KidVid case, the loathed nanny state was also attempting to intervene in advertising. In the 1965 incident, the culprit was a proposed ban on cigarette advertising.[60] While "nanny state" dates back at least to then, the complaint was not especially common in political language until the late 1970s and early 1980s.[61] By the 1970s, almost any regulation could be nannying. Tories "took another step towards the nursery in which nanny takes care" with a mandatory seatbelt law, one editorial explained.[62] Elsewhere in the conservative media, issues from regulating public smoking to encouraging the hiring of racial minorities to the expansion of social welfare programs all seemed evidence not only of a state overreaching but also of a state that infantilized—a nanny.

When Margaret Thatcher won the 1979 general election and became prime minister, anxieties about a British nanny state moved from an opposition cudgel to a leadership concern. In the 1980s, Thatcher's use of that and similar phrases brought the concept to the center of British politics and garnered international attention.[63] She took office amid growing internal condemnation of British state social welfare. This meant that the denigration of the "nanny state" was not only an attack on regulatory programs but also bound up with concerns about the growth of the welfare state, anxieties over feminism and antiracist activism, and general antistatist rhetoric. While in office, Thatcher excoriated the idea of a state interfering in the lives of citizens, both in social welfare and in regulatory capacities. The government "must nurture, not nanny; stimulate, not stifle," she said in a 1982 speech.[64] Elsewhere, opting for related metaphors, she argued that "we should not expect the state to appear in the guise of an extravagant good fairy at every christening, a loquacious and tedious companion at every stage of life's journey, the unknown mourner at every funeral."[65] Bidding adieu to the combined "nanny" of social welfare benefits and federal regulation, Thatcher promised the 1980s would be economically "invigorating" at the same time that the years would make Britain a "chillier, bumpier, less cozy place" for anyone reliant on big government.[66] Thatcher promised a Britain of manly self-reliance, one that celebrated the "vigorous virtues" of independence from state control.[67]

Thatcher's dismissal of fairies and nannies resonated across the Atlantic, as Americans grew increasingly opposed to visible regulation. As one *New York Times* reporter defined it in 1979, they were tired of "the assumption that the consumer is incompetent to take care of his own affairs."[68] When Ronald Reagan took office in 1981, this criticism of the nanny state emerged as a regular feature of political discourse. "Runaway government threatens our economic survival, our most cherished institutions, and the very preservation of freedom itself," he argued.[69] It was time, Reagan continued, for Americans to end "the great myth that our national nanny always knows best." Deregulation and smaller government, sometimes described as a reining in of the nanny state, were major goals for his administration.[70]

As Americans came to distrust the "national nanny" in the late 1970s and 1980s, it was not only a rejection of regulation but also an amplification of the critique of a "feminized" politics—of the changing public. The "national nanny" connotes a particular relationship between citizen and state, one both familiar and extrafamilial. In the modern American context, where fears of nonfamilial childcare are extreme, the national nanny is inherently a dangerous and unwanted figure. This was especially true in the early 1980s, when moral panics over nannies and day cares constantly made headlines.[71] These panics illustrated anxieties over the boundaries of the American family, heightened by the growth of the middle-class dual-income family. The nanny state was therefore typically not imagined as a helpful and efficient Mary Poppins but as a figure who appeared to threaten the private family or the autonomy of that family's male bread-winner. The possibility of an equal rights amendment undermined Christian gender roles, some complained.[72] The spread of seatbelt laws, proof "nanny will stand you in the corner," was "an abomination" encroaching on the private space of the car.[73] Many policies were read as attacks on the family, but regulations that explicitly took aim at children and children's health produced even greater anxiety.

KidVid

The debate over KidVid was only sporadically fought over the ethics of advertising to children, the practicality of regulation, or the way children processed advertising. Instead, the crux of the argument was parent-child and government-child relationships. FTC advertising regulations seemed to some the agency's attempt "to usurp at least part of the parental role."[74] Even those sympathetic to the FTC's aims adopted this dichotomy between the governmental role and the parental role. For instance, Dr. Philip L. Calcagno, of the American Academy of Pediatrics, testified that the unregulated advertising of sugary foods to children was a problem. Even still, he stressed that parents have the ultimate responsibility of monitoring television's influence on children.[75] This aligned with what advertisers were saying. "Little children are not purchasers," the president of the American Advertising Federation reiterated.[76] Children cannot be harmed, or even treated unfairly, by advertising this line of argument went, because it is a parent or guardian who must ultimately make the purchase. Attempts to say otherwise, to critics of the nanny state, seemed to diminish the role of the parent and overemphasize the role of government.

While this claim was critiqued a bit—after all, why spend $15 billion a year advertising to children if you believe they make no purchasing decisions—the idea that parents were the real roadblock to children's health proved a popular line of argumentation.[77] At this moment of nanny-state anxiety and fears about the weakness of the family, the idea that parents were pushovers emerged as a major talking point. One advertiser at the FTC hearings put it bluntly. There was nothing wrong with advertising sugary foods to children, as a strong parent would intervene before it got to the point of consumer harm. "All a parent has to say," he explained, "is, 'shut up or I'll belt you.'"[78] Only parents unwilling to discipline their children would have problems with children's advertising-based demands. Mocking all sides of the argument, one reporter described the critics' insistence that parents lay down the law. "Say no, dammit. Tell your kid that hell will freeze over and Jimmy Carter will become a dialect comedian before a box of snappy, sugary, crunchies comes into your house. Be a man for crying out loud."[79] Even as working mothers were commonly the ones blamed for permissive parenting and lax discipline, this formulation gets at the key concern of many who opposed federal regulations: regulations were emasculating.

Reporters covering the hearings often took the side of FTC critics and wrote about the FTC's arguments for KidVid rule making with skepticism. As reporters recounted testimony for the FTC, they often grouped them with psychobabble. "Some witnesses have said that children get inferiority complexes when their parents refuse to buy the products advertised on television," one reporter recounted.[80] A professor who testified about the dangers of advertising to children said that children would grow skeptical and distrusting of parents who refused to buy what children believed, via advertising, to be products they needed.[81] The *Washington Post* summed up its frustrations by explaining that the FTC plan "is designed to protect children from the weakness of their parents—and the parents from the wailing insistence of their children. That, traditionally, is one of the roles of a governess—if you can afford one. It is not a proper role of government."[82] Reflecting on KidVid several decades later, critics described the situation as one in which the FTC "learned that protecting parents from their children's requests . . . is not a sufficient basis for government action."[83] The lines around the so-called nanny state were thus drawn.

The argument that liberal parenting was to blame emerged simultaneously with broader social pushback against such parenting. For decades, Dr. Benjamin Spock's liberal and sometimes permissive parenting had been mainstream. While Spock was never as permissive as some claimed, he importantly came to stand in for a broader parenting trend that focused on nurture over punishment, rejected spanking, and encouraged parents to hold and comfort children as desired.[84] The result, according to some conservative critics of the 1970s, was a generation of demanding and entitled children. Children whose entitlement, perhaps, led them to become leftists, antiwar protesters, and hippies. These were the children whom Vice

President Spiro Agnew described as "spoiled brats who have never had a good spanking."[85] Major magazines of the late 1960s and early 1970s asked if Dr. Spock was, in fact, to blame for this American crisis in authority. This anxiety about permissive parenting was at the heart of the concern over KidVid as well. For the FTC, the idea that you would protect children from the aggressive advertising of sugary foods was part of a narrative of otherwise sheltering and supporting children. For FTC critics, however, it seemed more evidence that parents were unwilling to raise their own children and break with their "permissive" attitudes to deny children their desires. Additionally, this frustration was tied to the belief that too many parents were permissive because of a larger breakdown in gender roles.

At the time of the KidVid hearings, this debate over child rearing was at a fever pitch. In 1977, James Dobson founded Focus on the Family and republished his "tough love" answer to Spock's childrearing advice: *Dare to Discipline*. As Spock came to represent the permissiveness movement, Dobson's insistence that children needed spanking and a strict Christian upbringing became the 1970s and 1980s answer to such permissiveness.[86] This insistence on stricter parenting in part relied on the idea of a tougher father figure, but it also included an insistence on the importance of a stay-at-home mother. Dobson insisted that "children needed their mothers" while a growing antifeminist right, mobilized by the fight against the equal rights amendment, worried about "an exodus of mothers and babies from the home."[87] At the heart of it, the concern over KidVid regulation was a panic in which concerns over the "nannying" of the state wed concerns over the imagined decline of mothering. Would the state become the cold replacement for the fictional traditions of the warm and maternal? If so, it seemed to many that such a state could be only an impersonal and authoritarian "nanny," that it would always be a mere simulacrum of mothering.

This conservative version of family values clashed with a more leftist—but still family-centric—model of the 1970s. The Carter FTC envisioned itself protecting children from predatory corporations and in turn protecting families from conflict and poor health outcomes. This was also the model a number of supporters of the FTC rules adopted. For instance, at the beginning of the KidVid affair, some wives of Democratic congressmen lobbied on behalf of the FTC. These eight women pushed back against the idea that advertising regulation emphasized the weakness of parents, instead arguing that the agency's rulemaking process might "help us raise wiser, healthier children."[88] Regulations could help them be better mothers, they insisted, flipping the more conservative approach to the issue on its head.

While the Congressional Wives Taskforce argued on behalf of themselves as mothers, other FTC supporters, with a similar aim as the taskforce,
made different arguments. A small but notable number of FTC supporters
accepted the same premise as FTC critics—that American parenting was
weak. One reporter explained that "there is considerable doubt . . . whether
parents themselves very carefully regulate their children's viewing habits."[89]
The claims the FTC was overstepping its role were based in rhetoric about
parents as the force that could shield children from potential threats of
industry. In a scenario in which these parents were not simply pushovers
but were not present, the FTC's justification might shift. "Television sets
in effect become parents-in-absentia to millions of American tots," the reporter explained, reflecting much broader concerns about family life.[90]
As a critic of KidVid later explained it, the issue was whether these unsupervised children will "believe what the reformers think they *ought* to believe, or will they be manipulated and exploited into believing the 'wrong'
things?" Additionally, she continued, "many parents are not to be trusted
to make the 'right decisions' for their children."[91] Even the lobbying of the
congressional wives could be framed this way, as a call for help managing
motherhood in a confusing commercial era. While some believed the FTC
should regulate on the basis of the idea that modern families needed this
assistance, others worried that the FTC was overstepping the boundaries
between the public and private.

In the end, the idea the FTC had not simply behaved as "big government" but also as a "national nanny" became the most powerful takeaway
of the whole affair. "The job of teaching a child what is right and what is
wrong is really the job of the parent, and the government should stop
trying to be a 'national nanny,'" one commentator wrote.[92] "The federal
government has better things to do than play national nanny," another
editorial insisted.[93] The KidVid case not only marked a declining American
acceptance of a regulatory state; it also marked growing anxieties over the
boundaries between family and state and between the private space of family and public space of the economy. The two concerns were intertwined.

The Nanny State after KidVid

KidVid marked the growth of the gendered rhetoric of nanny state, and
the phrase was adopted frequently in the decades that followed. At the
same time the Reagan administration fought nanny statism of many sorts,

liberals employed the charge against Reaganites. When the Department of Agriculture proposed rules that allowed ground bone to go unlabeled in meat, they were castigated for trying to replace a governmental nanny with a "national mommy," lying to her children about whether there were vegetables in their dinner.[94] In another case, Cold War regulations that denied visas for radicals seemed to the *New York Times* an example of "the national nanny knows best."[95] Americans should find this policy "insult[s] their intelligence," the paper argued, and that there was no need to decide whom Americans can hear speak.[96]

The charge of nanny statism was more commonly used against Democrats, though, and this was doubly true when the familiar themes of children and health arose. "Nanny statism" functioned as a regular criticism of First Lady Hillary Clinton's health-care plan in the early to mid-1990s, for instance. In 1993, lamenting their 1992 presidential loss, a few Republicans discussed concerns about the party's direction publically. North Carolina senator Jesse Helms argued that the Republican Party had not adequately tapped into "the frustration and anger of the American middle class at the nanny state's endless intrusions."[97] Helms said that public schools, run by the government and teachers' unions, were the main site of such intrusions and the space where Republicans needed to be focused. Ultimately, the party agreed. At a political moment when the school voucher had gained in popularity, the concept of school choice symbolized the major tenets of anti-nanny-statist politics: an emphasis on greater distance between the supposedly autonomous family unit and the state.

This interest in both individual (or parental) choice and a small state came to a head as Republicans grappled with how to address the Clinton agenda. In particular, Republicans were nervous that both the leadership of First Lady Hillary Clinton and the administration's interest in health care would decrease choice and increase government. As a result, Republicans in the 1990s embraced the "nanny state" phrase more aggressively than even Reagan-era Republicans had done. When Newt Gingrich argued against the Clinton presidency just a few months after the inauguration, he described Clinton's plan as "more than the 'nanny state.'" Instead, Gingrich argued, Bill Clinton wanted the state to "be the mother, father, banker, investor and credit allocator." As evidence of the blurred familial and gender boundaries of the Clinton reign, Gingrich then switched gears, arguing that Bill Clinton lacked an agenda for reform while Hillary Clinton brought her own agenda to the office.[98]

Amid the politics of the 1990s, though, it was not just Republicans wary of the nanny state. Over the course of Clinton's first term, he and Vice President Al Gore actually went to great lengths to attack the nanny state. Gore critiqued vague, historical liberal excesses, especially the "galloping bureaucracy" and "stifling regulation" of government. He accused mid-century politicians, left and right, of building an "activist government" that was to be a "national 'nanny.'" Contemporary leftists needed to dismantle this system, he explained.[99] President Clinton even attributed the phrase to Gore during a speech in which he praised the general idea of regulation, but he also critiqued the implementation of regulations by an aggressive bureaucracy. It is time, he said, to "move beyond the sort of national nanny that can always tell businesses, consumers, and workers not only what to do but exactly how to do it, when, and with a 100-page guideline."[100] The administration took pains to insist not only that they were not nanny staters but also that they actually hated the nanny state. At one point, Gore argued that what people needed was a "grandparent state," not a nanny state. He explained that grandparents are nurturing but not authoritative.[101] Clinton tried to redirect the nanny language toward governments he saw as more authoritative, notably the Chinese state.[102] Bill Clinton also tried to use the language of the family, not unlike the proponents of KidVid had attempted, to justify the need for health care. It was not a usurpation of the parental role in this rendering but a support to help parents and strengthen the family, especially financially. The administration made similar, family-centric arguments through home ownership and welfare-reform policies.[103] Still, while both Clinton and Gingrich opposed "nanny statism" in the early 1990s, it proved easier to argue that the autonomous family could be saved from government than saved by it.

It was Hillary Clinton's health-care fight that exposed the troubled relationship between the intimate and political at the heart of nanny-state anxieties. The "Hillarycare" campaign effectively embodied the tensions over state boundaries. As a woman and the first lady, her direct and visible involvement in policy making and agenda setting was itself a blurring of public and private realms. The fact that this blurring took place in the realm of health care, a topic that straddles the public and private, further fueled nanny-state complaints. A. Wayne Allard, a Republican representative from Colorado, objected to Hillary Clinton and other Democrats' approaches to health coverage, which suggested that they "do not think that individuals are capable of making their own health care decisions."[104] Such arrogance, he continued, "is the ultimate in what former British

Prime Minister Margaret Thatcher has called the nanny state." A University of Chicago law professor, writing in the *New York Times*, described Hillary Clinton's support for federally subsidized children's health care as "all that is wrong in public policy debates today." President Clinton had promised the end of big government, the professor explained, and yet his wife's programs allowed the nanny state "to spread its tentacles further."[105] To Hillary Clinton's most aggressive critics, her approach "would lead to a kind of nanny-state despotism."[106] The failed health-care initiative transformed Hillary Clinton into a symbol of the nanny state.

Two decades later, anxieties about the regulation of health were as strong as ever. The nanny-state trope was wielded aggressively against New York City mayor Michael Bloomberg over another public health issue: soda. Bloomberg's 2013–2014 ban on the sale of sweetened sodas larger than sixteen ounces earned him a great deal of attention, much of it negative. The idea of addressing perceived obesity problems through an outright ban, rather than through some of the gentler antisugar tactics like labeling and education, was what made critics so uncomfortable with Bloomberg's approach. Within the limits of "Nanny York," as one opponent dubbed the city under Bloomberg, city residents would have to buy smaller sodas, or else switch to diet drinks, fruit juice, or milk-based drinks.[107] This soda regulation was decried as government overreach, and, with the help of major soda conglomerates and their allies, crushed within a year of taking effect.[108] Still, the temporary existence of the legislation raised the ire of those who declared the mayor "Nanny Bloomberg." Political cartoons depicted a feminized Bloomberg as a Mary Poppins figure, telling infantilized New Yorkers what they could drink. "When the government takes over the health care sector, the personal truly is the political," one critic wrote in a conservative Washington newsmagazine.[109] The adaptation of this 1970s feminist slogan to fit conservative anxieties about nutrition and the state was a response to Bloomberg in 2012, but it could have as easily been a response to Hillarycare or KidVid.

As these post-KidVid examples illustrate, the accusatory term *nanny state* has become most popular as it refers to regulation, and occasionally selective taxation, meant to change health-related behaviors.[110] Sometimes nanny-state complaints are simply complaints about corporate paperwork or environmental protection, but more often than not they are specifically complaints about where the line is drawn between the intimate and the public. As a consequence, the regulation of choices around health has become an especially popular site for those worried about "nannying." It

FIGURE 11.1. Center for Consumer Freedom advertisement, 2012 (courtesy of the Center for Consumer Freedom)

is no coincidence that as the reality of a breadwinning man evaporated, the image maintained a stranglehold on the American political imaginary since a nanny state appeared to undermine masculine independence, self-sufficiency, and individual freedom.[111] These fears were at the heart of the KidVid fight, and they have shaped American regulatory politics since then.

Conclusion

While KidVid is not a household name, the scars it left on the FTC have been long lasting, and the nanny-state metaphor has become a staple of American politics, policing the boundaries between the state and the family. Even as concerns that junk-food advertising was promoting childhood obesity grew in the following years, the FTC expressed no interest in getting involved. David Clanton, who headed the FTC in the early 1980s, remarked decades later that "the FTC is too smart to head down this path again . . . we don't need a neo-1970s regulatory approach to this difficult subject." Howard Beales, who directed the FTC's Bureau of Consumer Protection in the early 2000s explained that "those of us who lived through KidVid remember the past and have no desire to repeat it. We will tread very carefully."[112] In retrospect, critics of KidVid focused on the idea that the regulatory arm of the state had reached into the purportedly autonomous family unit. "Seeing itself as the grand protector of children," two critics of the proceedings wrote, "the FTC sought to decide what is fair and then imposed its concept of fairness upon all American families."[113]

The KidVid controversy and the subsequent punishment of the FTC coincided with larger attention not simply to regulation but also to the specific idea of the "nanny state." By the early 1990s, the term was used with increasing regularity. It sometimes referenced parental rights, as in requests that parents, not the state, be given authority in issues ranging from vaccines to school lunches. In other instances, the nanny-state narrative was explicitly about the relationship between the male breadwinner and the state. In the 2000s, for instance, Rush Limbaugh argued that the nanny state leaves Americans "childlike" and does not prepare them for "adulthood and manhood."[114] Similarly, Ron Paul described the nanny state as "an imitation family nanny," who cannot be dismissed, and hangs around her charge as "a threat to his ability to make his own choices."[115] One writer described how the problem of the "compliant," publicly loathed nanny state might be solved with the introduction of a "Daddy State" that could use "tough love" to solve social problems.[116] Stifling independence and personal choice on the one hand while also not "tough" enough to solve problems on the other, the nanny state has rarely been a popular figure. The nanny state is "a total buzzkill" that is "not letting them do anything fun."[117] The imagined-female nanny state might be an "annoyance" one day and a "threat to freedom" the next. The broad phrase is applied to a range of political moments, but its gendered connotations are key to its import. Americans embraced the smear of "national nanny" in the late 1970s as both a rejection of "big government" regulations and an objection to changes in American families and gender roles.

Notes

1. Barry R. Weingast and Mark J. Moran, "The Myth of Runaway Bureaucracy: The Case of the FTC," *Regulation* 6, no. 3 (May–June 1982): 34.

2. Tracy Westen, "Government Regulation of Food Marketing to Children: The Federal Trade Commission and the Kid-Vid Controversy," *Loyola of Los Angeles Law Review* 39, no. 79 (May 2006): 79.

3. *Oversight of the Federal Trade Commission: Hearings before the Subcommittee for Consumers, of the Committee on Commerce, Science, and Transportation,* Senate, 96th Cong., 1st sess., September 19, 1979, 156.

4. Meg Jacobs, *Panic at the Pump: The Energy Crisis and the Transformation of American Politics in the 1970s* (New York: Hill and Wang, 2016); Allan Brandt, *The Cigarette Century: The Rise, Fall, and Deadly Persistence of the Product that Defined America* (New York: Basic Books, 2007); James K. Conant and Peter J. Balint, *The Life Cycles of the Council on Environmental Quality and the Environmental Protection Agency* (New York: Oxford University Press, 2016); Jameson Wetmore, "Delegating to the Automobile," *Technology and Culture* 56, no. 2 (April 2015): 440–63.

5. Daniel Carpenter, *Reputation and Power: Organizational Image and Pharmaceutical Regulation at the FDA* (Princeton, NJ: Princeton University Press, 2010); Julian Zelizer, "The Uneasy Relationship: Democracy, Taxation, and State Building since the New Deal," in *The Democratic Experiment: New Directions in American Political History,* ed. Meg Jacobs, William J. Novak and Julian E. Zelizer (Princeton, NJ: Princeton University Press, 2003), chap. 11; Judith A. Layzer, *Open to Business: Conservatives' Opposition to Environmental Regulation* (Cambridge, MA: MIT Press, 2012).

6. I draw on some fantastic texts that do put gender at the center of policy making, such as those of Alice Kessler-Harris, Margot Canaday, and Robert Self, as well as the rich feminist history of the welfare state. Unfortunately, the implications of these books—that gender and gendered ideas are central to policy making of all sorts—have not changed many mainstream policy histories.

7. For "bully state," see Brian Monteith, *The Bully State: The End of Tolerance* (London: Free Society, 2009); and Patrick Basham, "From the Nanny State to the Bully State," *Institute of Public Affairs Review* 62, no. 1 (March 2010): 24–25. The popularization of "Big Brother" comes from George Orwell's *Nineteen Eighty-Four* (New York: Harcourt Brace, 1949). On paternalism, see *Paternalism: Theory and Practice,* ed. Christian Coons and Michael Weber (Cambridge: Cambridge Univer-

sity Press, 2013). On maternalism, see *Mothers of a New World: Maternalist Politics and the Origins of Welfare States*, ed. Seth Koven and Sonya Michel (New York: Routledge, 1993); and Eileen Boris and S. J. Kleinberg, "Mothers and Other Workers: (Re)conceiving Labor, Maternalism, and the State," *Journal of Women's History* 15, no. 3 (Autumn 2003): 90–117. The "tutelary" state is a European term, from Alexis de Tocqueville, *Democracy in America*, vol. 2, pt. 4. This idea has manifest in the U.S. context as the "schoolmarm," and more generally through ideas of government-as-teacher. Patrick McGuinn, "The National Schoolmarm: 'No Child Left Behind' and the New Educational Federalism," *Publius* 35, no. 1 (Winter 2005): 41–68. There are of course many sources for discussions of an American "police state," often with very different meanings. For two wildly different uses of the phrase, see Gerry Spence, *Police State: How America's Cops Get Away with Murder* (New York: St. Martin's Press, 2015); and Cheryl K. Chumley, *Police State U.S.A.: How Orwell's Nightmare Is Becoming Our Reality* (New York: WND Books, 2014). For the therapeutic state see James L. Nolan Jr., *The Therapeutic State: Justifying Government at Century's End* (New York: New York University Press, 1998); and Andrew J. Polsky, *The Rise of the Therapeutic State* (Princeton, NJ: Princeton University Press, 1993).

8. *Federal Trade Commission Reauthorization: Hearings before the Subcommittee on Commerce, Transportation and Tourism*, House of Representatives, 97th Cong., 2nd sess., April 1, 1982, 21–22.

9. Rick Perlstein, *Before the Storm: Barry Goldwater and the Unmaking of the American Consensus* (New York: Hill and Wang, 2001); Lisa McGirr, *Suburban Warriors: The Origins of the New American Right* (Princeton, NJ: Princeton University Press, 2002); Judith Stein, *Pivotal Decade: How the United States Traded Factories for Finance in the Seventies* (New Haven, CT: Yale University Press, 2011).

10. "Republican Party Platform," August 18, 1976, http://www.presidency.ucsb.edu/ws/index.php?pid=25843.

11. Patricia Strach, *All in the Family: The Private Roots of American Public Policy* (Stanford, CA: Stanford University Press, 2007), 164.

12. Robert Self, *All in the Family: The Realignment of American Democracy since the 1960s* (New York: Hill and Wang, 2012), 309.

13. Self, *All in the Family*, 310.

14. Natasha Zaretsky, *No Direction Home: The American Family and the Fear of National Decline, 1968–1980* (Chapel Hill: University of North Carolina Press, 2007), 12.

15. Laura Briggs, *How All Politics Became Reproductive Politics from Welfare Reform to Foreclosure to Trump* (Berkeley: University of California Press, 2017), 13–14.

16. Melinda Cooper, *Family Values: Between Neoliberalism and the New Social Conservatism* (Brooklyn, NY: Zone Books, 2017), 11–12.

17. *Oversight of the Federal Trade Commission: Hearings before the Subcommittee for Consumers, of the Committee on Commerce, Science, and Transportation*, Senate, 96th Cong., 1st sess., September 19, 1979, 156.

18. For a discussion of the rise of hunger discourse in the 1960s, see Laurie B. Green, "'Hunger in America' and the Power of Television: Poor People, Physicians, and the Mass Media in the War against Poverty," in *Precarious Prescriptions: Contested Histories of Race and Health in North America*, ed. Laurie B. Green, John McKiernan-González, and Martin Summers (Minneapolis: University of Minnesota Press, 2014), 211–36.

19. *Dietary Goals for the United States: Select Committee on Nutrition and Human Needs*, Senate, 95th Cong., 1st sess., December 1977.

20. Bartow J. Elmore, *Citizen Coke: The Making of Coca-Cola Capitalism* (New York: Norton, 2015), 277.

21. *Food Safety and Nutrition Amendments of 1978: Hearings before the Subcommittee on Health and the Environment of the Committee on Interstate and Foreign Commerce*, House of Representatives, 95th Cong., 2nd sess., July 18, 1978, 106.

22. Harvey Levenstein, *Fear of Food: A History of Why We Worry about What We Eat* (Chicago: University of Chicago Press, 2012), 145–47.

23. Paul Pierson, "The Rise and Reconfiguration of Activist Government," in *The Transformation of American Politics: Activist Government and the Rise of Conservatism*, ed. Paul Pierson and Theda Skocpol (Princeton, NJ: Princeton University Press, 2007), 23–25.

24. Theda Skocpol, *Diminished Government: From Membership to Management in American Civic Life* (Norman: University of Oklahoma Press, 2003), 202.

25. Warren J. Belasco, *Appetite for Change: How the Counterculture Took on the Food Industry*, 2nd ed. (Ithaca, NY: Cornell University Press, 2007), 145–46.

26. Marian Burros, "Sugar's Sweet Saturation: Capping America's Sweet Tooth: Should Consumption Be Controlled?" *Washington Post*, May 19, 1977, F1.

27. Larry Kramer, "TV Ads Aimed at Children Not a Sugar-Coated Issue," *Washington Post*, February 10, 1979, A2.

28. Molly Niesen, "From Gray Panther to National Nanny: The Kidvid Crusade and the Eclipse of the U.S. Federal Trade Commission," *Communication, Culture & Critique* 8, no. 4 (December 2015): 580.

29. Burros, "Sugar's Sweet Saturation," F1.

30. Dolly Langdon, "FTC Chairman Mike Pertschuk Is the Bureaucrat Who Makes Some Businessmen Turn Blue," *People* 12, no. 11, September 10, 1979, http://people.com/archive/f-t-c-chairman-mike-pertschuk-is-the-bureaucrat-who-makes-some-businessmen-turn-blue-vol-12-no-11/.

31. Langdon, "FTC Chairman."

32. *Annual Report of the Federal Trade Commission, For the Fiscal Year Ended September 30, 1978* (Washington, DC: Government Printing Office, 1978), 4.

33. Chris Jay Hoofnagle, *Federal Trade Commission Privacy Law and Policy* (New York: Cambridge University Press, 2016), 64.

34. J. Howard Beales, "Advertising to Kids and the FTC: A Regulatory Retrospective that Advises the Present," *Remarks before the George Mason Law Review*

2004 Symposium on Antitrust and Consumer Protection Competition, Advertising, and Heath Claims: Legal and Practical Limits on Advertising Regulation, https://www.ftc.gov/public-statements/.

35. Meg Jacobs, *Pocketbook Politics: Economic Citizenship in 20th Century America* (Princeton, NJ: Princeton University Press, 2007); Emily E. LB. Twarog, *Politics of the Pantry: Housewives, Food, and Consumer Protest in Twentieth-Century America* (New York: Oxford University Press, 2017).

36. Lizabeth Cohen, *A Consumer's Republic: The Politics of Mass Consumption in Postwar America* (New York: Knopf, 2003), 370, 523n56.

37. Thomas Whiteside, *The Investigation of Ralph Nader: General Motors vs. One Determined Man* (New York: Arbor House, 1972), 76; *Federal Role in Traffic Safety: Subcommittee on Executive Reorganization; Committee on Government Operations*, Senate, 89th Cong., 2nd sess., March 22, 1966, 1535.

38. Rick Perlstein, *Nixonland: The Rise of a President and the Fracturing of America* (New York: Scribner, 2008), 695.

39. Stephen J. Ducat, *The Wimp Factor: Gender Gaps, Holy Wars, and the Politics of Anxious Masculinity* (New York: Beacon Press, 2004), 61.

40. Ducat, *Wimp Factor*, 9.

41. Susan Jeffords, *Hard Bodies: Hollywood Masculinity in the Reagan Era* (New Brunswick, NJ: Rutgers University Press, 2004), 10.

42. Strach, *All in the Family*, 165.

43. Warren J. Belasco, *Appetite for Change: How the Counterculture Took on the Food Industry*, 2nd ed. (Ithaca, NY: Cornell University Press, 2007), 147.

44. Theodore J. Jacobs, "What's Wrong with Children's Television," *New York Times*, December 27, 1970, 81.

45. Tracy Westen, "Government Regulation of Food Marketing to Children: The Federal Trade Commission and the Kid-Vid Controversy," *Loyola of Los Angeles Law Review* 39, no. 79 (May 2006): 81.

46. Westen, "Government Regulation," 79–92, 85.

47. Larry Kramer, "Hearings Begin on Children's TV Ads," *Washington Post*, January 16, 1979, A2.

48. Susan Bartlett Foote and Robert H. Mnookin, "The 'Kid Vid' Crusade," *Public Interest* 61 (Fall 1980): 90–105, 92.

49. *Reauthorization of the FTC: Hearings before the Committee on Commerce, Science, and Transportation*, Senate, 97th Cong., 2nd sess., March 18, 1982, p. 330.

50. Foote and Mnookin, "'Kid Vid' Crusade," 90–105, 93.

51. Kramer, "TV Ads Aimed at Children," A2.

52. Janice E. Rubin, *The Federal Trade Commission: Brief Background and Legal Overview*, CRS Report No. 81-125A (Washington, DC: Congressional Research Service, 1981), issued May 19, 1981, 1; Niesen, "From Gray Panther," 588.

53. Zaretsky, *No Direction Home*, 219; Pauline M. Ippolito, "Regulation of Food Advertising," in *The Oxford Handbook of the Social Science of Obesity*, ed. John Cawley (New York: Oxford University Press, 2011), 746.

54. William C. MacLeod and Judith L. Oldham, "Kid-Vid Revisited: Important Lessons for the Childhood Obesity Debate," *American Bar Association—Antitrust* 18 (Summer 2004): 31.

55. Merrill Brown, "New Head at FTC, New Era for Kid Ads," *Washington Post*, October 1, 1981, D11.

56. *Reauthorization of the FTC: Hearings before the Committee on Commerce, Science, and Transportation*, Senate, 97th Cong., 2nd sess., March 18, 1982, 330.

57. Chris Hoofnagle, though, has argued that the focus on the *Washington Post* as liberal is misleading, both because any theoretical threat to advertising might hurt them and because it took a more "establishment" than "liberal" line. Chris Jay Hoofnagle, *Federal Trade Commission Privacy Law and Policy* (New York: Cambridge University Press, 2016), 63.

58. Michael Pertschuk, *Revolt against Regulation: The Rise and Pause of the Consumer Movement* (Berkeley: University of California Press, 1982), 70.

59. Henry Fairlie, "Political Commentary," *Spectator*, June 14, 1956, 6.

60. "Bad Ban," *Spectator*, February 12, 1965, 10.

61. David Williams, "Too Much Government?" *Spectator*, October 9, 1970, 14; Patrick Cosgrave, "Clear Choice for the Tories," *Spectator*, January 25, 1975, 4; John O'Sullivan, "Discrimination," *Spectator*, December 6, 1975, 11; R. W. F. Holmes, Letter, *Spectator*, March 26, 1976, 18; Monson Society for Individual Freedom, Letter, *Spectator*, March 13, 1976, 18.

62. "Onwards the Nanny State," *Spectator*, March 6, 1976, 1.

63. "The British Nanny State," *New York Times*, June 9, 1985; Jo Thomas, "Britain Proposes Overhaul of Almost All Welfare Programs," *New York Times*, June 4, 1985; Michael Jacobs, "Thatcherism and Reform of Welfare State," *Economic and Political Weekly* 20, no. 30 (July 27, 1985): 1262–63.

64. Margaret Thatcher, "Speech Opening Conference on Information Technology," London, Barbican Centre, December 8, 1982, transcribed by the Margaret Thatcher Foundation, http://www.margaretthatcher.org/document/105067.

65. Margaret Thatcher, "Airey Neave Memorial Lecture," March 3, 1980, https://www.margaretthatcher.org/document/104318.

66. "Thatcher Vows to Make Britain Safer for Free Enterprise," *Associated Press*, December 27, 1983.

67. Shirley Robin Letwin, *The Anatomy of Thatcherism* (New Brunswick, NJ: Transaction Publishers, 1992), 33–34; Patricia Holland, Hugh Chignell, and Sherryl Wilson, *Broadcasting and the NHS in the Thatcherite 1980s: The Challenge to Public Service* (London: Palgrave Macmillan, 2013), 79; Harold D. Clarke, Marianne C. Stewart, and Gary Zuk, "Introduction: Three Political Economies in an Era of Economic Decline," in *Economic Decline and Political Change: Canada,*

Great Britain, and the United States, ed. Harold D. Clarke, Marianne C. Stewart, and Gary Zuk (Pittsburgh: University of Pittsburgh Press, 1988), 12.

68. Harry Schwartz, "The F.D.A.'s New Chief," *New York Times*, October 6, 1979, 23; "The Dangers of Budget Bloat: Washington's Free-for-All Spending Just Makes Inflation Worse," *Time* 111, no. 20 (May 15, 1978), 72.

69. Ronald Reagan, "Remarks at a Rally Supporting the Proposed Constitutional Amendment for a Balanced Federal Budget," speech, July 19, 1982.

70. Gil Troy, *Morning in America: How Ronald Reagan Invented the 1980s* (Princeton, NJ: Princeton University Press, 2005), 342.

71. Peter N. Stearns, *Anxious Parents: A History of Modern Childrearing in America* (New York: New York University Press, 2003); Majia Holmer Nadesan, *Governing Childhood into the 21st Century: Biopolitical Technologies of Childhood Management and Education* (New York: Palgrave, 2010); Richard Beck, *We Believe the Children: A Moral Panic in the 1980s* (New York: Perseus, 2015).

72. Donald T. Critchlow, *Phyllis Schlafly and Grassroots Conservatism: A Woman's Crusade* (Princeton, NJ: Princeton University Press, 2005), 221; J. Brooks Flippen, *Jimmy Carter, the Politics of the Family, and the Rise of the Religious Right* (Athens: University of Georgia Press, 2011), 37–38.

73. Michael S. Swisher, "Letter to the Editor—Life under Socialism: Nanny Will Spank," *Wall Street Journal*, December 6, 1989; Michael Barry, "Civil Liberties Take a Belting," *New York Times*, September 8, 1984, 21; Robert Lindsey, "Tough Seat-Belt System Awaits New-Car Buyers," *New York Times*, September 5, 1973, 1; "U.S. Seeks to Spur Use of Car Seat Belts," *New York Times*, September 17, 1972, 25.

74. Larry Kramer, "Hearings Begin on Children's TV Ads," A2.

75. Carole Shifrin, "Monitoring of Children's TV Urged, Parents Urged to Monitor Advertising for Children," *Washington Post*, November 15, 1978, F1.

76. Howard H. Bell, "Comments on the American Advertising Federation on the Staff's Final Report," IRR No. 215-60, In the matter of Children's Advertising 43 Fed. Reg. 17967 (May 26, 1981), 3.

77. Westen, "Government Regulation of Food Marketing to Children," 79–92, 88.

78. Larry Kramer, "TV Ads Are Said to Benefit Child by Developing Skepticism," *Washington Post*, January 17, 1979, A5.

79. Richard Cohen, "Commercial for Kids: A Way to Earn a Living," *Washington Post*, January 21, 1979, B1.

80. "Someone Does Need a Nanny," *Washington Post*, March 16, 1979, A18.

81. "The Children's Hour," *Washington Post*, January 19, 1979, A20.

82. "The FTC as National Nanny," *Washington Post*, March 1, 1978, A22.

83. MacLeod and Oldham, "Kid-Vid Revisited," 31.

84. Gary Cross, *The Cute and the Cool: Wondrous Innocence and Modern American Children's Culture* (New York: Oxford University Press, 2004), 193.

85. Ann Hulbert, *Raising America: Experts, Parents, and a Century of Advice about Children* (New York: Knopf, 2003), 258.

86. Matthew D. Lassiter, "Inventing Family Values," in *Rightward Bound: Making America Conservative in the 1970s*, ed. Bruce Schulman and Julian E. Zelizer (Cambridge, MA: Harvard University Press, 2008), 20–21.

87. Dobson and Phyllis Schlafly, quoted in Lassiter, "Inventing Family Values," 21–22.

88. Carole Shifrin, "8 Hill Wives Lobby on TV Ads Aimed at Children; 'Let the FTC Conduct Its Inquiry, It May Help Us Raise Wiser, Healthier Children'; Group Backs Effort to Curb Food Commercials," *Washington Post*, May 18, 1978, A3.

89. Tom Shales, "Getting 'Em While They're Young: Ads for the Young and the Vulnerable," *Washington Post*, June 4, 1978, H1.

90. Shales, "Getting 'Em," H1.

91. Foote and Mnookin, " 'Kid Vid' Crusade," 100–101.

92. Larry Kramer, "TV Ads Aimed at Children," *Washington Post*, February 20, 1979, A2.

93. "Farewell to the National Nanny," *Washington Post*, April 6, 1981, A14.

94. "Little White Lies," *New York Times*, August 6, 1981, A22.

95. "Nanny at the Gates," *New York Times*, June 9, 1983, A22.

96. "Nanny at the Gates," *New York Times*, June 9, 1983, A22.

97. Jesse Helms, "The Wisdom of Henry Hyde," 103rd Cong., 1st sess., *Congressional Record*, vol. 139, daily ed. (May 27, 1993): S6720.

98. Newt Gingrich, "Kemp's Plan for GOP Triumph," 103rd Cong., 1st sess., *Congressional Record*, vol. 139, daily ed. (June 28, 1993): E1638.

99. Al Gore, "Common Sense Government Works Better and Costs Less," *Third Report of the National Performance Review*, September 7, 1995, 16.

100. William J. Clinton, "Remarks on Regulatory Reform," February 21, 1995, at American Presidency Project, http://www.presidency.ucsb.edu/ws/?pid=51006.

101. Sandra Sobieraj, "Gore: Militias and 'Extreme Individualism,'" *Associated Press*, June 12, 1997. This "grandparent state" concept was requoted over and over again by the CATO Institute, as in David Boaz, "The Politics of Freedom," *The Freeman: Ideas on Liberty* (May 2008): 29.

102. William J. Clinton: "Remarks at the Paul H. Nitze School of Advanced International Studies," March 8, 2000, at American Presidency Project, http://www.presidency.ucsb.edu/ws/?pid=87714.

103. Cooper, *Family Values*, 140–42; Briggs, *How All Politics Became Reproductive Politics*, 48.

104. A. Wayne Allard, "Health Care Revisited," 103rd Cong., 2nd sess., *Congressional Record*, vol. 104, daily ed. (August 3, 1994): H6745.

105. Richard Epstein, letter to the editor, "Health Care Law Shows Big Government Lies," *New York Times*, August 10, 1997.

106. David Brock, *The Seduction of Hillary Rodham* (New York: Free Press, 1996), 162.

107. Stu Bykofsky, "I Love New York Is Banned," *Philadelphia Daily News*, June 1, 2012; Jill Colvin, "New York Soda Ban Approved: Board of Health OKs Limiting Sale of Large-Sized, Sugary Drinks," *Huffington Post*, September 13, 2012.

108. Bartow J. Elmore, *Citizen Coke: The Making of Coca-Cola Capitalism* (New York: Norton, 2015), 289; "Nanny State Fizzles," *Investor's Business Daily*, March 13, 2013, A12.

109. "Notes on Nanny Bloomberg," *Weekly Standard* 17, no. 37 (June 11, 2012), 2.

110. For a discussion of taxes as "nanny state" taxes, see William F. Shughart II, "The Economics of the Nanny State," in *Taxing Choice: The Predatory Politics of Fiscal Discrimination*, ed. William F. Shughart II (Oakland, CA: Independent Institute, 1997), 13–25.

111. Marian Sawyer, "Gender, Metaphor, and the State," *Feminist Review* 52 (Spring 1996): 119.

112. MacLeod and Oldham, "Kid-Vid Revisited," 31.

113. Foote and Mnookin, " 'Kid Vid' Crusade," 102.

114. Rush Limbaugh, "De Tocqueville on the Nanny State," January 14, 2008, http://www.rushlimbaugh.com/daily/2008/01/14/de_tocqueville_on_the_nanny_state.

115. Ron Paul, *The School Revolution: A New Answer for Our Broken Education System* (New York: Grand Central Publishing, 2013), 21–22.

116. Notably, in his discussion, the "social problems" are primarily the problems of low-income Americans. He is not actually suggesting increased federal intervention for middle- or upper-income Americans. Paul Starobin, "The Daddy State," *National Journal*, March 1998, 678.

117. Lindsay F. Wiley, Micah L. Berman, and Doug Blanke, "Who's Your Nanny? Choice, Paternalism and Public Health in the Age of Personal Responsibility," *Journal of Law, Medicine & Ethics* (Spring 2013): 90.

Conclusions

The History of Neoliberalism

Kim Phillips-Fein

For historians trying to understand the ways that the political economy of the world changed in the late years of the twentieth century, the idea of neoliberalism has caught on far more slowly than in other disciplines. The term, which refers to the triumph of free market policies, the accompanying denigration of collective action and public institutions, and a social order that becomes ever more harshly unequal and savage as a result, has become one of the key concepts used to define our age. Yet while the idea of neoliberalism has been widely used by sociologists and anthropologists, popularized by the geographer David Harvey, and deployed by countless journalists on the left, historians have been much more tentative about adopting it. This is in part because it is generally used to describe our contemporary political economy, whereas the historical literature on the years after 1980—the era that might be described as neoliberal—is just beginning to come into being.

But it may also reflect a certain wariness among historians, a reluctance (even among politically sympathetic scholars) to adopt the idea fully, an appreciation of what might be its limits as well as its gifts. After all, the term contains within itself an implicit historical narrative about the late twentieth century: an argument that in the 1970s, a new way of organizing and thinking about political and economic life came into existence, one that sets the time period from then until now apart as a "neoliberal" age. The idea of neoliberalism is, at heart, an idea about how to periodize and conceptualize recent history. It may be that as historians take up the concept, their approach and their thinking will reshape its meaning for other fields as well.

Early in the 1990s, Daniel T. Rodgers wrote an essay for the *Journal of*

American History dealing with the rise and fall of what he called the "paradigm" of republicanism for thinking about the history of the American Revolution and American history more broadly.[1] Key to his analysis was that the concept of republicanism—a political framework distinct from liberalism which emphasized ideals of citizenship, emotionally charged concepts of the "public good" and an embrace of a passionate democratic politics— emerged and gained popularity as a way of understanding eighteenth- and nineteenth-century American history because it helped historians cope with a range of analytic problems and difficulties that otherwise proved elusive and maddening. Earlier visions of the American Revolution had seen it as the working out of a Lockean paradigm, a restrained revolution that professed great tolerance for commercial freedom and economic self-interest that was somehow able to avoid a broad popular politics. Their vision of American politics more generally was one of basic consensus around the ideals of capitalism and the market. In the context of 1960s America, such ideas started to break down, and as they did, historians were impressed anew by the impassioned rhetoric of the American Revolution, the fraught and paranoid images of power it contested, and what a generation saw as a vision of "labor republicanism" that joined the rights of citizens to concepts of economic democracy running well into the nineteenth century.

Eventually, "republicanism" was stretched so far and used to explain so much that it ceased to have persuasive power—but what was of interest to Rodgers was the reasons for its flourishing in the first place. As Rodgers put it, republicanism was a "paradigm" in the language of the historian of science Thomas S. Kuhn. It helped to fulfill certain critical intellectual needs and spoke to complexities and difficulties that had challenged scholars of earlier generations, that had emerged as prior modes of understanding broke down. Most centrally, it sought to redress a vision of American history that placed liberalism as the only tradition of the country. Republicanism answered "a breathtakingly wide array of questions"; in this regard, its "success and its weakness were one and the same."[2]

The history of the idea of neoliberalism is very different from that of republicanism, in part because it is a sociological concept as much as a historical one, focused on the pressing problems of contemporary society rather than those of an earlier era. But many of the dynamics around the spread and rise of the term—as well as some of the tensions around it now—resemble those Rodgers described regarding the career of the idea of republicanism. Neoliberalism is a way of thinking about the recent past that emerged out of a range of problems that are both intellectual and political in scope, and it speaks to the need to find a way of describing in broad terms the distinctive dilemmas of the present.

For historians in particular, the turn toward neoliberalism reflects frustration with arguments about the rightward shift in American politics that focus on the partisan triumph of the Republican Party in the 1980s, and the problems and limits of explaining American politics in terms of an oscillation between "conservative" and "liberal" poles. It arose, too, out of deep dissatisfaction with the mainstream way of describing the key economic and political shifts of the 1990s in terms of "globalization" and rising economic competition—ideas that connoted an inevitable, spontaneous and natural set of shifts that benefited all, even though the world that was being created seemed to be growing ever more starkly divided. And it contains within itself a powerful critique of the sharp and destructive economic polarization of recent years, the shredding of what there was of a social safety net in the United States, the rise of prisons as a way to contain poor people, and the fracturing of democratic institutions as inequality has grown. The idea of neoliberalism is so powerful and appealing that some scholars, such as Jackson Lears, have suggested that "there is simply nothing else so succinct and precise to describe the seismic shift that has occurred in the world political economy since the 1970s."[3]

But like all frameworks, that of neoliberalism offers a way of illuminating some features of the social world while obscuring others. The desire it reflects to describe the transformation of the world economy since the 1970s at the level of policy, economics, and psychology at the same time— to capture the changes that have taken place in a way that goes beyond partisanship, to suggest that they are larger than the triumph of any one political faction—also raises a set of questions about where this epochal shift emerged from, what its antecedents were, and what its future might be. What insights does the idea of neoliberalism afford historians, and what does the paradigm exclude or make difficult to see clearly? And how might historians reshape what is meant by neoliberalism?

* * *

The idea of neoliberalism, like the historical moment it describes, is a product not so much of the election of Ronald Reagan in 1980s as it is of the end of the Cold War. According to the sociologist Rajesh Venugopal, the word *neoliberalism* makes few appearances before the 1990s, with just over one hundred entries in English in Google Scholar between 1980 and

1989. Over the 1990s, the number grew to more than one thousand, and then in the first decade of the twentieth century, it expanded to well over seven thousand.[4] Why should the idea of neoliberalism have flourished at this moment? What intellectual needs might have called it forth?

Prior to the 1990s, *neoliberalism* had been used in a much more narrow sense.[5] As scholars such as Angus Burgin have written, this was the label chosen by some of the economists and intellectuals in the orbit of Friedrich von Hayek who organized around the Mont Pelerin Society in the wake of the Great Depression and the rise of communism, fascism, and Nazism. The word *liberalism*—with its eighteenth- and nineteenth-century emphasis on individual freedom—that had once been associated with John Stuart Mill and Adam Smith had been claimed in the 1930s by Franklin Delano Roosevelt and others who argued that the social rights that could be secured only by a welfare state were preconditions for individual freedom.[6] Recognizing that the older insistence that the market was sufficient alone would no longer be persuasive in the wake of the economic and political devastation of the 1930s, some of the scholars in Hayek's orbit (in particular Wilhelm Röpke) called for a reborn liberalism that would actually have room for the government to play a certain role in economic life, but that nonetheless rejected socialism and state ownership of industry. By rejecting dogma they would be able to save the principles that mattered most. Hayek himself said that he was not a "conservative," but he saw little reason to call himself a "neoliberal," instead preferring not to cede the old term and to define himself as a Whig. But others wanted a word that explicitly connoted a rebirth, an approach that sought to bring old ideas back into circulation in changed circumstances. As Raymond Moley put it in 1951, seeking to criticize the liberals of the New Deal era who seemed to have laid claim to the term permanently, a "neoliberal is someone who has stolen the good word 'liberal' out of an honored past."[7]

Neoliberalism as it emerged out of the 1930s and 1940s was but one strain of thought in the broader conservative universe. The early neoliberal thinkers (such as Hayek) were ambivalent toward later believers, most importantly Milton Friedman, who codified their ideas far more rigidly. The first people who toyed with (and by no means universally identified with) the term *neoliberal* were plagued by doubts about the viability of capitalism, impressed by its fragility, and uncertain about its future. As Burgin writes, "The more strident market advocacy of recent years emerged only after an extended period of contestation and debate."[8]

THE HISTORY OF NEOLIBERALISM

The term *neoliberalism* was then given new life in the United States in the late 1970s and early 1980s, when a group of rising stars in the Democratic Party embraced it as a way of describing their distinctive politics— one that was willing to turn away from an automatic endorsement of labor and the welfare state and the civil rights movement, in favor of what its proponents proclaimed was a new pragmatic flexibility and idealism in the face of changed circumstances. As Charles Peters, editor of the *Washington Monthly*, put it in a 1982 editorial in the *Washington Post*: "We still believe in liberty and justice and a fair chance for all, in mercy for the afflicted and help for the down-and-out. But we no longer automatically favor unions or big government or oppose the military and big business."[9] Just as the neoconservatives were liberals who had revisited their old politics, neo-liberals (so the story went) had taken a hard scrutiny of their faiths and found them wanting. They sought to find a way back to the White House by rejecting their old sympathies and demonstrating a new pragmatism and sympathy to market-based solutions. With Bill Clinton's election in 1992, it seemed they had succeeded.

* * *

Neither of these earlier claims to the political label of "neoliberal" is really what is meant by the contemporary use of the term. On the contrary, the turn to the idea of neoliberalism is a way not just of thinking about how particular individuals might identify politically but also of describing the broadest dynamics of contemporary politics, and the emergence of a political sensibility that spans both political parties.

For historians of the post–World War II United States, the key shift is away from a framework of analysis that treats the political shifts of the late twentieth century primarily in terms of the rise of conservatism and the "unraveling" (to quote Alan Matusow) of liberalism. After Ronald Reagan won the presidential election of 1980, many historians (mostly hailing from a liberal perspective themselves) concerned about the future of the country put forward the idea that the postwar liberal order had given way, in the mid-1970s, as it came under increasingly serious political challenges from left and right alike. They told a political, and partisan, narrative about the collapse of the Democratic Party and the rise of the right. The civil rights and black freedom movements, feminism, gay and lesbian politics, and the antiwar movement all criticized the terms and norms of postwar liberalism, highlighting its elisions and evasions, its prejudices and failures. At the same time, a mobilization at once grassroots and elite, organized around an antigovernment critique, took shape and gained momentum. It was especially able to do so once it was joined by a populist "backlash" against the successes of civil rights in particular, a furious reaction by displaced white Southerners and white ethnic voters in cities who feared their displacement by African Americans and Latinos. The implosion of liberalism and victory of Reagan in 1980 marked the end of the "New Deal order" and the emergence of a new era in the country's history.[10] The earliest historians of the rightward shift focused primarily on racism and the racial backlash to explain the victories of the Republican Party, looking at the white working-class voters who became known as "Reagan Democrats," and whose defection from the party of Roosevelt made possible Reagan's victory in 1980.

But by the 1990s the partisan intellectual framework and the emphasis on the white working class ceased to be as appealing. The presidency of Democrat Bill Clinton, after all, only highlighted how much had changed since the postwar years. The transformations of the 1980s were only beginning to become fully visible in the 1990s: the decline of manufacturing, the rise of the service sector, the development of global supply chains and the flight of capital offshore, the increasing weight of the financial sector in economic life, the dominance of an intellectual regime centered on a methodological individualism. These could not be explained simply in terms of the ascendance of free-market conservatism. Something more was needed.

There was also a key intellectual push that motivated the turn toward neoliberalism. As Daniel Rodgers has argued, throughout the 1970s and 1980s there had been a shift within the academy away from older ideas of society that had emphasized power, structure, and class as the key determinants of social life. The rise of postmodernism, the impact of Michel Foucault, and the new concepts of power as something that was omnipresent but not emerging from a single source all changed basic ideas about how society operated. Culture rather than class or economy came to seem increasingly important as a motive force, and thinkers began to elevate language as something that had the capacity to determine reality. The body came to be figured as the critical site of political contest, as important as the state. At the same time, economists increasingly turned against Keynesian macroeconomics to embrace a market framework of analysis that treated the economy as an agglomeration of individuals, each acting rationally, atomistically, and alone, and their ideas and approach spilled out to political science as well.[11]

Yet even as these modes of thinking rose and gained popularity, the actual politics of the United States, and indeed the world, was becoming more stratified, as one nation after the next seemed to turn against the welfare state and the tradition of social democracy, as inequality began to rise and to harden, and as the global dominance of the United States and Western models of capitalism became clear following the Iraq War of the early 1990s. Market metaphors seemed to hide the reality of a single superpower. Just as the oscillation between a static liberalism and conservatism no longer seemed adequate to describe the central trends of American politics, the dominant ways of writing about social relations no longer appeared sufficient to capture the growing power of the wealthy.

The rise of the idea of neoliberalism thus represented the resurgence of a framework that addressed power relations, approached the connections between the economy and political life, and sought to bring the breathless discourse about globalization into contact with the ever-widening gap between the rich and the rest of the world. It was deeply connected to a revival of interest in Marx, in ways that reflected the preoccupations of the 1990s and early 2000s, when the end of the Cold War made possible the celebration of capitalism on a global scale but also opened the possibility for a new critique.

The book that did the most to bring the idea of neoliberalism into broad circulation was David Harvey's 2005 *A Brief History of Neoliberalism*.[12] As Harvey put it, neoliberalism is a theory that "proposes that human well-being can best be advanced by liberating individual entrepreneurial freedoms and skills within an institutional framework characterized by strong private property rights, free markets and free trade."[13] Harvey emphasizes that this is an idea with implications for the state, namely that it should play a minimal role. But it is an idea with importance for more than social policy. Neoliberalism connotes a way of conceiving of society as a whole—a "hegemonic discourse," which has been "incorporated into the common-sense way many of us interpret, live in and understand the world," with implications for everything from the division of labor to "reproductive activities, attachments to the land and habits of the heart."[14]

Class politics is inextricable from this idea of neoliberalism. While it may be that the idea contains within itself "a utopian project to realize a theoretical design," it is more centrally "a political project to re-establish the conditions for capital accumulation and to restore the power of economic elites"—and it has been accompanied by the stunning rise in economic inequality that has characterized the United States over the past four decades, as documented by Thomas Piketty and others.[15] Although Harvey is careful to characterize the uneven, slow rise of neoliberalism (which he suggests was only adopted in tentative and chaotic experiments and did not really exist as a coherent orthodoxy until the 1990s), his work also emphasizes the ways that powerful economic elites sought to advance those idea associated with neoliberalism as solutions to the various crises of capitalism in the 1970s. In his interpretation, the rise of neoliberal thinking and of neoliberal approaches to social policy was made possible by, and helped to further, the growing power of capitalist elites.

Since the publication of Harvey's 2005 work, other thinkers have taken up his approach and pushed it farther still. Key to this turn has been a new interest in looking at the ways that neoliberalism has reshaped basic concepts about society, democracy, and the self. Scholars have melded Harvey's approach with that of Foucault to treat neoliberalism as a "governing rationality," not simply a specific set of economic policies (deregulation, privatization, hostility to unions) but a way of understanding social life itself. This has been articulated most fully by political theorist Wendy Brown in her work arguing that neoliberal regimes, despite their apparent focus on individual rights, are ultimately antithetical to democratic politics.[16] As she noted in a 2015 interview with *Dissent*, neoliberalism is "a governing rationality through which everything is 'economized' and in a very specific way: human beings become market actors and nothing but, every field of activity is seen as a market, and every entity (whether public or private, whether person, business, or state) is governed as a firm."[17] Envisioning all of life as a series of market exchanges corrodes the capacity of human beings to be self-governing actors, to participate in the radical acts of creation that define democratic politics. "Neoliberalism," as she puts it, "is the rationality through which capitalism finally swallows humanity— not only with its machinery of compulsory commodification and profit-driven expansion, but by its form of valuation."[18] It is the way that people take into themselves the logic of the marketplace and are affected by it at the most intimate levels—as they evaluate their educations, their romantic and familial choices, their deepest sense of who they are.

Finally, some scholars writing about race and the continued prevalence of racial inequalities given the putative adoption of a color-blind politics have been drawn to the idea of neoliberalism. This work has been driven by the paradox that an age focused on free markets has also seen an explosion of incarceration. By emphasizing the dependence of the seemingly free market on state policies, and by suggesting that laissez-faire can easily coexist with a repressive government that polices and contains people deemed incapable of realizing themselves as economically useful individuals, these historians have been drawn to the idea of neoliberalism as a way of making sense of the continued power of racial and sexual divisions in an age that on the surface rejected these.[19]

Neoliberalism, in other words, offers a powerful framework for thinking about the rise of inequality, both economic and political, connecting the two realms to each other and to a way of understanding social relationships that encompasses both individual experience and the highest reaches of government policy. It connotes a way of thinking about policy and changes in state action, doing so in terms that link ideas and agency to structure and power, and ultimately to a broad vision of society as a whole. Other frameworks for thinking about the post-1970s moment—in terms of the rise of the right or conservatism, or "financialization," or the shift to a "service economy"—do not possess the same capacity to link economy and politics. A focus on the rise of finance alone, for example, does not seem adequate to capture the broader ideological shifts taking place; an emphasis on the emergence of a service economy misses the political transformations; and an interpretation that rests entirely on the partisan conflict between left and right, and ascendancy of conservatism, does not help us make sense of the ways that the entire political landscape has shifted since the 1970s in ways that implicate liberals as much as anyone else and which affect left and right alike.

*   *   *

Yet despite the usefulness of the framework of neoliberalism, especially its capacity to signal the power relationships that lie behind the economy, to call attention to the role of government in adopting policies that promote the free market at the expense of institutions that encourage economic redistribution, historians have adopted it with some trepidation. At the heart of this discomfort may be a certain anxiety about the totalizing nature of the term. Because it appears to explain so much, because it has been applied to so many discrete aspects of social life, the idea of neoliberalism cannot help but raise questions.

The first area of uncertainty has to do with the question of how to conceptualize political labels and ideologies and put this history into the frame of neoliberalism. Part of the appeal of the idea of neoliberalism is that it de-centers self-identified conservatives from the history of the rightward shift, to emphasize the broader context and transformation of both political parties and the entire spirit of the times. But this raises the question: Who are the neoliberals? Are they best understood as those people—intellectuals, business leaders, activists, politicians—who actively promoted free-market politics and did so from the perspective of a rising conservative movement? Are they the people who may have called themselves neoliberals (e.g., Bill Clinton) whose liberalism sought to undo and rethink older features of the welfare state? Or is neoliberalism not really useful as a political label or identity, so much as it is a way of referring to the broader context in which these two poles come to seem the limits of organized politics—a way of describing the entire spirit of the age? And if the latter, how to think about the proliferation of self-defined conservative politics within an age of neoliberalism? Does the conservative reaction that was once associated with Reagan's rise ultimately come to seem a confused backlash to neoliberalism itself—as with the Trump voters who endorsed what they believed within some part of themselves to be a reaction against the free trade that had decimated their industrial towns?

This issue of political definition is linked to a question about chronology. When, exactly, did neoliberalism emerge? On the one hand, scholarship on the 1970s and 1980s suggests a political transformation that was gradual and contested, not a sudden turn. Historical writing on the 1970s—the moment that Harvey and others isolate as the crisis of the postwar regime and the turn toward neoliberalism—has suggested the protracted and conflict-ridden nature of the shift toward the market. The crises that defined that era—the pressure on the welfare state that manifested itself as fiscal crisis, the labor unrest that frightened executives and impinged on profit margins, the increasing competition that fueled fear among industrialists—did not lead in a straightforward way to the triumph of market ideology or even to policies of privatization. Although there were certainly powerful business leaders and free-market intellectuals who trumpeted laissez-faire and spread hostility to labor unions, the turn to the right was far from rapid or straightforward in historical terms. Public spending continued; austerity brought forth renewed calls for government assistance from both citizens and businesses; even fiscal crises were not capable of bringing about the large-scale privatization of public services in cities such as New York; many manufacturers continued to hope and to lobby for some kind of protection against international competition in order to secure and build up industrial strength. Neoliberal policies were adopted only slowly, gaining popularity in some areas and regions more rapidly than others. Although this might be most self-evident at the level of policy, it could be even truer in inner imaginaries and personal calculations and relationships: the family, for example, may be far more impervious and resistant to the ideology of neoliberalism than the rhetoric of human capital would suggest. Far from acting as though they are autonomous individuals, people in reality remain deeply bound to communities and conceive of well-being through them rather than only in terms of their own economic gain. What is more, even the most ardent believers in economic individualism often in fact embrace the idea that family responsibility should take the place of government protection through the welfare state. Even for them, the logic of neoliberalism is ultimately incomplete.[20]

Another question is whether recent history really is so different. Scholars have traced out the ways that elements and themes often associated with neoliberalism can be found deep in the twentieth century (and perhaps further back as well), throughout the "liberal" postwar order.[21] Public-private partnerships, the use of the state to subsidize private enterprise and enforce market relationships, the celebration of individualism and property ownership as the route to general wealth and prosperity, the importance of business engagement in local affairs—all these can be seen as key elements of postwar liberalism even at its height. Many of the same ideas that we see now as central to neoliberalism appear to have been equally central, albeit perhaps in different ways, to the order that preceded it.[22] Taken together, this raises an important question: if the same basic faith characterizes both the liberal and neoliberal moments, how difficult was it really to make the move from liberalism to what came after? Are there ways of thinking about liberalism and neoliberalism in relation to each other that avoid collapsing them into each other altogether, so that the direction of public resources toward private development during the New Deal, for example, comes to seem no more than an antecedent of the neoliberalism that lies ahead in the 1980s and 1990s? Are there ways to think about the history of the twentieth century that avoid a teleology in which everything winds up resolving into neoliberalism in the end, giving the sense that there are, or were, no real alternatives—as though "neoliberalism" has been present all along in waiting, a shadow politics long before it could come into full existence?[23]

A different difficulty with the idea of neoliberalism is the opposite: the concept seems to be too uncritical of the liberal economy of the postwar years. It runs the risk of setting the post–World War II era apart as some kind of "golden age" or ideal economic order, overlooking the many structural commonalities—economic concentration in the hands of a small elite, the stultifying nature of much work, the turn toward the carceral state, the emergence of consumerism as an ideology and the depletion of environmental resources—that link the present with that earlier time. What is more, all of these issues formed the subject of much social criticism and activism during the 1950s and (especially) the 1960s.

Perhaps most notable, the idea of neoliberalism—with its emphasis on the rise of economic insecurity and precariousness of economic life today—might avoid the extent to which the economic protections available during the post–New Deal era (the strong labor unions, the activist federal state) were far more easily available to white men than to African American and women workers. Part of what has happened over the last forty years is that the terms and conditions of labor that had predominated for these groups during the postwar years became the ones that white men had to accept as well. As N. D. B. Connolly has put it in his critique of neoliberalism published in *Dissent* magazine, for many theorists "the revision of the white social contract gets cast as universal."[24] How to think about the changes of the late twentieth century in a way that avoids the easy temptation of simply celebrating the labor unions and activist ideals of the postwar era, in ways that actually overstate the contrast between the present and the past?

One possibility raised by some of the recent work on the 1970s is whether the transformations of that time were far less ideologically coherent and confident than the idea of neoliberalism might imply. As the state no longer seemed capable of delivering steady economic growth and mastery in the international arena, as the society was roiled by conflict abroad and deep unrest and mistrust at home, the market emerged as an alternate arena almost by accident. Rather than seeing the rise of the power of finance in the economy as the product of the active efforts of the financial industry, for example, Greta Krippner's work on financial deregulation in the 1970s, for example, suggests that lawmakers deregulated the industry as they sought ways to evade directly confronting or coping with the economic slowdown of the decade. Judith Stein's history of deindustrialization argues that industrialists, unions and policy makers all sought a solution to the problem of declining productivity in the 1970s, and that the key development is less the self-confident ascendance of neoliberalism than the failure to adopt a key industrial policy.[25] The real story was not so much the ideological, passionate emergence of the free-market right and its efforts to remake the social order. It was the crisis of the liberal state, which faced serious internal challenges regardless of the assaults on it from outside. People with power sought to consolidate their authority, but they did so less out of a set of messianic ideas about the virtues of the market than simply because as the old order veered out of control and faced a set of political and economic challenges, they knew they could trust one another. The result is a haphazard neoliberalism, one that comes into existence without the sharply defined ideological politics we associate with the term—which in a sense only comes into existence after the fact.[26]

Taking this approach need not mean ultimately downplaying the role of politics and ideology—the extent to which there was a self-conscious class-based politics emerging, one that was not yet dominant but in fact was quite self-aware regarding its intentions and interests. Attending to the partial victories of neoliberalism might also ultimately shift our attention to the struggles of the 1970s and 1980s—the very different visions that people critical of the direction of the country had about what was happening, the many efforts to stave off the ascendance of business power, the revival of ideas of class even in a new context. Neoliberalism remains a powerful paradigm, but explaining its fraught rise might help open up new glimpses of alternatives—as well as revealing the active efforts that went into building the new order in the first place. The chapters collected in this book have sought to approach political history with an eye toward continuity rather than crisis, to explore some of the deep structures that are so constitutive of political life that they can be difficult even to see clearly outside. Although they do not by any means all take up the framework of neoliberalism, the idea, like these essays, reflects some of the underlying tensions in current thinking about the recent past. They point to the need to hold together in our minds the self-aware, movement-building strategies of the right, the ways these evolve in dynamic relationship to the changes within liberalism, and the larger historical context that shapes and presses down upon the whole political order. This project may be overwhelming at times, and perhaps it may be best to imagine different scholars working in relation to each other rather than any single person trying to author a work that manages to take on the whole. But to bring together a simultaneous awareness of agency and structure, political strategizing and changing context, conscious power and the substratum of wealth, resources, ideas, and culture that shapes and constrains how any group exercises political authority is the only way to begin to make sense of contemporary political history. The idea of neoliberalism, in short, is less an answer than it is a vital invitation to keep asking the deepest questions about the origins and the limits of our age.

Notes

1. Rodgers has also, more recently, written about the problems and limits of the idea of neoliberalism, in "The Uses and Abuses of 'Neoliberalism,'" *Dissent* (Winter 2018). His essay, and the four responses to it by Julia Ott, Tim Shenk, N. D. B. Connolly and Mike Konczal, are all well worth reading for their subtle and critical unpacking of the concept.

2. Daniel Rodgers, "Republicanism: The Career of a Concept," *Journal of American History* 79 (1992): 11–38.

3. Jackson Lears, "Technocratic Vistas: The Long Con of Neoliberalism," *Hedgehog Review* 19, no. 3 (Fall 2017), http://iasc-culture.org/THR/THR_article _2017_Fall_Lears.php.

4. Rajesh Venugopal, "Neoliberalism as Concept," *Economy and Society* 44, no. 2 (Fall 2015): 165–87. My discussion here follows and draws on Venugopal, Rodgers, and also Taylor C. Boas and Jordan Gans-Morse, "Neoliberalism: From New Liberal Philosophy to Anti-Liberal Slogan," *Studies in Comparative International Development* 44, no. (June 2009): 137–61.

5. See Lawrence Glickman, "Everyone Was a Liberal," *Aeon*, July 5, 2016; also George Monbiot, "Neoliberalism: The Ideology at the Root of All Our Problems," *Guardian*, April 15, 2016, for capsule histories of the evolution of the term.

6. This was of course an oversimplified reading of Smith and Mill, and hardly a realistic description of the political economy of the nineteenth century.

7. Glickman, "Everyone Was a Liberal."

8. Angus Burgin, *The Great Persuasion: Reinventing Free Markets since the Depression* (Cambridge, MA: Harvard University Press, 2012), 10. Also see Daniel Stedman Jones, *Masters of the Universe: Hayek, Friedman and the Birth of Neoliberal Politics* (Princeton, NJ: Princeton University Press, 2014); and Dieter Plehwe and Philip Mirowski, *The Road from Mont Pelerin: The Making of the Neoliberal Thought Collective* (Cambridge, MA: Harvard University Press, 2009). Some Chilean economists also drew on the term in the late 1960s and early 1970s, referencing the German use of it and German postwar economic growth. See Boas and Gans-Morse, "Neoliberalism."

9. Charles Peters, "A Neo-Liberal's Manifesto," *Washington Post*, September 5, 1982. Also see Randall Rothenberg, *The Neoliberals: Creating the New American Politics* (New York: Simon and Schuster, 1984).

10. See Steve Fraser and Gary Gerstle, *The Rise and Fall of the New Deal Order, 1930–1980* (Princeton, NJ: Princeton University Press, 1990).

11. Daniel Rodgers, *Age of Fracture* (Cambridge, MA: Harvard University Press, 2003).

12. Harvey's work built on and summarized debates that had been going on within Latin American studies and anthropology in particular, where scholars had used the term "neoliberalism" to make sense of Augusto Pinochet's regime in Chile, in which free market economic policies were implemented from above

without even the forms of political freedom which had been intrinsic to theories of nineteenth-century liberalism. Meanwhile, anthropologists critical of mainstream development theory described the World Bank and the International Monetary Fund in terms of "neoliberalism"—institutions that sought to impose market logics from above.

13. David Harvey, *A Brief History of Neoliberalism* (New York: Oxford University Press, 2005), 2.

14. Harvey, *Brief History*, 3.

15. Harvey, *Brief History*, 19.

16. Another key work to take this approach is Jamie Peck, *Constructions of Neoliberal Reason* (New York: Oxford University Press, 2010); also see Philip Mirowski's work on the history of economic ideas and neoliberalism.

17. *Dissent*, April 2, 2015, interview with Timothy Shenk.

18. Wendy Brown, *Undoing the Demos: Neoliberalism's Stealth Revolution* (New York: Zone Books, 2015), 44.

19. Among other works, see Loïc Wacquant, *Punishing the Poor: The Neoliberal Government of Social Insecurity* (Durham, NC: Duke University Press, 2009); Elizabeth Hinton, *From the War on Poverty to the War on Crime* (Cambridge, MA: Harvard University Press, 2016); Julilly Kohler-Hausmann, *Getting Tough: Welfare and Imprisonment in 1970s America* (Princeton, NJ: Princeton University Press, 2017).

20. See, e.g., Gabriel Winant, "A Place to Die: Nursing Home Abuse and the Political Economy of the 1970s," *Journal of American History* 105, no. 1 (June 2018). Anthropologists have been among those most deeply critical of the idea that the market calculations associated with neoliberalism have in reality so deeply reshaped family and psychological life. For example, see Caitlin Zaloom, "Finance," *Cultural Anthropology*, August 7, 2017, https://culanth.org/fieldsights/1163-finance.

21. For some of the recent work that treats the evolving ideology of postwar liberalism, see Robert Collins, *More: The Politics of Growth in Postwar Liberalism* (New York: Oxford University Press, 2000); Lily Geismer, *Don't Blame Us: Suburban Liberals and the Transformation of the Democratic Party* (Princeton, NJ: Princeton University Press, 2014); Suleiman Osman, *The Invention of Brownstone Brooklyn: Gentrification and the Search for Authenticity in Postwar New York* (New York: Oxford University Press, 2011); Brent Cebul, " 'They Were the Moving Spirits': Business and Supply-Side Liberalism in the Postwar South," in *Capital Gains: Business and Politics in Twentieth-Century America*, ed. Richard R. John and Kim Phillips-Fein (Philadelphia: University of Pennsylvania Press, 2017); Benjamin Holtzman, "Crisis and Confidence" (PhD diss., Brown University, 2016); Timothy Shenk, "Inventing the American Economy" (PhD diss., Columbia University, 2016).

22. For one exploration of these ideas, see Amy Offner, "Anti-Poverty Programs, Social Conflict and Economic Thought in Colombia and the United States, 1948–1980" (PhD diss., Columbia University, 2012).

23. Although he does not frame his exploration in terms of neoliberalism, this is similar to the line of questioning in Jefferson Cowie, *The Great Exception: The New Deal and the Limits of American Politics* (Princeton, NJ: Princeton University Press, 2016).

24. N. D. B. Connolly, contribution to "The Uses and Abuses of Neoliberalism," *Dissent*, January 22, 2018.

25. Greta Krippner, *Capitalizing on Crisis: The Political Origins of the Rise of Finance* (Cambridge, MA: Harvard University Press, 2011); Judith Stein, *The Pivotal Decade* (New Haven, CT: Yale University Press, 2010); Bethany Moreton, *To Serve God and Wal-Mart: The Making of Christian Free Enterprise* (Cambridge, MA: Harvard University Press, 2009).

26. I am indebted to Caitlin Zaloom for the term *haphazard* here.

Ten Propositions for the New Political History

Matthew D. Lassiter

This anthology emerged from a fall 2015 conference, "Seeing beyond the Partisan Divide," sponsored by the Miller Center at the University of Virginia and organized by the editors to reassess the metanarratives of twentieth-century U.S. political history. The diverse group of historians who gathered in Charlottesville engaged in productive debate about methodology and historiography, most notably the concept of political orders and specifically the utility of chronologically bounded frameworks such as the liberal New Deal era, the rightward turn or conservative triumph, and the alternative "rise" of neoliberalism. We discussed the benefits and pitfalls of organizing modern American history through sequential orders triggered by economic crisis-generated restructuring (the Great Depression of the 1930s and the global shocks of the 1970s), or through the critical elections and realignment models adapted from political science, or through conceptual shifts in structures of meaning as emphasized by intellectual and cultural historians. Our task as scholars, of course, is to historicize conceptual structures and not operate within them, to identify the durable patterns of state power and racial capitalism that persist despite partisan conflict in particular policy areas, to remain informed by the present without overreacting to contingent election outcomes and reproducing the binary oppositions of journalism and punditry. For example, many (otherwise excellent) books about political culture, political economy, and public policy in the 1960s and 1970s culminate in oversimplified narratives of right turns, conservative triumphs, and election maps misconstrued as proof of partisan, popular, and geographic polarization. The historical distortion arises, most of all, from imposition of an artificial red-blue binary drawn from the discourses of the two-party system that predesignates policy outcomes as liberal or conservative rather than hybrid political processes shaped by broad and diverse groups of actors and forces across the spectrum.[1]

The scholarship generated by the metropolitan turn in urban history illustrates the advantages of writing a more expansive political history while moving beyond the red-blue divide by linking grassroots identity formation to political economy and state processes. Back in the 1990s, social history dominated, the cultural turn was consolidating, and political historians mostly focused on the party system, election analysis, and top-down policy making. A cohort of scholars who identified primarily with the subfields of urban, social, labor, and African American history began researching issues of metropolitan development, local white politics, and civil rights challenges to state-supported housing and school segregation. Books such as Robert Self's *American Babylon* (2003), my own *The Silent Majority* (2006), and David Freund's *Colored Property* (2007) sought to connect the pioneering emphasis on neighborhood-level white politics in Thomas Sugrue's *Origins of the Urban Crisis* (1996) with the exploration of segregationist federal policy and suburban political culture in Kenneth Jackson's *Crabgrass Frontier* (1985). These case studies deliberately emphasized policy outcomes over electoral realignment, especially the persistence of racial and spatial inequality under both liberal and conservative governance. *Colored Property* found that "the politics of [racial] exclusion helped unify a suburban population that was remarkably diverse," while *The Silent Majority* concluded that "the partisan affiliation of voters as Republicans or Democrats has often mattered less than the populist identification of suburban residents as homeowners, taxpayers, and schoolparents." Despite explicit arguments that the grassroots "color-blind" defense of white suburban privilege shaped the strategies of both political parties and all three branches of the federal government, academic historians all too often lumped these books together with the "right turn" and "conservative ascendance" scholarship. This reductionist application of the paradigm of red-blue polarization and sequential political orders obscures how liberalism, conservatism, and many other forces at multiple scales produced ideologies and policy outcomes that sustained white class privilege, naturalized racial capitalism, and channeled state power toward suburban and corporate beneficiaries.[2]

In "Beyond Red and Blue," the introduction to this volume, the editors label the liberal-conservative paradigm a hegemonic binary and call on political historians to decenter crisis-inflected partisan frameworks by focusing on more durable patterns of governance and lived experience in the overlapping realms of state-economy, state-society, and state-subject relations. Many of the essays in this anthology seek to transcend liberal-conservative binaries by investigating the broad middle ground of political culture and policy formation in modern U.S. history. This revisionist move away from partisan-driven interpretations of rightward turns and red-blue polarization has also been evident, and urgently needed, in the booming literature on the carceral state and the nation's long and racially selective wars on crime and drugs. Recent books have critiqued the historiographical overemphasis on conservative "frontlash" and Republican law-and-order campaigns by demonstrating the fully bipartisan support for crime and drug wars as racial state-building projects, the deep continuities in the political and cultural construction of nonwhite urban criminalization and white suburban victimization, and the reconstitution rather than the "rise" of punitive policies of discretionary social control. The nation's long war on drugs is sustained by a basic political consensus behind criminalization, enforced through both law enforcement and coercive public health mechanisms, where the equally racialized "conservative" and "liberal" approaches of punitive versus rehabilitative policy have always been intertwined and far removed from the genuine alternatives of civil liberties and human rights.[3] To illustrate this consensus mode through recent history, consider President Barack Obama's reformist stance that "nonviolent drug offenders" should be diverted into treatment programs—through the apparatus of arrest—while violent criminals and drug dealers deserved tough prison sentences and international interdiction must continue to escalate. Obama did criticize racial discrimination in criminal justice, but on a policy spectrum his administration's overall approach to the "drug crisis" was much closer to the precedents set by Nixon and Reagan, as well as to Trump's law-and-order platform, than to the anticriminalization agenda of the American Civil Liberties Union and Human Rights Watch.[4]

The ten methodological and conceptual propositions that follow seek to distill the insights of this volume, alongside an extensive range of additional scholarship, into an admittedly partial set of best practices for the study of political history very broadly defined. These proposals are drawn in part from my own research but much more from what I have learned from other scholars, especially as a member of dozens of dissertation committees at the University of Michigan and as an instructor in three different graduate seminars in twentieth-century U.S. history: Urban/ Suburban History, New Political History, and most recently U.S. in the World. In all these courses, my own thinking about the field of political history has evolved productively by making connections between the state-centered "new political history" and American political development scholarship, the linkage of political culture and political economy in urban and suburban history and metropolitan studies, and the emphasis on identity formation from the individual to the imperial scales in the interdisciplinary American studies literature. Scholars of ethnic and cultural studies also have "brought the state back in" by interrogating boundaries such as public-private and national-imperial, highlighting bureaucratic discretion at every scale of regulatory encounter, and emphasizing continuities across regimes of governance in the racial, gender, and sexual norms of citizenship, knowledge production, and distribution of rights and retribution.[5] Whether or not they self-identify as political historians, a broad spectrum of scholars across many subfields now pursue the methods and subjects of political history writ large, generally along one or more of the axes of state-economy, state-society, and state-subject—the fields of inquiry that encompass topics of political economy, political culture, power relations, public policy, and identity formation.

   1. *All boundaries are artificial.* In the 2002 anthology *Rethinking American History in a Global Age*, Thomas Bender took the unusual step of resurrecting Frederick Jackson Turner as a model for historical conceptualization across boundaries, based not on the infamous frontier thesis but on the lesser-known 1891 essay "The Significance of History." Turner wrote that in history, and therefore to historians, "there are only artificial divisions"—a manifesto for always analyzing "inextricably interconnected" forces across both time and space, for comparative thinking about all historical categories and chronological eras, because "each is needed to explain the others" and "local history can only be understood in the light of the history of the world." For Bender, historicizing both time and space requires a theoretical flexibility that bridges cultural studies and the social sciences "by being diligently empirical, accepting no artificial boundaries" as historians follow the flows of people, capital, commodities, and ideas "across national and other boundaries."[6] In this volume, Suleiman Osman's conceptualization of an alternative politics of scale questions scholarship that deploys categories of "*local, regional, national,* and *global* as if they were natural and fixed," instead emphasizing the "institutional and symbolic" features of political boundaries. Sarah Igo's exploration of Social Security similarly highlights

the always "unfixed boundary between state and society, public and private." All political boundaries are simultaneously real and imagined, permeable even if consequential, a give-and-take between the need for clarification and the inevitability of oversimplification. Attention to boundaries may well be unavoidable in order to bring coherence to our narratives and analytical frameworks, but political historians should always be explicit about the costs as well as the benefits and ultimately seek to transcend rather than reinforce artificial divisions.

2. *History operates along spectrums, not through binaries.* Locating and analyzing the categories and actors of political history along spectrums, rather than as oppositions, is critical to thinking comparatively and operationalizing the insight that all boundaries are fluid, contested, and distort even as they reveal. In the state-economy realm, the pervasive discourse about government "intervention" and (de)regulation, often linked to false binaries of activist liberalism and "free market" conservatism, obscures the more fundamental role of the state and the law in creating and managing capitalist markets, as David Freund argues in his work on both the monetary and housing sectors.[7] Other essays in this volume move across the borders of public and private, foreign and domestic, liberal and conservative—most notably in Osman's powerful insight that the reigning binary frameworks for assessing the political culture and political economy of the 1970s all depend on declension and/or polarization narratives that conceal key continuities across time and space. The spectrum approach to political history also reveals that on many fundamental policy issues during the twentieth century, the competing positions of mainstream conservatism and liberalism in the two-party system were much closer to one another, and to the priorities of corporations and racial capitalism, than to the ideologies and social movements of the progressive left. As Daniel HoSang observes in *Racial Propositions* (2010), a study of the consensus ideology of "political whiteness" in modern California, "no large gulf existed between so-called racial liberalism and racial conservatism. Both understood white racial power as an individual rather than structural and historical phenomenon."[8] A spectrum-based approach also avoids the simplified binaries of geographical region-centered arguments, such as the "singular causal variable" of how the segregationist Southern Democrats distorted American political development, in favor of comparative models that operate across time and space, expand beyond the black-white divide, and consider the local, national, transnational, and imperial dimensions of power and ideology.[9]

3. *Comparative analysis is essential.* Political historians should always provide comparative frameworks to assess the representativeness and portability of case studies, evaluate and when necessary modify causal arguments, and avoid reproducing the artificial boundaries and binary oppositions highlighted above. Notwithstanding the discursive turn, political history should continue to value the social science method of rigorous cost-benefit analysis of the geographic, temporal, and topical parameters of the research project—with the cautionary note that comparative frameworks in political science and historical sociology, with their tendency to valorize the European welfare state and the allegedly "independent" variable, often reproduce various exceptionalisms (e.g., Southern, American) and reinforce what William Novak has called the "myth of the weak American state."[10] Instead of overemphasizing contrasts, important recent work in political history (especially in cultural and ethnic studies) has examined patterns and flows across local, regional, and national boundaries and fruitfully compared the governance and experiences of racialized groups such as African Americans, Asian Americans, Mexican Americans, and imperial subjects. Impressive examples of comparative analysis in this volume include Cebul and Williams's emphasis on key commonalities between urban liberalism and Sunbelt conservatism, Andrew Kahrl's analysis of predatory taxation in Chicago as a subset of longtime and nationwide projects of racial capitalism and the administrative state, and Stuart Schrader's linkage of U.S. imperial power, the national security state, and urban policing and carceral practices on the home front. Robust comparative frameworks generally mitigate against reductionist causal arguments that attribute the complex processes of political development and policy formation to a limited set of historical actors and places or regions, or to partisan and ideological formations such as liberalism or conservatism, not to mention neoliberalism and individualism. Comparative analysis makes causal claims more precise and compelling.

4. *Periodization always shapes, and distorts, arguments.* The challenge to the organizing framework of sequential political orders issued in the introduction to this volume is at heart a call for more rigorous comparative analysis across time as well as space. The artificial boundaries of periodization unavoidably introduce distortions and simplifications, in large part because of the demands of narrative storytelling, but also because the deliberate selection of starting and ending points always shapes the causal arguments and especially the typically normative conclusions about culminations and legacies. In his influential meditation on periodization and

storytelling, William Cronon observes that historical narrative "inevitably sanctions some voices while silencing others," and "the historical analysis derives much of its force from the upward or downward sweep of the plot."[11] As the editors of *Shaped by the State* point out, the ascension and declension frameworks of the New Deal order and the rise of conservatism schools each centers the experiences of white subject categories— the unionized working-class male breadwinner and the middle-class suburban professional family. This narrow rendering of political history has led to unproductive debates about class politics versus identity politics and excessive attention to election cycles as historical turning points. The "rise of neoliberalism" metanarrative has the advantage of recasting liberal-conservative dualities but too often exaggerates the novelty of privatization in the 1970s and conflates state power for multinational corporations as the restoration of the (fictitious) "free market." The essays by N. D. B. Connolly and Julie Weise provide additional characters and offer chronological correctives to the neoliberal frame, as in terms of statecraft there was little new about hybrid public-private modes of governance dominated by corporate interests and racial capitalism, from railroad construction in the nineteenth century to urban renewal and housing markets in the post–World War II decades. Political historians should regularly justify and reassess the costs and consequences of their periodization schemes and be wary, as Osman warns, of "too clean a break from the past."

5. *Policy outcomes and modes of governance are never inherently liberal or conservative but rather are shaped by multiple forces across the political spectrum.* The tendency to define specific policy outcomes in partisan or ideological terms leads to analysis that reads those labels backward into history in ways that reproduce the binary and flatten the complexity of political processes. For sometimes competing and often overlapping reasons, political formations and historical actors from across the spectrum have supported regulation and deregulation, tax revolts, private property rights, racial segregation, formal legal equality, immigration control, national security, imperial power, law and order, selective drug wars, family values, high-tech panaceas, and much more. In the introduction's useful framing, these political contests reconstructed the cultural meanings of liberalism and conservatism but represented broader state interactions with the economy, society, and citizens or subjects—an insight reinforced by every essay in this volume. Vibrant examples of political history beyond the red-blue divide include the wide spectrum of localist, antistatist,

and globalist orientations in Osman's analysis; the long history of public-private cooperation on international refugee policy in Melissa Borja's account; and the gendered conflicts featured by Sarah Milov and Rachel Moran in their reinterpretations of the trajectory of the regulatory state. The broader takeaway is that modes of governance—such as centralization, localism, privatization, regulation and deregulation, associational-ism, imperialism, disciplinary projects, and so on—are themselves politically neutral and therefore can and do serve many different agendas and often intersecting purposes in American political development, policy formation, and identity formation on the ground.[12] Centering the state, capitalism, citizenship, governance, and law reveals that partisan conflict over legislative or executive branch policy making takes shape within broader structures of power, meaning, and historical development itself. Even if the two parties seem bitterly divided on, for example, health-care policy, the compromise outcome still has been shaped by a fusion of many interest groups and lobbies, ideas and structures of meaning, legal constraints, forces of consensus, and path-dependent processes.

6. *Polarization is shaped by political structures more than it is a reflection of public opinion.* The reigning thesis of a deeply polarized nation takes its cues from political science and popular journalism, which over-emphasize partisan conflict and ideological divisions and often understate the role of political structures and institutions. As with the liberal con-sensus school of midcentury, the polarization thesis has evolved into a hegemonic framework that reinforces artificial boundaries and locates policy formation and political conflict within binaries rather than along spectrums. The red-blue divide as imagined in the national election maps is a particularly simplistic way to split the United States into warring camps, given the winner-take-all nature of the undemocratic electoral college and the considerable malapportionment of the U.S. Senate in favor of small states and rural areas. Political polarization has increased by some mea-sures in recent decades, but less because of a deep ideological schism sepa-rating red and blue America, and more because of the extreme partisan gerrymandering in the U.S. House of Representatives and state legis-latures, the influence of interest groups and committed partisans in low-turnout primaries, and the legalization of unlimited corporate and plu-tocratic money in politics and therefore policy making. Even the Pew Research Center's documentary project on political polarization—labeled the "defining feature of American politics" in recent decades, the "vast and growing gap between liberals and conservatives, Republicans and

Democrats"—acknowledges that the ideologically committed wings represent a minority of public opinion, contrasted with a "center that is large and diverse, unified by frustration with politics and little else."[13] The two-party system is institutionally incapable of representing the policy preferences of many citizens—much more so than a multiparty parliamentary democracy, for example. Rather than taken as given, polarization itself should be historicized as a product of institutional development and structural forces to assess the causes and scope of partisan conflict with more precision.

7. *Consensus remains a useful concept, but when applied to specific topics not entire eras.* Polarization frameworks recede in explanatory power when the research agenda shifts from liberal-conservative plotlines to investigation of broader historical problems, such as the persistence and evolution of various forms of inequality, the disproportionate power of corporations under all regimes of modern governance, the relationship between capitalism and state formation, the projection of American power in the global arena, and the normative as well as legal boundaries of citizenship and exclusion. The polarization thesis that supplanted the liberal consensus model has highlighted partisan conflict and various backlashes, in the process marginalizing historical inquiry into aspects of political culture, political economy, and public policy shaped more by consensus ideologies along a truncated spectrum of the possible. Many of this volume's essays feature consensus politics in operation, deeply embedded in the history of capitalism and state development, including Connolly's genealogy of racialized private property rights, Cebul and Williams's examination of New Deal national-local growth partnerships, Freund's analysis of the widespread acceptance of federal transformation of the banking sector and monetary policy, Weise's reminder of the centrality of exploitable migrant labor to the American (indeed global) economy, and Schrader's account of a national security-oriented "consensus that would guide the reconfiguration of governance that the carceral state embodies." A consensus sensibility reorients assessments that mainstream liberalism turned rightward or found itself co-opted by law-and-order conservatism on the road to mass incarceration—instead recognizing that disciplinary projects of social and racial control have long been central to both political traditions, as subsets of American state building and imperial processes. Partisan affiliation does not define public opinion or policy continuities on a significant number of topics, and for many others even the "polarized" conflict takes place within broader structures of consensus forged by state-building processes, capitalist development, and not least cultural structures of meaning.

8. *Culture is also a structural force in American political history.* I started and ended the most recent version of my New Political History graduate seminar with books by Daniel Rodgers, to illuminate how insights of cultural and intellectual history offer alternative models of periodization and historical causation by focusing on the circulation of ideas and consequent shifts in structures of perception and meaning. *Atlantic Crossings* (1998) argues that policy formation in the Progressive and New Deal eras depended on conceptual breakthroughs that "denaturalize[d] the 'laws' of economics," based on a model that transnational flows of ideas can "transform a tragic but incurable condition into a politically solvable problem."[14] *Age of Fracture* (2011) brilliantly transcends the current historiographical wars over the 1970s, and plotlines of red-blue partisan warfare, with a method attuned to the "intellectual construction of reality" through transformations in dominant "conceptions of human nature" and metaphors to understand the state, economy, society, and experience.[15] Sarah Igo's chapter in this volume similarly charts the shift in the meaning of social "security" from a new marker of state protection and economic citizenship in the 1930s to a symbol of popular distrust of state surveillance and control by the 1960s and 1970s, "voiced by groups on both the left and right" in a popular political culture broadly skeptical of political institutions and technologies of power. Scholars of ethnic studies and transnational accounts of U.S. empire also have played a major role in connecting state-centered scholarship to cultural history's formative insights that identity has been "a central object of political struggle" and of the "construction of normative categories as a fundamentally political process."[16] Political historians who study grassroots actors and social movements tend to trace how the structures of political economy and public policy produce and reshape local cultures and identities, but the American studies–influenced scholarship also demonstrates the deeply embedded structures of culture in state processes, policy formation, and knowledge production.

9. *Modern American political history encompasses the "United States in the World."* Recent scholarship in many subfields has located the twentieth-century United States in more expansive contexts through the subjects and methods of transnational, international, and global history. In American studies, cultural historians of empire have urged scholars to conceptualize their projects "against the naturalized frame of the nation" and recognize that "the boundaries of the 'domestic' are illusory and ideological." These powerful insights recognize the ubiquity of governance technologies of legal "states of exception" inside and outside national

borders, position even the private family as an explicitly transnational site of analysis, and have demonstrated that domestic and imperial strategies of racial segregation and uplift converged in the Jim Crow South, Native American reservations, Mexican American barrios, Asian American enclaves, and imperial encounters.[17] In Paul Kramer's parallel move beyond the domestic-foreign and black-white binaries, "racialized power" has operated along a spectrum of "absolutizing to civilizing modes" that incorporates both conservative and liberal traditions of capitalist governance, in contrast to antiracist and anti-imperial visions.[18] The customary divide between domestic politics and foreign relations in twentieth-century U.S. history has reinforced many of the artificial boundaries and binaries challenged in this volume, whereas conceptual models attentive to broad spectrums and border crossings will help interpret "every dimension of American life as entangled in other histories."[19] The revisionist value of transnational methods and international topics can be found in Julie Weise's analysis of labor rights and citizenship status across the U.S.-Mexico border and Stuart Schrader's foregrounding of imperial practices in the development of domestic urban policing. As a rule, even if the empirical research base is necessarily contained, political historians can and should develop more capacious comparative frameworks that reassess domestic topics in transnational, international, and global contexts.

10. *Against exceptionalisms.* Every proposition in this list involves either an explicit rejection of exceptionalist frameworks or a methodological and conceptual approach that will inhibit their deployment. It is important to note that there is a fundamental difference between empirical evidence of distinctiveness—the presence of unique characteristics in every individual, case study, and process—and exceptionalist narratives that portray one nation (or region) as "not simply different from all others . . . [but] a deviation from a rule." Social scientists, in particular, have assessed American political economy and state development against an idealized version of the European welfare state, as William Novak and Daniel Rodgers have critiqued.[20] Political historians then often applied these insights through monocausal arguments about black-white racism (lacking multiracial and imperial comparisons), the ideology of individualism (without attention to contingencies of law and political structure), or Southern exceptionalism (an essential foundation of the myth of American exceptionalism). Intellectual and cultural historians have shown that popular and scholarly narratives of American exceptionalism flourish in times of national crisis connected to perceptual shifts about the United States on the world stage,

such as celebrations of the "American way of life" in the politically constructed consensus ideology of the early Cold War years and the post–September 11 acknowledgment of the imperial responsibilities facing a lone superpower. In Rodgers's useful formulation, the exceptionalist narrative is "an easy and reflexive category of analysis" that "highlights the intense contrasts of the moment" by ignoring connections across political (or otherwise-constructed) boundaries and silencing inconvenient voices and processes.[21] Like polarization tropes, exceptionalist narratives are embedded in structures of cultural meaning, produced by binaries rather than spectrums, operationalized through artificial boundaries, retreats from transnational and global history, and a misapplication of comparative analysis. They are also, always, unconvincing.

Notes

1. Matthew D. Lassiter, "Political History Beyond the Red-Blue Divide," *Journal of American History* (December 2011): 760–64.

2. Kenneth T. Jackson, *Crabgrass Frontier: The Suburbanization of the United States* (New York: Oxford University Press, 1985); Thomas J. Sugrue, *The Origins of the Urban Crisis: Race and Inequality in Postwar Detroit* (Princeton, NJ: Princeton University Press, 1996); Robert O. Self, *American Babylon: Race and the Struggle for Postwar Oakland* (Princeton, NJ: Princeton University Press, 2003); Matthew D. Lassiter, *The Silent Majority: Suburban Politics in the Sunbelt South* (Princeton, NJ: Princeton University Press, 2006), 7–8; David M. P. Freund, *Colored Property: State Policy and White Racial Politics in Suburban America* (Chicago: University of Chicago Press, 2007), 41. For a more recent example, see Lily Geismer, *Don't Blame Us: Suburban Liberals and the Transformation of the Democratic Party* (Princeton, NJ: Princeton University Press, 2014). For urban and suburban case studies that do emphasize "right turn" and "rise of conservatism" frameworks, see Lisa McGirr, *Suburban Warriors: The Origins of the New American Right* (Princeton, NJ: Princeton University Press, 2001); Kevin M. Kruse, *White Flight: Atlanta and the Making of Modern Conservatism* (Princeton, NJ: Princeton University Press, 2005).

3. Naomi Murakawa, *The First Civil Right: How Liberals Built Prison America* (New York: Oxford University Press, 2014); Elizabeth Hinton, *From the War on Poverty to the War on Crime: The Making of Mass Incarceration in America* (Cambridge, MA: Harvard University Press, 2016); Julilly Kohler-Hausmann, *Getting Tough: Welfare and Imprisonment in 1970s America* (Princeton, NJ: Princeton University Press, 2017); Matthew D. Lassiter, *The Suburban Crisis: Crime, Drugs, and White Middle-Class America* (Princeton, NJ: Princeton University Press, forthcoming). For the traditional view, see Vesla M. Weaver, "Frontlash: Race and the Development

of Punitive Crime Policy," *Studies in American Political Development* (Fall 2007): 230–65; Katherine Beckett, *Making Crime Pay: Law and Order in Contemporary American Politics* (New York: Oxford University Press, 1999).

4. See, for example, Barack Obama, "Remarks at International Association of Chiefs of Police Annual Conference," October 27, 2015, American Presidency Project, http://www.presidency.ucsb.edu/ws/index.php?pid=110995; Office of National Drug Control Policy, *National Drug Control Strategy 2010*, https://obamawhitehouse .archives.gov/sites/default/files/ondcp/policy-and-research/ndcs2010.pdf.

5. In particular, see the books published by the University of California Press in the American Crossroads series, at http://www.ucpress.edu/series.php?ser=ac.

6. Thomas Bender, "Historians, the Nation, and the Plenitude of Narratives," in Bender, ed., *Rethinking American History in a Global Age* (Berkeley: University of California Press, 2002), 1–21; Frederick Jackson Turner, "The Significance of History" (1891), http://teachingamericanhistory.org/library/document/the-signifi cance-of-history/.

7. Freund, *Colored Property*.

8. Daniel HoSang, *Racial Propositions: Ballot Initiatives and the Making of Postwar California* (Berkeley: University of California Press, 2010), 86.

9. Kimberly S. Johnson, "Race and the Study of American Politics," in *The Oxford Handbook of American Political Development*, ed. Richard M. Valelly, Suzanne Mettler, and Robert C. Lieberman (New York: Oxford University Press, 2016), 597.

10. William J. Novak, "The Myth of the Weak American State," *American Historical Review* (June 2008): 752–72.

11. William Cronon, "A Place for Stories: Nature, History, and Narrative," *Journal of American History* (March 1992): 1348, 1350.

12. Brian Balogh, *The Associational State: American Governance in the Twentieth Century* (Philadelphia: University of Pennsylvania Press, 2015).

13. Pew Research Center, "Political Polarization," http://www.pewresearch .org/packages/political-polarization/.

14. Daniel T. Rodgers, *Atlantic Crossings: Social Politics in a Progressive Age* (Cambridge, MA: Harvard University Press, 1998), 6.

15. Rodgers, *Age of Fracture* (Cambridge, MA: Harvard University Press, 2011), 2–3.

16. James W. Cook and Lawrence B. Glickman, "Twelve Propositions for a History of U.S. Cultural History," in *The Cultural Turn in U.S. History: Past, Present, Future*, ed. James W. Cook, Lawrence B. Glickman, and Martin O'Malley (Chicago: University of Chicago Press, 2008), 3–39 (their introduction also inspired the title of this essay).

17. Laura Briggs, Gladys McCormick, and J. T. Way, "Transnationalism: A Category of Analysis," *American Quarterly* (September 2008): 625–48; also see the special issue edited by Mary L. Dudziak and Leti Volpp, "Legal Borderlands:

Law and the Construction of American Borders," *American Quarterly* (September 2005).

18. Paul A. Kramer, "Shades of Sovereignty: Racialized Power, the United States and the World," in *Explaining the History of American Foreign Relations*, 3rd ed., ed. Frank Costigliola and Michael J. Hogan (New York: Cambridge University Press, 2016), 245–70.

19. Bender, "Historians, the Nation, and the Plenitude of Narratives," 6.

20. Novak, "Myth of the Weak American State"; Rodgers, *Atlantic Crossings*; Daniel T. Rodgers, "American Exceptionalism Revisited," *Raritan* (Fall 2004): 21–47, quote on 23.

21. Wendy Wall, *Inventing the "American Way": The Politics of Consensus from the New Deal to the Civil Rights Movement* (New York: Oxford University Press, 2008); Rodgers, "American Exceptionalism Revisited."

Contributors

MELISSA BORJA is an assistant professor in the Department of American Culture at the University of Michigan. She is completing a book about the impact of United States resettlement policy on refugee religious life.

BRENT CEBUL is assistant professor of history at the University of Pennsylvania. He is the author of *Illusions of Progress: Business, Poverty, and Development in the American Century* (University of Pennsylvania Press, forthcoming).

N. D. B. CONNOLLY is the Herbert Baxter Adams Associate Professor of History at Johns Hopkins University and author of *A World More Concrete: Real Estate and the Remaking of Jim Crow South Florida* (University of Chicago Press, 2014), which received 2015 Liberty Legacy Foundation Book Award from the Organization of American Historians and the 2014 Kenneth T. Jackson Book Award from the Urban History Association. He is currently working on two new projects, *Four Daughters: An America Story* and *Black Capitalism: The "Negro Problem" and the American Economy*.

DAVID M. P. FREUND, associate professor of history at the University of Maryland, is the author of *Colored Property: State Policy and White Racial Politics in Suburban America* (University of Chicago Press, 2007), which was awarded the 2008 Ellis W. Hawley Prize from the Organization of American Historians, the 2007 Kenneth Jackson Book Award from the Urban History Association, and the 2009 Urban Affairs Association Best Book Award. He is currently completing *State Money*, a history of financial policy and free-market ideology in the modern United States.

LILY GEISMER is associate professor of history at Claremont McKenna College and the author of *Don't Blame Us: Suburban Liberals and the Transformation of the*

Democratic Party (Princeton University Press, 2015). She is currently working on a new project that examines the promotion of market-based solutions to problems of social inequality since the 1960s.

SARAH IGO, associate professor of history and director of the Program in American Studies at Vanderbilt University. She is the author of *The Averaged American: Surveys, Citizens, and the Making of a Mass Public* (Harvard University Press, 2007), which was an Editor's Choice selection of the *New York Times* and one of *Slate*'s Best Books of 2007, as well as winner of the President's Book Award of the Social Science History Association and the Cheiron Book Prize. Her new book is *The Known Citizen: A History of Privacy in Modern America* (Harvard University Press, 2018).

ANDREW KAHRL, associate professor of history at the University of Virginia, is the author of *Free the Beaches: The Story of Ned Coll and the Battle for America's Most Exclusive Shoreline* (Yale University Press, 2018) and *The Land Was Ours: African American Beaches from Jim Crow to the Sunbelt South* (Harvard University Press, 2012), winner of the 2013 Liberty Legacy Foundation Award from the Organization of American Historians.

MATTHEW D. LASSITER is Arthur F. Thurnau Professor of History and Urban and Regional Planning at the University of Michigan. He is the author of *The Silent Majority: Suburban Politics in the Sunbelt South* (Princeton University Press, 2006), winner of the 2007 Lillian Smith Award presented by the Southern Regional Council. He is the coeditor of *The Myth of Southern Exceptionalism* (Oxford University Press, 2009) and *The Moderates' Dilemma: Massive Resistance to School Desegregation in Virginia* (University of Virginia Press, 1998). He is currently completing a book titled *The Suburban Crisis: The Pursuit and Defense of the American Dream* (Princeton University Press).

SARAH MILOV is assistant professor of history at the University of Virginia. Her current book project, titled *Smoke and Ashes: From Corporatism to Neoliberalism in Tobacco's Twentieth Century* (under contract at Harvard University Press), examines how American tobacco farmers have shaped the economic, legal, and cultural significance of the cigarette.

RACHEL LOUISE MORAN is assistant professor of history at the University of North Texas. She is the author of *Governing Bodies: American Politics and the Shaping of the Modern Physique* (University of Pennsylvania Press, 2018).

SULEIMAN OSMAN, associate professor of American studies at George Washington University, is the author of *The Invention of Brownstone Brooklyn: Gentrification and the Search for Authenticity in Postwar New York* (Oxford University Press, 2011). The book received the Hornblower Prize from the New York Society Library.

KIM PHILLIPS-FEIN is an associate professor at the Gallatin School of Individualized Study at New York University. She is the author of *Invisible Hands: The Making of the Conservative Movement from the New Deal to Reagan* (W. W. Norton, 2009) and *Fear City: New York's Fiscal Crisis and the Rise of Austerity Politics* (Metropolitan Books, 2017), a finalist for the Pulitzer Prize for History.

STUART SCHRADER is a lecturer in Africana studies and assistant research scientist in sociology at Johns Hopkins University. He is completing a book titled *American Streets, Foreign Territory: How Counterinsurgent Police Waged War on Crime* (University of California Press).

JULIE WEISE, associate professor of history at the University of Oregon, is the author of *Corazón de Dixie: Mexicanos in the U.S. South since 1910* (University of North Carolina Press, 2015), which won the 2016 Merle Curti Award for best book in U.S. social history from the Organization of American Historians and was cowinner of the CLR James book award from the Working Class Studies Association (2016). Her next project, *Citizenship Displaced: Migrant Political Cultures in the Era of State Control*, explores diverse migrant workers' political consciousness and relationships to origin and destination states in the post–World War II period.

MASON B. WILLIAMS is an assistant professor of political science and leadership at Williams College. He is the author of *City of Ambition: FDR, La Guardia, and the Making of Modern New York* (W. W. Norton, 2013), which was named a *New York Times Book Review* Editor's Choice. He is working on a book examining the politics of schools, policing, and housing in late twentieth-century New York.

Index

Aaron, Henry, 196, 197
ABC-TV, 234
Abraham, Itty, 48
Action for Children's Television, 320, 322, 324
Action on Smoking and Health (ASH), 220, 224, 225, 231, 235
addiction, 236, 288, 316n56, 320
administrative state, 27, 368
advertising, 40, 219, 317, 319–25, 327–29, 335, 340n57
affirmative action, 85–87, 220
AFL-CIO, 39, 229, 321
Africa, 265
African Americans, 39, 63, 79, 87, 298, 299, 358, 368; as activists, 69, 177, 243, 244, 246, 252, 254; and black freedom movement, 68, 293, 351; and the carceral state, 16, 292, 297–99, 308; and Emancipation, 164, 165, 166, 177, 191; and governance, 78, 83, 189, 193, 195, 247; history of, 9, 242, 292, 364; and liberalism, 13, 62–63, 65–67, 70, 71, 74, 76, 80, 81–82, 84, 86, 162, 248, 250; and migration to northern cities, 107, 166, 176, 177, 191, 352; the New Deal, 29, 30, 33, 34, 37, 38, 47, 66, 75, 76, 77; as property owners, taxpayers, and tenants, 15, 78, 190–207, 211; as workers, 75, 165, 168, 169, 175, 176, 177. *See also* agricultural laborers; antiracism; Black Power; Jim Crow; race; white privilege; white supremacy
Agency for International Development (AID), 301, 304, 306

Agnew, Spiro, 329
Agricultural Adjustment Act, 75
agricultural laborers, 14, 84, 172, 179; exclusion of from New Deal, 30, 74, 118n18, 162–64, 176, 180. *See also* Bracero program; sharecroppers; Southern Tenant Farmers Union (STFU); undocumented workers
Alabama, 66, 83, 102, 104
Alexandria, VA, 243
Alinsky, Saul, 198
Allard, A. Wayne, 332–33
Allegheny Conference on Community Development (Pittsburgh), 113
alt-right, 6
American Academy of Pediatrics, 327
American Advertising Federation, 327
American Bankers Association (ABA), 129, 130, 154n23
American Cancer Society, 219, 226
American Civil Liberties Union (ACLU), 232, 365
American Council of Nationalities Service, 271
American Dental Association, 321
American Enterprise Institute's Center for the Study of Government Regulation, 324
American exceptionalism, 6, 82, 252, 373–74
American Lung Association, 219, 227, 230
American Refugee Committee, 268, 269
American Revolution, 150n1, 242, 348
American Revolution Bicentennial Administration, 242

Ames, Jessie Daniel, 72–73
Anslinger, Harry, 305, 316n56
anticommunism, 5, 68, 290, 296, 302–3, 318
antiracism, 68, 83, 326, 373
antistatism, 11, 31, 97, 100, 244, 253, 255, 317, 326, 369
antiwar activism, 242, 328, 351
Appalachian Regional Commission, 112
Area Planning and Development Commissions (GA), 113
Aristotle, 142
Arizona, 167
Arkansas, 66, 162, 166–75, 177, 180, 182n27
Arkansas Delta, 14, 162, 164, 176, 179
Arkansas State Employment Office, 174
Arlington Park Race Track, 200
asbestos, 229–30
Asia, 252, 265, 316n56
Asian Americans, 368, 373
associational state, 8, 103, 108, 117n11, 263, 370
Association of Southern Women for the Prevention of Lynching (ASWPL), 73
AT&T, 220, 237n5
Atlanta, GA, 28, 37, 79, 105, 111, 178, 196
Atlanta Constitution, 40–41, 43
Atlantic Charter, 67
Atomic Energy Commission, 111
Attica State Prison rebellion, 307–8
Atuahene, Bernadette, 190, 210
Augusta, GA, 97, 111
austerity, 86, 102, 109, 189, 255, 356
Austin, TX, 255

Baker, Ella, 10, 22
Baltimore, MD, 40, 113, 197, 298
Banking Act of 1935, 14, 138, 146, 151n4
banking sector, 123, 125, 132, 371
bankruptcy, 47, 113, 189
Ban Vinai refugee camp, 269
Banzhaf, John, 226, 231, 232, 234, 235
Baptists, 274, 279. See also religion
Baruch, Bernard, 139
Bay Area Council (San Francisco), 113
Bell System, 234
Bennett, James V., 304–5
Berkeley, CA, 245, 305
Berrios, Joseph, 210
Bethlehem Lutheran Church, 273
Bethune, Mary McLeod, 73, 76

Big Brother state, 33, 318, 320, 336n7
big government, 8, 17, 126, 163, 246, 254, 317, 322, 326, 330, 333, 336, 351. *See also* antistatism; nanny state
Big Tobacco, 229, 236
Bill of Rights, 224
blacklisting, 173–74, 176
black nationalism, 255
Black Panther Party, 255
Black Power, 194, 244–45, 293
black sites, 294
Black Taxpayers' Federation, 203–4
Bloomberg, Michael, 333, *334*
Blumrosen, Alfred, 231–32, 239n34
Boas, Franz, 169
bonds (fiscal policy), 124, 128–30, 132–36, 139, 144–45, 147, 155n32, 159n77, 190
Booth, Paul, 200
Border Patrol, 10, 300
Boston, MA, 30–31, 113, 196–97, 230, 242, 243, 254, 320, 324
Boston Women's Health Book Collective, 254
Bracero program, 10, 14–15, 168–77, 179–80
Brazil, 28, 301, 304
Breen, Stanley, 268
Bretton Woods, 251, 252
Bridgeton, NJ, 223, 228
Bronander, Roy, 174–76
Broward County, FL, 83
Brown v. Board of Education, 63, 74, 80, 87
Buckley, William F., 83
Buddhism, 253, 265, 280, 282
Bureau of Consumer Protection, U.S., 335
Bureau of Indian Affairs, U.S., 169
Bureau of Labor Statistics, U.S., 45
Bureau of Narcotics and Dangerous Drug, U.S., 300
Bureau of Refugee Programs, U.S., 268
Bureau of Social Science Research, 301
Burgess, W. Randolph, 147
Burlington, VT, 245
Byrne, Jane, 201, 208

Caballero Calderón, Dagoberto, 163, 170
Cabrini-Green housing project, 210
Cadell, Patrick, 253–54
California, 46, 110, 111, 167, 206, 289, 320, 367
Calumet Township, IN, 193–95
Cambodia, 261–62, 275, 280–81

Campaign against Pollution (CAP), 198–200, 205

Campbell Soup, 234

Camp Concern, 298

Cano del Castillo, Ángel, 163, 170, 172–76

capital accumulation, 192, 208, 353

capitalism, 3, 6, 125, 163, 172, 245, 250, 348, 350, 354, 370; concerns over the viability of, 350, 353; history of, 3, 17, 18n3, 248, 371; and race, 7, 64–67, 70, 78, 255, 363, 367, 368, 369

carceral state, 6, 289–310, 316n56, 358, 371; influence of Japan on, 289–91, 294, 305–6; race and gender hierarchies of, 292, 295, 297; scholarship on, 7, 16, 291–95, 297, 308–10, 365; and Vietnam War, 291, 298–99, 302, 305, 309; and War on Poverty, 293, 297–99, 301. See also Cold War; imperialism; law enforcement; national security state

Cárdenas, Lázaro, 169

Caribbean, 67

Carter, Jimmy, 253, 261–62, 280–81, 318, 320, 322, 324, 328–29

Catholic Bulletin, 274

Catholic Charities, 268, 271, 276, 280

Catholicism, 33, 53n37, 201, 265, 272–73, 275, 279–80

Catholic Relief Services, 269

Cedartown, GA, 59n110, 178

Census, U.S., 27, 30–31, 44–45, 50n6, 61n124

Center for Science in the Public Interest (CSPI), 320, 322

central banking, 123–25, 132–34, 136, 139, 143, 147

Central Intelligence Agency (CIA), 304, 306, 310n3

Chamberlain, Lawrence, 128, 147

Chamber of Commerce, U.S., 101, 102

chambers of commerce: Augusta, GA, 97; Liberty, TX, 97; New Orleans, LA, 108; Phoenix, AZ, 105; Portland, OR, 108; Seattle, WA, 104

Charitable Choice laws, 264

Charter of the United Nations, 306

Chase Economic Bulletin, 137

Chase Economic Review, 138

Chase Manhattan Bank, 138, 234

Chicago, IL, 78, 104–7, 198–210, 215n48, 217n72, 314n33, 368

Chicago Council on Foreign Relations, 253

Chicago Daily Tribune, 34

Chicago Defender, 39, 75, 208

Chicago Transportation Authority (CTA), 201

Chicago Tribune, 209–10

Chicago Urban League, 207

Chile, 307, 360n8

Christian and Missionary Alliance, 269

Christian Connection Center, 273

Christ Lutheran Church, 276

Churchill, Winston, 67

church-state partnership, 262–82. See also refugee resettlement; voluntary agencies

Church World Service (CWS), 270–71, 274, 277

citizen and state, 326

citizenship, 7–10, 15, 17, 18n3, 110, 221, 235, 348, 366, 370, 371; of African Americans, 77–78, 106, 177; and Mexican immigration, 10, 164, 169–70, 177–79, 373; and social security, 13, 38, 48, 372

Civil Aeronautics Board (CAB), 219

Civilian Works Administration (CWA), 75, 96

civil rights, 75, 83, 191, 202, 220, 297, 318, 352, 364

Civil Rights Act of 1964, 87

Civil Rights Act of 1983, 207

civil rights movement, 10, 13, 64–66, 76, 82, 87, 104, 105, 164, 179, 222, 237n6, 252, 291, 293, 351

Civil War, U.S., 132, 135

class, 5, 8, 11, 12, 30, 38, 68, 69, 73, 107, 110, 180, 244–45, 248, 369; and ideas about the nanny state, 325, 327, 331; and Mexicans, 164, 165, 167, 170; and middle-class African Americans, 69, 79; neoliberalism and politics of, 352–53, 359; and smoking, 224–25, 228, 235, 236; white homeowners as middle-, 192–93, 197, 204, 206, 208, 209. See also agricultural laborers; domestic workers; white workers; working women

Clean Air Act, 226

Clearing the Air at Work, 233, 235

Cleveland, OH, 104–5, 108, 139

Clifton, NJ, 235

Clinton, Bill, 86, 331–33, 351–52, 356

Clinton, Hillary, 95n106, 331–33

Coalition to End Unconstitutional Tax Foreclosures, 210

Cobb County, GA, 114–15

Cold War, 267, 281, 296, 307, 311n9, 331, 374; and carceral state, 298, 305, 307; end of, 349, 353; and liberalism, 246, 248, 252; and the national security state, 281; and race, 67–68, 85, 250

collateral, 14, 124–26, 128–34, 137, 138, 140, 146–49

collective bargaining, 221, 227–30, 302

Colombia, 307

Colorado, 37, 332

Columbia University, 125

Columbus, OH, 104, 280

Combahee River Collective, 254

Commager, Henry Steele, 241–42, 256n1

commercial bankers or banking, 128, 129, 134, 135, 138, 140, 160n77

commercial paper, 128–30, 133, 136–38, 147, 149, 154n25

Committee on Civil Rights, 83

Communications Workers of America (CWA), 218, 227–29, 231, 234

communism, 350

Communist Party, U.S., 10

Community Action Programs (CAPs), 84

Confederate States of America, 132

Congressional Wives Taskforce, 330

conservatism, 7, 14, 116n5, 118n21, 172, 191, 270, 371; and deregulation, 236, 333; and fiscal policy, 125, 126, 149, 151n6, 152n8, 352, 367; and neoliberalism, 13, 17, 77, 243, 349–51; opposition of to liberalism, 318, 319, 322, 325, 328, 329; rise of, 4–6, 64, 97, 114–15, 244, 245, 246, 254, 294, 355–56, 363–65, 369; scholarship of, 6, 18n7, 18n21, 20n15, 97, 119n34, 369; shift in meaning of the term, 81, 85, 95n106; Sunbelt, 13, 97, 99, 108, 368; and support for carceral state, 296, 308. See also free-market economics; law-and-order politics; liberalism-conservatism paradigm; neoconservatism; New Right

Constitution, U.S., 66, 74

consumer economy, 9, 17

consumerism, 248, 252, 358

consumer rights and activism, 98, 107, 194, 232, 246, 319–21, 326, 328, 332

consumption, 6, 139, 141, 324

contingency, historical, 8, 62, 64, 164, 180, 250, 298, 373

continuity, historical, 6–9, 11–13, 15–17, 21n21, 62, 66, 119n27, 248, 290, 296, 359, 365–67, 371

Cook County, IL, 198–99, 201, 203–5, 207–10, 214n31, 217n72

Coordinating Committee (Boston), 113

Copenhagen, 253

corporate relocation, 194, 195, 208

corruption, 78, 193, 194

Cose, Ellis, 254

council wars (Chicago), 208

counterinsurgency, 298

credit, 28, 41, 45, 46, 125, 127, 130, 135, 137–40, 143–49, 152n11, 153n19, 155n38, 156n41, 157nn51–52, 159n69, 160n79, 160n82, 161n83, 190, 331

crime, 7, 78, 195, 365. See also carceral state; law-and-order politics; law enforcement; mass incarceration; War on Crime

crisis, 16, 17, 164, 299, 329; Detroit foreclosure crisis, 189–90, 210; Gary budget crisis, 193–95; Great Depression as, 29, 124, 129–30, 138, 140, 143, 150; of liberalism, 358; mass incarceration as, 16, 289, 298; and Mexico's "Lost Decade," 178; narratives or paradigms of, 4–6, 10, 12–13, 15–17, 359, 365, 373; neoliberalism as of the white working class, 13; the 1970s as a period of, 15, 109, 244, 248, 251, 356, 363; scalar, 250–51, 255; urban crisis, 9, 109, 211. See also Gary, IN; Great Depression; refugee resettlement

cultural history, 4, 11, 372

currency, 14, 123–25, 127, 130–35, 138, 139, 145, 146, 148–49, 150n1, 154n26, 160n82

"currency" or "quantity" theory of banking, 126, 140, 141–43, 145, 146, 150

Currie, Lauchlin, 143–46, 159n69

Customs Service, U.S., 300

Daley, Richard J., 121n50, 201, 215n48

Daley, Richard M., 208

Dallas, TX, 97, 113, 230

Dallas Citizens' Council, 113

data, 29, 30, 32, 34, 35, 45–49, 54n45, 193, 226, 249, 302. See also privacy; surveillance

Davis, Bette, 39

debt, 14, 66, 67, 124, 126–38, 140, 146–49, 151n3, 158n66, 159n69, 160n79, 189, 202

declension narratives, 243, 244, 247, 251, 293, 367, 369. *See also* "rise and fall" narratives

decolonization, 68

defense economy, 105, 110, 111, 112, 113, 121n58, 290, 307

deflation, 142

deindustrialization, 109, 195, 236, 358

democracy, 7, 12–15, 17, 21n19, 117n6, 221, 348, 371; and neoliberalism, 115, 349, 354; and New Deal federalism, 98, 102, 104, 105–7, 110, 250; racial contradictions of, 64, 67–68, 71, 86, 89n14, 293

Democratic Party: and African Americans, 65, 68, 74, 76, 162–63; as a coalition, 163, 296; and liberalism, 68, 85, 152n8; and neoliberalism, 351–52; and rhetoric around regulation, 318, 320, 321, 324, 329, 331, 332; southern wing of, 46, 51n18, 64, 65, 68, 75, 81, 84, 85, 163, 172, 176, 367; as urban machine, 201, 207, 208. *See also* red-blue divide

Department of Agriculture, U.S., 169, 331

Department of Health, Education, and Welfare, U.S., 220, 270

Department of Health and Human Services, U.S., 270

Department of Housing and Urban Development, U.S., 195, 197

Department of Justice, U.S., 309

Department of Labor, U.S., 298

Department of State, U.S., 268

Department of the Navy, U.S., 74

Department of Treasury, U.S., 52n26, 53n36, 54n45, 123–24, 127–29, 131–38, 146, 147, 150n1, 154n4

deregulation, 245, 246, 324, 326, 367, 369, 370; as neoliberal policy, 8, 86, 354, 358

desegregation, 63, 78, 80, 87, 293

Detroit, MI, 113, 189, 190, 210

Detroit Renaissance, 113

devolution, 97, 248, 254

Dewey, John, 169

Dinkins, David, 115

Displaced Persons Act of 1948, 267

Dobson, James, 329

Doctors without Borders, 253

domestic workers, 30, 51n19, 74, 84, 163, 172, 173, 176, 183

Dominican Republic, 307

Drug Enforcement Administration, U.S., 300

DuPont, 111, 234

Durham, NC, 70, 76

Eastland, James, 75, 85

Eccles, Marriner, 146

economic collectivism, 221

economic depression, 8, 12, 29, 74

economic redistribution, 15, 70, 169, 355

economic rights, 37, 40, 165

Ecuador, 307

Eisenhower, Dwight, 307

Election of 1936, 30, 36, 76

electoral malapportionment, 105, 370

Emanuel, Rahm, 208

Emergency Banking Act of 1933, 138

enganchadores (labor recruitment agencies), 166, 167

England, 318

England, AR, 175

enterprise zones, 246

Environmental Defense Fund, 226

Environmental Improvement Associates (EIA), 234, 235

environmentalism, 222, 226, 231, 243, 247, 248, 249, 252, 253; and regulation, 198, 225, 333

Environmental Protection Agency (EPA), 225, 226

Episcopal Migration Ministries, 274

Epton, Bernard, 208

Equal Employment Opportunity Commission, 231

Ervin, Sam J., Jr., 46, 47

evangelical Christians, 244, 245, 253, 260n30, 264–66, 269, 270, 280. *See also* religion

Evanston, IL, 202

Expendable Americans, 229

Fadell, Tom, 193, 194

Fair Assessments for Beverly, 199, 200

Fair Deal, 252

fair employment laws, 79, 83, 85, 98, 106

Fair Labor Standards Act, 162

FAIR v. McNary, 207

family, 67, 84, 168, 176, 189–91, 193, 202, 210, 261, 369, 373; and neoliberalism, 354, 357, 361n20; and the state, 318–27, 329–32, 335–36. *See also* nanny state; refugee resettlement

fascism, 67, 206, 350

Federal Bureau of Investigation (FBI), 27, 35, 300, 302, 306

Federal Bureau of Prisons, U.S., 304

Federal Council on Negro Affairs, 76

Federal Emergency Relief Administration, 75

Federal Employment Practices Commission, 68

Federal Housing Administration (FHA), U.S., 74

federalism, 13–14, 97, 99, 101, 105, 106, 108, 111, 112, 114–15, 116n5, 249–50

Federal Open Market Investment Committee, 137

Federal Reserve, 45, 123–26, 129–39, 143–48, 150, 150n1, 154n26, 159n73

Federal Reserve Act of 1913, 123, 125, 131–34, 138, 145, 154n26

Federal Reserve Board, 45, 138

Federal Trade Commission (FTC), 17, 317–25, 327–30, 335

Federal Trade Commission Improvements Act of 1980, 324

feminism, 9, 10, 222, 243, 244, 245, 247, 248, 250, 252–54, 326, 333, 336n6, 351. *See also* gender; working women

"fiat currency," 137, 149

Fifth Circuit Court of Appeals, 230

financialization, 8, 160n82, 355

Fine, William, 289–91, 294, 306, 307, 310n1

Finney, Leon, 207, 208

First National Bank, 200

Fish, Hamilton, 268

Fisher, Irving, 142, 143

Florida, 43, 68, 69, 77, 80, 83, 84, 234

Florsheim, Milton, 139

Florsheim Shoe Company, 139

Focus on the Family, 329

Food and Drug Administration (FDA), 319, 320

Ford, Gerald, 242, 243

Fordism, 9

foreclosure, 76, 189, 190, 191, 210

Foreign Affairs, 67

Foreign Intelligence Advisory Board, 307

foreign policy, U.S., 252, 253, 290–93, 294. *See also* imperialism

Fortune magazine, 125

Foucault, Michel, 50n11, 352, 354

France, 28, 309

Franken, Mark, 272, 280

Franklin, John Hope, 87

free enterprise system, 123, 124, 132, 143

Free Finnish Mission, 269

free-market economics, 246, 347; and conservatism, 114, 367; and neoliberalism, 255–56, 353–56, 358, 360n12, 369; and New Deal, 5, 12, 14, 150

Friedman, Milton, 148, 350

Friends of the Earth, 253

Frum, David, 245

Fulbright, J. William, 174

Gadsden, AL, 102

Gainesville, GA, 178

Galbraith, John Kenneth, 135

Gary, IN, 193–95, 245

Gathings, E. C., 172, 174

gender, 11, 15, 292, 366, 370; inequality or hierarchies of, 6, 8, 98, 297; language around regulation or the nanny state, 318–19, 321–22, 325–27, 330–36; and policy, 17, 41–42, 57n87, 292, 336n6; and scale, 250, 295; scholarship on, 6–7, 9, 18n3; and smoking, 224–25, 238n18. *See also* feminism; "KidVid" or Children's Advertising Rule; LGBTQ politics; nanny state; working women

general equilibrium theory, 141, 142, 145

General Motors, 321

gentrification, 200, 203, 208, 248, 254

geography, 18n11, 248, 249, 292

George III (king), 242

George Washington University National Law Center, 232

Georgia, 66, 71, 72, 91n45, 97, 104, 110–14, 168, 178, 196

Gingrich, Newt, 5, 114, 115, 294, 331, 332

Glass, Carter, 138–40, 143, 148

Glass-Steagall Act, 14, 138, 145

global civil community, 252

globalism, 242, 243, 251, 253, 254, 256, 370

globalization, 7, 164, 241, 252, 349, 353

Global South, 252

glocalization, 243, 244, 251, 252, 255, 256
Gold Reserve Act of 1934, 138
gold standard, 124, 138
Good Neighbor Policy, 67
Gore, Al, 332
Great Britain, 67, 144, 246, 317, 325–26
Great Depression, 10, 27, 40, 43, 107, 133, 137, 140–41, 143–44, 150, 179, 189, 350; as crisis, 138, 143, 146, 149, 363; New Deal as response to, 74, 101, 102, 124–27, 145, 146
Greater Baltimore Committee, 113
Greater Philadelphia First, 113
Greater Phoenix Leadership, 113
Great Recession, 3, 189
Great Society, 15, 64, 83, 163, 164, 252
Green Bay, WI, 279
Greenpeace, 253
Group Against Smoking Pollution (GASP), 219, 220, 224
Gruccio, Philip, 218, 232, 233
Guam, 294
Guatemala, 304, 305

Hall, Stuart, 68
Hamilton, John D. M., 30, 31
Harrington, Michael, 246
Hartsfield, William B., 37, 250
Harvard University, 143, 146, 196
Harvey, David, 264, 347, 353–54, 356, 360n12
Hatcher, Richard, 193, 194, 195
Hayek, Friedrich, 350
Head Start, 84, 85
health, 10, 15, 34, 194, 243, 270, 271, 277, 333, 365; effects of smoking, 218, 223–26, 230, 235; and New Deal initiatives, 15, 101, 106, 111. See also health care; "Kid-Vid" or Children's Advertising Rule; tobacco; and specific figures, laws, and organizations
health care, 331–33, 370
Health Consequences of Involuntary Smoking, 233
Hearst, William Randolph, 30
Heart Association, 219
Helms, Jesse, 331
Hesburgh, Father Theodore, 262
Hinduism, 265. See also religion
Hitler, Adolf, 31, 41

Hmong people, 269, 272, 274, 275, 279, 280, 281
Holocaust, 58n102, 261
Home Owners Loan Corporation (HOLC), 74, 75
Honduras, 307
Hoover, Herbert, 14, 124, 138, 143
Hoover, J. Edgar, 302, 305
Hopkins, Harry, 96, 102, 103
House Subcommittee on Health and the Environment, 319
Housing Act of 1949, 108
Housing Act of 1954, 111
housing markets, 80, 189–90, 192, 197, 199, 369
housing policy or programs, 7, 67, 74, 76–80, 84, 105, 108, 196. See also public housing
housing regulation, 108, 163, 170, 171, 172
human rights, 66, 243, 247, 251, 253, 254, 256, 290, 306, 365
Human Rights Watch, 365
Hungarian uprising of 1956, 267
Hynes, Thomas, 204, 207, 208

Idaho, 173
Illinois, 203, 205
Illinois Department of Local Government Affairs, 203
immigration, 7, 9, 18n3, 165, 252, 265, 313n20, 369; of Chinese to the Deep South, 164; of Europeans in the 1890s and 1900s, 100–101, 165. See also Bracero program; Mexican Americans; refugee resettlement
imperialism: connection between and domestic oppression, 17, 67, 297, 299, 302, 313n25, 368, 369, 370, 371, 372, 374; and its effect on Japan, 305–6; and Latin America, 307–8; need for its consideration in U.S. history, 366, 367, 368, 369, 370, 371, 373–74; as the origin of the carceral state, 294–95, 303–4, 308–10. See also carceral state; foreign policy, U.S.; and specific conflicts, laws, and figures
Indiana, 43, 46, 193, 245
Indiana Board of Tax Commissioners, 193
indigenismo, 169
individualism, 352, 357, 368, 373

Indochinese Migration and Refugee Assistance Act of 1975, 269
Indochinese War, 16. *See also* Vietnam War
Indonesia, 309
industrialization, 100, 116n6, 119n34
industrial workers, 98, 162, 171, 172, 177
inflation, 142, 143, 146, 251, 253, 281, 296, 302
infrastructure development or spending, 98, 100, 102, 104, 105, 108, 110, 111, 112, 169
intellectual history, 160n78, 302, 372
Interagency Task Force, 268
intercommunalism, 255
interdependence, 241, 253
interest (finance), 124, 128, 136, 190
Internal Revenue Service, 45, 46
International Association of Chiefs of Police (IACP), 302–4
International Association of Machinists, 230
International Brotherhood of Electrical Workers, 234
International Cooperation Administration, 306
International Corrections and Prisons Association, 302
International Institute, 271
International Monetary Fund, 250
International Red Cross (IRC), 261, 262
International Sugar Research Foundation, 320
internment of Japanese Americans, 296
Interpol, 300
Interstate Commerce Committee (ICC), 219
Iraq War, 353
Islam, 265. *See also* religion

Jackson, Maynard, 247
Jamaica, 307
Japan, 289–91, 294, 296, 305–7, 310n1, 315n48, 316n56
Jefferson, Thomas, 66, 68, 255
Jim Crow: and extralegal violence, 68–69; as a labor system, 164, 179; liberalism, 65, 67, 74, 80, 82; and the New Deal, 7, 12, 14, 79, 98–99, 101, 105; opposition to, 81, 82; outside of the South, 85, 110; and paternalism, 81, 83; the persistence of, 64, 86–87, 89n14, 116n6, 191–92; and segregation, 63, 66, 373. *See also* Bracero program; Juan Crow; lynching; segregation; South, U.S.

job training, 108, 270, 271
Johns Hopkins Club, 62, 65
Johns Hopkins University, 62, 87
Johns-Manville Corporation, 230
Johnson, Lyndon, 65, 83, 84, 85, 231, 297, 301, 302, 303
Jones, Pearl, 274, 275
Juan Crow, 105, 110, 164, 179
Judaism, 33, 34, 53n37, 262, 265, 273, 275, 280. *See also* religion

Kanawha, WV, 254
Kennedy, Edward, 294
Kennedy, John F., 82
Key, V. O., 87
Keynesian economics, 86, 101, 110, 126, 251, 252, 352; post-, 140, 248
Khmer language, 277
"KidVid" or Children's Advertising Rule, 317, 319, 321–24, 325, 327–30, 332, 333, 334, 335. *See also* nanny state
King, Martin Luther, Jr., 82, 293
Kiwanis International, 102
Koop, Everett, 233
Kosel, Tom, 276, 278, 279
Ku Klux Klan, 73, 75

labeling, 319–20, 333
Labor Department, U.S., 171, 175, 176
labor unions, 106, 120n41, 162, 163, 238n26, 239, 331, 369; and erosion of, 221, 235–36; and neoliberalism, 351, 354, 356; and race, 67, 74, 79, 358; and smoke-free workplaces, 15, 218, 222, 223, 227–31, 235–36; and social security, 29, 30, 31, 33, 34, 36, 47, 54n40. *See also* collective bargaining
Lake Worth, FL, 43
Landon, Alfred, 37
Lange, Dorothea, 42
Lansing, MI, 40
Laos, 272, 275, 277, 279, 281
La Porte, IN, 43
la revolución institucional, 164, 169, 175, 179
Latin America, 265, 290, 306–8
Latinx history, 9
Latinx people, 9, 210, 252, 254, 292, 352. *See also* Bracero program; Mexican Americans

law-and-order politics, 9, 290, 293, 304, 312n14, 365, 369, 371. *See also* carceral state; crime; Rockefeller drug laws

law enforcement, 16, 86, 290, 293, 296–305, 365

Law Enforcement Assistance Act of 1965, 301, 302

Lawndale Peoples Planning and Action Committee (LPPAC), 199–200

LGBTQ politics, 9, 245, 351

liberal consensus, 9, 243, 246, 296

liberalism, 5, 7, 97, 221–22, 231, 251, 352, 359, 367, 369; attacks on, 318, 348; Cold War liberalism, 246, 248; gendered meanings of, 17, 322; geography of liberalism, 164, 169; maintenance of white supremacy through, 13, 62–68, 70–72, 74, 77, 79–82, 84–87, 364, 371; Mexican liberalism, 163, 169, 177, 179–80; New Deal liberalism, 5, 65, 67, 112, 244, 246, 248; as a paradigm, 6, 171; post-WWII liberalism, 192, 221, 243, 245, 351, 357; racial liberalism, 68, 367; relationship with neoliberalism, 13, 180, 348, 350, 351, 356, 357; urban liberalism, 13, 98, 99, 108, 109, 114, 368. *See also* liberal consensus; liberalism-conservatism paradigm; New Deal order

liberalism-conservatism paradigm, 6, 9, 10, 65, 103, 108, 116n5, 349, 353, 355, 364, 365, 370, 371. *See also* New Deal order; red-blue divide

libertarianism, 82, 85, 255

Liberty, TX, 97

Limbaugh, Rush, 335

Lions Club International, 102

loans or lending (fiscal policy), 124, 126, 128–39, 144–48, 160n82

localism, 65, 73, 249, 369, 370; and New Deal, 97–99, 102–3, 108, 112, 114–15, 251; in the 1970s, 242, 243, 250, 252–56

Lockhart, Charles, 84

Longview Farms, 173

Los Angeles, CA, 106

Louisiana, 166, 167

Lutheran Immigration and Refugee Services (LIRS), 270–75, 277–78

Lutheranism, 272, 276–80. *See also* religion

Lutheran Social Service, 271, 276, 280

lynching, 68–74, 81, 82

Lyons, Arthur, 199–202, 204, 208

managerialism, 222

Mandelbaum, Rabbi Bernard, 262

marginal theory of value, 141, 142

Marlboro, 224

Marshall, Alfred, 141–42

Marshall, Thurgood, 73

Marshals Service, 300

Martin, Isaac William, 192, 206

Marx, Karl, 353

Marxism, 69, 250

Massachusetts, 139, 234, 254

Massachusetts Institute of Technology (MIT), 234

mass incarceration, 64, 66, 67, 245, 349, 354, 371. *See also* carceral state; crime; law-and-order politics; War on Crime

McCarthyism, 252. *See also* Red Scare

McClaughry, John, 255

McClellan, John, 174

McDuffie, Lizzie, 76

McGovern, George, 319–20

McNamara, Robert S., 298

Medicare, 192

Memphis, TN, 163, 170, 173, 176, 177

Merle Norman Cosmetics, 235

Merriam, Charles E., 101, 103

Merrick, John, 70

Methodism, 279. *See also* religion

metropolitan history, 6, 364, 366

metropolitan politics, 110

Mexican Americans, 164, 167, 255, 368, 373

Mexican consulate in the United States, 167–79

Mexican Revolution, 166, 167, 169

Mexican state, 15, 163–73, 175, 176, 177, 179

Mexico City, 253

Mexico-U.S. border, 164, 166, 168, 179, 373

Miami, FL, 77, 78, 79, 80, 82, 84

Miami-Dade County, FL, 196

Michigan, 40, 47, 189

Middle East, 10

Midwest, 97, 109, 167

migrant labor, 10, 14, 371. *See also* agricultural laborers; Bracero program

Migration and Refugee Assistance Act of 1962, 267

military, U.S., 6, 100, 110, 252, 265, 294, 298, 302, 303, 307, 309, 310n3, 351

Mill, John Stuart, 350

Miller, James C., 324

Millville, NJ, 218, 230–31, 232

Milwaukee, WI, 104, 196

Mine Safety Appliance Company of Pittsburgh, 223

minimum wage, 162, 164, 172, 175, 177, 179, 183n47

Minneapolis, MN, 273

Minnesota, 241, 270–73, 276, 279, 280

Minnesota Business Partnership, 113

Mississippi, 74, 75, 80, 84, 165–68, 171, 172, 179, 214n32

Mobil Oil, 234

Model Cities, 297

modernization theory, 252

monetary orthodoxy, 14, 126–27, 139–44, 148–50, 160n82

Money, MS, 74

money supply, 14, 123, 126–27, 129, 131–32, 137, 139, 142, 145

Monroe doctrine, 306

Mont Pelerin Society, 255, 350

Moses, Robert, 106–7, 118n17

Mother Earth News, 255

Moton, Robert, 71

Moynihan, Daniel Patrick, 113–14, 298

multinational corporations, 251, 252, 256, 369

Murray, James Anderson, 37

Nader, Ralph, 194–95, 226, 231–32, 246, 321

nanny state: and Bloomberg soda ban, 333; and the coding of regulation, 317, 321–24, 335; and fears over the decline of parenting, 328–30; and labeling, 319–21; and masculinity, 334, 335; origins of the term, 325–26; other nicknames for regulatory state, 318; and political rhetoric about the family, 318–19, 320, 322, 326–27; use of the term around Clinton, 331–33; use of the term by Democrats against Reagan, 330–31

National Association for the Advancement of Colored People (NAACP), 33, 68, 71, 73, 76, 104, 202, 232

National Association of Evangelicals, 270

National Banking Act of 1863, 133

National Banking Act of 1864, 133

National Bank Note, 133, 135, 150n1

National Cancer Institute, 226

National Council of Churches, 270

National Dairy Council, 320

National Guard, 300

National Institutes of Health, 220

nationalism, 167, 169, 177, 178, 179, 241, 255, 256, 292, 294, 303

nationalization, 169

National Labor Relations Act, 106

National Recovery Act, 75, 106

National Resources Defense Council, 226

National Resources Planning Board, 103, 112, 119n34

National Retail Merchants Council, 323

National Review, 83

national security, 84, 110, 111, 369, 371. *See also* carceral state; national security state

National Security Act, 310n3

national security state, 292, 294–96, 302–3, 305, 307–9, 310n3, 368

National Taxpayers' Union of Illinois, 205

National Urban League, 76, 80

nation-state, 241–44, 249–53, 296

Native Americans, 242, 248, 252, 254, 373

Nazism, 206, 306, 350

Negro Officers for Negroes, 82

neighborhood movement, 254

neoclassical economics, 141, 158n58

neoconservatism, 255, 351

neoliberalism, 15, 17, 77, 97, 248, 297, 319, 368; as an approach to urban governance, 115, 190, 192, 206, 208, 210; as a defining feature of an era, 5, 103, 266; emergence of, 16, 64, 244, 248, 251, 351, 352, 356, 363, 369; historiography of, 5, 6, 8, 122n71, 255–56, 347–59, 360n1, 369; and liberalism, 8, 13, 16, 64–66, 86, 110, 191–92, 350, 357; policies, 264, 356, 359; political culture of, 211, 243–44; as a transnational process, 164, 165, 177, 180, 318, 360n12

Netherlands, 309

New Deal, 4–10, 16, 51n17, 226, 232, 252, 372; and African Americans, 65, 66, 67, 73, 75–77, 79, 293; and federalism or local governance, 13–14, 31, 96–115, 119n27, 250, 371; and financial reform, 14, 125, 127, 131, 138–39, 144, 146, 149; and labor regulation, 162–64, 169, 171–73, 175; legacy of, 15, 21n21, 350, 357–58; and Mexican liberalism, 14–15, 169, 175, 179–80; and Social Security,

13, 27, 29, 34, 35, 44, 48; transformation of, 244, 246, 248, 293, 296. *See also* New Deal order; New Deal state
New Deal order, 15, 115, 244, 363; fall of, 163, 180, 221–22, 296, 352; as a paradigm, 4–6, 9, 97, 108, 115, 293, 369. *See also* liberalism-conservatism paradigm
New Deal state, 7, 12, 14, 16, 29, 98–99, 101, 106, 112, 115, 119n27
Newhouse, Richard, 203
New Jersey, 34, 222–24, 225, 228, 230, 232
New Jersey Bell Telephone, 218, 220, 222–23, 226–28, 231–34. See also *Shimp v. New Jersey Bell*
New Jersey Department of Health, 225
New Jersey Department of Labor, 225
New Jersey Superior Court, 218, 232
New Left, 242, 301, 305. *See also* student activism
New Orleans, LA, 108, 166, 167, 170, 179
New Republic of Africa, 255
New Right, 244, 245, 255, 293, 296. *See also* conservatism
Newton, Huey, 255
New York, 38, 46, 113, 195, 307, 308, 316n56
New York Amsterdam News, 38
New York City, NY, 9, 40, 43, 104, 105, 109, 114–15, 139, 162, 193, 195, 226, 254, 302, 333, 356
New York City Citizens Housing and Planning Council, 195
New York City Parks Department, 106, 107, 118n17
New York Commission of Investigation, 193
New York Police Department (NYPD), 302
New York Post Office, 37
New York Public Interest Research Group, 195
New York State Identification and Intelligence System, 46
New York Telephone, 234
New York Times, 36, 143, 234, 289, 290, 291, 326, 331, 333
Ngô Đình Diệm, 305
Nixon, Richard, 224, 233, 255, 301, 307, 365
nongovernmental organizations (NGOs), 16, 247, 253, 256
nonsmokers' rights, 219–22, 224–31, 233–34, 236

nonviolent direct action, 65, 78, 82
North, U.S., 13, 73, 76, 82, 83, 97, 98, 100, 104, 106
North Carolina, 76, 112, 113, 331
North Carolina Mutual Life Insurance Company, 70, 76, 77
nutrition, 319–22, 333

Oak Terrace Nursing Home, 273
Obama, Barack, 365
Occupational Safety and Health Administration (OSHA), 225, 226, 227, 229, 232
Occupy Wall Street, 6
Office of Inter-American Affairs, U.S., 306
Office of Refugee Resettlement, U.S., 269, 270
Office of the Surgeon General, U.S., 234
Offices of Economic Opportunity, 84
Ohio, 137, 280
Oklahoma, 68, 280
Oldman, Oliver, 196, 197
Omnibus Crime Control and Safe Streets Act, 303
"open market" operations, 124, 136–38, 143, 155n39
Operation PUSH, 202
orders and critiques of, 4, 5, 7, 9, 222, 244, 251, 252, 255, 296, 347, 351, 357, 358, 363, 364, 368. *See also* New Deal order
Oregon, 42, 172, 280
Organization of Petroleum Exporting Countries (OPEC), 252
Our Revolution, 210
Oxfam America, 253

Pacific Northwest, 168, 169
parenting, 236, 318–19, 321–22, 327–30, 331, 332, 335
Parkin Farmers' Association, 172
Partido Revolucionario Institucional (PRI), 169, 177–78
paternalism, 13, 67, 71, 73, 79, 81–84, 86, 167, 170, 308, 318
patriarchy, 6, 9, 245
Paul, Ron, 335
pension, 40, 41, 189
Pentagon, 298, 299
Pentagon Papers, 302

People's Bicentennial Commission (PBC), 242
periodization, 249, 292, 296, 297, 299, 309, 368–69, 372
Pertschuk, Michael, 320–25
Peters, Charles, 351
Pew Research Center, 370
Philadelphia, PA, 104, 107, 109, 113, 200, 219, 220, 234, 241, 242
Philippine-American War, 27
Philippines, 309
Phoenix, AZ, 105, 112, 113
Piketty, Thomas, 354
Pine Bluff, AR, 174
Pittsburgh, PA, 113, 195, 223, 279
Pittsburgh Courier, 33
Planning Grant Program, 112
planters, 67, 75, 85, 162, 165–66, 168, 170–74, 176, 179
Plessy v. Ferguson, 74
polarization, 248, 349, 360, 370, 371, 374
police state, 309, 318
policy feedbacks, 11, 108
political economy, 5, 15, 141, 142, 248, 250, 347, 349, 363–64, 365, 366, 371, 372, 373
political history, U.S., 3–17, 18n4, 21n19, 21n21, 21n23, 23n27, 97, 99, 108, 116n5, 126, 242, 248, 249, 291–92, 303, 308–9, 317, 359, 363–74
pollution, 198, 200, 219, 221, 225, 226, 252, 253
Pol Pot, 261
populism, 9, 69, 114, 169, 177, 352, 364
Portland, OR, 43, 108
post-Fordism, 248
postindustrialism, 248
postmaterialism, 248
postmodernism, 246, 248, 352
Post Office, U.S., 33, 100
poverty, 7, 76, 84, 112, 114, 231, 281, 293, 297, 301
privacy, 27, 35, 46, 49, 63
private property, 65, 70, 353, 369, 371
private security, 302
privatization, 8, 16, 45, 64, 86, 248, 254, 354, 356, 369, 370
probation, 297, 304
Progressive Era, 13, 64, 67, 98, 100, 134, 372
progressivism, 97, 98, 106, 112, 162, 206, 250, 367

prohibition, 225
Project Transition, 298, 303
protección, 167, 170, 173, 175, 178
Protestantism, 265, 272, 273, 280
Public Health Service, 225, 227
public housing, 77, 79, 98, 106, 110–11
Public Housing Administration, 74
public-interest law, 219, 222, 226, 231, 232
Public Interest Research Group (PIRG), 232
public-private partnerships, 134, 357, 366, 369, 370; as part of neoliberalism, 86, 255; as part of New Deal, 97, 103, 109–13, 115, 357; and refugee resettlement, 262–64, 266–67, 281
Public Works Administration (PWA), 96
Puerto Rico, 294

Quigg, H. Leslie, 78

race, 15, 33, 51n18, 53n32, 89n14, 98, 110, 295, 297, 308, 325, 354–55, 364–65; scholarship on, 6–10, 11, 292, 307, 352, 363–73. *See also* African Americans; Bracero program; capitalism; carceral state; imperialism; Jim Crow; Juan Crow; Latinx people; lynching; race; segregation; taxation; white privilege; white supremacy; *and specific figures, laws, and organizations*
radicalism, 6, 10, 15, 69, 84, 124, 242, 245, 252, 254, 256, 293, 297, 307, 331
RAND Corporation, 301–2
Reagan, Ronald, 206, 253, 255, 289, 293, 324, 330–31, 356, 365; age of, 5, 86, 114, 180, 331; election of, 256, 326, 349, 351, 352
"real bills" or "commercial" theory of banking, 126–28, 134–40, 144, 145, 147, 148, 153n13, 154n29, 155n39, 157n52
realignment, 5, 17, 363, 364
Reconstruction, 63, 77, 79, 81, 83
red-blue divide, 6, 7, 11, 12, 13, 97, 99, 244, 245, 251, 364–65, 369, 370, 372. *See also* liberalism-conservative paradigm
rediscounting (finance), 133, 134, 136, 137, 139, 146, 147
Red Scare, 68
Refugee Act of 1980, 269–70

refugee resettlement, 16, 370; and Carter administration, 261–63, 280–81; and the costs of religious involvement, 262, 267, 276–80, 282; before the crisis in Southeast Asia, 267; reasons for turning to voluntary agencies for, 268–70, 281–82; by United States, as reflective of neoliberalism, 264, 266; use of congregations for, 271–76. *See also* church-state partnership; public-private partnerships; voluntary agencies; *and specific countries, churches, denominations, figures, laws, and organizations*

regulation, 17, 35, 52n26, 83, 84, 245, 317, 367, 369, 370; of African Americans, 65–66, 80, 86; environmental, 198, 225–27; as feature of New Deal, 13, 98, 105–9, 132; and the limitations of the nation-state, 241, 251, 366; resistance to, 8, 113, 236; workplace safety for labor, 162–63, 168, 169, 173, 176, 218–19, 221, 231. *See also* deregulation; housing regulation; "KidVid" or Children's Advertising Rule; nanny state; regulatory state; *and specific figures, laws, lawsuits, and organizations*

regulatory state, 106, 318, 319, 320, 325, 330, 370

rehabilitation, 290, 308

Reich, Charles, 231

religion, 5, 16, 29, 30, 33, 34, 51n19, 52n37, 54n40, 80, 85, 261; and freedom or pluralism, 262, 263, 265, 267, 282. *See also* refugee resettlement; Religious Right; *and specific denominations, institutions, and figures*

Religious Right, 16, 264, 265. *See also* evangelical Christians

rent control, 106

Report on Smoking and Health, 219, 224

republicanism, 70, 348

Republican National Committee, 30–32, 36

Republican Party, 4, 37, 75, 176, 208, 255; ascendancy of in the 1980s, 5, 349, 352; and crime policy, 289–90, 301, 306, 365; opposition of to New Deal policies, 29, 30–32, 36, 39; opposition of, to regulation, 317, 318, 331–32; and Southern Democrats, 84, 85. *See also* red-blue divide; Republican National Committee; *and specific politicians*

reserves (finance), 124, 131, 132, 133, 137, 138, 146

Riddick, George E., 202

rights revolution, 15, 221

"rise and fall" narratives, 5, 179, 180, 221, 348. *See also* declension narratives

Rockefeller, Nelson, 289–91, 305–8

Rockefeller drug laws, 289, 306, 308. *See also* carceral state; mass incarceration

Rodgers, Daniel, 23n28, 246, 248, 347, 348, 352, 372–74

Roosevelt, Eleanor, 73, 76

Roosevelt, Franklin Delano, 43, 65, 96–97, 101, 102, 113, 169, 350, 352; financial policy of, 14, 124, 125, 129, 138, 146, 151n5; and imperialism, 67, 74, 306; and racial liberalism, 68, 73–76, 82; and social security, 29, 30, 37, 45, 51n17, 75. *See also* New Deal; *and specific laws*

Rosewood, FL, 69

Rotary International, 102

Rust Belt, 112, 114, 252–53

Rustin, Bayard, 82

Rutgers University, 231

Salas Ochoa, Heriberto, 163, 170

Saldaña, Esteban, 171

Salem, NJ, 222, 223, 225

San Antonio, TX, 170

San Francisco, CA, 10, 43, 113, 137, 245, 255

Santa Monica, CA, 245

scale and "politics of scale," 16, 23n28, 27, 169, 243–44, 247–52, 255–56, 295, 296, 300, 301, 308, 309, 364, 366

school choice, 331

School of Criminal Justice, 305

School of Criminology, 305

School of Police Administration and Public Safety, 305

Schumacher, E. F., 253, 255

Scott, Coy E., 162, 163, 165, 170, 174–76

Scott, James C. (mayor), 77

seatbelt laws, 325, 327

Seattle, WA, 104

Secretaría de Relaciones Exteriores (Mexican Secretariat of Foreign Relations), 170

Secret Service, 300

securities (finance), 67, 123, 124, 128–38, 144–48, 154n22, 160n77

segregation, 63–66, 74, 81, 83, 85, 110, 304,
    369, 373; in housing, 66, 79, 98, 190, 192,
    196, 199, 364; and redlining, 77, 86, 254;
    in schools, 63, 364; and white power, 81–
    82. *See also* desegregation; Jim Crow
Senate's Select Committee on Nutrition and
    Human Needs, 319
September 11 attacks, 374
service economy, 355
sexuality, 11, 18n3, 292, 297, 366. *See also*
    LGBTQ politics
sharecroppers, 10, 75, 86, 173
Shimp, Donna, 218–35
Shimp v. New Jersey Bell, 218, 220, 221,
    231, 234
Silicon Valley, 111
Simpson, Alan, 317, 319
slum removal and urban renewal, 105, 108,
    109, 111, 113, 203, 369
Smathers, George, 68, 82, 83, 85
Smith, Adam, 350
Smuts, Jan, 67
social democracy, 101, 109, 250, 251, 252,
    256, 353
social history, 4, 7, 9, 10, 11, 292, 300, 364
socialism, 68, 106, 350
social movements, 11, 46, 221, 243, 244, 248,
    251, 256, 301, 367, 372
social safety net, 86, 264, 349
Social Security, 13, 27–49, 169, 192, 366, 372
Social Security Act of 1935, 28, 29, 38, 39,
    75, 86
Social Security Administration, 13, 45
Social Security Board, 31, 32, 34, 35, 36, 37,
    39, 42, 52n26
Social Security Number (SSN), 28–31, 33,
    36–40, 41–48
Social Security Task Force, 47
South, U.S., 10, 73, 75, 76, 78–85, 97, 100,
    107, 255, 373; conservatism, 13, 65; effect
    of New Deal localism in, 98, 104–5, 110–
    14, 116n6, 119n34; and liberalism, 68,
    70–71; Mexican workers in the South,
    163–80; New South, 68, 74, 82; post-
    Emancipation South, 164, 166, 191; and
    segregation, 63, 65, 69. *See also* Bracero
    program; Democratic Party; Jim Crow;
    lynching; *and specific figures, organiza-
    tions, and states*
South Africa, 67

South Carolina, 46, 70, 111, 112, 234
Southeast Asia, 261–62, 266, 268–75, 281–
    82. *See also* refugee resettlement; *and
    specific conflicts, countries, and peoples*
Southern Growth Policies Board, 112
Southern Tenant Farmers Union (STFU),
    163, 171, 177
Southwest, U.S., 104, 164, 165, 168, 173, 179
Soviet Union, 68, 252, 304, 306
Spaulding, Charles, 70, 76
speculative investment, 127–30, 137, 139
Spock, Benjamin, 328–29
Springfield, IL, 203
Springfield, MA, 139
Stable Money League, 142
stagflation, 86, 113
State Department, U.S., 271, 273
Steinfeld, Jesse, 224, 232, 233
Stennis, John, 85
St. Paul, MN, 272, 273, 276
student activism, 178, 222, 232, 245, 248
suburban history, 366
suburbs, 78, 84, 111, 197, 208, 290, 309; and
    decentralization, 246, 248; politics of, 85,
    114, 191, 204, 244, 245, 252, 364–65, 369;
    and segregation, 67, 192, 196; taxation
    of, 191–93, 195, 197, 205, 209, 211. *See
    also* suburban history
Summers, Edna, 202
Sunbelt, U.S., 13, 14, 97, 98, 99, 100, 105,
    108, 110, 111, 112, 114, 368
Sunflower County, MS, 75
Supreme Court, U.S., 63, 207
surveillance, 8, 12, 13, 27, 47, 49n2, 297; by
    corporations, 34, 35; by the state, 16, 29,
    31, 36, 45, 46, 372. *See also* data; privacy;
    Social Security

Tamm, Quinn, 302, 303
tattooing, 42, 43, 47, 58n92, 58n98, 58n102
taxation, 29, 45, 50n11, 67, 81, 106, 109,
    113, 128, 131, 229, 236, 317, 318, 333,
    343n110, 363; and discriminatory assess-
    ment, 15, 86, 189–210, 368; organizing
    around, 77–78, 191, 200, 202, 205–6,
    211n2, 369
Taylor, Robert, 77
technocracy, 75, 245, 246, 255
Techwood Homes, 79
tenant unions, 84–85

Terry, Luther, 218–20, 232–34
Texas, 40, 97, 166, 167, 168, 172, 173
Thailand, 261, 268, 269, 304
Thatcher, Margaret, 325–26, 333
think tanks, 255, 301
Third World Conference on Smoking and
    Health, 226, 227
Till, Emmett, 73–74
Tlatelolco Massacre, 178
tobacco, 70, 218–19, 222–26, 229, 233–35.
    See also Big Tobacco; Shimp, Donna;
    Shimp v. New Jersey Bell; and specific
    organizations
Tobacco Institute, 229
Tobacco Workers International Union
    (TWIU), 229
Tocqueville, Alexis de, 102
Tories (Great Britain), 242, 325
To Secure These Rights, 83
transnationalism, 169, 247, 252, 300, 302,
    318; as an approach to history, 14, 16–17,
    19n12, 249–50, 308, 367, 372–74
TransWorld Airlines, 234
Treaty of Chapultepec, 306
Triangle Shirtwaist Factory fire, 162
triangulation, 86
Triborough Bridge, 106
Truman, Harry, 65, 67, 68, 76, 83, 267, 307,
    310n3
Trump, Donald, 3, 4, 356
Tuitán, Durango, 175
Tulsa, OK, 44, 69
Turner, Frederick Jackson, 366
Turner, Lana, 39
Tuskegee Institute, 71

undocumented workers, 164, 168, 169, 173,
    178, 179
unemployed workers, 29, 42, 96, 104, 298
"unfairness" principle, 323–24
United Community Housing Coalition, 210
United Nations, 241, 253, 261, 300, 306
United Nations Children's Fund (UNICEF),
    261
United States Army's Special Operations
    Research Office, 301
United States Catholic Conference (USCC),
    270, 272
United States Conference of Catholic
    Priests, 274

United States Conference of Mayors
    (UCSM), 101
University of California, Los Angeles, 234
University of Illinois at Chicago (UIC),
    School of Urban Sciences, 201
University of Michigan, 365
University of North Carolina, 75
University of Pennsylvania Medical School,
    219
University of Virginia, Miller Center, 363
urban history, 366
urbanization, 100, 112
U.S. Employment Service (USES), 163,
    166, 174
U.S. Steel, 193–95, 198–200
Utah, 146

Venezuela, 307
Vietnam and Vietnamese people, 273, 275,
    277, 279, 280, 281, 299, 305, 309
Vietnam War, 10, 46, 47, 244, 268, 273, 274,
    291, 298, 299, 302
Virginia, 138
Vollmer, August, 305
voluntary agencies, 16, 263, 266–78, 280–82,
    286n56. See also church-state partner-
    ship; public-private partnerships; and
    specific organizations

Wagner Act, 74
Walras, Marie-Esprit-Léon, 141, 142
Walter, Ingrid, 270, 275, 276
war, 8, 12, 29. See also specific conflicts
War Between the States, 114
War on Crime, 297, 301, 365
War on Drugs, 365, 369
War on Poverty, 84, 114, 293, 297, 314n36
War Relief Control Board, 267
Washington (state), 168, 234, 280
Washington, Booker T., 69, 71
Washington, DC, 43, 66, 74, 76, 84, 96, 101,
    104, 107, 109, 113, 115, 124, 125, 174,
    176, 245, 307, 321
Washington, Harold, 201–5, 207, 208
Washington Post, 42, 138, 235, 325, 328,
    351
Watergate, 10
Waxman, Henry, 320
Wayne County, MI, 189, 190, 210
Weaver, Robert Clifton, 76, 77

welfare programs, 10, 16, 47, 84, 86, 206; and
     carceralization, 297–99; and the nanny
     state, 318, 322, 325, 326, 332; and the
     New Deal, 28, 96, 102, 106, 109, 172; and
     the Progressive Era, 98, 100; and public-
     private cooperation, 263–64, 268, 271
welfare state, 29, 41, 42, 86, 336n6; Euro-
     pean, 326, 368, 373; and neoliberalism,
     350–52, 356–57
Wells, Ida B., 73
West, U.S., 76, 100, 106, 110, 111, 164
West Germany, 251
West Virginia, 254
White, Walter, 76
White House on Balanced Economic
     Growth, 113, 114
"White Man's Burden," 67, 82, 86
white privilege, 6, 190, 191, 211, 364
white supremacy, 6, 8, 9, 13, 62, 64–66,
     69. *See also* African Americans; Jim
     Crow; lynching; race; segregation; white
     privilege
white workers, 13, 83, 162, 163, 165, 169,
     171, 177, 352
Wichita Falls, TX, 40

Williamsport, PA, 37
Willis, Henry Parker, 125, 133, 138, 139
Will See, 210
Wilson, O. W., 305
Wilson, Woodrow, 71, 74, 82
Woodward, C. Vann, 62–65, 68, 87
working women, 10, 29, 33–34, 38, 42, 47,
     53n38, 84, 162, 220, 238n18, 325, 358
workplace rights, 15, 220–22, 231, 236. *See
     also* nonsmokers' rights; Shimp, Donna;
     Shimp v. New Jersey Bell
work-relief labor, 96, 100, 101, 107
Works Progress Administration, 75, 96–97,
     104, 106, 107, 118nn17–19
World Affairs Council of Philadelphia, 241
World Court, 241
World Relief, 270, 277, 278
World Vision, 269
World War I, 27, 124, 128, 129, 134, 136,
     145, 166
World War II, 9, 14, 27, 67, 68, 107, 109, 140,
     163, 166–68, 192, 229, 266, 267, 294, 296,
     305, 306, 351, 357, 369

Yale University, 142, 291

Lightning Source UK Ltd.
Milton Keynes UK
UKHW010051130419
340944UK00005B/16/P